CLARENDON PLATO SERIES

Laws 1 and 2

CLARENDON PLATO SERIES

Volumes published

Gorgias
Terence Irwin

Laws 10
Robert Mayhew

Phaedo
David Gallop

Philebus
J. C. B. Gosling

Protagoras
C. C. W. Taylor

Theaetetus
John McDowell

Plato

Laws 1 and 2

Translated with an Introduction and Commentary
by
SUSAN SAUVÉ MEYER

OXFORD
UNIVERSITY PRESS

OXFORD
UNIVERSITY PRESS

Great Clarendon Street, Oxford, OX2 6DP,
United Kingdom

Oxford University Press is a department of the University of Oxford. It furthers the University's objective of excellence in research, scholarship, and education by publishing worldwide. Oxford is a registered trade mark of Oxford University Press in the UK and in certain other countries

First Edition published in 2015
Impression: 1

Published in the United States of America by Oxford University Press
198 Madison Avenue, New York, NY 10016, United States of America

British Library Cataloguing in Publication Data
Data available

Library of Congress Control Number: 2015934067

ISBN 978–0–19–960408–1

Printed and bound by
CPI Group (UK) Ltd, Croydon, CR0 4YY

To Hannah

Preface

Why the present volume? Students of Plato's *Laws* already have the benefit of several excellent commentaries and translations produced in the last century. England's magisterial commentary on the Greek text (1921) continues to be a valuable resource to readers in English, as is the more limited set of notes on the text in Saunders (1972). Neither, however, offers much guidance on points of philosophical, as opposed to philological, interpretation. On many fronts both have been superseded by the excellent commentary in German, with accompanying translation, recently completed by Schöpsdau (1994–2011). The latter contains considerably more historical material than England, and is an indispensable resource for any serious scholarship on the *Laws* today. Readers of Spanish or French have the benefit of up-to-date scholarly translations with accompanying notes by Lisi (1999) and Brisson/Pradeau (2006), respectively. While readers in English have in recent years had the benefit of a number of pioneering studies (such as Bobonich 2002) and collections of essays (Lisi 2001; Scolnicov and Brisson 2003; Bobonich 2010; Horn 2013; Peponi 2013b; and Sanday 2013), the closest we have to a philosophical commentary on the *Laws* in English are the notes and long interpretive essay that accompany the translation by Pangle (1980) and the detailed analysis by Strauss (1975); however, the aggressively 'Straussian' orientation of these two works makes them less helpful to readers of other philosophical persuasions. Of course, no philosophical commentary can plausibly claim to be without theoretical presuppositions, and the orientation of the present work reflects presuppositions characteristic of scholarship on Plato by so-called 'analytic' philosophers in the English-speaking world over the last half-century. The translation aims to be more idiomatic than Pangle's, and is heavily indebted to the very elegant and readable translation by Saunders (1970). The latter displays a detailed and nuanced appreciation of Plato's Greek that it would be a formidable task to match, but on points crucial to the interpretation of the philosophical and psychological doctrines, it is often less precise than is optimal for the Greekless philosophical reader. It is to the needs of such a reader that the present translation is addressed, while still striving to maintain a fluent and readable English style. The main concern of the commentary is to understand how the work is structured as a complex piece of argumentation, and to appreciate the theories (legal, ethical, and psychological) expounded and criticized within it. For the most part, it pays attention to textual or philological issues only when these have implications for philosophical issues. (The present volume went into production simultaneously with the appearance of Prauscello 2014, and thus too late to benefit from this welcome addition to the scholarship on Book 2.)

Introduction

THE PLACE OF THE *LAWS* IN PLATO'S PHILOSOPHY

Our ancient sources tell us little about the date and composition of Plato's *Laws* other than that it was written after the *Republic* (*Pol.* 1264b26) and that it was 'in the wax' when Plato died, after which it was 'copied out' by Philip of Opus (DL 3.37). Stylometric analysis groups it with other dialogues generally considered to be late works, such as *Philebus*, *Sophist*, *Statesman*, and *Timaeus* (Kahn 2002), and the dialogue's style, syntax, and organization bear the marks of a work left unrevised on the author's death. Only a minority of scholars today doubt its authenticity (see Nails and Thessleff 2003), a view that was widespread among nineteenth-century scholars (see Guthrie 1978: 321–3).

The *Laws* revisits many themes of the *Republic*. It articulates a detailed law code for a city state that has much in common with the ideal state described in the *Republic*, even though it is avowedly 'second best' in comparison to the former (739e). It contains many extended reflections on psychology, education, art, legislative theory, criminology, and theology. For a general introduction to the work, see Stalley 1983, Laks 2000, and Brisson/Pradeau 2007. On the relation between *Republic* and *Laws*, see Schofield 1999, Bobonich 2002, Kahn 2004, Laks 2005, and Zuolo 2012; on the development of Plato's political philosophy more broadly, see E. Barker 1918, Bolot 2006, Klosko 2006, and Schofield 2006.

OVERVIEW OF THE DIALOGUE

On the island of Crete three elderly men begin a lengthy pilgrimage on foot to the sacred cave of Zeus. They are citizens of three different Greek city states—Athens, Sparta, and the Cretan city of Knossos—who agree to occupy their time on the journey with a discussion of 'law codes and legislation' (625a6–7, 641d9). In particular, their concern is to investigate what makes for good legislative practice (637d2, 630d8–632c7), and to compare the relative merits of different '*nomoi*' or laws (627d3–4, 638b4–7). Much of Books 1 and 2 is devoted to a comparative evaluation of institutions distinctive of the interlocutors' home cities, for example the characteristically Dorian[1] institution of communal meals (*sussitia*) practised in Sparta and Knossos, and the paradigmatically Athenian institution of the drinking party (*sumposion*). The Athenian here develops the themes that a city's laws and institutions shape the character of its citizens, that the legislator's goal is to inculcate virtue in the citizens, and that choral song and dance has an important role to play in ethical training. Book 3 investigates the origins of the practice of legislation, and attempts to explain the successes and failures of different types of constitution. Book 4 turns to the task of devising legislation for a soon-to-be founded Cretan colony, later described as 'the city of the Magnesians' (860e). This project occupies the remainder of the twelve books of the work, which in fact contain at least as much methodological discussion as they do actual legislation, along with extended discussions of education and culture (Books 7–8), penology (Book 9), and theology (Book 10).

THE RANGE OF 'LAW' (*NOMOS*)

The 'laws' (*nomoi*) under examination are not restricted to the products of a legislator or a formal legislative process, but include a

[1] On the label 'Dorian', see note on 624a1–2 and on 625e2–7.

wide variety of social norms, both written and unwritten (see note on 625a6–7). For example, the Dorian norm that forbids the youth to inquire into legislation and requires everyone to 'sing out their agreement' in praise of the laws (634d–e) is hardly likely to be a statute of these cities, and the practice under examination in much of Books 1 and 2, the after-dinner drinking party (*sumposion*) prevalent in Athens and other non-Dorian cities, is what we might call an institution or a social practice, but it owes neither its origin nor its continued existence to legislation (except to the extent that legislation does not forbid it). By and large, Plato's *Laws* (especially Books 1 and 2) is a sustained examination of the goals and merits of such norms and practices. While the interlocutors are particularly interested in methodological and epistemological problems faced by those who devise legislation and seek to implement it, even these issues cluster around the focal question of what makes for a good or bad norm or social practice, broadly construed. The semantic range of the Greek term '*nomos*' (generally rendered as 'law' in this translation, but occasionally by 'custom', as at 637c7) is broad enough to encompass this extension; other terms used to refer to this object of inquiry include '*nomima*' (customs, norms) and '*epitêdeumata*' (practices).

THE THREE INTERLOCUTORS

The three interlocutors are an unnamed Athenian, a Spartan named Megillus, and a Cretan named Clinias who is identified as a citizen of Knossos. Plato's refusal to give a name to the Athenian (who comes from Plato's home city) has roused considerable speculation as to whether he is intended to be recognized as a philosopher (thus Zuckert 2009: 31–3)—perhaps even Plato's teacher Socrates, the main speaker in many other Platonic dialogues (Strauss 1975: 1–2, Rowe 2012; rejected by Nightingale 1993: 294–6). At any rate, it is clear that, first of all, the Athenian is the dominant speaker in the dialogue (pretty much the exclusive speaker after Book 2); it is the views he articulates that comprise the 'doctrine' of the work, such as there is any. Second, the stubbornly generic classification of the Athenian in terms of his home city is in line with the fairly stereotypical characterization of Clinias and Megillus as paradigmatic exemplars of their own home cities' national characteristics. While it is possible that Megillus is based on a historical figure, nothing is known about Clinias (see note on 642b4). In any case, their names add no greater depth to their characterization than does the minimal characterization of the Athenian in terms of his native city. Clinias and Megillus are portrayed from the outset as products of their Dorian upbringing (625a5)—whence their preference for militaristic institutions and distaste for luxury (628e, 636e–637b). Plato depicts their intellectual tastes and ethical notions in line with the familiar stereotypes of Spartans as brief and wooden in discourse and Cretans as similarly disinclined to verbal elaboration (641e, 721e; cf. *Protag.* 342c–343c). The loquacity of the Athenian and his greater intellectual fluency are also in keeping with the stereotype of Athenians articulated in the same context in *Laws* (641c–d). While the differences between Knossian and Spartan norms turn out not to be of great interest to the Athenian (see note on 624a1–2), the characteristically Dorian features that these cities share and their differences from non-Dorian cities such as Athens are a topic to which Plato consistently directs our attention throughout Books 1 and 2.

As paradigmatic products of two very different types of institutions, the three interlocutors replicate almost exactly the position of the original legislators in the natural history of legislation set forth at the beginning of Book 3: they are members of societies that prize different and conflicting norms who come together to select which norms are best to implement as written laws (681a–d; see Meyer 2006). Even the term the interlocutors use to address each other, *xenos*, highlights this feature of their respective relations. The term is a respectful form of address to a foreigner. It is often translated 'visitor' or 'guest', which reflects its link to a deeply rooted norm of offering hospitality to strangers (718a). But this won't do for the present translation, since all three interlocutors address each other as *xenoi*, and only Clinias is on his home turf. For want of a more idiomatic alternative, the term is consistently rendered 'Stranger' in this volume. In keeping with their status as *xenoi* to each other, the three interlocutors of *Laws* are engaging in a cross-cultural inquiry premised on mutual respect. And unlike so much of the discourse that goes by that name in the present day, Plato's interlocutors proceed on the assumption that it is possible for such inquiry to yield results of universal significance.

SYNOPSIS OF BOOK 1

The book opens with Clinias and Megillus claiming a divine pedigree for the law codes of their respective cities. The Athenian asks Clinias to identify what the divine legislator had in mind when devising Cretan institutions. Clinias replies that victory in war is the legislator's primary concern, since war and conflict are the human condition (624a–627c). The Athenian counters by arguing that reconciliation and friendly relations between citizens are better than victory of one faction over another (627c–628e), and so the legislator will seek to equip the citizens with the full range of virtues, including justice and moderation, not just the courage touted by poets such as the Spartan Tyrtaeus (628e–630c). These virtues, together with wisdom, are 'divine goods', on which all 'human goods' such as wealth, power, and strength depend (630d–631c). This ranking and dependence are what the proper legislator will have in view when devising institutions and giving instructions to the citizens. So, the Athenian concludes, the divine lawgivers for Crete and Sparta must have had more in view than cultivating courage in the citizens (631d–632d).

The problem for the interlocutors then becomes to identify laws or institutions of Knossos and Sparta that promote the full range of virtues, with the discussion to proceed one virtue at a time (632e). Megillus is able to identify many Spartan institutions that promote courage, conceived of as resistance to pain and fear, but neither he nor Clinias is able to identify any Spartan or Knossian institution designed specifically to cultivate moderation, conceived of as resistance to pleasure and desire (633a–636e). In response to Megillus' proposal that Spartan laws forbidding drinking parties (*sumposia*) promote moderation, the Athenian makes the provocative claim that such parties in fact provide an important educational benefit, provided they are properly led (637a–641d). A proper defence of this claim, he warns, will require an extensive discussion of education (641d–643a). He proceeds to define education (*paideia*, 643a–644b), and then provides a model of the human subject trained in that education: we are like divine puppets pulled by opposing cords of pleasure, pain, and anticipation on the one hand, and by the golden cord of calculation (*logismos*) on the other (644b–645c). While drunkenness has the temporary effect of weakening the golden cord, a properly supervised drinking party is a training ground in which a person may cultivate resistance to shameless pleasures and desires (645d–649d). In fact, it is an especially safe forum in which to reveal a person's character (649e–650b).

SYNOPSIS OF BOOK 2

Book 2 opens with the announcement that there is an even greater benefit to be had from drinking parties than the diagnostic function mentioned at the end of Book 1. True to his earlier claim that the practice has an important educational function (641b–d), the Athenian now announces that it is a safeguard to education (653a). He follows up with a more precise and detailed account of education than the one he sketched in Book 1: fully fledged virtue consists in the 'agreement' (*sumphônia*) of correctly trained pleasures and pains with one's rational judgement (*logos*), while 'education' (*paideia*) consists in having correctly trained pleasures and pains (653a–c). The training is to be done by choral performance (*choreia*)—ensemble song and dance regularly performed by citizens at festivals to the gods (653c–654a). Since only beautiful or admirable (*kalon*)[2] music will have the requisite training effect, the question of how to safeguard education thus becomes, for much of the rest of Book 2, the question of what makes choral music beautiful, and of what institutions will ensure that only beautiful music is selected for choral performance. In a long and complicated argument directed mainly against the thesis that music is beautiful insofar as it gives pleasure, the Athenian insists instead that beautiful choral music trains performer and audience alike to enjoy what is actually good and beautiful; thus musical composition must be strictly controlled (654b–660a). He faults Crete and Sparta for failing to live up to this standard on the ground that their music, however regimented, fails to teach the appropriate lessons about virtue and goodness—most importantly, that the just life is happy and most pleasant, and the unjust life miserable (660b–664a). He then specifies the institutions that should structure musical education if a city is to avoid such errors (664b–670e). These are the three choruses, composed respectively of children, young adults, and elders. The first two will perform choral song and dance in festival settings while the third, identified as the chorus of Dionysus, will vet choral compositions for performance. The criteria on which they will do so are articulated at length by the Athenian (666d–670b) in a discussion that amounts to a general theory of what is beautiful in representational art. The chorus of Dionysus is thereby an important safeguard to education, although its activities as described so far have no obvious role for the drunkenness associated with Dionysus and with the drinking parties whose importance the Athenian has proposed to defend. Accordingly, the Athenian concludes by explaining that the chorus of Dionysus will function as a drinking party, where wine 'loosens up' the singers and makes them amenable to the educational effects of song (671a–674c).

[2] On the nature of the *kalon* (beautiful, admirable, noble), see note on 630c7.

Outline of the text

BOOK 1

I. Introductory conversation (624a1–625c5)
The divine origin of legislation, and the human project of inquiring into laws.

- (624a1–625a3) Zeus and Apollo credited with the origin of Cretan and Spartan laws.
- (625a4–c5) A discussion of 'law codes and legislation' proposed to fill the journey to the sacred cave of Zeus.

II. Peace not war is the proper focus of legislation (625c6–632d7)
Articulation then criticism of the thesis that war is the human condition and victory in war the ultimate aim of the legislator. The legislator aims not only at producing citizens who excel in battle against external foes, but also, more importantly, at endowing them with the virtues that enable them to live peacefully with fellow citizens and cooperate in the project of self-government.

- (625c6–626c5) A survey of Cretan practices, from which it is inferred that war is the human condition and victory in war the primary concern of the legislator.
- (626c6–627c2) Development of the idea that war and conflict are the human condition: between states, villages within states, families within villages, siblings within families, and within individual persons (the better part struggling against the worst).
- (627c3–628c8) Reconciliation of warring parties proposed as preferable to victory of the better over the worse;

- (628c9–e1) Hence peace is a goal superior to victory.
- (628e2–630d1) Application of this result to criticize the military ethic propounded by the Spartan poet Tyrtaeus.

- *The goals and practice of the proper legislator*
    - (630d2–631b2) Proper legislation aims at virtue in its entirety (wisdom, moderation, justice, and courage), not just courage.
    - (631b3–d1) These virtues are the ***divine goods*** on which all ***human goods*** (health, wealth, etc.) depend.
    - (631d1–632b8) The legislator instructs citizens in this ranking of goods, and monitors and evaluates their emotional responses, financial dealings, etc.
    - (632c1–d7) 'Finishing touches' to that legislation, including guardians of the laws.

III. Institutions to cultivate courage and moderation (632d8–643a8)

A survey of Spartan institutions identifies many designed to cultivate endurance of pain, but none to cultivate resistance to pleasures.

- (632d8–633a3) Proposal to identify the ways in which Dorian institutions satisfy the larger legislative goals identified at 630d–632d; discussion to proceed one virtue at a time.

Courage

- (633a4–c7) *Courage as resistance to pains*
  Many Spartan institutions noted for cultivating resistance to pain and fear.
- (633c8–634c4) *Courage as resistance to pleasures*
  No Spartan or Cretan institutions cultivate resistance to pleasures.
    - (634c5–635b3) *Interlude: etiquette and credentials for criticizing norms.*
    - (635b4–e3) Cultivating resistance to pleasures requires exposure to pleasures.

Moderation

- (635e4–636d4) Practices that cultivate courage undermine moderation.
- (636d5–637c3) Happiness is not a matter of simply resisting pleasures (or enduring pains). Rather it depends on intelligent selection of pleasures and pains. Are drinking parties among the pleasures to be selected or rejected?
- (637c3–639a1) How to evaluate the merits of drinking parties and other social practices?
- (639a2–641a3) A drinking party, like any communal undertaking, must have a leader; its goal is to cultivate friendly relations among its participants.
- (641a4–643a8) The benefit of a properly conducted drinking party can be explained only in the context of a theory of education—which will require a lengthy discussion.

IV. **Education, virtue, and self-mastery** (643b1–646e2)

- (643b1–644b5) *Education* (*paideia*)
  Defined as channelling of pleasures and desires from childhood via play. In the strict sense, it cultivates virtues of citizenship.
- (644b6–c3) Self-mastery proposed as a paradigm for virtue.
- *The psychology of self-mastery*
  - (644c4–d6) Pleasure, pain, anticipation, and calculation.
  - (644d7–645c8) The divine puppets.
- (645d1–646e2) *Drunkenness and self-mastery*
  Drunkenness weakens self-mastery in the short term, but this is a temporary debility, to be offset by a resulting strengthening—on analogy with physical training, which weakens the body in the short term, but ultimately strengthens it.

V. **Drinking parties as training for moderation** (646e3–650b10)

Drunkenness simulates the conditions that elicit in citizens the shameless pleasures and desires that moderation requires them to resist.

- (646e3–647c2) *Varieties of fear and daring*
  The legislator must not only cultivate the daring required by courage, but the sense of shame (a type of fear) required by moderation and justice.

- (647c3–d8) *Cultivating shame by exposure to shamelessness*
  Cultivating moderation requires exposure to 'shamelessness' and practice at battling against it.

- (647e1–649d7) *Wine as a drug to induce shamelessness*
  Inebriation simulates the conditions in which we are prone to such shamelessness.

- (649d7–650b10) *Drunkenness as a test for character*
  A drinking party therefore provides a way of testing people's character, without exposing fellow citizens to danger.

BOOK 2

I. **Education, virtue, and choral performance** (652a1–654d4)

- (652a1–653a4) Drinking parties are a safeguard of education (*paideia*).

- (653a5–c6) Education (*paideia*) is properly trained pleasures and pains—v. virtue, which is agreement (*sumphônia*) between properly trained pleasures and pains and the account (*logos*) that one grasps.

- (653c7–654a8) It is by singing and dancing in choruses at festivals to the gods that we maintain our education.

  - *The natural origins of choral dance* (653d5–654a3)
    The natural youthful exuberance of voice and gesture, together with the distinctively human enjoyment of harmony and rhythm, makes us eager to engage in song and dance.

- (654a9–d4) The finely educated person sings and dances finely, and as a result feels appropriate pleasure and pains.

II. Virtue, not pleasure, is the standard of beautiful choral art (654d5–660a8)

- (654d5–655b8) Beautiful song and dance depict the speech and actions of virtue.
- (655b9–656b8) Taking pleasure in wicked characters shapes one's own character accordingly.
  - opinions about the pleasant and the beautiful or admirable (655c4–d4).
  - enjoying what one thinks shameful (655d5–656a6).
  - benefits and harms from choral pleasures (656a7–b8).
- (656c1–657c2) Thus it is important for the legislator to establish what correctness in music consists in, and to require that composers conform to it (as e.g. in ancient Egypt).

The problem with using pleasure as the standard

- (657c3–658a3) The intimate relation between feelings of pleasure, judgements about goodness, and choral music gives initial plausibility to the thesis that the finest choral music is that which gives the most pleasure.
- (658a4–e5) But on this criterion, those of different age, sex, and education would give different verdicts. However, the most authoritative judgement would be from those with the best education: the elders.
- (658e6–659c8) Thus in musical education the pleasures of the better should be used to shape those of the inferior; the reverse is what happens when the mass audience delivers the verdict in choral competitions.

Conclusion

- (659c9–660a8) The job of the poets is to put into pleasant vehicles (beautiful phrases, harmony, and rhythm) the speech and actions of virtue. Songs are 'charms' to make serious matters pleasant.

III. The teachings of beautiful choral art (660b1–664b2)

Beautiful choral works must teach that the just person is happy and lives a pleasant life, while the unjust are unhappy and live unpleasant lives.

- (660b1–d10) Clinias proposes that only Crete and Sparta conduct music according to the principles above.
- (660d11–663e2) The Athenian clarifies what composers must teach:
  - *Justice, happiness, and so-called goods*

    The just are happy, the unjust unhappy, and so-called goods and bads are such only for the good person (660d11–661d5).
  - But this is not what Cretans and Spartans are taught (661d6–662a8).
- (662b1–664b2) *Pleasure, persuasion, and compulsion*
  To teach that the just life is good, composers must present it as pleasant; this makes citizens willing to pursue it.
  - Such a view will be obvious to those with a proper musical education, and composers must be compelled to teach it (662b1–c5).
  - Four arguments to the effect that the just life is most pleasant (662c5–663e2).
  - The ease with which poets can be expected to persuade children of these salutary doctrines (663e3–664b2).

IV. The institutions of correct education: the three choruses (664b3–666d2)

- (664b3–665d8) Three choruses introduced: of the Muses, of Apollo, and of Dionysus.
- (665d9–666d2) *Where the chorus of Dionysus will perform*
  These elders will not sing in choruses at public festivals, but in drinking parties, where wine will lessen their reluctance to sing, which naturally accompanies advancing age.

V. **The 'finer' music of the Dionysian Chorus** (666d3–671a1)

- (666d3–667b4) *What the Chorus of Dionysus will 'sing'*
  Rather than perform choral works, they will sing a 'finer music'.

That finer music identified

- (667b5–668b8) Music, as a representational art, is not to be judged by the standard of pleasure, but by the accuracy of its representation of admirable (*kalon*) behaviour.
- (668b9–669b4) A wise judge of a piece of music must know three things:
  1. what the work represents.
  2. how accurately it represents it.
  3. how 'well rendered' it is in 'phrases, tunes, and rhythms'.
- (669b5–670a3) *The third criterion explained*
  Are the harmony and rhythm employed appropriate to each other and to the gestures and tunes of the choral song and dance?
- (670a3–671a1) The finer music of the Dionysian chorus requires expertise in the third criterion, which is distinct both from the expertise of the composers, and from that of choral performers.

VI. **Drinking parties** (671a2–674c7)

- (671a2–672d10) Drunkenness replicates, in the elderly, the youthful exuberance that makes one eager to participate in music. When drinkers are in this malleable condition, a capable leader of a drinking party can lead them in the songs that will repair and renew their education.
- (672e1–673d9) The discussion so far has focused on music, which concerns the movements of the voice. Still to be addressed is athletics (*gumnastikê*), which concerns the motions of the body.
- (673d10–674c7) Drunkenness is a serious business, not a recreational activity. The consumption and production of wine should occupy a very small part of the activities of a society.

Translation

Persons in the dialogue

ATH: An Athenian

CL: Clinias of Crete

MEG: Megillus of Sparta

Book 1

ATH: Is it a god or a human being, Strangers, who gets the credit for 624a
establishing your laws?

CL: A god, Stranger, most assuredly a god! Here on Crete we say it is Zeus, while in Sparta, where our friend here comes from, I believe they say it is Apollo. Isn't that so?

MEG: Yes.

ATH: Don't you say, as Homer does, that Minos made a pilgrimage to
his father every nine years and formulated the laws for your cities by b
following the oracles he received from him?

CL: That is exactly what we say here. You will also have heard of his
brother, Rhadamanthus, who was a paragon of justice. We Cretans
would say he deserves this accolade from the excellent way he adjudi- 625a
cated legal disputes.

ATH: A fine reputation indeed, most appropriate to a son of Zeus.
Now since you and our friend here have been raised under such
distinguished laws, I expect you would not find it unpleasant if we
whiled away our journey today in a conversation about law codes and
legislation. In any case, we are told that the road from Knossos to the b
sacred cave of Zeus is fairly long, with shady places under tall trees along
the way where one can rest, which is a good idea in this hot weather.
Those at our stage of life would do well to take frequent breaks in those
spots and refresh ourselves with conversation. That way the distance will
pass quite easily.

CL: You are right, Stranger. There are indeed amazingly tall and
beautiful cypress trees in the sacred groves up ahead, as well as meadows c
in which we might spend time and rest.

ATH: A very good idea.

CL: Yes, indeed. When we see for ourselves, we shall think so all the more. So let us be off, and may good fortune go with us.

ATH: May it indeed. Now let me ask you why the law has ordained your communal meals, your regime of athletic training, and your style of armament. What is their point?

CL: I think our ways are pretty easy for anyone to understand, Stranger.
The nature of the terrain all over Crete, you may observe, is unlike the
d flat land of the Thessalians, which is why they train mainly on horseback
and we train on foot, since our uneven ground is well suited to foot
racing. Our arms accordingly have to be lightweight, so that we aren't
unduly burdened while we run. The lightness of bows and arrows, then,
makes them the perfect weapons for us to use. All this equips us well for
e war, and it is with the same end in view, I believe, that the lawgiver
devised all our institutions—even our communal meals. He organized
these, I would venture, based on the observation that an army on
campaign is compelled to eat together in order to maintain a proper
guard—and he dismissed the folly of most people, who fail to grasp that
every city is engaged in a continuous lifelong war against every other. If
we must dine together in order to be on our guard during times of war,
626a with a roster of sentinels and their officers to keep watch, we should do
likewise in peacetime—for what most people call peace exists only in
name, while in fact every city is by nature always in an undeclared war
against every other. If you look at it this way, you will discover, I submit,
that it is with war in mind that the Cretan lawgiver established all the
institutions that govern our public and private life. He endowed us with
b laws to guard us on the understanding that those who fail to prevail in
war derive no benefit from anything else they practise or possess, since all
the goods of the vanquished go to the victors.

ATH: You evidently have a well-trained understanding of Cretan in-
stitutions, Stranger. But please clarify one point about the criterion you
c gave for being a well-governed city. You are saying, I gather, that its
affairs must be arranged to make it victorious in war over other cities.
Isn't that so?

CL: Absolutely, and I think our friend here agrees with me.

MEG: How could a Spartan answer any differently, Sir?

ATH: Now, suppose you are right about the relations between cities. Is it any different between villages?

CL: Not at all.

ATH: So is it the same there?

CL: Yes.

ATH: What about relations between households within villages, and between individual men? Is it still the same?

CL: The same.

ATH: And a man in relation to himself—should we think of him as d
one enemy pitted against another? What is our position here?

CL: Well done, Stranger from Athens—I wouldn't want to address you as hailing from Attica, when you so clearly deserve to be called after the goddess! You have gone right to the heart of the matter and made it easy to see the truth of our present contention. Everyone is the enemy of everyone else in public life, and in private each person is pitted against himself.

ATH: My goodness! What do you mean? e

CL: In the latter contest, Stranger, victory over oneself is the highest and most excellent of all victories, and being defeated by oneself is the most shameful and wretched of defeats. These ways of speaking indicate that each of us is engaged in an internal war against himself.

ATH: Well, let's apply this thesis back to the previous cases. Since each of us as a single individual is either master of or defeated by himself,
should we say that the same thing happens in households, villages, and 627a
cities? Or should we deny it?

CL: You are asking whether some of them are masters of themselves and others defeated by themselves?

ATH: Yes.

CL: Another good question. This sort of thing most emphatically does occur, especially within cities. Where the better people are victorious over the inferior masses, the city would correctly be called 'master of itself'. This kind of victory is truly praiseworthy, while the opposite holds when the opposite happens.

b ATH: As to whether we should ever accept that it is possible for the inferior to be master over the superior, that would take too long to discuss—but what I take you to be saying is the following. It sometimes happens that a large number of unjust citizens collectively undertake to force their will on the just minority and enslave them—even though all are members of the same tribe and born into the same city. When the former prevail you say it is right to call the city 'defeated by itself' and bad, and when they are defeated, 'master of itself' and good.

c CL: While this way of speaking is decidedly odd, Stranger, it is undeniable that these things do happen.

ATH: Let's stay with that point. Presumably there could be many brothers born to a single man and wife and it would not be unheard of if the majority of them turned out to be unjust and the minority just?

CL: Not at all.

ATH: We are not seeking to mandate that the household or tribe as a whole be called 'defeated by itself' when the wicked parties win, and
d 'master of itself' when they are defeated. That wouldn't be fitting, since our concern is not with the felicity of this popular expression, but with what is correct and mistaken in the nature of laws.

CL: What you say is very true, Stranger.

MEG: I agree. Your remarks so far strike me as just right.

ATH: Now consider the following. These brothers we spoke of might find themselves before a judge?

CL: Certainly.

ATH: Now which would be a better judge: one who put the wicked
e parties to death and set up the better ones to rule themselves, or one who made the worthy ones the rulers and let the inferior ones live but made them agree to be ruled? Even better is a third judge—the sort who is able to take in hand this tribe at odds with itself and, without killing any of its
628a members, reconcile them by establishing laws that will secure their friendship with each other for the future.

CL: This sort of judge and lawgiver would be better by far.

ATH: And yet it would not be with a view to war but to its opposite that he establishes their laws.

CL: That is true.

ATH: Now what about the person who sets up a city? Is it more with a view to war against external foes that he arranges its life, or with a view to the type of war that from time to time arises within cities, and is called b
faction? No one would ever want this in his own city, and should it ever arise there he would want to be rid of it as quickly as possible.

CL: He will clearly be concerned with the second kind of war.

ATH: Now in which condition would you prefer that the city be forced to direct its attention to external enemies—with the faction resolved into peace because one side is destroyed and the other victorious, or with friendship and peace achieved through reconciliation?

CL: Anyone would prefer the latter for his own city. c

ATH: And the lawgiver would be of like mind?

CL: Certainly.

ATH: Now isn't it for the sake of what is best that any lawgiver will establish his institutions?

CL: Of course.

ATH: The best, however, is neither war nor faction (one should pray to be spared the necessity of either) but rather peace and mutual goodwill. Victory of a city over itself, it would seem, is not the highest achieve- d
ment but a necessity. To think otherwise is like supposing that a disease-ridden body is performing at its best after being flushed out by a purgative—with no thought to the case of a body that needs no such treatment. For the same reason no proper statesman will assess the happiness of either a city or an individual solely and primarily with a view to war against external enemies, and no lawgiver is any good unless he regulates military matters for the sake of peace, rather than regulating peacetime for the sake of war. e

CL: Your argument appears sound, Stranger, but unless I am much mistaken, our own institutions, as well as those of the Spartans, are fashioned entirely and emphatically with this goal in view.

ATH: That may well be. However, there is no need on our part to push 629a
the point aggressively. We should maintain a civil tone as we question

them, since we and they alike take these matters most seriously. Let us follow up the argument together, taking as our authority Tyrtaeus, who was of Athenian stock but became a Spartan citizen. He takes these matters most seriously, if anyone does, for he said:

> 'I would not memorialize a man nor take any account of him'

b —not even, he says, the richest man of all, or one who possessed good things in abundance (he enumerates virtually all of them)—'who did not always prove to be best in war'. Presumably you are familiar with his poems. Our friend here, I expect, knows them by heart.

MEG: I do indeed.

CL: They have made their way from Sparta to our shores as well.

ATH: Well then. Let's join forces and question our poet more or less like this: 'O Tyrtaeus, most divine poet, we think you are wise and good
c to have praised so highly those who distinguish themselves in war. All of us here—myself, this gentleman, and Clinias here from Knossos—are emphatically in agreement with you on this point, we think. But we'd like to be sure that we are talking about the same men. So please tell us whether or not in your view, as in ours, there are clearly two kinds of war.' I think that even a poet far inferior to Tyrtaeus would say,
d correctly, that there are two. One of these, which we call 'faction', is the hardest conflict, as we were saying just now. The other type of war we all posit, I believe—the kind we wage against external enemies and foreigners—is far milder.

CL: To be sure.

ATH: 'Well then, which kind of men and which kind of war do you have in mind when you praise some men so highly and censure others? It seems to be the one we wage against external enemies, inasmuch as you
e said in your poems that you cannot abide those who "fail to be emboldened by the sight of bloody slaughter" and do not

> "lay waste the enemy, assailing him at close quarters".'

So then next we'd say, 'It seems your praise, Tyrtaeus, is particularly directed at those who have distinguished themselves in battle against external and foreign enemies.' I gather he would say 'yes' and agree with us?

CL: Of course.

ATH: We, on the other hand, hold that while these men are good,
there are others who are better by far—those who show themselves to be 630a
best in the most important kind of war. We too can invoke a poet as our
witness: Theognis, citizen of Megara in Sicily, who says:

> A trustworthy man, O Kyrnus,
> is worth his weight in silver and gold,
> in times of hard faction.

This man, we say, is far better in the harder conflict than that other
one—to nearly the same degree as a blend of justice, moderation, and
wisdom along with courage is better than courage on its own. For no b
one would be trustworthy and dependable in the face of faction unless
he had all of virtue. While plenty of mercenaries are willing to march
forth and die fighting in the kind of battle Tyrtaeus mentions, the vast
majority of these are rash, unjust, insolent, and utterly witless, with very
few exceptions. Now, what point are these remarks intended to estab- c
blish? Clearly, and above all else, it is that the legislator from Zeus in this
country and any legislator who is any good will set his primary sights on
nothing other than the greatest virtue when he establishes laws. This,
according to Theognis, is trustworthiness in a crisis, which one might
call complete justice. By contrast, the virtue that Tyrtaeus singles out for
praise, although it is admirable and appropriately celebrated by the poet,
nonetheless comes fourth in rank and merit, strictly speaking. d

CL: Dear Stranger, we are casting our own legislator in a very poor light.

ATH: Not at all. It is we who are doing poorly by supposing that Lycurgus and Minos had war in view when establishing the institutions here and in Sparta.

CL: So what should we be saying instead?

ATH: What is only right and true to say on behalf of a divine lawgiver,
that he made the laws looking not to a part of virtue, and the most e
trifling one at that, but to virtue in its entirety. That is, he worked out
his laws according to different categories from the ones that guide
legislators today. These people seek out laws under the category of
whatever need arises, adding it in to the rest. One works out laws

about inheritance and heiresses, another about assault, and countless others in like manner. We, on the other hand, maintain that the
631a proper way to formulate laws is to start where our present inquiry began. I am altogether impressed, in fact, at your own first stab at legal interpretation. You were correct to begin with virtue and say that it was for its sake that the legislator framed his laws. However, you were clearly incorrect, in my view, to suppose that it was only to a part of virtue, and the smallest one at that, that he referred all his laws. That was the whole point of my subsequent argument so far. Now, shall
b I explain the sort of divisions I would have hoped to hear you make in your speech?

CL: Certainly.

ATH: You should have said: 'Stranger, it is for good reason that Cretan laws are held in such high repute among the Greeks. They are correct laws and bring happiness to those who live by them, since they provide them with every good. Now goods are twofold—some of them human, others divine—and the former depend on the divine. A city that receives
c the greater ones acquires the lesser as well; otherwise, it is bereft of both. Chief among the lesser goods is health, second beauty, and third is strength for running and other physical activities. Fourth is wealth that is not blind but clear-sighted, which comes from following wisdom. Wisdom itself is first and leader of the divine goods. Second is a moderate disposition of the soul involving intelligence. Third would be justice, which arises when these two are combined with courage, and
d fourth would be courage. The latter goods are naturally ranked above the former, and the lawgiver must rank them thus as well.

'Next, he must inform the citizens that all his other instructions to them have these goods in view, the human goods directed at the divine, and the divine ones directed at their leader, intelligence. When the citizens join together in marriage, when they beget and raise children,
e male or female, when they are young, and as they mature and reach old age, he must take care to mete out honour and dishonour correctly. In the citizens' dealings with each other, he must scrutinize carefully their
632a pains and pleasures, their desires, and the general intensity of their passions. He will praise and blame these correctly, through the laws themselves. As for their feelings of anger and fear, when their souls are disturbed on account of misfortune, and relief from these in times of prosperity—the sorts of feelings people have in illness, war, poverty, and

their opposites—for all of these he must define and teach what is admirable and what is not in different people's responses.

'Next, the lawgiver must safeguard the ways the citizens acquire and b
dispose of property. He must review joint enterprises and their dissolutions, both voluntary and involuntary, indicating where justice is to be found and where it is missing in such transactions. He will award honours to those who are receptive to the laws, and ordain penalties for those who are resistant to persuasion. Finally, he will put the
finishing touches on his constitution by determining what sort of burial c
rites should be performed and what sorts of honours awarded to different people when they die. With his survey complete, the author of these laws will appoint guardians for them all. Some will operate with wisdom, others with true opinion—so that intelligence will bind it all together to follow moderation and justice rather than wealth and
ambition.' This, Strangers, is how I was hoping to hear you explain d
the laws attributed to Zeus and Pythian Apollo, which Minos and Lycurgus established. Indeed, I still wish to hear how these features are present in those laws, and how it is that their order is obvious to anyone experienced in the law—whether the experience is due to knowledge or results from some training—but is completely obscure to the rest of us.

CL: And how are we to go about doing that, Stranger?

ATH: I think we need to return to our original starting point and
examine first the practices to do with courage. After that, if the two of e
you are willing, we will then go through the next kind of virtue, and after that the next. Our exposition of the first will serve as a model for the rest, and we will lighten our journey, so far as we can, with conversation. In the end we will have gone through virtue in its entirety and shown it to be the focus of the things we were just discussing—provided the god is willing.

MEG: An excellent proposal. Let our admirer of Zeus here be the first 633a
one you set out to examine.

ATH: I shall try, but I'll be examining you and myself at the same time, since our discussion is a group effort. So tell me. We say that it is with war in mind that the legislator devised your communal meals and your regime of athletic training?

MEG: Yes.

ATH: And what practices shall we list third and fourth? We will no doubt need to enumerate them just as thoroughly for virtue's other parts—or whatever we should call them; it doesn't matter so long as what we mean is clear.

b MEG: Well third, like any other Spartan, I would say that he invented the hunt.

ATH: Let's try to list a fourth, and if possible a fifth.

MEG: Now fourth, I would venture to say, is our large set of activities that involve endurance of pain. For example, we have our boxing matches and the raids that regularly involve a severe beating. In addition, our so-called 'secret service' involves amazingly heavy practice in
c endurance—going barefoot and sleeping without bedding during the winter, ministering to one's own needs without the help of servants, and ranging over the whole countryside night and day. Our 'naked games' are also gruelling exercises in endurance as we compete in the worst heat of the summer—not to mention a great many additional examples too numerous to go through separately.

ATH: Well done, Spartan Stranger. But let's consider what we take courage to be. Does it amount quite simply to a battle against fears and
d pains alone? Or does it also oppose yearnings and pleasures, those powerfully seductive flatterers that can melt the resolve even of those who consider themselves highly dignified?

MEG: That's what I think. It opposes all these things.

ATH: Now, if I recall our previous discussion correctly, our friend here spoke of a city being 'defeated by itself', and likewise a man. Isn't that so, Stranger from Knossos?

CL: Quite true.

e ATH: So now, is it the person defeated by pains whom we call bad, or also the one defeated by pleasures?

CL: Even more so, I think, in the case of pleasures. Pretty well everyone has in mind the person controlled by pleasures when we speak of being 'defeated by oneself' in the reprehensible sense, rather than the person defeated by pains.

ATH: But surely Zeus and the Pythian lawgiver did not legislate for a lame form of courage, able to attack only on the left and incapable of doing battle against the insidious pleasures ranged to its right? Didn't they equip it to fight in both directions? 634a

CL: Yes, in both, I think.

ATH: So let's go back and identify in your two cities the practices that engage with pleasures rather than flee them. Where pains are concerned, your practice isn't to avoid them but to thrust a person into their midst, where he is compelled and persuaded by honours to master them. What arrangement is there in your laws to do likewise concerning pleasures? b
Please tell me what practice you have that makes the same person courageous in the face of pains and pleasures alike, so that he defeats the ones he ought to and is never defeated by the enemy that is hardest and closest at hand.

MEG: Well Stranger, I was able to mention a large number of laws directed against pains, but I don't think I could as easily come up with c
large-scale and striking examples in the case of pleasures, although perhaps I might succeed at finding some small ones.

CL: Nor would I find it any easier to identify a clear case among Cretan laws.

ATH: That's not surprising, Strangers. Now, sirs, if one of us criticizes something in the laws of the others' home city, but his intent is to discover what is true and best, we should accept this criticism mildly rather than harshly.

CL: Quite right, Athenian Stranger—a persuasive point.

ATH: At our age, Clinias, acting otherwise would hardly be fitting. d

CL: Indeed it wouldn't.

ATH: Now whether it is right to criticize the Spartan and Cretan constitutions is the topic for another discussion—although I would probably find it easier than either of you to voice what is generally said. That's because, as soundly based as the rest of your legal arrangements are, one of your finest is the law that forbids the young to inquire into what is and isn't admirable among those arrangements. Instead, e
everyone must join voices and sing out their agreement that all the laws

are beautifully arranged, since they are edicts of the gods. If anyone says otherwise, they must absolutely refuse to listen. An old man, however, if he has any misgivings about your institutions, is allowed to communicate them to a state official, or to someone else his own age, as long as he is out of hearing of the young.

CL: Absolutely correct, Stranger, and spoken like a diviner. Even at this
635a great remove from our legislator, you have hit upon exactly what he was thinking and articulated it most truly.

ATH: Well, there are no young men present now, and we are at an advanced age, so your legislator would allow us to discuss these matters among ourselves without striking a discordant note?

CL: That's right—and don't hold back at all in your criticism of our laws. There is no dishonour in recognizing that something is less than admirable. Indeed, it gives one the opportunity to correct it, provided
b one receives the criticism with goodwill rather than resentment.

ATH: Very good. What I'm going to say, in any case, is not a criticism of your laws. I wouldn't do that without first giving them a thorough examination. I simply express my puzzlement. Among all the Greeks and foreigners known to us, your legislator is the only one who commands abstinence from the greatest pleasures and enjoyments and forbids you to taste them. But when it comes to pains and fears, which we were just discussing, his view was that if from an early age a
c person avoids these on every occasion, when he does encounter those hardships, fears, and pains that are unavoidable he will be put to flight and enslaved by people with training in such matters. That same lawgiver, in my view, should have thought the same thing about pleasures. He should have said, 'If our citizens grow up without experience of the greatest pleasures, they will have no practice at enduring in the face of pleasures and refusing to be compelled into shameful conduct. Their weakness in the face of pleasures will subject them to the
d same fate as those who are defeated by fears, only their enslavement will be different and more shameful, since it will be to men who are both able to endure in the face of pleasures and also well versed in matters of pleasure—utterly bad people, some of them. Our citizens' souls will be slaves in one respect and free in another, unworthy of being called courageous and free without qualification.'

Consider, now, whether you two think anything in those comments is on the mark.

CL: Well, it seems so on first hearing, but I worry about rushing to judgement on such a weighty matter, like foolish adolescents. e

ATH: Well, Clinias—and you too, Stranger from Sparta—if we might proceed to the next item on our agenda, let us talk about moderation next after courage. What will we find in your legal systems that makes them superior on this front to the system of any randomly governed people, as in the military matters we were just discussing? 636a

MEG: That's hardly easy. Still, it seems that our communal meals and athletic training are well designed to achieve both effects.

ATH: What really seems hard, Strangers, is that constitutional matters are as contradictory in their effects as they are controversial in discussion. The same problem arises in physical training, where there is hardly a single regimen one can prescribe for a given body that does not evidently harm our bodies in some respects, while benefiting them in others. Take your system of athletic training and communal meals. b
They benefit your cities in many ways, but constitute a danger in times of faction, as the youth of Miletus, Boeotia, and Thurii have made clear. What's more, it seems the great antiquity of these practices has corrupted the sexual pleasures that are natural to humans and beasts. Your cities in particular are to be criticized for bringing about this effect, yours and any others that put such great emphasis on athletic training. c
Whether it is right to be playful or serious about such matters, it is imperative to keep in mind that it seems natural for male and female to experience pleasure when they have intercourse for procreation, but that the pleasure of males coupling with males or of females with females is unnatural, one of the greatest outrages arising from failure to control one's pleasures. Indeed, we all fault the Cretans for coming up with the story of Ganymede. Convinced as they are that their laws come from d
Zeus, they saddle him with this tale so that they can be following the god even when reaping this particular pleasure.

Enough now about stories. The upshot for our legislative inquiry is that virtually the whole subject concerns pleasures and pains, those in cities and those in individual characters. These two springs flow freely by nature, and whoever draws from the right one at the right time and to

e the right extent lives a happy life—whether a city, an individual person,
or an animal—while the one who draws from them unintelligently and
at the wrong time lives the opposite way.

MEG: That's more or less right, Stranger; at any rate, we are at a loss to
say anything against it. Nonetheless, I still think that the lawgiver for the
Spartans quite rightly commanded us to avoid pleasures. As for the laws
in Knossos, our friend here, if he wishes, will come to their defence. To
637a me, the Spartan legislation concerning pleasure is the finest in all the
world. For example, our law has entirely banished from the country the
activity in which people are most likely to indulge in extreme pleasures,
outrageous behaviour, and utter folly. In neither the countryside nor any
town under Spartan control will you find drinking parties, with all that
they involve, stirring up every possible pleasure. Nor is there anyone
b who, on encountering a drunken reveller, will not visit upon him a
severe and immediate punishment, even if he has the festival of Dio-
nysus as his excuse. I have seen revellers of this sort piled into wagons in
your city, and in Tarentum among our own colonists I once saw the
whole city drunk at the Dionysian festival. At home we do nothing of
the sort.

ATH: But, Spartan Stranger, such activities are all perfectly commend-
able when practised with discipline, although I admit they are the height
c of stupidity when practised without restraint. In fact, someone defend-
ing our own ways might well take a shot at you, pointing to the lack of
restraint in your women at home. Of course, for all such practices—
whether in Tarentum, in my home, or in yours—there is thought to be a
single reply that acquits a practice of the charge that it is faulty rather
than correct. To the stranger who is shocked at the unfamiliar ways that
he observes in their home, everyone will respond, 'Don't be shocked,
Stranger. This is our custom here and no doubt you do things differently
d where you come from.' But our present discussion, my dear friends, is
not about what other people do but about the excellence or deficiency of
their lawgivers.

Now, let us continue with the general topic of drinking, which is a
practice of no small importance and requires a good legislator to under-
stand it. I'm not talking simply about whether drinking wine should be
allowed, but about drunkenness itself. Should a people indulge in this,
as the Scythians and Persians do, as well as the Carthaginians, Celts,
e Iberians, and Thracians—warlike peoples, all of them—or follow your

practice instead? While your people, as you say, abstain completely, the Scythians and Thracians take their wine unmixed. Women and men alike spill it all over their clothes and think this an admirable and happy practice to engage in. The Persians too, although they imbibe in a more orderly manner, still engage most assiduously in this and the other indulgences that you reject.

MEG: When it comes time to take up arms, sir, we put all these peoples 638a
to flight!

ATH: Don't say that, sir! There have been and will be many cases of flight and pursuit that tell us nothing, so this is a dubious criterion to invoke. In fact, it is highly disputable that victory and defeat in battle show whether a people's practices are admirable. For instance, larger
cities defeat smaller ones in battle. The Syracusans subjugated the b
Locrians, whose laws were thought to be the best in that region, and the Athenians did the same to the Ceians, with many other examples easy to find. So let's set aside talk about victory and defeat and focus on the specific practices themselves, attempting to persuade ourselves that such-and-such a kind of practice is admirable, while such-and-such another is not. To begin with, let me tell you something about the right way to determine the value of these practices.

MEG: What do you mean? c

ATH: My own view is that anyone who is ready to criticize or praise a practice as soon as it is mentioned is not going about this business in the right way. It is as if one person praises cheese as a wholesome food and another immediately denounces it—without first finding out its effects and its presentation: how and to whom it is served, with what accompaniments and in what condition, as well as the condition of the person
who eats it. That's just what's going on in our discussion, if you ask me. d
Drunkenness is barely mentioned and right away some of us are criticizing it and others praising it, quite absurdly. Each of us invokes witnesses and advocates for our own side, some thinking the large number on their side settles the matter, others taking it to be conclusive that those who don't engage in the practice are victorious in battle
(although even here we might dispute the facts). If this is the way we e
are going to treat all the other institutions we examine, it makes no sense, in my opinion. Let me show you instead, if I can, the different approach that I think we must follow in all such matters, and illustrate it

in the case of drunkenness. After all, thousands upon thousands of peoples who dispute the position of your two cities on this topic would combine forces against you in argument!

MEG: Well, if there is a correct way to investigate matters of this sort,
639a we ought not to balk at hearing about it.

ATH: We should conduct our inquiry more or less along the following lines. Suppose one person praises goat-keeping, and praises the animal itself as an admirable possession, while another reviles the practice because he has seen goats untended by a herdsman and causing damage as they graze in cultivated fields. In the same way he disparages any animal that he has seen unsupervised or tended by incompetent masters. In our opinion, are the denunciations of such a critic soundly based at all?

MEG: How could they be?

ATH: Now, is someone a good ship's captain as long as he is skilled at
b navigation, regardless of whether he is prone to seasickness? What should we say about that?

MEG: He is no good at all if his skill is combined with the affliction you just mentioned.

ATH: What about a leader of armies? Is he fit to lead as long as he is skilled in military science, even if he is a coward in the face of dangers, seasick, and drunk with fear?

MEG: How could he be?

ATH: And what if he is both unskilled and a coward?

MEG: That's a thoroughly rotten leader, only fit to command women!

c ATH: Now take any gathering you like that naturally has a leader and is beneficial when it does. Suppose someone praises or disparages it, but has never seen a properly conducted instance of it, only cases where there is no leader or a bad one. Do we think that praise or criticism from this kind of observer of this kind of gathering is of any value?

MEG: How could it be, if the critics have never observed or partici-
d pated in a properly conducted assembly of this sort?

ATH: Hold on to that point a moment. Would we say that drinking companions, or a drinking party, are one kind of gathering?

MEG: Most emphatically.

ATH: Now, has anyone ever observed one that was properly conducted? The two of you can easily reply with a resounding 'No', since the practice is not native or lawful in your countries. I, by contrast, have encountered many of them in many places and examined them all quite thoroughly,
but pretty well none of those I have observed or heard of was conducted e
properly in its entirety, except perhaps for a few short bits here and there. On the whole, they were almost entirely off the mark.

CL: What do you mean, Stranger? Could you be more precise? Our lack of experience, which you have noted, hardly equips us to recognize
what is correct and incorrect in such a gathering, even if we were to 640a
attend one.

ATH: Most likely not, but see if you can learn from what I have to say. You grasp the point, don't you, that in any gathering, or collective activity of any kind, the correct thing is for the participants to have a leader?

CL: Yes, of course.

ATH: Now we were just saying that a leader of warriors has to be courageous.

CL: Of course.

ATH: And a courageous man is less disturbed by fears than cowards are.

CL: That too is true. b

ATH: If there were a way to appoint a completely fearless and undisturbed general to command an army, wouldn't we make every effort to employ it?

CL: We surely would.

ATH: Now the leader we are concerned with at present is not one who will lead an army into battle against enemies in wartime. Rather, in peacetime, he will lead friends gathered together in mutual goodwill.

CL: Right.

ATH: Now such a gathering, if it is to involve drinking, will not be c
without disturbances, will it?

CL: Of course not—quite the contrary, I should expect.

ATH: So, first of all, they too are in need of a leader?

CL: They are indeed, like nothing else.

ATH: And shouldn't they be provided with a leader who is himself undisturbed, if possible?

CL: Of course.

ATH: And also, it would seem, one who is wise about social gatherings,
for his job is to safeguard the existing friendly relations among the
d participants and use the present gathering to strengthen them for the
future.

CL: Very true.

ATH: So we must set up as ruler over our drinkers a leader who is sober and wise, rather than the opposite? With a party of drunks led by a drunk, or by a young and inexpert leader, it would be a stroke of great luck if things failed to turn out badly.

CL: Absolutely.

ATH: If someone were to fault these gatherings in cities where they are
conducted as correctly as possible, and he directed his criticisms against
e the practice itself, he might, perhaps, be correct in his criticisms. But if
someone were to abuse the activity because he sees it done all wrong, it is
clear that he fails to realize two things—first, that the activity is not
being done correctly, and second, that any practice will appear perni-
cious when conducted, as this one is, without a sober leader as its master.
Surely you understand that an intoxicated captain, or leader of anything
641a at all, will overturn the ship or the chariot or the army, or whatever he is
in charge of?

CL: What you have said is all very true, Stranger, but please move on to
the next point. What possible good could we get from this drinking
practice, even supposing it is conducted correctly? For example, take
that army under correct leadership that you mentioned: those who
follow the leader reap the not inconsiderable benefit of victory in war,
b and similarly with the other examples. But what is the great benefit that
a city or private citizens would reap from a properly led drinking party?

ATH: Well, if you are asking what great benefit we would say a city derives from having a single pupil or chorus properly trained, our answer would be that from a single case the benefit is fairly small. But if you are asking what benefit a city derives from educating people in general, then it is not hard to say that those who are properly educated become good
men, and as a result do admirably in all things. They even defeat their c
enemies in battle! Education, you see, delivers victory, although victory sometimes undermines education. For many are made insolent by their victories in war, and this in turn fills them with myriad other vices. Many have won, and will win, Cadmean victories, but there is no such thing as a 'Cadmean' education.

CL: You seem to be telling us that the practice of drinking wine
together is important for education, provided it is conducted properly! d

ATH: I am indeed.

CL: Are you in a position to affirm, next, that this claim is true?

ATH: As for the truth, Stranger, in such a contentious matter only a god may insist that this is how things are. But if I am simply to say how things seem to me, I won't begrudge you an answer, seeing as we are already embarked on a conversation about laws and constitutions.

CL: That is exactly what we are trying to ascertain—your opinion on
the point at issue! e

ATH: Then we are doing the right thing; you are trying to figure out what my view is, and I am doing what I can to present it clearly. Now let me say this as a preliminary. Every Greek is of the opinion that my city loves argument and long discussion, while Sparta is brief of speech and Crete more given to extended thought than extended exposition.

Now, I don't want to give the impression that I am going on and on 642a
about a trifling matter, stretching out my discussion of drinking with fussy elaboration. However, a correct and natural treatment of the topic is impossible without first giving a clear and adequate treatment of correctness in music, and this, I'm afraid, is impossible without first discussing education as a whole—a very long discussion indeed. So what do you think we should do? Should we abandon this topic of discussion
for the time being and shift to a different issue about laws? b

MEG: Perhaps you aren't aware, Athenian Stranger, that my family
holds the position of *proxenos* for your city. Now maybe all children,
upon learning that they are *proxenoi* of a particular city, are imbued with
a feeling of goodwill towards it right from youth, as if it were a second
fatherland after their own city. In my case, that's just what happened. I
c would hear other children say, when Spartans praised or criticized the
Athenians for something, 'O Megillus, your city has treated us badly' or
'treated us well'. From listening to this and always defending you against
those casting aspersions on your city, I acquired broad feelings of
goodwill towards you. Even your accent is dear to me, and I hold to
be most true the popular saying that 'good Athenians are exceptionally
d so'. They alone are good not by compulsion but of their own nature, by
divine allotment, truly and without pretence. So don't hold back on my
account. As far as I'm concerned you may speak as long as you like.

CL: That goes for me too, Stranger. After you've listened to what I have
to say, don't hold back: go ahead and speak at whatever length you wish.
You have heard, presumably, of Epimenides, a divinely good man native
to this area and in fact my kinsman. He visited your city on a mission
from the god's oracle ten years before the Persian war, and performed
sacrifices commanded by the god. The Athenians were alarmed at the
e time about the military preparations in Persia, but he assured them that
the Persians would not invade for another ten years and that when they
did, they would be driven back without accomplishing any of their
objectives and would suffer greater damage than they inflicted. My
ancestors formed ties of hospitality with you then, and ever since my
643a people and I have been well disposed towards yours.

ATH: Well, it seems that you, for your part, are ready to listen. I for mine am ready as well, at least as far as intentions go. As for whether I am able to carry it off, that's more difficult, but I must try nonetheless. As a first step in our argument, then, let us define education, what it is and what it can do, since we said that the discussion on which we are embarked needs to go through this topic before reaching the god that is its destination.

CL: Certainly, let's do it that way, if it pleases you.

b ATH: Let me tell you how we should understand education. See
whether you are pleased with that.

CL: Please tell us.

ATH: My view is that anyone who will be good at anything at all when
he is grown must practise it right from childhood; both his playtime and
his serious attention must be occupied with its activities. Those who will
be good farmers or builders should build toy structures or work the soil c
in their play, and their caregivers should supply them with miniature
tools of the trade, replicas of the real ones. What they must learn, in
particular, are the essential preliminary skills. The future carpenter
learns to take measurements, and the warrior to ride a horse, by doing
these things (or things like them) when they play. It is through playful
activities that their caregivers try to direct children's pleasures and
desires towards what they must do when they are fully grown. Indeed,
it is of the utmost importance for education, on our view, that one
receives a correct upbringing, since this inculcates as far as possible in the d
soul of the child at play a passion for the occupation in which the grown
man will need to be completely good.

So tell me, are you pleased with my account so far?

CL: How could we not be?

ATH: Now, let's be precise about what we are calling education. As it
is, when we praise and disparage the upbringing of different people,
saying this person is educated and that one uneducated, the latter is
often quite thoroughly 'educated' in retail trade or merchant shipping or e
some other such thing. But our discussion, presumably, is not with
those who consider that sort of thing to be education. Rather, it
concerns the education that, right from childhood, directs a person
towards virtue, giving him an appetite and passion to become a perfect
citizen, one who knows how to rule and be ruled with justice. I think it
is clear that this sort of upbringing is what our present account aims to 644a
single out with the title 'education'. By contrast, an upbringing directed
at making money or cultivating strength—or any other skill that does
not involve intelligence and justice—it classifies as 'mechanical', 'slav-
ish', and unworthy of the name 'education'. Rather than quibble over
labels, let us stick with our present agreement that as a rule those who
are properly educated become good and that education is never to be
disparaged, since it is the first of the very finest things bestowed upon b
the best of men. If it ever goes off course and there is the possibility of

correcting it, then anyone, at any time of life, must devote all his energies towards correcting it.

CL: You are right. We agree with what you say.

ATH: Now, we previously agreed that those who are able to rule themselves are good, while those who are unable to do so are bad.

CL: Exactly.

ATH: Let us return to this phenomenon and clarify further what we
c take it to be. I hope you will allow me, if I can, to illustrate by means of
an image.

CL: Go ahead.

ATH: We assume each of us is a single individual?

CL: Yes.

ATH: But we each have inside ourselves two opposite and witless advisors, which we call pleasure and pain.

CL: That's the case.

ATH: Besides these two, we have opinions about the future, whose
common name is 'anticipation' and whose particular names are 'fear',
d the anticipation before pain, and 'daring', the anticipation before the
opposite. And against all of these we have calculation as to which of
them is better or worse. When it becomes the common view of a city, it
is called 'law'.

CL: I am barely able to follow you, but please continue as if I did.

MEG: That's what I'm feeling too.

ATH: Let's think about it this way. Consider each of us, living beings
that we are, to be a divine puppet—whether constituted as the gods'
plaything or for a serious purpose, we have no idea. What we do know is
e that these various experiences in us are like cords or strings that tug at us
and oppose each other. They pull against each other towards opposing
actions across the field where virtue is marked off from vice. Our
account singles out one of these pulls and says that each of us must
follow it and pull against the other cords, never loosening our grip on it.
645a This is the sacred and golden guidance of calculation, also called the

city's common law. The other pulls are hard as iron, but this one is soft because it is golden, while the others resemble all kinds of different material. One must always pitch in with the noblest guidance, that of law, since calculation—although it is noble—is gentle rather than violent, so its guidance requires helpers if our golden element is to be victorious over the others.

Here is how we may vindicate the tale of virtue that likens us to b
puppets. It makes clearer, in a way, what is meant by 'self-mastery' and 'self-defeat', as well as the manner in which a city and an individual person ought to live—a person must grasp within himself the true account concerning these pulls and live in accordance with it, while a city, having received this account from a god or from the person who understands these matters, must establish it as law and conduct its internal and external affairs accordingly. In addition, the tale gives us a
more lucid articulation of virtue and vice, and greater clarity here will c
perhaps shed light on education and various other practices, particularly the drinking party. While it might appear that, in the latter case, we have said too much about a trifling matter, it might equally turn out to be worth the lengthy treatment.

CL: You are right. Let's finish whatever in our present enterprise is worth the effort.

ATH: So tell me, what sort of effect will we produce by getting our d
puppet drunk?

CL: What are you getting at with that question?

ATH: Nothing in particular yet. I'm just asking what generally results when the one is combined with the other. I'll try to state more clearly what I have in mind. My question is this. Doesn't drinking wine make our pleasures and pains, our angry feelings, and our passions more intense?

CL: Very much so.

ATH: What about our perceptions, memories, opinions, and cogni- e
tions? Are they likewise intensified? Or don't they, rather, completely abandon a person who is full of drink?

CL: You are right; they abandon him completely.

ATH: So his soul returns to the same condition as when he was a young child.

CL: Indeed.

ATH: Wouldn't he then be least in control of himself?

646a CL: Yes, least.

ATH: Don't we affirm that this sort of person is the worst?

CL: Very much so.

ATH: So it is not only an old man who becomes a child again, but also, it seems, a man who is drunk.

CL: Well said, Stranger.

ATH: So is there any argument that could even try to convince us that we should partake of this practice rather than flee it with all our strength and ability?

CL: I gather there is. So you say, at any rate, and you were only a moment ago prepared to give it to us.

b ATH: You remember correctly. I am in fact still prepared to give it, since the two of you have emphatically declared your willingness to listen.

CL: How could we not listen—if only for the bizarreness of the proposal that a man should willingly launch himself into utter degradation!

ATH: You mean degradation of soul, don't you?

CL: Yes.

ATH: Well, my friend, what of the body and its degradations—emaciation, disfigurement, and weakness? Would we find it bizarre if
c someone willingly brought such things upon himself?

CL: Of course we would.

ATH: What about people who present themselves for medical treatment with drugs? Are we to suppose they don't know that starting shortly thereafter and continuing for many days their bodies will be in such a state that they would be unwilling to go on living if it were a permanent condition? Or consider those who go in for strenuous athletic training. Don't we know that they become weaker immediately afterwards?

CL: Yes, we know all that.

ATH: And we also know that it is for the sake of the resulting benefit that they willingly go in for these things.

CL: Precisely. d

ATH: So, shouldn't we think about other practices along the same lines?

CL: Of course.

ATH: So this is how we should think about the practice of wine drinking—provided it is correct to place it in the same category.

CL: No doubt.

ATH: If it turns out to provide us with a benefit not inferior to what is produced in the bodily case, then wouldn't it have the advantage over bodily exercises that, in the initial stage at least, the latter is painful, while it itself is not?

CL: Correct. But I should be surprised if we were able to discover any e
such benefit in it.

ATH: That's the very task incumbent upon us at the moment, it would seem. Now tell me: are we able to distinguish two roughly opposing kinds of fear?

CL: What kinds do you mean?

ATH: The following. On the one hand, we fear bad things when we expect them to befall us.

CL: Yes.

ATH: On the other hand, on many occasions we fear for our reputation, believing that people will think ill of us if we do or say something
that is ignoble—a kind of fear that we call 'shame', and I dare say 647a
everyone else does too.

CL: Certainly.

ATH: These are the two fears I was talking about. The latter opposes not only pains and other fears but also the most prevalent and strongest pleasures.

CL: Very true.

ATH: So doesn't the legislator, and anyone else worth his salt, hold this
fear in great esteem, calling it 'shame', and calling the daring that is
b opposed to it 'shamelessness'—the latter being, in his view, the greatest
evil in private or public life?

CL: You are right.

ATH: Not only does this fear safeguard us in many other and important respects, but nothing is more effective, man for man, at securing victory and safety in war itself. For there are two things that secure victory—daring in the face of the enemy and fear of being disgraced in front of one's friends.

CL: That is the case.

ATH: So each of us needs to become both fearless and afraid, for the
c reasons we have explained in the two cases.

CL: Absolutely.

ATH: Now when we want to make someone unafraid of various things, we achieve this effect by exposing him to fear in a controlled manner.

CL: Certainly.

ATH: What about when our task is to make someone justly afraid? To
make him victorious in the fight against his pleasures, don't we need to
throw him into the ring with shamelessness and make him wrestle
against it? In order to become perfect in courage, a person must face
d off against the cowardice within him and defeat it, since without
experience and practice in struggles of this kind, no one would get
even halfway towards virtue. So will anyone become perfect in moderation if he has not done battle against the many pleasures and desires
that urge him to commit shameless and unjust actions—if he has not
defeated them by dint of argument, effort, and skill, both in play and in
earnest—if he has, on the contrary, never experienced such things?

CL: It hardly seems likely that he could.

e ATH: Well then, has any god given humans a potion for fear? I have in
mind the sort of drink that the more one is willing to imbibe, the more
one comes to suppose, with each drink, that he has fallen into misfortune, a drink that makes him fearful about everything in his present and
648a future circumstances, one that ultimately delivers even the most

courageous person into absolute and total dread, but once he has slept it off, he is back to his usual self?

CL: And where in the world might one find such a drink, Stranger?

ATH: Nowhere, I'm afraid. But if there were such a drink somewhere, wouldn't it be useful to the legislator for inculcating courage? For example, we could put the question to him, 'Legislator—whether you make laws for the Cretans or for any other people—wouldn't you b
welcome, first of all, a test for courage and cowardice in your citizens?'

CL: Any legislator would clearly say yes.

ATH: And if we asked whether he would prefer a test one could conduct in safety and away from danger, as opposed to the opposite?

CL: He would undoubtedly agree to the safe option.

ATH: 'Wouldn't you employ it to lead your citizens into fears and test their reactions, so that by exhorting, chastising, and bestowing honour upon them, you would compel them to become fearless? You would c
heap disgrace upon the disobedient for failing to be exactly as you command. Whoever performed well and courageously in these training exercises would escape punishment, but those who did badly would be penalized. Or would you decline to make use of the potion, even if you found no other reason to find fault with it?'

CL: How could he not use it, Stranger?

ATH: As a method of training, my friend, this would be much easier than present methods, whether for individuals, small groups, or however many one might want. A single person training by himself in peacetime d
who was bashful about being observed by others before he was in good condition might train against his fears in this way. He would do well to supply himself with this one drink instead of a lot of other equipment. A person who was confident that he was well equipped by nature and practice would not hesitate to strip and train with fellow drinkers so that he could demonstrate his ability to escape and overcome the compulsive e
shaking induced by the potion. His virtue would keep him from being seriously tripped up or led astray by impropriety, although he would leave off drinking before the final round, since he would fear the drink's power to defeat any human being.

CL: Yes, Stranger, that would be very moderate of him.

649a ATH: Let's return to address our legislator. 'Well then, Legislator, I gather no god has gifted us with such a potion for fear, and we have not managed to devise one for ourselves (setting aside the claims of quacks). But what about fearlessness, the excessive and untimely daring to do what we should not? Is there any drink for this, do you think?'

CL: He will presumably answer that there is such a drink, and that it is wine.

ATH: Now isn't this drink exactly the opposite of the one we were just discussing? The immediate effect of drinking wine is to make a person
b more affable than he was before, and the more he drinks, the more he is filled with optimistic expectations and belief in his abilities. In the end he is brimming over with unchecked speech and freedom, in conceit of his own wisdom, and full of every kind of fearlessness, so that there is absolutely nothing that he would hold back from saying, and likewise from doing. Everyone would agree, I think, that this is what happens?

CL: Of course.

ATH: Recall now the two things that we said should be cultivated in our souls: the first is that we should be supremely daring, while the
c second, its opposite, is that we should be supremely afraid.

CL: We gather this is the shame you were talking about?

ATH: You remember well. Since it is in the presence of fears that we must practise being courageous and fearless, we should consider whether the opposite condition is to be cultivated in the opposite circumstances.

CL: That seems likely.

ATH: So it is in the presence of things that naturally make us especially daring and bold that it seems we must practise at *not* being shameless
d and full of audacity, but rather afraid of daring to say, undergo, or do anything shameful at all.

CL: So it seems.

ATH: Well, all these things have such an effect on us: anger, passion, insolence, ignorance, greed, and cowardice—along with wealth, beauty, strength, and everything that by making us drunk with pleasure drives

us out of our minds. Now for an inexpensive and relatively harmless
way, first of all, to test ourselves, and second, to get practice in these
matters, what more suitable pleasure can we name than the recreation e
and testing afforded by wine—provided it is conducted with some care?
Look at it this way. Suppose we wanted to put to the test an ill-tempered
and savage soul, prone to all kinds of wrongdoing. Would it be more
dangerous to do so by entering into a business deal with the man and
exposing oneself to the attendant risks, or by keeping company with him 650a
at a festival of Dionysus? The same goes for testing a soul in thrall to
sexual passion by entrusting to its care our own daughters, sons, and
wives. We would be endangering what is most precious to us in order to
discern the soul's character. No further examples are necessary to
establish the superiority of testing through this relatively innocuous
form of recreation. And in fact, as far as this feature of the activity
is concerned, we think neither Cretans nor any other peoples would b
dispute that it is a fitting way of testing each other, superior to other
testing methods in its low cost, safety, and speed at delivering results.

CL: That at any rate is true.

ATH: Now, to be able to discern the natures and dispositions of people's souls—wouldn't this be extremely useful to the discipline that cares for these matters? We agree, I take it, that this is the task of politics?

CL: Of course.

Book 2

ATH: Presumably the next thing to consider is whether the only good 652a
thing about drinking parties is that they reveal our natures. Or is there
also some great benefit, which we must take very seriously, that arises
from properly conducted communal drinking? What do we say? The
present argument evidently aims to establish that there is, but we need
to listen attentively if we are not to get tripped up by it. b

CL: Go on, then.

ATH: Well, I want to recall what we said correct education is in our
case. My proposal is that this drinking practice, when properly conduct- 653a
ed, is its safeguard.

CL: That is a very large assertion.

ATH: Here's what I mean. When we are children, the first sensations
we experience are pleasure and pain, and it is in our pleasures and pains
that virtue and vice first develop in our souls. By the time we are old, we
are lucky if we have also developed wisdom and stable true opinions, for
these goods and all that they involve complete a person, but it is the b
virtue that first develops in children that I am calling education. If
pleasure and liking and pain and hatred develop correctly in our souls
when we are not yet able to grasp the account, and when we do grasp the
account they agree with it because they have been correctly trained by
appropriate habits, this agreement is virtue in its entirety. But the part of
virtue that consists in having properly nurtured pleasures and pains, so
that we hate what we should hate and love what we should love from c
beginning to end, if you separated this off in your account and called it
education, you would be exactly right, in my view.

CL: And in our view too, Stranger. Your earlier remarks about education as well as your present comments strike us as quite correct.

ATH: Very good. Now this condition of having correctly nurtured
pleasures and pains—that is, education—tends to slacken and be un-
done over the course of human life. However, the gods took pity on the
d sorry lot of humankind and ordained intervals of respite from their toils
in the form of festivals to the gods. To set them back on the correct
course, they gave them the Muses, their leader Apollo, and Dionysus as
fellow celebrants. They are nurtured during these festivals in the com-
pany of the gods.

Here's a hymn we hear—let's see whether its message is true to nature
or not. It says that every young creature is practically unable to sit still or
e keep quiet, always straining to move about and make noise. Some leap
and bound as though they were dancing in playful glee, while others
break out in sounds of every sort. Now the other animals do not sense
order and disorder in movement (what we call rhythm and harmony).
654a But the gods whom we said were given to us as partners in the dance
gave *us* pleasure in rhythm and harmony, and that is how they set us in
motion and lead our choral dance. When they link us together in song
and dance we call it a chorus—from the name for delight, which fits its
nature. So shall we accept this as our first point, that our initial
education is through the Muses and Apollo, or what?

CL: Just what you said.

ATH: So in our view the uneducated person will be unversed in choral
b dance, and the educated person will have a proper choral training.

CL: Of course.

ATH: Now choral performance as a whole is a matter of dancing and singing.

CL: Necessarily.

ATH: So the well-educated person would be able to sing and dance well.

CL: So it seems.

ATH: Let's see what this thing we've just said amounts to.

CL: What thing?

ATH: 'He sings well', we say, and 'he dances well'. Should we add,
c 'provided the things he sings and the things he dances are beautiful'? Or
shouldn't we?

CL: We should add it.

ATH: Now suppose that what he considers beautiful really is beautiful and what he considers ugly really is ugly, and he treats them as such. Do we hold him to be better educated in choral dance and music than a person who is able to comply in particular cases with what is thought to be beautiful, using his body and his voice, but who fails to enjoy beautiful things and fails to hate their opposites? Or is the better educated person the one who gets it right in his pleasures and pains, d
embracing what is beautiful and offended by what is not, even if he is not quite able to get it right in voice and body or to grasp it in his thought?

CL: You describe a far superior education, Stranger.

ATH: So if we three can identify what is beautiful in song and dance, we can also discern who is correctly educated and who is not. Without this knowledge, however, we could never know whether there is any safeguard for education, or where it is to be found. Isn't that so? e

CL: Very much so.

ATH: Next we must, like hounds in the hunt, track down beautiful gesture, tune, song, and dance. For if these elude us, any further discussion of correct education, whether it be for Greeks or for barbarians, will be in vain.

CL: Yes.

ATH: Well then, what should we say is a beautiful gesture or tune? Consider a courageous soul encountering great hardships, and a cowardly soul in the equivalent circumstances. Will their gestures and 655a
utterances be alike?

CL: How could they, since not even their colouring is?

ATH: A nice phrase, my friend. However, it is not correct to speak of gestures or tunes as having 'good colour' (in the image employed by chorus masters). Rather, since gestures and tunes are in music, which is a matter of harmony and rhythm, it is correct to speak of them as having good rhythm or good harmony. As for the gesture or tune of the cowardly or courageous person, the correct thing to say is that those b
of the courageous are beautiful and those of the cowardly are ugly. Now,

to avoid going on at great length about every case, let us posit the general principle that all the gestures and tunes connected with virtue of soul or of body are beautiful—whether this is the virtue itself or its representation—while all those connected with vice are the opposite.

CL: A very good proposal. Let our answer for now be that this is how things stand.

ATH: Now a further question. Do we all get the same enjoyment from
c every choral work, or is this far from the case?

CL: Very far indeed.

ATH: Now what do we say is the cause of this divergence? Is it that the
same works are not beautiful for everyone? Or that they are, but they just
don't seem to be so? Presumably no one would say that the choral dances
of vice are more beautiful than those of virtue, or avow that *he* takes
pleasure in the gestures of wickedness while others find enjoyment in a
contrary Muse. Of course, most people do say that the power to bring
d about pleasure in the soul is what makes music correct. Their view is
insupportable and altogether impious to pronounce, but another doctrine is even more likely to lead us astray.

CL: What doctrine is that?

ATH: Well, choral dances imitate different types of character found in
all kinds of actions and fortune, the performers drawing both on their
respective characters and on imitation. When the words, songs, or any
other component of the choral work comport with a performer's char-
e acter—either with his nature or with his training or with both—he will
necessarily enjoy them and praise them and call them beautiful. But if
the choral components run contrary to his nature, type, or training the
inevitable result will be that he cannot enjoy or praise them but will
instead call them ugly. In cases where a person's nature is correct, but his
training is the opposite, or his training is correct but his nature the
656a opposite, his praises will conflict with his pleasures, and he will call such
choral dances 'pleasant but wicked'. People like this, when they are in
the presence of those they think wise, are ashamed to move their bodies
in such dances, and ashamed to sing out their hearty approval, although
they do enjoy doing so when they are on their own.

CL: What you say is most correct.

ATH: So does any harm come to a person who enjoys the gestures or tunes of wickedness, or any benefit accrue to those who welcome the opposite pleasures?

CL: It seems likely.

ATH: Likely, or is it in fact necessary? It's just like what happens to b
someone who associates with bad men of wicked character and comes to enjoy and welcome their company instead of disliking them. When he condemns their wickedness it is as if he is playing a game or dreaming. When this happens, surely it is inevitable that the person who is pleased becomes like the sort of person he enjoys, even if he is ashamed to praise him. Indeed, can we name any greater good or evil that befalls us than this absolutely necessary consequence?

CL: I can think of none.

ATH: So, in places where there are good laws concerning musical c
education and recreation (either now or in the future), do we think composers will be allowed to put whatever rhythm, tune, or phrases they please into a work and teach it to the youths and children of the law-abiding citizens in their choruses, regardless of the effect it may have on their development towards virtue or wickedness?

CL: This makes no sense at all. How could they be allowed?

ATH: They are in fact allowed to do this in practically every city— d
except in Egypt.

CL: In Egypt, you say! How have they regulated these matters there?

ATH: It is really quite astonishing. A long time ago, it seems, they recognized the principle that we are now affirming, that the youth of the city must be trained to practise beautiful gestures and songs. Having established which ones are beautiful, and what they are like, they put
these on display in their temples, permitting no painter or anyone else e
who depicts gestures to introduce new forms or to invent anything that departs from the ancestral tradition. Even today this is not allowed in those arts, or in music quite generally. If you examine the artworks there, you will find painting and sculpture that have lasted a thousand years—not practically a thousand, but actually a thousand—with the
works produced today no more beautiful or ugly than those of the past, 657a
since they are produced by exactly the same art.

CL: What you describe is astonishing.

ATH: An extreme feat of legislation and statecraft indeed! Now you may find fault with other matters over there, but as far as music is concerned, this truth is worth noting—that it is possible to provide enduring stability to songs that have a natural correctness, provided the legislator is bold enough. This is a task for a god, or a divine man (in
b Egypt, they say it is Isis who composed the songs that have lasted this great expanse of time). Now, as I was saying, if someone were able somehow to grasp the standards of correctness in these matters, he should be bold enough to regiment them into law. After all, the pursuit of pleasure and pain in the constant striving after novelty in music has little power to undermine *sanctified* choral dancing by branding it 'old fashioned'. In Egypt at any rate it has turned out to have no such power—indeed, quite the opposite.

c CL: Such would seem to be the case, from what you are saying now.

ATH: So are we bold enough to describe roughly as follows the correct use of music and recreation in choral dance? When we think we are doing well we are pleased and, conversely, when we are pleased we think we are doing well. Isn't this the case?

CL: It certainly is.

ATH: And in such circumstances, feeling pleasure, we are unable to keep quiet.

CL: That is so.

d ATH: Isn't it the case that the young among us are eager to dance in a chorus, while those of us who are elders think the proper way to conduct ourselves is as their audience? We take a vicarious pleasure in their recreation and revelry now that our own agility has left us, and out of nostalgic longing for it we set up competitions for those who are most able to evoke in us the memories of our youth.

CL: Very true.

ATH: So we don't find entirely off the mark, do we, the opinion about
e festival performers widely expressed today, that the most accomplished and deserving of victory is the one who gives us the greatest pleasure and delight? These festivals are occasions of recreation for us, so the performer who most delights the most people should be honoured most

highly and, as I said, carry off the victory prize. Isn't this the correct 658a
thing to say, and the right way of proceeding on these matters?

CL: Perhaps.

ATH: In these matters, sir, 'perhaps' is not good enough. Let us divide the matter into its parts and examine it along the following lines. Suppose someone were to set up a completely open contest, restricted neither to athletics, nor music, nor horsemanship. After assembling everyone in the city, he would set up a prize and proclaim that anyone who wished could compete in a contest that is simply about pleasure.
Whoever most pleases the spectators will be victorious, with no require- b
ments on how he is to do this. He will win by being best at achieving this result—that is, he will be judged the most pleasing of the contestants. What do we think would result from such a proclamation?

CL: What kind of result do you have in mind?

ATH: It is likely, I suppose, that one person will perform as a rhapsode, in the manner of Homer, while others will play the lyre, stage tragedies, and put on comedies. It wouldn't even be surprising if someone thought
that putting on a puppet show gave him the best shot at victory. Now c
with these and other contestants advancing in droves, can we say which one is rightly the winner?

CL: That's a strange question to ask. How could anyone answer, as if he could tell without having listened to each of the contestants himself?

ATH: Shall I tell you the strange reply?

CL: Sure.

ATH: Well, if the very small children are delivering the verdict, won't they select the puppeteer?

CL: Of course. d

ATH: And if it is the older children, they will choose the producer of comedies, while tragedy will be the choice of the educated women, adolescent boys, and pretty well the majority of the crowd.

CL: Yes, probably.

ATH: But we old men would probably get the most pleasure from listening to a rhapsode reciting beautifully from the *Iliad* and *Odyssey* or from some work of Hesiod. We would declare him to be the overwhelming winner. Now the next point to raise, isn't it, is which of these would be the rightful winner?

CL: Yes.

e ATH: It is clear that you and I at any rate must declare the proper winners to be those selected by our own age group. For our training seems to be the best by far in any city anywhere today.

CL: Of course.

ATH: I agree with the majority this far at any rate: that music is to be judged by pleasure—not, however, the pleasure it affords any random person. My view is, roughly, that the finest Muse delights the best people, those who are properly educated, and especially the single person
659a who is pre-eminent in virtue and education. We say the judges of these events need virtue because they must possess not only wisdom but courage as well. For a true judge must not take his lessons from the audience, dazzled by the clamour of the crowd and by his own lack of education. Nor, if he has come to the correct verdict, should he be so
b spineless and cowardly as to lie and deliver a shoddy judgement through the very lips through which he has sworn he will deliver the verdict of the gods! A judge is rightly the spectators' teacher, not their pupil. He sits in judgement of them, and opposes them if their pleasures are unseemly or incorrect. This used to be possible under the ancient law of the Greeks. Today, however, in the manner of the Sicilian and Italian law, the verdict is entrusted to the mass of spectators, with the winner determined by a show of hands. This practice has not only corrupted the
c poets—for they compose with an eye to the base pleasures of the judges, and thus the spectators are educating *them*—it has corrupted the pleasures of the spectators as well. Their pleasures are supposed to improve from listening to better characters than their own, but quite the opposite is in fact what befalls them, and by their own doing.

Now that we have given a thorough treatment to that topic, let's consider what significance it has for our discussion. See whether you think it is this.

CL: What?

ATH: I think this is the third or fourth time that our discussion
d has come round to the same point, that education is the drawing and

guidance of children towards the correct account that is articulated by
the law and accepted as correct by the worthiest and eldest citizens on
the basis of their experience. The soul of a child must not become
trained to feel pleasure or pain that opposes the law, or opposes those
who accept the law. Rather, it must follow the law and be pleased and
pained at the same things as are the elderly. Bringing about this e
'agreement', as we call it, is the very serious purpose of the things
that we call 'songs' (which are really charms for our souls). Children's
souls, you see, can't abide seriousness, so we perform these charms in
the playful guise of songs. We are like those who care for the ill and
infirm, who deliberately use pleasant-tasting dishes and drinks to 660a
deliver wholesome foods and put unhealthy foods in bad-tasting dishes
so that their charges will become trained, correctly, to enjoy the
one and hate the other. The correct legislator will persuade the
composers to do the same thing with their lovely and laudable phrases,
and if he fails to persuade them he will compel them to compose
correctly—by setting into rhythms the gestures of people who are
moderate, courageous, and completely good, and couching their
tunes within harmonies.

CL: By Zeus, Stranger, is this how you think poets compose in b
other cities today? As far as I can tell, except in my own home and in
Sparta, I don't see that things are done in the way you describe. Rather,
there is always something new going on in dance and in the other
branches of music, with the changes guided not by law but by unregu-
lated pleasures. Things are so far from remaining the same and following
the same forms, as in your Egyptian example, that they are never c
the same!

ATH: Very good, Clinias! If I gave you the impression that I was
describing how things are actually done these days, I wouldn't be
surprised if it's my own fault for failing to express my point clearly.
Perhaps I presented what I wish to happen in such a way as to make
you think that I was affirming it to be the case. After all, it is never
pleasant to inveigh against errors that are irremediable or far advanced,
although sometimes it is necessary to do so. Now since you and I are of d
like mind on this question, tell me this. You say that this is how things
are done in your city and in that of our friend here, in contrast to the rest
of Greece?

CL: Of course.

ATH: What if other cities were to do it this way too? Would we say their practice would be more admirable than at present?

CL: It would be a vast improvement if they did it as his city and mine do it, and, what's more, as you say they ought to be doing it.

ATH: Now, let's be sure we are thinking along the same lines. Is this
e what is proclaimed in all the musical education in your cities? You compel
your poets to say that the good man, since he is moderate and just, is
happy and blessed—whether he is tall and strong or short and weak, and
whether or not he is wealthy—but that the unjust man, no matter
whether he is 'richer than Cinyras and Midas', is wretched and lives
miserably? Your poet says, if he speaks correctly, 'I would not memorial-
ize, nor take any account of a man' who fails to accomplish with justice all
his so-called admirable achievements— even one who in such a condition
661a 'lays waste the enemy and assails him at close quarters', but is unjust, or
who is 'emboldened by the sight of bloody slaughter', or 'outruns the
North Wind of Thrace', or achieves any other of the so-called goods.

You see, the things most people call good are incorrectly so called.
They say that being healthy is best, having good looks is second, and
wealth is third. Many other things too get called goods: keen sight and
b hearing, along with acuteness of the other senses; acting the tyrant,
doing whatever one desires; and, as the summit of all blessedness,
achieving immortality upon acquiring all these goods. Now you and I
on the other hand presumably say this: that all these things are the best
possessions for just and pious men, but to unjust men they are the worst,
c starting right with health. In fact, seeing, hearing, and perceiving, even
simply being alive, are the worst things for the person who, though
immortal for all time and endowed with the rest of the things called
good, lacks justice (that is, virtue as a whole), although they are less bad
for such a person if he lives only for a very short time.

These views of mine, I gather, are what you persuade and compel the
poets in your cities to affirm and cast into corresponding rhythms and
harmonies in the education they provide for your youth? Isn't that so?
d Look, my obvious point is that the things called bad are good to the
unjust, but bad to the good, while the good ones are genuinely good to
those who are good, but bad to those who are bad. So, to return to my
question, are you and I in agreement, or not?

CL: As I see it, we are more or less in agreement on some points, but not at all on others.

ATH: Presumably our disagreement concerns the person who possesses
health, wealth, and absolute tyranny? I'll even add in for you that he has
superlative strength and courage, and is free from death and all the other e
so-called bad things, but within him there is nothing but injustice and
insolence. Do I fail to persuade you that a person living like this is
obviously wretched rather than happy?

CL: Exactly.

ATH: Well! How should we go on from here? Take the man who is
courageous, strong, handsome, wealthy, and does whatever he likes his 662a
whole life long. If he is unjust and insolent, don't you think it necessary
that he lives shamefully? This much, perhaps, you would concede, that
he lives shamefully?

CL: Certainly.

ATH: And also badly?

CL: I am not prepared to go that far.

ATH: Would you at least agree that his life is unpleasant and of no benefit to him?

CL: How could we possibly concede this further point?

ATH: How indeed, my friends? We are so badly out of tune with one b
another that it would take a god to bring us into agreement! As far as I'm
concerned, my dear Clinias, these things appear so necessary that not
even 'Crete is an island' is as obvious. If I were a lawmaker I would do
my best to compel the poets, and everyone in the city, to abide by these
doctrines in their utterances. I would mete out virtually the highest
penalty to anyone in the land who spread word that there are wicked
people who live pleasantly, or that while some things are beneficial and c
profitable, others are more just. I would persuade the citizens to pro-
claim the opposite of what it seems Cretans and Spartans are saying
these days, and no doubt other peoples as well.

In the name of Zeus and Apollo, my excellent friends, suppose we
asked these very gods, your lawgivers, 'Is the most just life the most d
pleasant, or are there two lives, one of them the most pleasant, the other
the most just?' If they answered that these are two different lives, the
right question to ask next would be, 'Should we call happiest those
leading the life that is most just, or the life that is most pleasant?' If they
replied that it was those living the most pleasant life, their position

would be very strange; however, I would prefer not to attribute such a
position to the gods, but rather to our ancestral legislators. So let the
e preceding question have been posed to our ancestral legislator and let
him be the one to reply that the person living the most pleasant life is
most blessed. I would then say, 'Didn't you wish for me to live the
happiest life? But you never stopped exhorting me to live most justly!' A
legislator or father who took such a position would be very strange and
quite at a loss to stay in agreement with himself. If instead he declared
that the life that is most just is the happiest, anyone hearing this, I think,
would want to find out what good and admirable thing the law com-
663a mends in such a life that outstrips pleasure. For what good could there be
for the just person that is separated from pleasure? Look, in the eyes of
men and gods, are renown and praise good and admirable but unpleas-
ant, while ill repute is the opposite? We will hardly assent to that, my dear
legislator. Well, what about neither wronging anyone nor being wronged
by anyone? It is surely not the case that this is unpleasant but good and
admirable, while the contrary is pleasant but shameful and bad?

CL: How could it be so?

b ATH: Surely the doctrine that does not divorce the pleasant and the
just or the good and the admirable, even if it accomplishes nothing else,
can persuade a person to be willing to live a just and pious life. So, as far
as the legislator is concerned, any doctrine that denies this is the most
shameful and is to be resisted to the utmost, since nobody would
willingly be persuaded to do anything that failed to yield more pleasure
than pain. Now objects viewed from a distance appear hazy to most
people, especially to children, but the legislator will dispel the haze and
c clarify our judgement. He will persuade us, however he can, by means of
training, praises, and doctrines, because matters of justice and injustice
are subject to perspective. When considered from the perspective op-
posite to the just person's—that is, from the standpoint of one's own
injustice and wickedness—unjust actions seem pleasant and just ones
unpleasant. From the standpoint of the just person, the situation is
completely reversed on both counts.

CL: So it seems.

ATH: Now which judgement shall we say is more authoritatively true—that of the worse soul or that of the better?

CL: Necessarily, I suppose, that of the superior person. d

ATH: So it is necessary that the unjust life is not only more shameful and more depraved, but also in truth more unpleasant than the just and pious life.

CL: So it would seem, friends, at least as far as the present argument goes.

ATH: But even if matters were not as the present argument maintains, could any halfway decent legislator, if he dared to lie to the youth for the sake of the good, tell a lie more beneficial than this? Is there any lie with greater potential to make everyone always act justly—not because they e
are forced, but willingly?

CL: Truth is a beautiful thing, Stranger, and an enduring one. But persuasion, it seems, is not an easy matter.

ATH: Well, haven't people been easily persuaded of the Sidonian's tale, implausible though it is, and of many others as well?

CL: What kind of tales?

ATH: About armed warriors growing from teeth sown in the earth—a perfect example to show the legislator that if he tries he can persuade the souls of the young of whatever he wants. All he needs to figure out is 664a
what doctrine will deliver the greatest good to the city should he convince them of it. Then he must use every means at his disposal to ensure that the whole community, all their lives long, are of one voice on this topic—in their songs, in their stories, and in their judgements. Of course if you think at all differently, no one will begrudge you the chance to dispute the argument.

CL: I don't see either of us as capable of disputing these points. b

ATH: Then I will take it on myself to continue. For I maintain that all choruses (and there are three of them) should direct their charms at the souls of children, which are still young and pliable. They should affirm all the beautiful doctrines we've gone through, and still others we could mention, but the most important point—let it be noted—is this. In affirming that the gods call the same life both most pleasant and most excellent, we will be speaking truth to the highest degree and we are c more likely to persuade those whom we need to persuade than if we were to proclaim any other doctrine.

CL: What you say must be conceded.

ATH: To begin with, the chorus dedicated to the Muses and consisting of children would rightly be the first to take the stage, singing out such doctrines with all their heart before the entire city. Second will be the chorus of those up to 30 years old, calling upon Paean Apollo as witness for the truth of what they affirm, and praying that he grace the youth
d with persuasion. In addition to these two, a third chorus must also sing. It will consist of those over 30 and up to 60 years of age. Those who are beyond all that and no longer up to the challenge of singing will be allotted the role of storytellers. They will recount divinely inspired stories about these same characters.

CL: What's this you say about the third choruses, Stranger? We don't quite follow what you mean to say about them.

ATH: They are, in fact, pretty much the whole point of most of the preceding discussion.

e CL: We don't understand at all. Please try to explain more clearly.

ATH: At the beginning of our discussion, if you recall, we said that all young creatures have a fiery nature. They are unable to keep their bodies or their voices still, and are always uttering noises and jumping about in disorder. A sense of order in both domains, we said, is missing in the other animals, and belongs to human nature alone. Rhythm is the name
665a for order in movement; order in voice, a blend of high pitch and low, is called harmony; and the combination of the two is called a chorus. The gods took pity on us, we said, and gave us Apollo and the Muses to join and lead our choral dance. And third, if you recall, we said they gave us Dionysus.

CL: How could we not remember!

ATH: Now that we've spoken of the chorus of Apollo and that of the
b Muses, we need to discuss the third and remaining chorus, that of Dionysus.

CL: What do you mean? Please tell us. A Dionysian chorus of elders sounds exceedingly strange, on first hearing. Will those over 30, 50, and even up to 60 years of age really dance a chorus in his honour?

ATH: That is exactly what I mean. Now, I do owe you an account, I think, of the way in which it would be reasonable for this to take place.

CL: I should say!

ATH: Are we agreed on the points that we took up before?

CL: Which ones? c

ATH: That every man and child, free person and slave, female and male, indeed the whole city, should perpetually sing to itself those charms that we discussed—always with some alteration or other and at any rate with sufficient variety to please the singers and make their thirst for the hymns insatiable.

CL: How could one not agree with this way of doing things?

ATH: Now as for this best element of the city, whose collective age and d
wisdom makes it the most persuasive group of citizens, where should it sing those finest songs, if it is to bring about the most good? Or will we be so foolish as to overlook those with the greatest command of the finest and most beneficial songs?

CL: We cannot let them go, according to our present argument.

ATH: So what would be the appropriate way for them to sing? See whether it is this.

CL: What way?

ATH: As a person advances in age, doesn't he become increasingly
reluctant to sing? That is, he enjoys it less and, when compelled to do it, e
he feels especially embarrassed—the more so the older and more moderate he has become. Isn't this so?

CL: Very much so.

ATH: And he would feel even more embarrassed if he sang in the theatre, standing up before all kinds of people. Even worse, suppose such men had to be lean and sing on an empty stomach, like choruses who are engaged in competition. Wouldn't they find singing the height of unpleasantness and humiliation, and carry out their task with no eagerness at all?

CL: Most necessarily. 666a

ATH: So how shall we encourage them to sing eagerly? Shouldn't we
legislate, first of all, that children 18 years old and younger are forbidden
to partake of any wine at all? We would explain that one should not pour
additional fire into the bodies or souls of our youth, but rather be
mindful of their excitable condition in the period before they engage
with the burdensome toils of life. Next, our law will allow those up to 30
b years of age to drink wine in moderation, but the young must abstain
completely from drunkenness and from drinking large quantities of
wine. A person approaching 40, however, when invoking the gods at
the end of a communal dinner, will call upon Dionysus in particular,
inviting him to that rite and recreation for the elders which he gave to
humans as a remedy for the crabbedness of old age. It makes us grow
c young again and forget our ill temper as our souls' hardened character
softens, like iron that becomes pliable when placed in the fire. In such a
condition, wouldn't a person be less embarrassed about singing—if he is
not in a large gathering, but a moderately sized one, and among familiars
rather than strangers? Wouldn't he be more willing to sing with enthusiasm those songs that we have repeatedly said are charms?

CL: Very much so.

ATH: To the extent that it leads them to join with us in song, then, this
d practice would not be at all unseemly.

CL: Not at all.

ATH: Now what kind of sound, or music, will issue from these men? Surely it must be suitable for them?

CL: Of course.

ATH: Well, what kind of music would suit divine men? Would it be that of a chorus?

CL: Well, Stranger, speaking for my own city and that of the Spartans, the only type of song we are capable of is what we learned to sing in our own choral training.

ATH: So it would seem. As a matter of fact, you are missing out on the
e finest kind of song. I mean, your legal systems are fit for an army camp,
rather than the inhabitants of a city. You keep your youth herded
together like colts at pasture, and none of you lays hold of his own
colt, drags him wild and kicking away from his fellow grazers, and
commits him to the individual care of a groom who will stroke him

and tame him and give him all the elements of an upbringing that will make him not only a good soldier but a capable participant in the affairs 667a
of a city or town. This is the sort of person whom we said earlier was even more warlike than the warriors of Tyrtaeus, one who consistently values the possession of courage as fourth in virtue, not first, both for individuals and for the city as a whole.

CL: If I'm not mistaken, Stranger, you are again casting aspersions on our lawgivers.

ATH: If I do, sir, it is not my intent. Let us simply follow the argument where it leads, if you are willing. Now, if there is a kind of 'music' finer
than that of choruses and public theatres, let us try to assign it to those b
whom we said were embarrassed by the latter kind but eager to partake of the finest variety.

CL: Yes, indeed.

ATH: Now, in the case of anything that brings us enjoyment, mustn't we first of all say the following? Either this very feature on its own is the most important thing about it, or else what is most important is a certain correctness or, third, a benefit? Consider eating and drinking, for example, and taking in nourishment quite generally. These bring us enjoyment, which we might call 'pleasure', but if we are talking about
correctness and benefit, we talk of what is healthy in a given meal, and c
this is what is most correct in it.

CL: Absolutely.

ATH: Learning, too, has its pleasure, an element of enjoyment that comes along with it. But its correctness and benefit, what is good and beautiful in it, derive from its truth.

CL: That is so.

ATH: Now consider the representational arts. Their business is to
produce likenesses, and when they succeed, any pleasure that accom- d
panies their product, should any pleasure arise, is appropriately called 'enjoyment'.

CL: Yes.

ATH: But presumably the correctness in such cases would be produced, roughly speaking, by accuracy in quantity and quality, not by pleasure.

CL: You are right.

ATH: So the only thing that would be correctly judged by pleasure is
what provides neither benefit nor truth nor likeness when it is achieved
e (nor harm either, for that matter). Rather, it comes to be solely for the
sake of this very thing, enjoyment, which those other things bring in
their wake, but when it occurs without them, is best called 'pleasure'.

CL: You mean only harmless pleasure.

ATH: Yes. I also call it 'recreation' when it produces neither harm nor benefit worthy of serious mention.

CL: Quite correctly.

ATH: On the basis of our present discussion, wouldn't we say that no
imitation is to be judged by pleasure and false opinion? In particular,
668a accuracy should never be. For it is never the case that something is
accurate, or in general proportional, simply because someone thinks so,
or fails to enjoy something. Rather, an imitation is to be judged in terms
of its truth above all else, and least of all by any other standard.

CL: Absolutely, indeed.

ATH: Now all music, we say, is representational and imitative?

CL: Of course.

ATH: So we should be least prepared to accept it when someone says
that music is to be judged by the pleasure it gives. That sort of music, if
b there should be any, is unworthy of our serious attention. We should
seek instead the kind that achieves likeness in imitating what is beautiful.

CL: Very true.

ATH: So those who seek out the finest song and music must not search for the kind that is pleasant but the kind that is correct. For, as we said, correctness of imitation consists in rendering the actual dimensions and qualities of the object imitated.

CL: How could it not?

ATH: Now anyone would agree on this point about music, that all of
c its compositions are imitations and representations. Surely all com-
posers, audiences, and actors would agree on this?

CL: Certainly.

ATH: So, in order not to misjudge a particular composition, it seems, one must recognize just what it is. Without recognizing its nature—just what it intends, what it actually represents—one will hardly discern whether the intention is carried out correctly or misses the mark.

CL: Hardly indeed.

ATH: And if one fails to recognize whether it is correct, will one ever be d
able to discern whether it is good or bad? I'm not expressing myself very clearly here. Perhaps this way of stating the point is clearer.

CL: What way?

ATH: There are no doubt myriad likenesses involving our sense of sight.

CL: Yes.

ATH: Suppose, in these cases, a person did not know the bodies being imitated. Would he ever recognize what is correct in their rendering? I mean, for example, the dimensions of each body and, if it has parts,
their position, number, and proper arrangement, as well as their colours e
and shapes. Is it rendered with these things all mixed up? Do you think that a person completely ignorant of what the imitated creature is could make these discriminations?

CL: How could he?

ATH: Now suppose we recognized that the drawn or sculpted figure is a human being, and that all its parts, colours, and shapes have been
captured by the art. Is it necessarily the case that someone who recog- 669a
nizes these things is thereby in a position to recognize whether the work of art is beautiful, or whether it falls short of beauty in some way?

CL: But then, virtually all of us would recognize which pictures are beautiful!

ATH: You are quite correct. So, for each representation, whether in painting or in music as a whole, doesn't a wise judge need to have the
following three things? One must know first of all, what it is, next how b
correctly it is rendered, and third, how well the particular representation is rendered in phrases, tunes, and rhythms.

CL: So it would seem.

ATH: Now, let us not omit to state the difficulties we face in the case of
music. It gets talked about more than any other kind of representation,
but in fact it requires the greatest care of all. Not only is making a
mistake here extremely harmful, since one will come to welcome evil
c characters, but it is extremely difficult to notice. This is because the
composers are inferior poets to the Muses. The Muses would never
make the blunder of composing words suitable for men and then giving
them the colour or tune of women, or attaching rhythms of the servile
and slavish to the tune and gestures of the free. Nor, having composed
rhythms and gestures of a free person would they attach to them a tune
or speech that conflicts with the rhythms. Furthermore, they would
d never mix together animal and human voices, the sounds of instru-
ments, and every kind of noise, yet purport to be imitating a single
thing. Human composers, however, eagerly spin these elements into a
great jumble devoid of reason, a source of laughter for people who are in
what Orpheus calls the 'prime season of delight'. It is not enough that
composers confound these things, they also wrench them apart—when
they separate rhythm and gesture from tune and set bare speech into
e metre, or separate tune and rhythm from words when they employ
bare lyre or reed pipe. This makes it extremely difficult to recognize
what the wordless rhythm and harmony intends, what worthy object of
imitation it resembles. You must understand, however, that it is utterly
crude to be so enamoured of speed, dexterity, and animal cries that
670a one employs reed pipe or lyre other than to accompany dance and song.
The bare employment of either instrument is completely unmusical
showmanship.

Well, enough said on that topic. After all, our inquiry is not into what
we *shouldn't* do when we have reached our thirties or gone past 50 and
are availing ourselves of the Muses, but rather what we should do. Our
discussion has already indicated this much, I think: that those who have
b reached 50 and are fit to sing must have received an education better
than that of the choral Muse. They must have keen perception and
knowledge of rhythms and harmonies. How else could one recognize the
correctness of tunes—which of them should be in the Dorian harmony,
and whether the rhythm the composer has attached to a tune is correct
or not?

CL: Clearly, there is no way.

ATH: So it's laughable for the general crowd to think that they are able
to recognize what is and isn't harmonious and well rhythmed, simply
from having been drilled at singing to the reed pipe and marching in
rhythm. They fail to appreciate that they don't know a single thing c
about what they are doing. Presumably the tune with the appropriate
features is correct, while the one with inappropriate features is in error.

CL: Most necessarily.

ATH: Suppose a person does not even recognize what features a tune has. Will he ever be able to do what we said—that is, recognize whether it is correct in any given case?

CL: By what means could he do so?

ATH: That is exactly what we are discovering now, it would seem.
Those singers of ours, whom we encourage and in a way even compel to
sing willingly—they must be educated to the point that each is able to d
follow closely the feet of the rhythms and the notes of the melodies.
Thus, with a synoptic grasp of harmonies and rhythms, they will be able
to select what is appropriate. This is what is fitting for people of their age
and character to sing, and when they do, they not only enjoy the
harmless pleasures of the moment, they also guide the younger singers
towards the appropriate embrace of worthy characters. They will have e
been educated to the point that the skill they practise is more exact than
that of the common run, and even that of the composers themselves. For
there is no need for a composer to recognize the third thing, whether the
imitation is beautiful or not. All he needs to know, basically, are
harmony and rhythm. These people, by contrast, must know all three,
in order to select what is most beautiful as well as what is second.
Otherwise, their incantations will never succeed in drawing the youth 671a
towards virtue.

Our argument has done its best to establish that we were right in our
earlier defence of the chorus of Dionysus, so let us consider whether it
has succeeded. Now, a gathering of this sort inevitably becomes more
boisterous as the drinking proceeds—an unavoidable feature, we ori-
ginally supposed, of these events as they take place nowadays. b

CL: Necessarily.

ATH: Anyone who participates in such a gathering loosens up and becomes merry. Bursting with unchecked speech and unwilling to listen to his neighbours, he thinks he is fit to rule both himself and the rest of the company.

CL: Indeed.

ATH: Didn't we say that when this happens the souls of the drinkers
are like iron in the fire? They become softer and more youthful,
c receptive to the influence of a skilful educator who can shape them
anew, just as when they were young. The one who moulds them, the
same as before, is the good legislator. His task is to make laws about
drinking parties. These are laws that can take in hand that cheerful
drinker—who is emboldened, unduly shameless, and unwilling to abide
by the order of taking turns at listening, speaking, drinking, and
singing—and make him willing to do just the opposite. Against the
shameful boldness that is filling him they can send in the finest oppon-
d ent: fear with justice. This is the divine fear that we have called 'modesty'
and 'shame'. Isn't that so?

CL: That is so.

ATH: As guardians and assistants of these laws, there will be undis-
turbed and sober commanders for the inebriated. To battle against
drunkenness without these commanders is more dangerous than taking
the field against an enemy army in the absence of undisturbed officers.
And he who cannot willingly obey his leaders in the realm of Dio-
e nysus—those over 60 years old—bears an even greater shame than he
who disobeys his officers in the realm of Ares.

CL: Correct.

ATH: Now, with this sort of drunkenness and recreation, aren't
the drinking companions benefited by participating? Don't they
part company better friends than when they started—unlike today,
672a when they part as enemies—since they behave in a lawful and com-
pliant manner throughout, given that the sober are in charge of the
inebriated?

CL: Correct, provided the gathering is as you describe.

ATH: So let us no longer roundly condemn the gift of Dionysus as a bad thing that should not be allowed into the city. Indeed, I could go on and recount the greatest good he has given us—only I am hesitant to do so in front of the general public, since people have difficulty understanding the point and take it in the wrong way. b

CL: What sort of thing do you mean?

ATH: According to a widespread oracular tale about this god, it is in revenge for being driven out of his mind by his stepmother Hera that he inflicts us with Bacchic frenzy and all that manic dance, and it is for this purpose that he gave us the gift of wine. For my part, I leave it to those who think they have sound judgement about the gods to pronounce on such matters, but this much I do know: that no creature is born with the c
degree of intelligence that is appropriate to it when it is fully grown. During the time before it possesses its proper intelligence, it raves and shouts at random and as soon as it gets to its feet it jumps about in disorder. Let us remember that we called these the origins of music and athletics.

CL: We surely do remember.

ATH: Do we also remember saying that in the case of us humans, this d
origin gives rise to a sense of rhythm and harmony, and that Apollo and the Muses and Dionysus among the gods are responsible for this?

CL: Of course.

ATH: On the subject of wine, the situation seems to be this. The story other people tell is that wine was given to human beings in an act of revenge, to drive us mad. But the story we are telling now is quite the opposite. It says that wine was given to us as a potion for instilling shame in the soul and health and strength in the body.

CL: An excellent recapitulation of our discussion, Stranger!

ATH: So much for one half of choral dancing. As for the other half, we e
will either continue with it or pass over it, depending on how the matter strikes us.

CL: What sort of halves do you mean? How do you divide them?

ATH: Well, we said that choral performance as a whole is pretty much the whole process of education, and one part of it, the vocal part, involves rhythm and harmony.

CL: Yes.

ATH: The other part concerns bodily movement. Like vocal move-
ment, it involves rhythm, but its distinctive feature is gesture. The other
673a part, vocal movement, has tune as its distinctive feature.

CL: Very true.

ATH: Now, in the case of the vocal activities that reach the soul and cultivate virtue, we ventured to call this 'music'.

CL: And rightly so.

ATH: As for bodily movements, which we call 'dance' when they are performed as recreation, when such movement leads to virtue of the body, let us call the skilled guidance towards that bodily condition 'athletics'.

CL: That would be quite correct.

b ATH: So much for our account of music, which is the half of choral
performance whose treatment we said we had completed. As for the
other half, shall we discuss it too, or how should we proceed?

CL: Sir, you are talking to Cretans and Spartans here! If we have dealt with music, but omitted athletics, what do you expect us to answer to your question?

ATH: I would say that your question gives me my answer loud and
c clear. I take your question to be not only a reply but also an order to
complete the discussion of athletics.

CL: You have understood me perfectly. Do just that.

ATH: Yes, we must. It will not be a very difficult discussion, since both of you are familiar with this discipline and considerably more experienced in it than in the previous one.

CL: That is pretty much the truth.

ATH: Now this kind of recreation has its origin in the natural propen-
d sity of all animals to jump about. Add in the human sense of rhythm
that we mentioned, and you have the genesis and birth of dance. Since
tunes remind us and rouse us to rhythm, the union of these with each
other gives birth to recreation in choral dance.

CL: Very true.

ATH: Having gone through one part of the subject, as we said, we will next try to go through the other.

CL: Absolutely.

ATH: Let us first put the finishing touches on our discussion of the use
of drunkenness—that is, if you agree. e

CL: What do you have in mind?

ATH: Suppose a city treats the activity in question as a serious matter:
they employ it in an orderly and law-governed manner—as a means to
practise and cultivate moderation. And suppose it treats other pleasures
along the same lines; it does not abstain from them but cultivates
mastery over them. That is what it should be doing. But suppose it
treats the activity as a form of recreation, allowing anyone who wishes to
drink whenever and with whomever he wishes and in conjunction with 674a
any activity whatsoever. I would not vote to let this city, or man, engage
in any drunkenness whatsoever. Indeed, I would go beyond even the
Cretan and Spartan practice and vote for the Carthaginian law that
prohibits all wine drinking to soldiers on campaign. It requires that their
gatherings during this period serve only water, and that even in the city
itself no slave, male or female, shall taste it, nor shall any of the officials
during their year in office. Ship captains and jurors shall drink no wine b
when they are on active duty, nor shall any person who is about to
participate in important deliberations, or anyone at all during the day
(except for purposes of bodily training or medical treatment), or even at
night if they are intending to beget children (this holds for women as
well as men). There are many other circumstances one could mention in
which no one in their right and lawful mind should drink wine. The
upshot of all this is that a city does not need many vineyards. Once all c
agricultural and dietary matters have been arranged, those involving
wine will turn out to be the most measured and to comprise the smallest
part.

With your agreement, Strangers, let this be the finishing touch to our discussion of wine.

CL: Well put. We do agree.

Commentary

A NOTE TO THE READER

The line numbers cited in the commentary are keyed to the Greek text of des Places, and will not correspond precisely to the lines in the English translation. In order to reduce visual clutter, the philosophical convention of using single quotes to mark the mention of a term is not employed for transliterated Greek terms, which are in italics.

Book 1

I
INTRODUCTORY CONVERSATION

(624a1–625c5)

The divine origin of legislation, and the human project of inquiring into laws

624a1 'A god or a human being'
The theme of the divine origin of the law runs throughout the *Laws*. The Athenian will describe law as management by reason (*nous*), which is the spark of the immortal in us (713e–714a; cf. 644d2–3 (and note ad loc), 645a1–2, 645b4–8). The so-called 'divine' goods identified at 631b–d are all expressions of wisdom (*phronêsis*). The Athenian's project in Books 1–2 is to draw out the implications of assuming that the Spartan and Cretan constitutions meet the standards of such a 'divine' origin, and ultimately to reject the assumption. Note that the Athenian does not take the assumption of divine origin to preclude a rational human investigation into the basis of law; indeed, the assumption that identifies reason and god presumably licenses such an investigation. Nowhere in *Laws* is it assumed that correct norms are based on divine fiat inaccessible to human reason or immune to moral evaluation. Thus the position put forth in Plato's *Euthyphro* (that what is holy is not thus because the gods command it—10d) is completely consistent with the *Laws*. On the nature and existence of the gods, as well as their concern for human affairs, see the extended arguments in Book 10. These

arguments are recapitulated at the end of the *Laws*, where the Athenian reiterates the importance of divine guidance for human legislation (966c–968b).

624a1 'Strangers (*Xenoi*)'
A polite form of address to a foreigner. The dialogue's three interlocutors are *Xenoi* to each other (see Introduction) and repeatedly address each other as such throughout Book 1. In subsequent books, the frequency of the term drops significantly.

624a1–2 'your laws'
The Athenian addresses Clinias and Megillus together, as is typical in Books 1–2 (e.g. 625a5–6, 643b1–2), and each typically replies on behalf of both—e.g. 626c3, 628e2–5, 636e5, 644b5. The two men are citizens of different city states—Clinias of the Cretan city of Knossos (629c3) and Megillus of Sparta (624a4)—but the Athenian takes Cretan and Spartan law codes to be 'akin' (*adelphois nomois*, 683a2). Their law codes are characteristically Dorian in that they are distinctive of the cities whose population was believed in Plato's day to descend from so-called Dorian invaders who settled the Peloponnese and Aegean Islands (including Crete) after the collapse of Mycenean civilization (*Laws* 682e–683a; Thuc. 1.12.3; see O. Murray 1993: 9–15.) The common historical roots of the Dorian cities in Greece are explored in Book 3 and their characteristic features are the subject of study (and criticism) in Books 1 and 2. On the characteristic features of Cretan law codes, see Griffith 2013.

624a7–b3 'Don't you say, as Homer does, that Minos made a pilgrimage to his father . . . ?'
Zeus is the father of Minos. The question, addressed to Clinias, inquires into specifically Cretan stories about the divine source of legislation. On Minos, see Homer, *Odyssey* 11.568–71 and 19.178–81. Like Minos, the three interlocutors in *Laws* are embarked on a pilgrimage to the cave of Zeus (625b2; see Nightingale 1993: 282 and Morrow 1960: 27–8). The human legislator in the corresponding Spartan stories is Lycurgus (630d6).

625a2 'legal disputes'
This prefigures Clinias' general point that conflict is the context for all norms and laws (625e–626b). The Athenian, like Socrates in *Republic* 3 (405a–410a), will denigrate legal disputation (*Laws* 11, 937d–938a), although, in keeping with the attention to practical realities that distinguishes the *Laws* from its more utopian predecessor, he makes provisions for litigation in the city of Magnesia (e.g. 766d–768e, 932d–938c). In any case, the lived experience of the laws envisioned by the Athenian will not be battles in court, but correct living and the shaping of character. On the Athenian's version of the proper judge, compare 627d–628a.

625a4 'a fine reputation (*kalon . . . to kleos*)'
alternatively: 'a noble [or admirable] reputation'
On the range and translation of the term *kalon*, see note on 630c7.

625a5 'raised under such distinguished laws (*en toioutois êthesi tethraphthe nomikois*)'
more literally: 'raised in such lawful training (alt: habits, *êthesi*)'
The parallel language at 695d8–e1, 708c8, and 751c9 (cf. 752c3–5, 770d2) indicates that *êthos* is used here, not in its typical sense of 'character' (as e.g. at 636d7, 650a5, 655d6, 656b2, 666c1), but as the training or practice that shapes character (a reversal of the terminology of 792e2: 'all *êthos* is due to *ethos*'). On *ethos* as training, see note on 655d7–e1. On the reputation of Cretan and Spartan laws for producing good citizens who are obedient to the laws, see Aristotle, *EN* 1102b9–12.

625a6 'not . . . unpleasant'
Pleasure and its relationship to laws and institutions is a persistent theme throughout the *Laws* (631e–632a, 636d–e, 643c–e, 653a–c, 732e–733d). See Stalley 1983: 59–70; Bobonich 2002: 350–73.

625a6–7 'in a conversation about law codes and legislation (*peri te politeias . . . kai nomôn*)'
more literally: ' . . . about government (alt: political constitution) and laws'

Politeia, here translated 'law code', sometimes refers to constitutional law, but it often (as at 632c1, 634d5, 635e7, 676a1) simply refers to a body of laws. The discussion will address not only written laws (the products of legislation) but also a wide variety of social norms and practices (see Introduction); on what counts as a social norm, see Bicchieri 2006: 8–28. 'In a conversation' (more literally, 'speaking and listening'—*legontas te kai akouontas*) implies that the interlocutors will take turns in each role. In fact, the conversation will be decidedly one-sided, with the Athenian doing almost all the talking. But here, as England points out, the Athenian's initial invitation to engage in a legislative inquiry invokes his interlocutors' credentials, not his own.

625b4 'Those at our stage of life (*tais hêlikiais*)'
The three interlocutors are self-proclaimed old men (*gerontes*) (634e, 658d; see note on 664d1–2). As such, they are at the proper age to engage in legislative inquiries (634d–635a) and their views on legislation and education are to be accorded a special authority, according to the Athenian in Book 2 (658e–659d, 670b–e). The significance of different stages of life is marked in the institution of the three choruses (664b–665d).

625b6–7 'refresh ourselves with conversation (*logois te allêlous paramuthoumenous*)'
alternatively: 'encourage ourselves . . . ' cf. 632e4–5 and note ad loc

II
PEACE NOT WAR AS THE PROPER FOCUS OF LEGISLATION

(625c6–632d7)

Clinias indicates that the institutions of his home city, Knossos, are organized to promote victory in war (625c–626c). This is a mark of their excellence, he argues, since war and conflict are a ubiquitous and inevitable feature of human life at every level (626c–627c). The Athenian responds that reconciliation of warring parties is preferable to victory of the better party over the worse, and hence that peace is a superior goal compared with victory (627c–628e). The military ethic propounded by the Spartan poet Tyrtaeus is criticized in this light (629a–630c) and the Athenian concludes that a correct legislator will aim at cultivating 'the whole of virtue' in the citizens, which will involve training them in wisdom and justice, not just courage (630d–632d).

The military focus of Cretan institutions

625c6–9 'let me ask you why the law has ordained your communal meals (*ta sussitia*), your regime of athletic training (*ta gumnasia*), and your style of armament. What is their point?'
more literally: 'on what principle (*kata ti*) has the law ordained your common meals . . . '
The question is asked of Cretan city states in general, not just of Clinias' own city, Knossos. See note on 624a1–2. On the communal meals (*sussitia*), see note on 625e2–7. 'Athletic training' here renders *gumnasia*—which includes military training; on the scope of the related term *gymnastikê*, see note on 673a8–10.

625e2–7 'our communal meals . . . [he] organized . . . based on the observation that . . . every city is engaged in a continuous lifelong war against every other'
Here Clinias passes from specifically military institutions to familiar features of Dorian societies even in peacetime: the communal meals (*sussitia*) in which all male citizens participate, instead of dining in private at home. On the classification 'Dorian', see note on 624a1–2. On the difference between Cretan and Spartan *sussitia*, see Aristotle, *Politics* 1271a26–37, 1272a1–27. A version of *sussitia* plays a role in the ideal city outlined in *Republic* (416e), and will be included in the plan of legislation endorsed by the Athenian in *Laws* 6 (780a–781d, 783b–c; cf. 7, 806e), but not without criticism of the institution's

potential for undermining the norms of a peaceful and law-abiding society (636b–c). On *sussitia* in *Laws* see David 1978, Samaras 2010, Schöpsdau 2003. Even if the *sussitia* are not in fact of Dorian origin (as argued by O. Murray 1993: 176–7), Plato still took them to be a distinctive feature of the Dorian societies of his day.

626a3–4 'exists only in name'
literally: 'is nothing but a name'

626a4–5 'every city is by nature always in an undeclared war against every other'
Aristotle reports that city states on Crete were in persistent conflict with each other (*Politics* 1269a40–b1).

626a6–8 'it is with war in mind that the Cretan lawgiver established all the institutions (*nomima*) that govern our public and private life'
Aristotle concurs with this diagnosis of the goal of Cretan constitutions (*Pol.* 1324b6–9). As at 630d7, 'institutions' translates *nomima*, which differs little in meaning here from *epitêdeumata* (practices) at 626b2. These need not themselves be the result of legislation; in Book 3 (681a–b) national or ethnic temperament is cited as a source of *nomoi*.

626a8–b1 'endowed us (*paredôke*) with laws (*nomous*) to guard us (*phulattein*)'
Thus Clinias portrays the laws as performing the function of *phulakê* (defence, standing guard), which he has just identified (625e–626a) as the central function of Cretan institutions. (Thanks to Brad Inwood for pointing this out.) While Clinias has in mind the defence against military foes, the Athenian will later use the vocabulary of guardianship to invoke the role that legislation or institutions play in supporting peacetime objectives such as friendship, justice, or education (628a2, 632b2, 640c10, 654d8; for a further extension of the use, see 705d3). See note on 632b2–3.

The present translation takes *tous nomous* (b1) to be the subject of the infinitive *phulattein* (a8). By contrast, most translators take *tous nomous* to be the object. Herodotus 1.73.12–14 shows that the latter construal is not necessary. In the present case it would yield either the translation 'and commanded us to abide by (*phulattein*) the laws' (England, followed by Schöpsdau and Lisi)—an odd use of *phulattein*—or 'commanded us to preserve the laws' (Brisson/Pradeau). The latter sense would prefigure the Athenian's later theme that laws require guardians (632c, 752e; see note on 632c4).

626b3–4 'all the goods of the vanquished go to the victors'
Clinias implies here that the point of victory in war is to 'possess goods'—presumably material possessions such as money and property. The Athenian will reject this view when he affirms the doctrine of divine and human goods at 631b–d, claiming instead that any benefit to come from possessing such 'human goods' depends on the proper use of and attitude towards them, which issue from moderation and justice. A militarized analogue of the Athenian's principle by the Spartan poet Tyrtaeus is quoted at 629a7–b3; see Bobonich 2002: 131–6. The value Clinias implicitly places on material possessions explains why he will later balk when the Athenian proposes (661d–662a) that someone might possess such things in abundance without being happy.

626b5–6 'a well-trained (*kalôs . . . gegumnasthai*) understanding of Cretan institutions (*nomima*)'
The training is that invoked at 625a5–6. The Athenian's choice of words here recalls the athletic training (*gumnasia*) invoked at 625c7. Given the traditional understanding that *gumnasia* is training of the body, while 'music' is training of the mind (673a, 764c, 795d, *Rep.* 376e; cf. 441e), there is also a suggestion here that Clinias' views are inculcated by rote (e.g. a 'well-rehearsed understanding'). See also note on 632d5–6.

626c1–2 'its affairs must be arranged to make it victorious in war over other cities'
By contrast, the Athenian will argue that peace is the proper goal of law (627d–628d).

626c6–627c2

War and conflict as the human condition

Responding to Clinias' and Megillus' proposal that victory in war is a city's ultimate aim, and thus the primary focus of a legislator (626c1–5), the Athenian asks whether war or conflict also characterizes the relations between villages within the domain of a city, between households within villages, and between siblings within a household (626c6–13). After his interlocutors answer 'yes' in all cases, he asks whether the same applies to an individual person's relation to himself—again an emphatic 'yes' (d1–9). Victory in the battle against oneself, Clinias declares, is 'the highest and most excellent of all victories' (626e2–3). Victory over oneself, Clinias clarifies, consists in the better part (or party) defeating the worse (627a3–c2), although the point is not developed in the context of psychological conflict within a person, but in that of civil strife within a city state. The analysis of internal psychological conflict will not occur until 644b–645c.

626d3–4 'hailing from Attica . . . called after the goddess'
The city of Athens (in the region of Attica) is named after Athena, the goddess of wisdom. With the main speaker now identified as stereotypically Athenian, Plato has completed his presentation of the three interlocutors as displaying the distinctive features of their respective home states.

626d5–6 'You have gone right to the heart of the matter (*ep' archên*) and made it easy to see the truth of our present contention' more literally: 'You invoke quite correctly (*orthôs*) the fundamental principle (*archên*) that clarifies the matter (*logon*)'

The 'heart of the matter' (*archên*, d5) is stated by Clinias at 626d7–9: 'everyone is the enemy of everyone else in public life, and in private each person is pitted against himself'—on which see note on 626e5. This principle supports Clinias' original contention (625e–626b) that victory in war is the primary focus of the legislator.

626e1 'my goodness (*ô thaumasie*)'
literally: 'you amazing man'

626e2–3 'victory (*to nikân*) over oneself is the highest and most excellent of all victories'
This affirmation is consistent with Clinias' earlier claim (626a–b) that victory in battle against external foes is the ultimate aim of the legislator, even though the present claim invokes a victory over internal psychological forces. As Clinias and Megillus understand it, the victory-over-oneself that they praise—later to be called 'self-mastery' (*to kreittô heautou* 645b2; cf. 626e8)—is displayed by the warrior who conquers his fears in battle (cf. 635b–c, 649c). By contrast, Schöpsdau (1994: 159–60) proposes that the present introduction of the personal case provides the Athenian with the basis on which he will criticize the militaristic focus of Dorian institutions. However, the Athenian's criticisms of the victory ideal (articulated at 627c–628d and 629c–630c) make no mention of conflict internal to a person; the conflict invoked in those contexts is internal to a city or a family (see note on 628c9–11, and 'A tactical concession?' in the general note on 628e2–630d1). While the Athenian is responsible for the line of questioning that leads to the present focus on internal conflict within a person, it is not the Athenian but his interlocutors who embrace victory in such conflict as a paradigm for virtue. While the Athenian will later exploit his interlocutors' belief that virtue, quite generally, is displayed in victory over opposing internal impulses (633d–634b, 644b), he will himself endorse a very different conception of virtue in Book 2 (653a–b)—also implicit in the account of education he offers in Book 1 (643b–644b)—on which virtue consists in 'agreement' (*sumphônia*) between internal

elements. These very different conceptions of virtue will be referred to below as the 'victory' and 'agreement' models. See notes on 626e5, 627a6–7, 628c9–11, 632d8–643a1, and 643b1–646e2.

626e4 'These ways of speaking (*tauta*)'
These are the common locutions, 'defeated by oneself' (*hêttôn heautou*) and its contrary 'master of oneself' (*kreittôn heautou*)—used, for example, in *Protag.* 358c–d and *Rep.* 430e–431b. The Athenian will substitute the latter at 626e8 for Clinias' locution, 'victory (*nikan*) over oneself' (e2). He will later use *akrateia* and *enkrateia* respectively, as synonyms for these terms (636c7, 645e8). The latter is the term Aristotle uses for continence, in contrast to *akrasia* (incontinence, weakness of will, *EN* 1145a15–18). The phenomena here invoked, which will be a recurring focus of the Athenian throughout Book 1 (633c–634b, 644d–646a, 647c–648e), correspond roughly to what Aristotle calls *akrasia* and *enkrateia* in *EN* VII 1–3, conditions that the latter distinguishes from genuine virtue and vice of character. The Athenian too will propose a model of virtue in Book 2 that rejects mere *enkrateia* as sufficient for virtue. See notes on 626e2–3 and 636c6–7.

626e5 'each of us is engaged in an internal war against himself'
Under the prompting from the Athenian's questioning, Clinias has now extended his original proposal, that conflict is a universal feature of human life, to apply to an individual person's relationship to himself. The internal analysis of personal self-conflict, however, is not pursued in the present context and will not be addressed explicitly until 644d–645c. The assumption that such conflict is inevitable informs the paradigm for virtue invoked at 632e–636c and 644b. On the difference between that paradigm and the alternative conception that the Athenian will endorse in Book 2, see notes on 626e2–3, 628c9–11, 634e1–2, 643b1–646e2.

626e7 'let's apply this thesis (*logon*) back to the previous cases'
The thesis is that of 626d1–e5—that an individual person is subject to internal conflict. Instead of dwelling on the psychological

implications of this thesis in its application to an individual person (a point not raised until 644b ff.), the Athenian here will immediately apply it to the parties involved in the types of conflict just enumerated at 626c–d: 'households, villages, and cities' (627a1). It is the problem of internal conflict within cities, not within persons, that will allow the Athenian to conclude at 628c9–e1 that peace, not war, is the proper focus of legislation. On the Athenian's tactical reasons for not pressing the analogous point about individual virtue, see note on 626e2–3.

627a6–7 'This sort of thing most emphatically does occur, especially within cities'
This remark introduces the notion of *stasis* or civil faction, internal conflict within a city, which was a common problem in Greek city states in Plato's time, but has as yet not figured in the discussion between the interlocutors. The problem of civil strife also looms large in Plato's *Republic*, where it is deployed as an analogue to the psychological turmoil within the unjust person. Here, however, the Athenian conspicuously fails to draw the analogy between civic strife and the psychology of vicious character. No doubt this is at least in part because the Athenian's interlocutors are attracted to a model of virtue that involves—indeed presupposes—internal conflict. See notes on 626e2–3 and 643b1–646e2.

627a7–9 'Where the better people are victorious over the inferior masses, the city would correctly be called "master of itself" '
This passage invokes better and worse parts of a *political* entity, and it will not be until 644b–645c that the analogous parts of an individual person are identified.

627b1–2 'whether we should ever accept that it is possible for the inferior (*cheiron*) to be master (*kreitton*) over the superior (*ameinonos*)'
An allusion to the surface paradox more accessible in Plato's Greek than in English translation. 'Master' here translates *kreitton*, which is ambiguous in meaning between 'better' and 'stronger'—hence the

paradox is something like saying that the inferior are superior to their betters. Such a paradox is exploited by Socrates in Plato's *Gorgias* 488b–e; and a different paradox in the notion of self-mastery is articulated at *Rep*. 430e–431a, where it is solved by positing, as in our present passage, a 'better' and 'worse' part within a person's soul (see Dorion 2007). Schöpsdau, by contrast, following Gigon, proposes that the Athenian's doubts here rest on the conviction that a good person cannot be harmed by a bad one (*Ap*. 30c–d). However, the Athenian never endorses such a thesis, even at 660e–661e, where he allows that bad things can happen to a good person (661d).

627b3–4 'members of the same tribe (*suggeneis*)'
An imprecise kinship relationship that applies both to the fellow citizens in the present example and to members of a nuclear family in the following example (627c–628a), where the cognate term *suggeneia* is used (627c10 and e5). See also note on 627e5.

627b4–5 'unjust (*adikoi*) citizens . . . the just minority'
As is typical in Plato, justice and injustice are primarily conceived of as properties of persons, rather than features of institutions.

627c1 'this way of speaking is decidedly odd'
The expressions for self-mastery and self-defeat apply, in ordinary speech, to individual persons (see note on 626e4). Clinias is commenting on the anomaly of using them to describe a city.

627c3–628c8

Reconciliation of warring parties is preferable to victory

In response to his interlocutor's claim that victory in internal conflict is the 'highest and most excellent victory', the Athenian distinguishes three different ways in which such conflict might be settled, illustrated in the case of a feuding family brought before a judge (627d8–628a5). The first two are varieties of victory of a better party over its rebellious inferiors; the latter party are either (1) executed, or (2) politically subjugated (627d11–e3). On the third option (3) the parties are reconciled by laws that ensure their future peaceful and friendly coexistence (627e3–628a3). Only (3) is a legislative solution, and only in that case is the conflict eliminated rather than decided in favour of one of the warring parties. Clinias agrees that it is the preferable solution, both in itself (628a4–5), and for strengthening the city against external foes (628b6–c3). Thus the Athenian will conclude at 628c9–e1 that peace is the ultimate focus of the legislator. Drawing this conclusion puts him in a position to make the analogous point about an individual person: that internal harmony is a superior achievement to victory of the better part over a recalcitrant worse part; however, the Athenian conspicuously fails to draw the latter conclusion; see note on 628c9–11.

627c8–10 'We are not seeking to mandate that the household (*oikia*) or tribe (*suggeneia*) as a whole be called "defeated by itself" '
This would indeed be an odd way to use the expression in Greek (see note on 627c1). The primary application of the expression is to the self-control or lack thereof in an individual person (as at 644d–645c). Here the expression is extended to apply to interpersonal or inter-group conflict; 'seeking to mandate that' translates *thêreuein* 627c9 (more literally: 'hunting for').

627d5–7 'very true (*alêthestata*) . . . just right (*kalôs*)'
As at 625c4–5, Clinias displays his preference for practical over verbal matters, and the hitherto passive Megillus concurs. On the Dorian distaste for verbal elaboration, see 641e. Megillus' *kalôs [sc. legeis]* simply reiterates the sense of Clinias' *alêthestata . . . legeis*; he is endorsing the content, not the style of the Athenian's remarks (by contrast: Saunders translates it 'nicely put'). On the expression, see note on 630c7.

627e1 'the better ones to rule themselves (*archein . . . hautôn*)'
The expression 'rule themselves' (*archein hautôn*) will be used at 644b7 to refer to individual self-control or self-restraint, which is

then explained at 644d–645c as the victory of calculation's golden pull over the opposing 'iron pulls' of pleasure and pain (see note on 644b6–7). In the present context, by contrast, the expression has its ordinary meaning of political self-rule—with no implication that a better part is ruling a worse. Indeed, the self-rule invoked here is exercised entirely within the 'better part' of the family, since the worse part, on this first option, has been eliminated.

627e2–3 'made them agree to be ruled'
more literally: 'makes them . . . be ruled voluntarily (*archesthai hekontas*)'
While *hekôn* (voluntarily) is often correctly translated as 'willingly' (as at 663b4–6), this is too strong for the present context and would obscure the difference between the second and third judges' solutions (see note on 627e3–4). Even actions performed under duress or constraint may be classified as *hekousion* (voluntary) in ordinary Greek, provided they are performed intentionally; this is why such actions will constitute a grey area for Aristotle's discussion of the topic to exploit (*EN* 1110a4–b9). Given this elasticity of the notion of the *hekousion*, the Athenian's characterization of the wicked brothers as *hekontas* is consistent with their displeasure at being ruled. It is because the brothers prefer this arrangement to the alternative of being put to death that they are made to 'agree' to it.

The notion that citizens should be voluntary (*hekontes*) subjects to the laws will be a persistent theme of the Athenian's (e.g. 700a5), although the relevant notion of voluntariness in those contexts (captured by the translation 'willingness'), unlike the one at play in the present passage, implies the absence of constraint or reluctance (as at 663e1–2, 690c3, 832c3–5, 921d9); see Laks 2005. For further citations within *Laws*, see note on 663b4–6. On the different ways of marking the contrast between *hekousion* (voluntary) and *akousion* (involuntary), see Meyer 1993: 9–14.

627e3–4 'Even better is a third judge'
literally: 'third in excellence (*triton . . . pros aretên*)'

The excellence (*aretê*) is specifically that of a judge (cf. the *aretê* of a legislator at 637d2). Later (630a ff.) the more general human *aretê*, consisting of wisdom, moderation, courage, and justice, will become the focus of the discussion, where the term is translated 'virtue'. See notes on 629e9–630a2 and 630b2–3.

England and others puzzle over how the third judge is different from the second, but there is a clear contrast if we construe the evil brothers' attitude in the second case as in the note on 627e2–3. The first judge executes the evil parties, the second makes them submit to the rule of their betters (even if they are not entirely happy with this arrangement), and the third reconciles the two parties, making them friends (*philous*, 628a3) rather than masters and subjects (the importance of friendship (*philia*) among fellow citizens is stressed in Book 3). By contrast, England, followed by Schöpsdau, supposes that the third makes permanent, through laws, the arrangement instituted by the second. Strauss (1975: 5) takes the Athenian to present the third judge as the worst, on the grounds that the laws allow the bad as well as the good to rule; however, we may suppose that the reconciliation that establishes the friendship between the citizens (628a1–3) rehabilitates the wicked brothers and so makes all the brothers good.

627e5 'this tribe at odds with itself'

The term translated as 'tribe' (*suggeneia*) applies equally to the family invoked at 627c and the fellow citizens invoked at 627b (see note on 627b3–4). Thus the superiority of the third solution (reconcile the warring parties) applies to both family and city. Note that the language used at 627c8–d3 and 627d11–628a3 is not specific to the case of the family. The term 'brothers', which appears in some translations (Saunders, Taylor) is not in Plato's text.

628a1–2 'reconcile them by establishing laws'

The third alternative is the first truly legislative solution, in contrast to the first and second, which are judicial verdicts. The point of proper legislation, as the Athenian will explain in Book 3, is to raise citizens under institutions that will make them well disposed to each other and to the importance of following the laws; as a result, no conflict should arise in the first place.

628a6–7 'it would not be with a view to war but to its opposite that he establishes their laws'

The Athenian here neatly draws the conclusion that contradicts Clinias' initial claim that victory in war against other cities is the single focus of the legislator (625d7–e2, 626a5–8). This is not to say that victory in war is unimportant, but simply that establishing friendly relations among citizens is an important goal of the legislator. Since the issue in the immediate context concerns conflict *within* families or states, not between them, all the Athenian establishes here is that it is better to have a community whose members are reconciled to each other than one where a discordant element is kept under control. At 628c9–e1 he will draw the stronger conclusion that the goal of victory in war is subordinate to that of living in peace without faction. See also note on 628c9–11.

628a9 'the person who sets up (*sunarmottôn*) a city'

A transition from the case of the judge to the case of the legislator. The verb *sunarmozein*, here translated 'sets up' (with Taylor, Lisi), also evokes the 'harmonizing' functions of the 'third judge' above at 627e3–628a3, as well as the notion of *sumphônia* (agreement) that will be important later on (see notes on 628c9–11 and 634e1–2). Thus Saunders translates the verb as 'harmonizes', and similarly des Places and Brisson/Pradeau; however, the former meaning is likely to be operative here. Otherwise it prejudges the question that the Athenian is about to ask concerning the legislator (see note on 628a9–b2). Schöpsdau manages to capture both connotations of the verb.

628a9–b2 'Is it more with a view to war against external foes that he arranges its life, or with a view to the type of war that . . . arises within cities . . . ?'

This question is in superficial tension with the Athenian's claim that the proper legislator does not have war as his focus (628a, 630d). However, as the present context develops the point, it is clear that the legislator has civil war in mind as something to avoid.

628b6–9 'in which condition would you prefer that the city be forced to direct its attention to external enemies . . . ?'
Here the Athenian exploits the high value placed by his Dorian interlocutors on victory in war against external enemies, even though he does not endorse their view.

628c6 'for the sake of what is best (*tou aristou heneka*)'
Here Plato uses *aristos* to indicate not just the greatest good, but a goal—that for whose sake the other things are pursued; on the connection between good and goal, see Aristotle *EN* I 1094a18–22, 1097a18–24. *Aristos* in some contexts might alternatively be rendered by 'excellent' (as at 629b3 and 630a2, where for consistency's sake, it is also translated 'best'). Its cognate noun (*aretê*) is translated as 'virtue' at 630b3, c4, e1–3, 631a3–5; on the translation see note on 629e9–630a2.

628c9–e1

Peace, not victory, is the ultimate goal of legislation

In this difficult paragraph, the Athenian takes up his announced points in reverse order: victory over internal faction is not the best thing to aim at (628c11–d4); nor is victory in external war (d4–e1). His conclusion, that war is 'for the sake of' (*charin*) peace (d8), allows victory in external war to be a goal of the legislator, but one that is subordinate to the ultimate goal of peace.

628c9–11 'The best (*ariston*), however, is neither war nor faction . . . but rather peace and mutual goodwill'
Presumably 'war' and 'faction' are here shorthand for 'victory in war' and 'victory against faction'. The Athenian here articulates this

conclusion only as a claim about what is good for a city state (*polis*), not an individual person, notwithstanding the mention of the latter at 628d5. It is, of course, easy to make the analogous point in criticism of the ideal of self-mastery affirmed by Clinias at 626e2–3: while 'victory over oneself' is better than being 'defeated' by pleasures or pains, far superior to either is the condition of not being torn by opposing inclinations in the first place (thus Stalley 1983: 55 and 1994: 164). Indeed, the latter condition is captured by the conception of virtue as 'agreement' (*sumphônia*) that is implied in the account of education that will be presented later in Book 1 (see note on 643b1–646e2), and articulated explicitly in the fuller account of education in Book 2, 653a–b. In the present context, however, the Athenian conspicuously fails to apply his conclusions to the case of an individual person. Indeed, as the discussion proceeds, he will continue to appeal to his interlocutor's conception of virtue as victory over oneself at 633c–d, 635b–d, 644b. (On the tactical reasons for doing so, see note on 627a6–7 and general note on 628e2–630d1.) On 'victory' and 'agreement' as competing paradigms for virtue, see notes on 626e2–3 and 643b1–646e2.

628d1 'not the highest achievement (*tôn aristôn*) but a necessity (*tôn anankaiôn*)'
more literally: 'not one of the best things but a necessity'
If it was the best thing, it would be the legislator's goal (628c6–7). On the opposition between necessity and the good, see *Laws* 858a, *Rep.* 493c.

628d2–3 'a disease-ridden body is performing at its best (*arista prattein*) after being flushed out by a purgative'
Another analogy to a purgative is invoked at 646c. On 'performing (or doing) one's best' as a synonym for happiness (*eudaimonia*), see note on 628d5.

628d5 'the happiness (*eudaimonia*) of either a city or an individual'

'Happiness' (*eudaimonia*) is used as equivalent to 'performing at [one's] best' (*arista prattein*) at 628d3. It means 'living well' (*eu zên*) or 'doing well' (*eu prattein*—*Rep.* 354a1; *Euthyd.* 278e3, 279a2–3, 280b5–6; cf. *Laws* 657c5–6; Aristotle *EN* 1095a18–20) and is also captured by 'doing admirably' (*kalôs prattein*—641c1; see note on 637e5). Thus *eudaimonia* is a kind of well-being, or well-functioning, rather than subjective contentment, in contrast to what the English translation 'happiness' might suggest. It belongs not only to individual people (*Laws* 631b) but also to cities (*Laws* 636d–e, 683b, 697b, 710b, 781b, 927b, 945d; *Rep.* 500e), and it is the lawgiver's business to bring it about (*Laws* 628d, 631b, 742d–743c). The Athenian will explain at 631b–d that one is happy insofar as one has good things, and that the greatest of these are the virtues—hence his later remarks that one is happy (*eudaimôn*) insofar as one is good (*agathos*) or just (*dikaios*)—*Laws* 660e–661d; cf. 742d–743c. On the notion of 'happiness' in Greek ethics, see Kraut 1979; Annas 1993: 27–46. On the relationship between being good (or virtuous) and being happy, see Meyer 2008: 11–14. See also notes on 631b5–6, 636e1, and 660e7–9.

628d8–e1 'rather than regulating peacetime for the sake of war' A point repeated in Book 7, 803d. On the expression 'for the sake of' (*charin*—equivalent to *heneka* at 628c6), see notes on 631d5–6 and on 647c1.

628e2–630d1

Criticism of the military ethic of the poet Tyrtaeus

Clinias notes that, whatever the merits of the Athenian's remarks, Spartan and Cretan institutions obviously have war as their primary focus (628e2–5). The Athenian encourages him not to be defensive on the issue, but to proceed on the assumption that all parties to the discussion take military success 'most seriously' (629a2–3). As a device to make concrete this common sense of purpose, he shifts the conversation away from an examination of Clinias' and Megillus' views to a hypothetical conversation with the poet Tyrtaeus (629a–630c), whose alleged ties to both Athens and Sparta (629a5) make him an appropriate spokesman for the alleged shared concerns. It is Tyrtaeus, rather than the Dorian interlocutors or their legislators, who is criticized for eulogizing prowess in war against external foes instead of the broader range of virtues that include not only courage but also justice and moderation (629e–630d). The engagement with Tyrtaeus thus serves to introduce the notion of virtue (*aretê*) into the discussion. The issue is no longer whether peace or victory is the legislator's goal, but which virtues the legislator should aim to cultivate in the citizens—those for peace or those for war.

A tactical concession?

The Athenian's argument takes the curious tack of conceding the Dorian assumption that excellence in war is of the utmost importance (629a–c), and limiting the debate to the question of which kind of war (external or internal) is more important (629c–d). On the face of it, this concession contradicts the conclusion just articulated by the Athenian that war is not the legislator's ultimate focus (628c9–e5; to be reiterated at 630d4–7). Having previously established

(a) that civil conflict poses greater dangers than external war (628a–b), and
(b) that peace is a higher goal than victory in conflict (628c–d),

the Athenian now appears to conduct his 'conversation' with Tyrtaeus as if (b) had not been established. He argues simply that the person who excels in civil conflict is superior to Tyrtaeus' warrior against external foes (629e–630a). However, the Athenian's enumeration of the virtues required for success against internal faction (630a–c; developed further in 631c–e) makes it clear that these include the virtues of sociable cooperation during peacetime—in particular, moderation and justice. Rather than simply equipping a person for success in the battles of a civil war, these virtues will prevent faction and civil strife from arising in the first place. It is the combination of these that the Athenian presents to Tyrtaeus as superior to strictly military courage. However strained the assumption that this expanded range of virtue displays 'excellence in civil war', it fits with the Athenian's strategy of appealing to normative assumptions that his interlocutors find attractive.

628e4–5 'with this goal in view'
literally: 'are for the sake of these (*toutôn heneka*)', i.e. success in war against external enemies. See notes on 631d5-6 and 647c1.

629a2 'to push the point aggressively (*diamachesthai*) . . . maintain a civil tone'
more literally: 'to be contentious . . . '
(Cf. a similar contrast between contentious or combative argument and civilized discussion at *Meno* 75c–d). The Athenian's point here is that the present discussion is not a contest for victory but an inquiry into the truth. 'Civil' translates the adverb *êrema*—'gently', which invokes the gentleness (*praotês* or *hêmerotês*) that in Plato is typically associated with persuasion and reasoning and contrasted with force or violence (*Stsm.* 307a–b, *Rep.* 375b–e, 410c–411e; *Laws* 634c, 666e, 731b–d; cf. *Rep.* 399a–c). See also notes on 629d2, 634c7–8, 645a6. On the importance of balancing gentleness and forcefulness, see note on 631c7–8. On contentious argument (*eristikê*), see also *Lys.* 211b–c, *Euthyd.* 272a–b, *Soph.* 226a, 231e.

629a2–3 'we and they alike take these matters most seriously'
The antecedent of 'they' is not supplied by the context, but it is presumably the legislators of the Spartan and Cretan institutions invoked by Clinias at 628e2–5, who are the assumed object of *anerôtan* ('question' 629a2). 'These matters' (*tauta*, 629a3) are most likely the military goals (*toutôn*, 628e4) that Clinias has just cited as the focus of Dorian legislation. Thus Schöpsdau. By contrast, England proposes 'laws and government' as the antecedent. However, as Schöpsdau notes, Clinias' use of 'emphatically' (*spoudên*) in

628e4 (which concerns military matters) is picked up by the Athenian's 'take . . . seriously' (*spoudazontôn*) here at 629a3. The two occurrences of 'these matters' (*peri tauta*) in 629a3 and a6 both refer back to the '*toutôn*' in Clinias' remark at e4; cf. 629c2–4.

629a4 'Tyrtaeus'

An elegiac poet of the seventh century BCE whose martial poems glorifying valour in combat were a staple in Spartan culture. See Podlecki (1984). Pausanias 4.15.6 reports that Tyrtaeus transferred his allegiance from Athens to Sparta; the tale is not very flattering to the poet and reflects the centuries-long tension between Athens and Sparta. See also note on 634a2, where Tyrtaeus may be alluded to.

629a7–b3 'I would not memorialize a man . . . not even . . . the richest man of all . . . who did not always prove to be best in war'

The quotation-cum-paraphrase from Tyrtaeus (fragment 12 West) continues at 629e1–3 and is revisited in Book 2 at 660e–661a. The poet articulates a slightly skewed version of the principle that the Athenian will express in the doctrine of divine and human goods at 631b6–d2. In refusing to praise wealth and the other generally recognized standards of success unless it is combined with 'virtue', Tyrtaeus implies that there is no value in possessing such putative goods as wealth unless one also possesses virtue (*aretê*). By contrast, Clinias at 626b2–4 implies that military valour is to be prized because it secures and defends material possessions. For development of this point, see Bobonich 2002: 131–6. Tyrtaeus' error, attributed to the interlocutors quite generally at 630d4–e3, is an overly narrow conception of the requisite virtue or excellence. (On 'virtue' and its connection to being 'best in war', see note on 629e9–630a2.)

629b9 'most divine'

A typically Spartan locution, also used by Megillus at 626c4; see note on 642d5.

629d2 'the hardest (*chalepôtatos*) conflict'

'Hardest' translates the superlative of *chalepos,* which is regularly contrasted with *praos* (mild, gentle; see notes on 629a2, 634c7–8, 645a6) but also with 'easy' (*rhadion*) at 636a2–4; cf. 641b7. England prefers 'deadliest', but the Athenian's point is unlikely to be that external war causes less death and destruction than civil war, given the bloody carnage he has invoked to characterize external war just a few lines later in the quote from Tyrtaeus (629e2–3). Presumably *chalepos* is to be understood in the same sense as in the quote from Theognis at 630a4–5 where it (and its comparative form) is used to modify *dichostasiê* (faction) and *polemos* (conflict, a6): roughly, civil war is the most difficult battle to fight. In Book 2, the same term is used to describe the dangers posed by improper song and dance (see note on 669b5–6).

629d3 'as we were saying just now'—628a9–b4.

629d5 'far milder (*praioteron*)'—see note on 629d2.

629e9–630a2 'while these men are good (*agathôn*), there are others who are better (*ameinous*) by far—those who show themselves to be best (*aristous*) in the most important kind of war (*megistôi polemôi*)' *Agathos* is an ordinary adjective meaning 'good' and is used here along with its comparative (*ameinôn*) and superlative (*aristos*) forms (cf. 628c6–7, 629b3). Many translators, however, translate the terms here by forms of 'courageous' or 'brave' (Bury, Saunders, des Places, Brisson/Pradeau, but not Lisi or Schöpsdau). This is unwarranted. While the sort of goodness that Tyrtaeus has in mind is undoubtedly courage or bravery, it is important to distinguish the general notion of goodness that is invoked by *agathos* and its cognates from the specific kind of goodness that is manifest in the bravery extolled by Tyrtaeus. Even if, as the Athenian charges, Tyrtaeus and his ilk collapse all of goodness into courage (*andreia*), one cannot articulate this point without respecting the distinct meanings of the two terms.

At 630b–c, the Athenian will restate the present affirmation as a claim about 'excellence' or 'virtue' (*aretê*—the abstract noun cognate with the superlative *aristos*). In many literary contexts, including the poems of Tyrtaeus, *aristos*, the cognate verb *aristeuein*, and the noun *aretê* characterize warriors who are victorious over opponents (e.g. Homer *Iliad* 6.208, 11.784), and in such contexts *aretê* often refers to strength, speed, or military prowess (e.g. ibid. 8.535, 11.90, 22.268; cf. Tyrtaeus fr. 12.33 West). But in the political context of the fourth and fifth centuries BCE that Plato depicts in his dialogues, *aretê* connotes excellence much more broadly construed. For example, it is the object of pursuit by any ambitious participant in public life (dramatized by Plato in openings of *Protagoras* 310b–319a; see Meyer 2008: 8–11). Thus even if what Tyrtaeus has in mind when he uses the term *aretê* is bravery (as at Tyrtaeus fr. 12.13 West), we must translate the term as 'virtue' or 'excellence' rather than 'bravery'. On virtue, see also note on 630b2–3.

630a4 'Theognis . . . of Megara'
An elegiac poet of the sixth century BCE. The verse quoted is Book 1.76–77 (Diehl/Young).

630a7–b2 'a blend of justice, moderation (*sôphrosune*), and wisdom along with courage (*andreia*) is better (*ameinôn*) than courage on its own'
literally: 'justice, moderation, and wisdom coming to the same thing (*eis t'auton elthousa*), along with (*meta*) courage is better . . . '
This remark, together with the classification of courage as 'fourth in rank and merit' at 630c8, is elaborated and explained by the ranking of 'divine goods' at 631c5–d1 (on which see note on 631c7–8). The phrase 'than courage on its own' (b2) is missing from the MSS but quoted in Eusebius and Proclus. Whether or not the phrase was in Plato's text, the comparison the Athenian intends is clearly with the virtue singled out for praise by Tyrtaeus (630c6–7). The latter is exemplified in the behaviour of the rapacious mercenaries (b5–8). Unlike the virtues invoked by Socrates in *Protag.* (329c–333b, 349b–d), it does not depend on or imply the presence of the other virtues, and the same might be said of

the 'moderate disposition of a soul' invoked at 631c7 that must be combined with wisdom (*phronêsis*) to become a divine good (see note ad loc). Such isolated 'courage' and 'moderation' are rather like the traits that go by those names in *Euthyd.* 281c, *Stsm.* 306a–308a, 310d–e; *Laws* 661e, 696d, 710a; cf. 681b: tendencies to aggression and risk-taking on the one hand ('courage'), and to restraint and deliberateness on the other ('moderation'); see Irwin 1995: 340, 347–8, Lane 1998: 171–2, Carone 2002: 336–7, Bobonich 2002: 289–90; for a history of discussion on this point see Cairns 1993: 374n90. These tendencies do not always yield appropriate action (witness the case of the mercenaries, on which cf. Protagoras' initial position in *Protag.* 349d). Only when balanced against each other and tempered with wisdom do they amount to the conditions that are called 'courage' and 'moderation' in *Protagoras*, and are there argued by Socrates to involve wisdom (361b). By contrast, the Athenian counts the mercenary's imperfect trait as a virtue (*aretê*) at 630c6–7 (taking *aretên* at c4 to be the antecedent of *hên* at c6). It is still worth having, although less valuable than if it were part of 'complete virtue'. See also note on 661d8–e1.

630b2–3 'no one would be trustworthy and dependable in the face of faction unless he had all of virtue (*sumpasês aretês*)'
What is here called 'all of virtue' (*sumpasês aretês*) is called 'the greatest virtue' (*megistên arêten*) at 630c3–4. It is the blend of justice, moderation, wisdom, and courage invoked at 630a7–b2 (see note above) and called 'virtue in its entirety' (*pasan aretên*) at 630e2–3, 632e5–6; cf. *aretês hapasês* at 661c4. This is the virtue that the legislator should aim at (630c2–4). It is necessary for trustworthiness in times of civil strife because while courage alone might equip one to defeat the seditious party in battle, the other virtues (especially moderation and justice) equip one to resist the temptation to engage in sedition oneself. The latter virtues, moreover, if cultivated widely in the citizen body, are proof against the tendency for faction to develop in the first place. Thus Theognis' figure of the warrior who is trustworthy in times of faction nicely makes the transition from the

awkward assumption that prowess in war is, after all, the legislator's primary concern (see general note on 628e2–630d1) to the Athenian's main contention, that the legislator must aim at inculcating 'all of virtue'.

This is the first use in *Laws* of the noun *aretê* (virtue, excellence; cognate with the adjective *aristos*, best) to characterize the focus of the legislator. As in other works of Plato, *aretê* is used as a general term for the traits of wisdom, moderation, justice, and courage, and is not restricted (as in some Homeric contexts) to courage or military prowess (see note on 629e9–630a2). Also in keeping with this general usage (as at *Laws* 965d1–3, *Protag.* 325a1–2), the singular *aretê* (rather than the plural *aretai*) is used to invoke the totality of the virtues. Accordingly, justice, wisdom, etc. are not called 'virtues' (*aretai*—in contrast, for instance, with Arisototle's usage: *EN* 1114b26, 1144b18) but 'parts of virtue' (630e1, 631a5, 633a8). Unlike Socrates in *Protagoras* (329c–d), however, the Athenian will later disavow interest in making precise the notion of a 'part' of virtue (see note on 633a8–9).

630c2–4 'any legislator who is any good will set his primary sights on nothing other than the greatest virtue (*megistên aretên*) when he establishes laws'
That the legislator should aim at the 'greatest virtue', 'the whole of virtue', or 'virtue in its entirety' (see note on 630b2–3), is repeated at 688a–b and 705d–706a. On virtue (*aretê*), see note on 629e9–630a2.

630c5–6 'which one might call complete justice (*dikaiosunên* . . . *telean*)'
It is slightly odd that the trustworthiness invoked by Theognis is called 'complete justice' here, when just a few lines above it is called 'all of virtue'—a combination of justice with moderation, wisdom, and temperance (630a7–b3). The oddity evaporates in the light of 631c7–8, where the Athenian explains that justice is a combination of wisdom, moderation, and courage (rather than a trait that, like courage, can exist both in isolation from, and blended with, the other

traits); see note on 630a7–b2. Aristotle's too will invoke a notion of justice that includes all the other virtues, and may be called 'complete virtue' (*teleia aretê*, *EN* 1129b30).

630c6–d1 'The virtue that Tyrtaeus singles out for praise... comes fourth'

A point repeated in Book 2, 667a2–5 in a context less circumspect in its criticisms of Spartan institutions. There is even stronger criticism of the poet in Book 9, 858e1–3. The virtue in question is courage unmixed with moderation and wisdom (630b2; see note on 630a7–b2). The fourth place ranking is explained at 631c5–d1. See note ad loc.

630c7 'although it is admirable (*kalê*)'
alternatively: 'beautiful', 'noble', 'fine'

The thesis that virtue is something *kalon* (neuter adjective) is a frequent motif in Plato (e.g. *Charm.* 160e, *La.* 192c–d; see Irwin 1995: 37–8); the *kalon* is the central notion in Plato's *Symposium*, and Aristotle identifies it as the characteristic goal of virtuous action (*EN* 1115b12–13, *EE* 1230a26–33). On the meaning of the term in Plato and Aristotle, see Cooper 1996; Lear 2006; Irwin 2010; Barney 2010; Moss 2012; and Kraut 2013. The term and its cognates have a semantic range and force that are not captured by any single English term, and the same goes for its opposite, *aischron* (shameful, ugly, ignoble). In some contexts *kalon* simply means 'good' or 'correct' (see notes on 637e5 and on 634d9–e1); this is especially so in its adverbial form *kalôs*, which often means virtually the same as *eu* (well), and in the idiom *kalôs legeis* ('you are right'—627d6, 636e4, 646d1). In other contexts *kalon* has a strong expressive force, invoking both ethical and aesthetic goodness. The only English term that comes close to matching this range is 'fine'; however, except in its comparative and superlative forms, 'fine' in English can be a very pallid term of approval, and so fails to capture the dynamic and expressive force of the Greek term. The present translation therefore deploys a variety of English terms to render *kalon* and its cognates (with the author's thanks to an anonymous referee for urging this approach). It is occasionally rendered 'fine' (625a4), 'nice' (655a4), or 'noble' (645a4–6); 'finer' and 'finest' are retained for the comparative and superlative forms of the adjective (regularly over 665d–668b); 'admirable' is typically used in contexts that are predominantly ethical or political, and thus 'admirable' is the typical translation for *kalon* in Book 1 (although 634e2 is an exception); 'beautiful' is used in contexts concerning the arts (e.g. painting and sculpture at 669a), and hence is the predominant rendering in Book 2. In cases where both the ethical and the aesthetic dimensions of *kalon* are salient (either simultaneously, or in close succession, as at 654b–656a), or when the sense is not determinately one or the other (e.g. 663e, 664b, 667c), the default translation is 'beautiful' ('lovely' at 660a). The reader is invited to take any linguistic oddity that results as a reminder that the relevant notion of beauty encompasses both aesthetic and ethical norms. See also notes on 654b6–7.

630d2–631b2

The goals and practice of the proper legislator

The proper legislator, the Athenian explains—still leaving it open that the Dorian legislators fall into this category (630d–631a)—aims at cultivating 'virtue in its entirety', not just the military courage extolled by Tyrtaeus; the point is repeated at 688a–b without the polite supposition.

630d4–7 'It is we who are doing poorly by supposing that Lycurgus and Minos had war in view'

Lycurgus is the legendary Spartan legislator (mentioned unfavourably at 858e). Minos is identified as the legislator for Knossos at the opening of Book 1. The Athenian's generous assumption here (630d4–e3) that the Dorian constitutions do in fact aim at virtue in its entirety, not just military courage (repeated by implication at 632d1–4), will not be sustained in Book 2, where he will not mince words in castigating their societies for being organized on exclusively military principles (666e–667a). On the Athenian's reasons for insisting here on the authority of Minos, see Nightingale 1993: 283.

630d7 'when establishing the institutions (*nomima*)'
For consistency of translation, *nomima* is here and elsewhere rendered by 'institutions' and *nomoi* by laws, but no distinction is intended by the Athenian here between institutions, practices, and laws. See Introduction and note on 626a6–8.

630d9–e1 'What is only right and true to say on behalf of a divine lawgiver'
Translation following England, Schöpsdau, and Lisi. Although nothing in the MSS corresponds to 'lawgiver' and the transmitted text is problematic, it is clear from the context that the Athenian has in mind the divinely inspired legislators invoked at 624a—either a divine man (*theiou andros*) or divine legislation (*theias nomothesias*) or divine constitution (*theias politeias*). Des Places conjectures *euêthesias* (ingenuousness), followed by Saunders and Brisson/Pradeau.

630e1–3 'that he made the laws looking not to a part of virtue, and the most trifling one at that, but to virtue in its entirety (*pasan aretên*)'
A recapitulation of the conclusion about the proper goal of legislation just drawn at 630c1–6, in light of the conceit at 630d4–7 that it is the interlocutors rather than the Dorian legislators who have failed to note that legislation must be aimed at 'virtue as a whole' (*pasa aretê*); the latter locution is offered as equivalent to 'all of virtue' (*sumpasa aretê*) in 630b2–3. See note ad loc.

630e3–4 'he worked out (*zêtein*) his laws according to different categories (*eidê*) from the ones that guide legislators today'
The verb *zêtein* encompasses both seeking and inquiring; hence it is translated 'work out' in the present context and 'seek out' at 630e5; for stylistic variation it is rendered 'formulate' at 631a1.

The Athenian here articulates a general methodological principle licensed by the insight that legislation has virtue as its goal (630c1–5; 631a3–4). Current legislators devise laws piecemeal under heterogeneous categories (inheritances, assaults, etc.), which are introduced as the need for them arises. Instead of being goal-directed, this legislative practice is reactive, responding to problem cases. (An 'heiress' (*epiklêros*) is a fatherless, brotherless woman—and hence poses a problem for the typical Greek practice of passing on family wealth through the male line; see Pomeroy 2002: 84 and Cox 1998.) Such a reactive and disorderly procedure is contrasted with the type of inquiry (*zêtêsis*) that underlies proper legislation. The latter takes virtue as its focus, and devises laws with a view to what is required to inculcate it in the citizens. The proper methodology is specified more precisely at 632d8–e2 (see note ad loc): the legislator considers each virtue in turn, devising laws and institutions suitable for inculcating each. The use of *eidos* (translated as 'kind') at 632e2, repeating its occurrence here at 630e3, indicates that the different virtues (called 'parts of virtue' at 633a8; cf. 630e1, 631a5) are the 'categories' under which proper legislative practice or inquiry is to be organized. See note on 632d8–e2.

631a1–2 'to start where our present inquiry began'
literally: 'to begin as we did (*hôsper . . . êrxametha*)'

631a3–4 'You were correct to begin with virtue (*ap' aretês*) and say that it was for its sake that the legislator framed his laws'
Clinias did not in fact begin by invoking virtue (*aretê*), a notion which is introduced only by the Athenian, and not until 630b3, where it captures the considerations about what sort of person is 'good', 'better', and 'best' that are invoked in the dialogue with Tyrtaeus (629b3, 629e9–630a2); see note on 629e9–630a2. Clinias did affirm at 626e2–3 that 'victory over oneself' is the greatest kind of victory, a remark which the Athenian will later interpret as a proposal about what makes a person good (644b6–7), but Clinias does not

himself use the vocabulary of virtue when affirming that ideal. It is the Athenian who has redirected the conversation away from Clinias' emphasis on external results (victory over the enemy in war, 625d–626b) to virtue, considered as a personal trait. This transition prepares the way for the dialogue's next topic: education, the project of cultivating the virtues in the citizens.

631a5–7 'you were clearly incorrect . . . to suppose that it was only to a part of virtue, and the smallest one at that, that he referred all his laws'
See note on 630d4–7.

631a8–b1 'the sort of divisions (*pêi dielomenon*)'
alternatively: 'the way I would have hoped to hear you expound' (England)
One might suppose that in the sample speech that follows (631b–632c), the distinction between divine and human goods is an example of a 'division' that expresses the centrality of virtue to the legislative enterprise. Alternatively, one might expect, on the basis of *Stsm.* 262b–e, 285a–b, and *Phdr.* 273d–e, that the 'categories' (*eidê*) mentioned above at 630e3 and below at 632e2 mark the relevant divisions; see note on 630e3–4.

631b3–d1

Divine and human goods

The previous thesis that virtue is the focus of legislation (630d–631a) is now subsumed under the more general thesis that worthy laws benefit the community by 'provid[ing] them with every good' (631b6). The Athenian provides a taxonomy and ranking of goods that accords a central place to virtue and is to inform the legislator's practice: wisdom, moderation, justice, and courage (ranked in that order) are 'divine goods' on which all 'human goods' (wealth, health, etc.) depend.

631b5 'They are correct laws'
literally: 'they are in correct condition (*echousin . . . orthôs*)'
Presumably a synonym for *kalôs . . . echei* ('[they] are in admirable condition') at 634d9–e1; see note ad loc and on 667c6–7 and 668d1–2.

631b5–6 'and bring happiness to those who live by them, since they provide them with every good'
On happiness, see also note on 628d5. The Athenian here moves seamlessly from his prior claim that proper legislation aims at the virtue of the citizens (630d–631a) to claiming here that it gives them happiness. On legislation aiming at happiness, see also 662e.

Human goods depend on the divine

631b6–8 'Now goods are twofold—some of them human, others divine—and the former depend (*êrtêtai*) on the divine'
In what sense do the 'human goods' (health, beauty, strength, and wealth) depend on the 'divine goods' (wisdom, moderation, courage, and justice)? To the extent that the divine goods depend on wisdom (631c), one might find here an instance of the thesis, affirmed by Socrates in *Euthyd.* 278e–282a and *Meno* 87d–89a, that such things as health and wealth are good only if their use is directed by wisdom. For discussion, see Bobonich 2002: 136–53; he finds a better explanation in the theory of goods in the *Philebus* (2002: 153–79). On the relation between the present thesis of 'dependent goods' (Bobonich's term) and the Athenian's declaration in Book 2 that 'so-called goods' such as health and wealth are good only to the good person (661b–d), see note on 631c1–5 and general note on 660d11–661d5.

631b8–c1 'A city that receives (*dechêtai*) the greater ones acquires the lesser as well; otherwise, it is bereft of both'
alternatively: 'a city that welcomes the greater ones . . . '
One might suppose that this sentence explains or elaborates the dependence of human on divine goods affirmed in the previous

sentence, but the present sentence is in fact a conjunction of two theses: a sufficiency thesis (possessing the divine goods suffices for possessing the human ones) and a necessity thesis (possessing the divine goods is necessary for possessing the human ones). Only the latter affirms the dependence of human on divine goods. Moreover, both theses concern a city, not an individual person, as the recipient of the relevant goods. The latter fact has troubled many readers; England (endorsed by Bobonich 1995: 137 and 2002: 509n42) proposes to emend the MSS text to make a person the subject. Let us call the MS version of the thesis the 'political' version, and the emended version the 'personal' version.

While it is no doubt true, as England points out, that it is individual persons, not cities, who are the ultimate recipients of the divine and human goods here enumerated, it still makes sense for the Athenian to talk about a *city* receiving these goods, since this speech is supposed to articulate the goals with which a legislator devises laws for a city (see 630d1–e3). Moreover, the personal version of the sufficiency thesis is far stronger than any other claim affirmed in the *Laws* (or indeed anywhere else in Plato) about the relationship between virtue and the other goods. It would affirm that any person who has the divine goods (the virtues) will also have the human goods (health, wealth, etc.). But it is hardly plausible for the Athenian (or Plato) to suppose that a person who is wise, moderate, and courageous will never fall into illness and poverty.

The political version of the sufficiency thesis is considerably more plausible. Consider first the corresponding version of the necessity thesis: that without the divine goods, the city will lack the human ones. Even if it is not strictly impossible for health, wealth, and the like to be available in adequate quantity in a city whose inhabitants are unwise, immoderate, cowardly, and unjust, a legislator devising the basic institutions of a polity would be well advised to operate on the assumption that neglecting to cultivate 'complete justice' in the citizens will seriously impair their prospects for securing these human goods (for reasons made memorable by Hobbes many centuries later). The reason why the supply of human goods in a city might reasonably be expected to depend on the extent of wisdom, moderation, courage, and justice exercised by its inhabitants is that these virtues concern the ways in which one engages with the human goods. For example, moderation, courage, and justice concern the ways one pursues, uses, safeguards, disposes of, or risks losing such things as health, beauty, strength, wealth, and the like (thus the idea that wisdom, which the Athenian here insists is integral to 'complete justice', involves the correct 'use' (*chrêsis*) of such 'goods' in *Euthyd.* 281a–b; *Meno* 88a–d). On such a conception, it is not unreasonable to suppose that a city whose citizens have been taught to engage properly with the human goods will thereby *have* the human goods to engage with (the sufficiency thesis). To be sure, 'engaging' with the human goods extends to the limiting case where a person loses, gives up, or refrains from pursuing such a good, and thus it is conceivable that an individual person might, for example, be perfectly just in poverty and ill health; indeed, one of the legislator's tasks will be to teach the citizens to respond appropriately to such an eventuality (632a). But this is a problem for the personal version of the sufficiency thesis, not for the political version. From the perspective of a legislator aiming to inculcate the virtues in the citizens, which is precisely the perspective invoked in this passage, it is highly unlikely that the disposition to engage properly with the human goods could be cultivated in and exercised by the citizenry at large without there being an adequate supply of those goods. The Athenian is entitled to assume that the legislator whose primary goal is to inculcate complete virtue in the citizens will have to provide them with an adequate level of human goods, and this may be all there is to the sufficiency thesis. While supplying the city with the human goods is an important objective of his, this will be achieved in the course of carrying out his ultimate aim of supplying it with the divine virtues. Thus the political versions of both the sufficiency thesis and the necessity thesis are reasonable claims for the Athenian to make in this context.

The human goods

631c1–5 'Chief among the lesser goods is health, second beauty, and third is strength for running and other physical activities. Fourth is wealth that is not blind but clear-sighted, which comes from following wisdom.'

Compare the more open-ended enumeration of the 'so-called goods' in 661a–c, and in 649d and 716a, as well as in the popular drinking song reported at *Gorg.* 451e. Note that the goods listed in the present passage are not entirely independent of each other; the second and third items (beauty and strength) arguably depend on the first (health), and the fourth item ('wealth . . . clear-sighted to the extent that it is guided by wisdom') is explicitly marked as involving the primary divine good, wisdom (which recalls *Euthyd.* 280b–282a). Are we to understand a similar qualification implied for the other human goods? If the human goods involve the divine goods (and in this sense 'depend' on them), then they do not correspond to the 'so-called' goods of 661a–c. See note on 661a5–b3. The phrase, 'wealth (*ploutos*) that is not blind' invokes the familiar stereotype of the blind god Plutus (literally 'Wealth').

631c5–d1

The divine goods

The four virtues enumerated (wisdom, moderation, justice, and courage) recapitulate the four cardinal virtues enumerated in the *Republic* (427e). They are here ranked in order of priority:

(1) wisdom (*phronêsis*);
(2) moderation (*sôphrosunê*) tempered by wisdom;
(3) justice (= moderation tempered by wisdom plus courage);
(4) courage on its own (i.e. unaccompanied by moderation and wisdom).

631c5–6 'Wisdom (*phronêsis*) itself is first and leader of the divine goods'

'Wisdom' translates *phronêsis*, which the Athenian uses interchangeably with *nous* (translated as 'intelligence' at 631c7 and d5; see notes on 631d5–6 and 640d6). (This marks a terminological difference from the *Republic*, where the enumeration of the canonical four virtues uses *sophia* (e.g. 428b1—although the guardians are regularly descried as having *phronêsis*: 412c12, 431d1, 433d1). In *Laws*, the term *sophia* rarely occurs, and when it does it is typically used in a broad sense that applies to any learning or skill—e.g. 644a4, a context where it is distinguished from virtue; cf. 677c, 701a, 732a. In the *Republic*, *sophia* is the special province of the philosopher, but philosophy is notably absent from *Laws*; see note on 632d4–5.) Wisdom leads the divine goods not just in being the highest ranked, but in giving direction to the others—at least in the case of the second and the third divine goods, whose descriptions indicate that the third (justice) involves the second, and that the second involves the first. Perhaps wisdom leads the fourth, courage, in the same way that it leads the 'human goods'; see note on 631b6–8 and on 631c8–d1.

631c7 'a moderate (*sôphrôn*) disposition (*hexis*) of the soul involving intelligence (*meta nou*)'

Here, 'intelligence' (*nous*) stands for wisdom, the first of the divine goods (see 631d5–6). The translation reads *nou* with Eusebius, for the MSS' *noun*, following Schanz, Burnet, England, des Places, and Saunders. On the MS reading it would be 'a moderate disposition of the soul' that is 'second . . . after intelligence (*meta noun*)'; so described, the moderate disposition need not be accompanied (or informed) by intelligence, unlike the third-place divine good (justice), of which intelligence is identified as a component. The kind of moderation that is ranked second must therefore involve wisdom; otherwise instances of moderation that are foolish or otherwise lacking in wisdom (for instances of such moderation see *Euthyd.* 281c and *Stsm.* 306a–b; cf. 308b) would be divine goods second in rank only to wisdom—a position the Athenian explicitly rejects in later books (696d–e, 710a; see also note on 630a7–b2). It is still not clear, however, why intelligent moderation is ranked higher than justice (rather than, for example, equal to it). In any case, the Athenian's main point here (in support of his earlier assertions at 630b3–d1) is that justice is superior to the sort of courage lauded by Tyrtaeus (see note on 631c8–d1).

631c7–8 'justice, which arises when these two are combined with courage'

'These two' are the first two divine goods, wisdom and moderation (c6–7). The courage that is combined with them is the disposition that, when not so combined, is ranked fourth here at 631c8–d1 (see note ad loc) and at 630c8. That justice consists of such a combination implies that the just person has appropriately tempered and balanced the opposing dispositions of aggression (raw courage) and restraint (raw moderation)—see notes on 630a7–b2 and 661d8–e1. Thus justice arises from solving the problem articulated in Book 2 of the *Republic*: how to balance in the city's guardians the requisite but opposing tendencies of ferocity and gentleness (375b–d, 441e; cf. *Laws* 731b–d). Similarly, in the *Statesman*, the statesman's task (analogous to that of the legislator in *Laws*) is to balance and interweave the opposing tendencies of 'courage' and 'moderation' in the citizens (306a–308a). While in that dialogue true belief (*doxa*) is said to provide the proper direction, here in *Laws* is it wisdom (*nous* or *phronêsis*) that plays that role, although the Athenian seems willing to allow in some contexts that true belief can do the job of wisdom (632c5; see note on 630c5–6). In *Republic* 442a the means by which the opposing traits are balanced are 'harmony' (*harmonia*) and rhythm, which will loom large in the educational programme set forth by the Athenian in Book 2 (653e, 661c–d, 669b–670e); see note on 653e3–5.

631c8–d1 'fourth would be courage'

This is the courage ranked 'fourth in rank and merit' at 630c8–d1 in the criticism of Tyrtaeus. Courage, as it figures as the fourth good, is the ingredient added to wisdom and moderation in the recipe for justice, the third good. When not so combined, it is the disposition praised by Tyrtaeus and displayed by the mercenaries mentioned at 630b. On how wisdom 'leads' courage, see note on 631c5–6.

631d1–632d7

Legislating with a view to divine and human goods

The theory of divine and human goods just articulated (631b–d) should inform the practice of the proper legislator, who will instruct the citizens in this scheme of values, and monitor their compliance, using the laws to commend 'what is admirable and what is not' (632b1) in their emotional responses to each other and to the vicissitudes of life as well as in their financial dealings with each other (631d–632b). After describing the 'finishing touches' to such a legislative project (632c), the Athenian invites Clinias and Megillus to explain how the laws of their own cities are structured according to these priorities (632d).

631d2–4 'the lawgiver must rank (*takteon*) them thus as well . . . [H]e must inform the citizens that all his other instructions to them have these goods in view'
A suggestion that the legislator will deliver explicit instruction in this scheme of values, perhaps in the preludes to the laws that are mentioned in Book 4 (720a–724b); see also notes on 632b7–8 and 666a5–8 and Bobonich 2002: 97–118. On less didactic ways of inculcating the scheme of values, see note on 631e4–632a1.

631d5–6 'the human goods directed at the divine, and the divine ones directed at their leader, intelligence (*noun*)'
more literally: 'the human goods have the divine in view . . . '
'Directed at' translates *blepein eis* (with the verb understood from d4). It is a visual metaphor (literally 'looking at') which the Athenian regularly invokes over Books 1 and 2 to describe the goal or focus of

the legislator (625e–626a, 628a–d, 630c–631d, 632a). In the present context it captures two slightly different relationships of dependence:

(i) The relationship of laws to the taxonomy of goods that they implement (d3–4).
(ii) The dependence of human goods on the divine, and divine goods on wisdom (b7–d1).

The expression recalls the language that identifies the goal or focus of legislation at 625e, 626a, 628a, 630c–e; cf. 632e. The Athenian indicates that he takes it to be interchangeable with 'for the sake of' (*heneka* or *charin*) (628c6, 628d6-e5, 631a4). Thus we may understand the legislator to be instructing the citizens that the human goods are to be pursued 'for the sake of' the divine. To use or pursue wealth for the sake of the divine goods is to regulate one's pursuit and use of it via the standards of wisdom, justice, moderation, and courage. This is to limit one's pursuit or use of a 'human good' by the standards of the virtues. Plato uses *heneka* in a similarly limiting sense at *Gorg.* 506c9, where pleasure is to be pursued 'for the sake of' (*heneka*) the good, rather than vice versa (similarly, *Rep.* 403b4–c2, Aristotle *EN* 1102a23–25; see Meyer 2011: 56).

The present passage confirms that 'intelligence' (*nous*) here stands for wisdom (*phronêsis*), the first of the divine goods enumerated at 631c. The parallel passage at 688a–b identifies *phronêsis* as what the laws are *heneka* or 'directed at'. See note on 631c5–6.

631d6–e2 'When the citizens join together in marriage, when they beget and raise children . . . and as they mature and reach old age' The legislator's concerns range widely over the lives of the citizens: their private and family life, their financial dealings with each other (632b), and their burial rites (632c). Note the omission of the military matters that Clinias and Tyrtaeus have claimed to be the most important, except for the oblique reference to war on the list of misfortunes into which one might fall (632a6). Legislation concerning military matters is outlined in Book 8.

631e2–3 'he must take care to mete out honour and dishonour correctly'

The point that the laws apportion honour (*timê*) and dishonour (*atimia*) in connection with the proper ranking of goods is developed at greater length at the end of Book 3, 696d–697c; cf. 711b–c, 862d; the citizens are exhorted to give honour accordingly in the long prelude that opens Book 5, 726a–728a. In the present context, meting out honour and its opposite involves praising and blaming (632a) and calling things 'admirable (*kalon*) and not' (632b1; cf. 635a8, 655d5–656a5). These are not legally mandated rewards and sanctions, but expressions of praise and blame in the laws themselves, as 632a2–3 makes explicit. Here the Athenian anticipates the methodological point of Book 4 (720a–724b), that the laws will have preludes that instruct and persuade citizens before giving them orders backed up by threatened penalties. On persuasion, see note on 632b7–8. On the legislator's use of praise and censure, see notes on 648b8–c5 and 663c1–2; see also Morgan 2013.

631e4–632a1 'their pains and pleasures, their desires, and the general intensity of their passions'

The legislator's concern is not simply with the citizens' behaviour, but with their emotional responses and desires. It will later become clear, in the accounts of education (643b–644b, 653a–c), that the legislator's goal is not just to evaluate these affective responses but to train them, and that this training aims at inculcating the virtues, which are the 'divine goods' invoked in the present context. The emotions in question include anger, fear, and their opposites and are responses to the gain and loss of the human goods (632a3–7; see note ad loc). On the centrality of pleasure and pain to the legislator's concerns (a prominent theme in Book 2), see also 636d4–e3 and the notes on 644c6–7 and 649d4–7. On emotional responses as pleasures and pains, see note on 633c9–d2.

632a3–7 'As for their feelings of anger (*orgais*) and fear (*phobois*), when their souls are disturbed on account of misfortune, and relief from these in times of prosperity (*eutuchiais*)'

alternatively: '. . . and relief from these in times of good fortune' (des Places, Brisson/Pradeau, Pangle)
Anger, fear, and other 'disturbances' are further instances of the citizens' 'pleasures and pains' that the legislator is to scrutinize and evaluate (631e4–632a1). Anger and fear are presented here as responses to the loss of the 'human goods' (misfortune). Their opposites are presumably joy in (anticipation of) the possession of these goods (prosperity: *eutuchia*); see, for example, 649d6–7, where the human goods, wealth, health, and strength are said to 'make us drunk with pleasure'. The mention here of disturbances (632a4) recalls the account of pain and pleasure as disruption and restoration in *Philb.* 31d–32b. See Frede 2010: 118, 124–6. Fear and its opposite will be discussed in detail at 644c9–d3 and 646e–647e. It is linked to judgement about misfortune at 647e1–4. See also note on 649d4–7. On *eutuchia* (prosperity or good fortune), see *Euthyd.* 279d–280b.

632a7 'the sorts of feelings (*pathêmata*)'
While *pathêma* (plural, *pathêmata*) is not always a term for feeling or emotion, and could mean simply 'occurrence' (thus England, followed by des Places) or something that happens to one, it is used here as a general term to capture the angers and fears mentioned at 632a3. Thus Schöpsdau, Lisi, and Brisson/Pradeau translate.

632a7–b1 'he must define and teach what is admirable (*kalon*) and what is not in different people's responses (*diatheseôs*)'
more literally: 'in each person's condition'
The close connection between praising something and calling it admirable (*kalon*) is displayed in Book 2 (655d–656b); see also note on 631e2–3. *Diathesis*—used interchangeably with *hexis* at 791b1 and 792d3–4 (cf. *Philb.* 11d4, 32e3, *Tim.* 42d2)—could mean either the occurrent condition of the soul (what a person is feeling now), or a more settled disposition. Aristotle will reserve *diathesis* for the occurrent condition and *hexis* for the settled disposition (*Catg.* 8b26–28; *EN* 1105b19–1106a12). The Stoics will restrict *diathesis* to the latter—a usage that is reflected in the pseudo-Platonic *Definitiones* 411d.

632b2–3 'the lawgiver must safeguard (*phulattein*) the ways the citizens acquire and dispose of property'
more idiomatically: '. . . must look out for . . .'
The Athenian here uses the military language of standing guard (*phulattein*), originally invoked by Clinias, to apply instead to the activities of peacetime; see note on 626a8–b1. The present context uses that vocabulary to describe vigilance on behalf of the norms of justice. In contrast to the preceding lines, there is no mention of citizens' pleasures and pains. This would make sense if courage and moderation (the focus of the ensuing discussion in Book 1) are the virtues concerned with pleasures and pains.

632b7–8 'those who are receptive (*eupeithesin*) to the laws, and . . . those who are resistant to persuasion (*duspeithesi*)'
The resistant citizen is mentioned again at 648c2–3; see note ad loc. A recurring theme in *Laws* is that the citizens must be 'receptive to' or (more literally) 'easily persuaded by' the laws (*eupeitheis tois nomois*) (715c2, 718c8–10, 801e9, 880a6–9, 890c4; cf. 708c–d), or 'willing' (*hekontes, ethelontes*) subjects to the laws (700a5, 701b5–6; see notes on 663b4–6 and on 671d9–e1). That those who are not 'persuaded' by the laws are to be punished reflects the coercive aspect that must be joined with the persuasive aspect of the law embodied in the preludes mandated in Book 4 (711c, 718b, 722b–c). On what such persuasion amounts to, see Stalley 1983: 42–4; Bobonich 2002: 93–119; Laks 2005: 93–163; Mouze 2005: 317–23; Annas 2010: 75–91, Fossheim 2013, and notes on 662c3–5, 663b2–3, 663c1–2.

632c1 'put the finishing touches on his constitution . . .'
literally: 'when he reaches the end (*telos*) of the entire constitution . . .'—a pun on the root *telos*, which occurs in *teleutêsantôn* 632c2 ('when they die'; more literally: 'when they have reached their end'). The legislation regarding 'burial rites' and 'honours' bestowed upon the dead (c2–3) completes the treatment of life cycle milestones begun at 631d6. Legislation about marriage and childbearing is detailed in Book 4, 721a–d; 6, 771e–776b, 779e–785b; laws about

child-rearing and education occur throughout Book 7, and regulation of burial rites is addressed in Book 12, 958d–960b.

632c4 'will appoint guardians (*phulakas epistêsei*) for them all'
This military language recalls Clinias' original invocation of guards (*phulakes*) on the watch for enemy attack (625e–626a). While Clinias conceives of the laws as themselves standing guard (*phulattein*—see note on 626a8–b1), the Athenian here points to the necessity of guarding the laws themselves. That the laws require constant oversight and vigilance is a recurring theme later in *Laws*: see 769c–770a; the office of 'guardians of the laws' (*nomophulakes*) will be one of the most important in the constitutional legislation in Book 5 (752d–755b; cf. 961a–c); see Meyer 2006: 380–1.

632c5 'Some of them will operate with wisdom (*phronêseôs*), others with true opinion (*alêthous doxês*)'
Both *phronêsis* and 'stable true opinions' are described as rare achievements in Book 2 at 653a7–9. On true opinion as a substitute for wisdom see *Stsm.* 309c, a more optimistic assessment of true opinion than *Rep.* 477b–480a; cf. *Meno* 97a–98a, *Tim.* 51d.

Presumably the members of the 'nocturnal council' outlined in Book 12 (961a–b; 964e–969c) aspire to wisdom, but it is not made clear who else in the city will have (or lack) it. The Athenian regularly insists in Book 3 that *phronêsis* is a characteristic of the city (e.g. 693b), without specifying which citizens will possess it, or how it differs from correct opinion. Perhaps his self-deprecating comment at 859c relegates his own legislative competence into the latter category. But if England is right taking the true opinions invoked here to be cases of the 'experience (*empeiria*) in the law' resulting from training or habituation (*ethê*) at 632d5–6 (see note ad loc), then the Athenian's remark at 630d4–7 would imply that he and his interlocutors lack even the latter.

632c6–7 'intelligence (*nous*) will bind it all together to follow moderation and justice rather than wealth and ambition'

As at 631d5, *nous* is used as a substitute for *phronêsis* (wisdom), which is here reaffirmed in its role as 'leader' of the divine goods (631c6). The 'moderation and justice' in whose service it 'binds' the law code are the 'complete justice' that is the focus of the proper legislator (630c1–6). Courage, the only virtue of concern to Tyrtaeus, and the focus of Dorian legislation, is not even mentioned here. Instead, wealth and 'ambition' (*philotimia*: literally 'love of honour') stand in for the goals of the state as conceived of by Clinias, Megillus, and Tyrtaeus (see note on 626b3–4). On *philotimia* as characteristic of militaristic constitutions like Sparta, see *Rep*. 545a–b. On the connection between love of honour and love of wealth see *Rep*. 548a–b and Brennan 2012: 112–14.

632d2–4 'how these features are present in those laws . . . '
'[T]hese features' (literally: 'all this' (*panta tauta*—d4)) is a vague way of referring to the burden of the Athenian's speech at 631b–632c: that laws should comply with and communicate the relative priority of the divine and human goods (631b–d), and be organized into the categories of legislation enumerated at 631e–632c.

632d4–5 'how it is that their order is obvious . . . '
England takes the 'order' (*taxis*) to express a distinctively philosophical understanding of law. But there is no mention of philosophy in the present context (and barely any at all in the dialogue as a whole: 857c–d, 967c–d; but cf. Zuckert 2009: 31–3). The order in question is more likely the relative priority of divine and human goods invoked at 631b–d; indeed, the Athenian uses language to that effect (e.g. *tetakta* and *takteon* in 631d1–2).

632d5–6 'to anyone experienced in the law—whether this is due to knowledge or results from some training (*tôi . . . empeirôi technêi eite kai tisin ethesin*)'
alternatively: 'or results from some habituation (*tisin ethesin*)'
The adjective 'experienced' (*empeiros*) has positive connotations here, as well as at 692b3–4 and 741d7; so too the cognate noun *empeiria* at

659d4 (see note on 659d1–4). The non-pejorative use of the adjective is widespread in Plato: *Gorg.* 448b12, 465d5; *Protag.* 341a3; *Meno* 89e8; *Hipp. Min.* 367d6; *Rep.* 527a2, 533a9; *Parm.* 133b7; *Stsm.* 277e3, 291c4; *Tht.* 179e5, 206b5. This feature of Plato's idiom contrasts with his regularly pejorative use of the cognate noun, *empeiria*, to mark a 'knack' (*tribê*) as distinct from genuine knowledge (*Gorg.* 462c3–6, 463b4; *Phdr.* 270b5–6; *Philb.* 55e6; *Laws* 11, 938a4; cf. *Phdr.* 260e4–5, *Rep.* 493b5).

On legislation as a skill (*technê*), see Book 4, 709b–d. Proper legislators will be described as 'experienced in legislating' (*nomothesias empeiroi*, 692b3–4). In the present context, those whose legal experience comes from 'training' (alt: 'habituation'—*tisin ethesin*) are presumably those who have been, as the Athenian says, 'raised under' (*êthesi tetraphthe*, 625a5) the laws in question. Clinias' 'well-trained (*kalôs . . . gegumnasthai*) understanding of Cretan institutions' at 626b5–6 would be an instance of the latter, although the Athenian's remarks at 630d imply that Clinias has misconstrued the point of the institutions under which he was raised. The Athenian's main point in the long exposition to which the present comment is a peroration is that both parties to the legislative enterprise (lawgivers and the citizens for whom they legislate) must recognize the hierarchy of goods that structures the legislation in question. On the training (*ethos*) that will cultivate the values affirmed by the citizens, see note on 655d7–e1; on the alteration between *ethos* and *êthos*, see note on 625a5.

632d6 'completely obscure to the rest of us'
Schöpsdau and England construe as ironic the Athenian's inclusion of himself in the 'rest of us'. But while the actual structuring principle of the Dorian laws is no doubt evident to the Athenian, as it is to Clinias and Megillus, that principle is not the doctrine of divine and human goods, but a perversion of that ranking. The Athenian here persists in the polite fiction that the Dorian laws exemplify the highest legislative standards, as befitting their hypothesized divine origin (630d9–e1), and that the fault lies simply with

those who fail to recognize these standards as structuring those laws (630d4–7). The intended irony is that it is 'evident' to none of the interlocutors, including those trained under Dorian laws, that those laws exemplify the order of divine and human goods.

632d7 'how are we to go about doing that . . . ?'
more literally: 'what are we to say next . . . ?'

III
INSTITUTIONS TO CULTIVATE COURAGE AND MODERATION

632d8–643a1

Having established that the goal of correct legislation is to inculcate the whole of virtue, not just one part (630e–632c), the Athenian now invites his interlocutors to identify the Dorian institutions that train citizens in this expanded range of virtue (632d–e). The discussion begins with courage, conceived of initially as resistance to pain and fear (632e–633c), then expands to include 'resistance to pleasures' (633d–634a)—the latter eventually to be classified under the domain of moderation (see note on 635e5–6). While Megillus easily enumerates a range of Spartan institutions aimed at cultivating resistance to pains (633a–c), both he and Clinias are at a loss to name any that cultivate resistance to pleasures (634a–c). After an interlude about how best to conduct the delicate enterprise of criticizing the laws or institutions of one's own or another's city (634c–635a), the Athenian insists, against Megillus' objections, that exposure to the greatest pleasures is necessary for cultivating moderation (635b–637b). In particular, he makes the provocative proposal that drinking parties, condemned by Megillus as occasions for excessive indulgence (637a–b), in fact provide enormous social benefits (637b–e). As a prelude to identifying these benefits—which he will eventually allege to be the sought-after resistance to pleasures (649a–e)—the Athenian first expounds the proper methodology for settling disputes about the value of particular institutions or practices (638a–641d). His interlocutors respond by expressing their goodwill to the Athenian and to Athens (641e–642e).

Fighting against pleasures and pains

In treating virtue as a matter of victory in a fight against pleasures and pains (633c–d), the Athenian is appealing to the conception of virtue as self-mastery (to kreittô heautou) *that is endorsed by Clinias at 626e and that will be modelled in the figure of the divine puppets at 644d–645c. On whether this conception is one the Athenian endorses, see notes on 626e2–3 and 643b1–646e2. On the nature of the pains and pleasures to be resisted or fought against, see notes on 633c9–d2, 633e1–2, and 634a6–8.*

632d8–e2 'we need to return to our original starting point (*ex archês*), and . . . we will then go through the next kind (*eidos*) of virtue, and after that the next'
more literally: '. . . another (*heteron*) kind of virtue, and then another . . . '
A reiteration of the agenda announced at 630e–631a (see note on 630e3–4): organize the legislative inquiry according to the appropriate categories or kinds (*eidê*). Here the Athenian makes explicit a point implicit in the former passage: that the relevant 'categories' are the different virtues: courage, moderation, etc.

632e3–4 'Our exposition of the first will serve as a model for the rest'
The first case will be courage, treated as resistance to pains. It serves as a paradigm for the treatment of moderation, which will be construed as resistance to pleasures (634a–b, 635e–636e; see note on 635e5–6). On the alternative paradigm for virtue that will dominate the discussion in later books, see notes on 626e2–3, 643b1–646e2.

632e4–5 'we will lighten our journey (*paramuthia poiêsasthai tês hodou*), so far as we can (*peirasometha*), with conversation (*diamuthologountes*)'
A reiteration of the original proposal (625b6–7) that a conversation about laws will lighten the burden (*paramuthesthai*) of the long journey. Here the root *muth-* is repeated in *diamuthologein* (converse), making a pun on the double sense of *paramuthia* as both verbal exhortation and (derivatively) an alleviation. It is by filling up the time with talk that their journey will be made less onerous. The relevant notion of *muthologia* (storytelling) invoked here (and at 752a2) need not indicate that the content of the discussion will be fanciful, but rather that its participants have leisure to 'spin out the tale' at considerable length (as at *Rep*. 376d9; cf. *Rep*. 501e4). On the terminology, see Brisson 1982: 184–95.

632e5–6 'we will have gone through virtue in its entirety (*aretês pasês*), and shown it to be the focus (*ekeise bleponta*) of the things we were just discussing—provided the god is willing'
more literally: 'that it is what the things . . . are directed towards'
'Virtue in its entirety' (*aretês pasês*), in contrast to the narrow version of courage extolled by Tyrtaeus, is the focus of proper legislation (see note on 630b2–3). The 'things we were just discussing' are the regulations that govern citizens' personal lives, private property, financial transactions, etc. (631d–632c). These, referred to in summary as 'it all' (*panta tauta*, 632c6) are supposed to 'follow moderation and justice' (632c6–7), which are the elements of 'virtue in its entirety' overlooked by Tyrtaeus (630b–c). Thus Schöpsdau. But this does not mean that it is only the very general divisions of laws that are here invoked. It is also, as England claims, the specific instances of those laws that the Dorian legislators have ordained—and hence the specific Cretan institutions enumerated at 625d–626a and the Spartan ones about to be canvassed at 633a–d. To show that these bodies of law are in fact aimed at virtue in its entirety is to show that they adhere to the 'order' (*taxis*) invoked at 632d4–5 (see note on 632d5–6). Of course this aspiration will be unfulfilled, as the

ensuing discussion will identify no Spartan or Cretan institutions that cultivate moderation, and indeed will invoke some that undermine it (636a–c)—hence the ironic proviso, 'provided the god is willing'.

633a1–2 'Let our admirer of Zeus here be the first one you set out to examine'
Megillus acknowledges the Athenian's control of the discussion. In putting forward Clinias (who credits Zeus with the origin of Cretan laws and institutions at 624a) to bear the brunt of the Athenian's questioning, Megillus shows that characteristic Spartan fortitude does not extend to verbal engagements. He does, however, step forward to answer the Athenian's question at 633b–c.

633a3–4 'our discussion (*logos*) is a group effort (*koinos*)'
The discussion is also portrayed as a joint enterprise of the interlocutors at 629a4. The motif of a group undertaking (*koinônia*) will be important in the Athenian's later discussion of drinking parties (see note on 639c1).

Courage as resistance to pains

633a4 'So tell me (*legete*) . . . your communal meals and your regime of athletic training (*gumnasia*)'
The Athenian addresses his question to both Clinias and Megillus (second person plural), and the two institutions he mentions are common to both Sparta and cities on Crete (cf. 625c6–8). Megillus will answer first, citing specifically Spartan institutions (633a–c), thus balancing the earlier focus (625d–626b) on specifically Cretan norms. On 'athletic training' for *gumnasia*, see note on 673a8–10.

633a7 'And what practices shall we list third and fourth?'
That is, third and fourth examples of 'practices (*epitêdeumata*) to do with courage' (632e1), specifically those devised 'with war in mind' (633a5).

633a8–9 'for virtue's other parts—or whatever we should call them'
more literally: 'in the case of the parts of the rest of virtue (*peri tôn tês allês arêtes . . . merôn*) . . . '
Courage, moderation, and justice are described as 'parts' (*merê*) of virtue (630e1, 631a5, 705d8, 709e9–710a1, 936b5). The alternative is to call them 'kinds' or 'categories' (*eidê*—630e3, 632e2); see note on 630e3–4. On the terminology for the virtues, see also note on 630b2–3.

633b2 'the hunt'
On the importance of hunting in Spartan society, see Vidal–Naquet 1981: 169–75; Anderson 1985; and David 1993.

633b8 'raids that regularly involve a severe beating'
A ritual in which Spartan youth were supposed to 'steal as many cheeses as possible' while others were supposed to apprehend and whip them (Xenophon, *Lac.* 2.9.1–3; Plutarch, *Aristides* 17.10; Isocrates *Panathenaicus* 211–212). See Kennell 1995: 79–82; David 1993: 394–5; O. Murray 1993: 174.

633b9 'secret service (*krupteia*)'
On the Spartan *krupteia*, see Plutarch, *Lycurgus* 28.2–3. A version of this institution is proposed in the legislation of Book 6, 762e–763b. The Athenian will also commend the salutary effects of going barefoot and sleeping on the hard ground (942d).

633c4 'naked games (*gumnopaidiais*)'
These were not athletic but cultural competitions between choruses of male citizens (Athenaeus, *Deipnosophistai* 15.22.18–24). Competition between choruses at religious festivals was a familiar feature of life in Plato's day: see Morrow 1960: 302–3 and the references to choral competitions at 657d and 665e. Cultural competitions (fully clothed) will be prevalent in the city of the Magnesians (8, 828c–d); see Morgan 2013: 270–8.

633c8–634c4

Courage as resistance to both pleasures and pains

The Athenian here expands the conception of courage, originally construed as endurance of pains (633a–c), to include 'resistance to pleasures'. He challenges his interlocutors to identify Dorian institutions that cultivate the latter sort of resistance. Eventually the discipline of resisting pleasures will be classified under moderation (*sôphrosunê*) rather than courage (635e–637b). The Athenian's introduction of it here, under the rubric of courage, predisposes his interlocutors to endorse it as an excellence, since they readily see the importance of resisting pleasures that would distract one from the pursuit of military objectives.

633c9–d2 'Does [courage] amount quite simply to a battle (*diamachên*) against fears and pains alone? Or does it also oppose yearnings (*pothous*) and pleasures . . . ?'
Courage, on this expanded conception, involves fighting against two sorts of opponents: 'fears and pains' on the one hand and 'yearnings and pleasures' on the other (cf. *La.* 191d–e). Elsewhere (e.g. 633e–634b), the two kinds of opponents are more economically classified as 'pains' and 'pleasures'—most notably when these are identified as 'two opposite . . . advisors' at 644c and as 'two springs' from which we must draw wisely (636d–e). Sometimes pain's side of the contrast is expanded to include fears (635b–d, 647a), or pain is replaced with fear (647c, 648b–e); at other times pleasure's side is expanded to include appetite (*epithumia*), passion (*erôs*) (643c–d, 647d), daring (*tharros*) (644c–d), or yearnings (*pothous*), as in the present passage; cf. 631e–632a.

An ambiguity in 'pleasure' and 'pain'

What is the significance of invoking fears in addition to pains, and appetite or yearning in addition to pleasures? One might suppose that the expanded enumeration reflects a more precise account of the motivational factors at play in the endurance or 'battle' that the Athenian has in mind. For example, one might suppose:

(A) That pain and pleasure are pleasant and painful experiences—e.g. the pleasures of food, drink, and sex and the 'enjoyments' (*paidia*) mentioned by the Athenian at 635b5, and the pains of being cold and hungry, suffering in the heat, or receiving a beating, listed by Megillus at 633b–c.

(B) And that fear and yearning are affective responses in the agent to the prospect of the experiences in (A)—an aversion to pain, and attraction to pleasure.

But this would be a mistake, for 'pleasures' and 'pains', in the Athenian's usage, range over both (A) and (B). At 636d5–7 he will claim that 'pleasures and pains . . . both in cities and in individual characters' constitute the 'whole subject' of legislative study. What he understands there by 'pleasures and pains . . . in cities' (636d6–7) may well be pleasant and painful experiences of the sort Megillus has in mind at 633b–c and 636e–637a; however, those 'in individual characters' (636d7) presumably include affective responses such as those in (B). The latter are what he has in mind at 631e–632a when he describes the legislator's concern with the citizens' 'pains, pleasures, desires, and . . . passions', which include 'feelings of anger and fear' (632a3); the latter are classified as 'pains of the soul' at *Philb.* 47e. Indeed, in the account of *paideia* at the beginning of *Laws* Book 2, he uses 'pleasure and pain' as a general term for affective response, including such things as love (*philia*) and hate (*misos*) (653a–c; see note on 653a6).

Thus 'pleasure' and 'pain' are ambiguous in the Athenian's usage between (A) pleasant and painful experiences of the sort that Megillus has in mind, and (B) affective states (desires, fears, and other emotions) that may have (A), or anything else, as their intentional objects. The pleasures and pains that one 'battles' against in the struggle for self-mastery described in the present context need only be those of type (B); see notes on 633e1–2 and 634a6–8. (On a further ambiguity concerning fear and pleasure, see notes on 647c3–4 and 648b7–8.)

633d3 ‘melt the resolve (*thumous*)’
Note the similar use of the term *glukuthumia* (translated as ‘weakness in the face of pleasure’) at 635c8, which shares the root for *thumos* (here used in the plural). In the *Republic*, *thumos* (‘spirit’) invokes the toughness and ferocity of the warrior who is neither deterred by the pains he faces nor distracted by the prospect of pleasures (375a–b, 410d). The Athenian thus presents self-control in the face of pleasures—which he will eventually classify as moderation (*sôphrosunê*; see note on 635e5–6)—within the domain of the military values that his interlocutors endorse.

633d5 ‘our previous discussion . . . spoke of a city being “defeated by itself”, and likewise a man’
The notion of an individual person’s self-defeat is originally discussed at 626d–e, and it is transferred, with some awkwardness, to the case of a city at 627a–c. While Clinias proposes self-mastery (the opposite of self-defeat) as the highest achievement (626e), the Athenian criticizes that ideal at 627e–628d.

633e1–2 ‘the person defeated (*hêttô*) by pains . . . defeated by pleasures’
On being ‘defeated’ by pleasures or pains cf. *Protag.* 352b–353a, where the vanquishing force is more fully characterized as anger (*thumos*), pleasure, pain, passion (*erôs*), or fear (352b7–8). At 635d1 the Athenian uses ‘defeated by fears’ instead of the present ‘defeated by pains’. There, as in the present context, the Athenian is referring back to the condition that Clinias described as being ‘defeated by oneself’ (626e3–4). The defeat occurs in the sort of struggle modelled in the figure of the divine puppets at 644d–645c.

As argued in the note on 633c9–d2, the Athenian uses ‘pleasure’ and ‘pain’ to refer both to (A) pleasant and painful experiences such as sexual indulgence and bodily discomfort and to (B) pleasant and painful affective states that may have (A) as their intentional objects. One might reasonably ask which sort are the ones that can 'defeat' a person (for it is to these that a person will need to be exposed in order to develop the requisite resistance). The case can be made that it is, strictly speaking, pleasures of type (B) that are relevant. The sort of scenario Megillus describes at 633b–c under the heading 'endurance of pain' might be one in which a person is simultaneously experiencing a pain of type (A) and a pain of type (B), e.g. an affective response to flee the situation. But it might equally be one in which the (A)-pain is only in prospect (the enemy is advancing with gleaming swords, but one is as yet unscathed . . .) and the only pain the agent experiences is of type (B) (his fear and desire to flee). Thus it need only be pains of type (B) that one struggles against in the fight for self-mastery. Similarly, cases of being defeated by pleasures need not be ones in which one is actually engaging in an (A)-pleasure. All that is needed is that one experience a pleasure of type (B): an affective pleasure at the prospect of, or a desire to engage in, that (A)-pleasure. Indeed, in the case of many (A)-pleasures, the battle has already been lost when the agent actually experiences them. This is not to say that the (B)-pleasures and (B)-pains are not themselves extremely pleasant and painful, respectively, and thus possess strong motivational force. However, the distinction between (A)-pleasures and (B)-pleasures will be important to appreciating the Athenian's insistence that one must have experience of pleasures in order to learn to defeat them. See note on 634a6–8.

634a1 'the Pythian lawgiver'
Apollo, credited with the origin of Spartan laws at 624a and 632d.

634a2 'a lame form of courage (*cholên tên andreian*)'
An unflattering allusion to the poet Tyrtaeus (who is 'interrogated' at 629b–630c). Pausanias, in the second century CE, reports a story that Tyrtaeus was a dim-witted Athenian schoolteacher 'lame in one

foot' (*ton heteron tôn podôn cholos*, 4.15.6 line 10) sent by Athens to Sparta in grudging compliance with an oracle requiring that an Athenian advisor be sent there. On 'lame' courage, see also note on 634b4.

634a6–8 'practices (*epitêdeumata*) that engage with pleasures rather than flee them. Where pains are concerned your practice isn't to avoid them but to thrust a person into their midst'
'Engaging (*geuonta*) with pleasures' (more literally: 'tasting pleasures') is presumably intended to be analogous to the 'endurance (*karterêseis*) of pain' that Megillus cited at 633b6; cf. 'endure in the face of pleasures' at 635d3. But 'partaking of pleasures' hardly sounds like a feat of endurance or resistance—which the Athenian needs it to be, if it is to count as a 'battle against pleasures' analogous to the 'battle against pains' at 633d1–2. Nor would it be plausible of him to claim that one needs to partake of a given pleasure in order to develop resistance to its appeal (given his condemnation of same-sex intercourse at 636c–d as a pleasure that one must 'master'). The Athenian's point can be made both precise and plausible by distinguishing between the different senses of 'pleasure' and 'pain' that he employs ambiguously (see note on 633c9–d2). Cases of self-mastery (and self-defeat) where pleasure is the opponent need only be ones in which a person faces a situation in which inappropriate (A)-pleasures (e.g. adulterous sex) are available to him and he experiences a (B)-pleasure that urges him to indulge in those (A)-pleasures. Self-mastery in such cases involves 'defeating' or 'subjugating' (*kratein*, 634b1) the (B)-pleasure—i.e. 'enduring' its pull without acting on it. Thus it is reasonable for the Athenian to claim that one must have experience 'engaging with' or 'tasting' (*geuonta*) (B)-pleasures, not (A)-pleasures, in order to develop such self-mastery. Thus the legislator needs to devise institutions that expose citizens to situations that provoke those (B)-pleasures. Such training by exposure is described more fully at 647c–649d; see notes on 647c3–4, 647c8–10.

634a9 'where he is compelled and persuaded by honours'
The honours would include those meted out by the lawgiver at 632b–c, and would include the praises delivered by means of the laws at 632a. On the interplay between compulsion and honours in training, see notes on 648b8–c5 and 670c9. Once again, as at 632b, the dual coercive and persuasive aspects of the law to be mandated in Book 4 are foreshadowed. See note on 632b7–8.

634b4 'the same person'
more literally: 'the same people'
A person must be 'courageous' in both the face of pleasures and the face of pains; otherwise he will have the 'lame form of courage' invoked at 634a2. This would be either the courage that is not combined with moderation (criticized as fourth-rate at 630c8), or moderation unmixed with courage (as at 681b; see note on 630a7–b2).

634b4–5 'defeats (*nikan*) the ones he ought to (*ha dei*)'
Such a 'defeat' of pleasures or pains would be an instance of what Clinias and the Athenian have been calling 'self-mastery' (*kreittôn hautou*, 626e–627d). The qualification '[that] he ought to' (*ha dei*, b4) indicates that not all pleasures and pains should be resisted, anticipating the point at 636d–e that pleasure and pains are 'two springs' from which a person must draw intelligently. Indeed, 646e–647b advocates cultivating certain pains (fears), and 643c–d advocates cultivating certain pleasures. On the ambiguity in the pleasures and pains to be resisted and indulged in, see note on 633c9–d2. Identifying which pleasures and pains to resist and which to cultivate is the job for wisdom—hence the role of wisdom in properly cultivated courage and moderation at 631c–d and the call for 'intelligent selection' of pleasures and pains at 636d–e.

634b5–6 'the enemy that is hardest (*chalepôtatôn*)'
This description of pleasure invokes the previous characterization of civil war as 'the hardest conflict' at 629d1–2 (see note ad loc and on

669c1). As at 633e1–2, the pleasure that defeats a person from within need only be of type (B), an affective response, rather than type (A), a pleasant experience that is the intentional object of the former. See note on 633e1–2.

634b8 'a large number of laws (*nomous*) directed against pains'
As at 634d7–8 and 637c7, the 'laws' (*nomoi*) invoked here need not be written statutes, but only practices and institutions (*epitêdeumata*, as at 632e1, 634a6). See note on 634d8–9.

634c5–635b3

Etiquette and credentials for criticizing norms

Having exposed deficiencies in the home institutions of his Dorian interlocutors, the Athenian now cautions his interlocutors not to interpret this as an expression of hostility (634c–d). Indeed, he proposes, such critical inquiry by men of their age is in fact authorized by Dorian norms (634d–e). The interlocutors agree to proceed with both frankness and goodwill (635a–b).

634c5 'That's not surprising'
Translation following Schöpsdau, contra England, who reads this as a tactful comment to the effect that no constitution is perfect. Both Clinias and Megillus have proved unable to identify Dorian institutions for cultivating an important part of virtue, and it is this that the Athenian says is not surprising. His comment suggests, at least to the dialogue's audience, that there are no such institutions to be found in the Dorian cities, and hence that they are imperfect. The Athenian here begins to abandon the pretence that Dorian legislation is unimpeachable (630d–e, 631b), and he begins to articulate direct criticisms of those laws, although he will first adopt the pretence of simply repeating 'what is generally said' (634d5–6). Compare the direct and unmitigated criticism of Dorian educational institutions in Book 2 at 666e–667a.

634c7–8 'we should accept this criticism mildly (*praiôs*) rather than harshly (*chalepôs*)'
A similar point is made at 635a6–b1. On the contrast between *chalepôs* (harshly) and mildly (*praiôs*) or gently (*êrema*), see notes on 629a2, 629d2, 645a6. The aggression implied in *chalepôs* is connected to anger or defensiveness, hence its invocation in the present context.

634c9 'a persuasive point (*peisteon*)'
Persuasion is the project in 'gracious' or 'gentle' (*praiôs*) discussion, in contrast with the violent or coercive methods involved in aggressive argument (on the aggression implicit in *chalepôs*, see note on 634c7–8). On the theme of coercion v. persuasion, see notes on 629a2, and 634a9.

634d5–7 'I would . . . find it easier than either of you to voice what is generally said'
'What is generally said' (*ta legomena . . . pros tôn pollôn*) is presumably what is generally said in criticism of Spartan and Cretan norms (thus Schöpsdau). The Athenian is better placed to state these criticisms than his Dorian interlocutors because they have been trained from youth to reject any criticism of their own laws, as he is about to note.

634d8–9 'one of your finest (*tôn kallistôn*) is the law that . . . '
For consistency, 'law' translates *nomos*, although 'norms' would be more appropriate here, for it is unlikely that what is being reported here is a written statute (see Wilamovitz 1920: vol I, 661). On the translation of *kallistôn*, see note on 630c7.

634d9–e1 'what is and isn't admirable (*poia kalôs . . . ê mê kalôs echei*) among those arrangements'
Like *kalôs keithai* in the next line (634e2; see note ad loc), *kalôs echei* recalls the expression *orthôs echein* ('is correct') used at 631b5; see note ad loc and on 667c6–7. The Athenian has characterized the subject

of their present inquiry as 'what is . . . correct and mistaken about laws' (627d3).

634e1–2 'everyone must join voices and sing out their agreement (*sumphônein*)'
more literally: 'with one voice and from a single mouth all must agree'
While the dominant meaning of *sumphônein* is 'agree', *sumphônia* also has musical connotations, which are probably latent in the present passage, given the musical metaphor ('striking a discordant note') at 635a5; the metaphor of 'singing out agreement' will be given a concrete application in the institution of the three choruses in Book 2 (664b–665c). The verb *sumphônein* in the sense of 'agreement' can apply to (a) interpersonal 'agreement' (as in the present context and likewise at 661d, 662b, 664a) as well as to (b) intrapersonal harmony, as in the conception of virtue articulated in Book 2: a person's pleasures and pains should *sumphônein* ('agree') with their *logos* (653b; cf. 689d, 696c, and note on 653b4–5). These two kinds of *sumphônia* are connected at 659d–e. On the differences between conceiving of virtue as 'agreement' and Clinias' conception of virtue as victory over self, see notes on 626e2–3, 628c9–11, 643b1–646e2. The unanimity described here is endorsed as a desirable effect of education at 659d–e.

634e2 'that all the laws are beautifully arranged (*hôs panta kalôs keitai*)'
alternatively: 'that they are all admirably (*kalôs*) arranged'
This unanimous endorsement of the laws provides a direct answer to the forbidden question: 'which of the legal arrangements *kalôs echei* [literally: are admirable or beautiful]?', 634d9–e1. On the range of the term *kalon*, see note on 630c7.

634e4 'An old man'
The advanced age of the interlocutors (cf. 625b, 635a) is here invoked as a credential for engaging in the critical inquiry into the

laws; cf. 635e1–3. On the corrupting effects of political criticism on the young, cf. *Rep*. 538d–539c. On the special role for the elderly in education, see *Laws* 664e–666c.

635a5 'without striking a discordant note'
Continues the choral metaphor of 634e1–2.

635b2–3 'not a criticism of your laws . . . I simply express my puzzlement (*aporôn*)'
This disclaimer notwithstanding, the ensuing paragraph (635b2–d8) provides the foundation for a trenchant criticism of those Dorian institutions: their failure to train citizens at resisting pleasures makes them 'slavish'. What the Athenian finds puzzling can only be interpreted as a 'puzzle' on the strained assumption (implied at 632e, and articulated explicitly at 635e) that the Dorian legislators do aim at inculcating moderation as well as courage, and hence that they do cultivate resistance to pleasures. The expression of puzzlement (*aporia*) is a common trope in Plato's portrait of Socrates in dialogues such as *Euthyphro*, *Laches*, *Charmides*, and *Republic* I.

635b4–e3

Cultivating resistance to pleasures requires exposure to pleasures

Having expanded the range of courage to include not just resistance to pains but also resistance to pleasures (633d–634a), and raised doubts about whether Dorian institutions are equipped to train citizens in the latter (634a–c), the Athenian now claims that such training must involve exposing citizens to 'the greatest pleasures'—something that Dorian institutions do not allow.

635b5 'enjoyments (*paidiôn*)'
more literally: 'recreations'

Elsewhere in this translation the term *paidia*, here translated as 'enjoyment', is rendered 'recreation', although for stylistic or contextual reasons it and its compounds is occasionally translated as 'play' or 'playful' (as at 643b–d, 653e2–3, 659e4). The term in Greek (*παιδιά*) is distinguishable only in accent from the term for childhood (*παιδία),* both deriving from the root *παῖς* (child); see D'Angour 2013. *Paidia* will play a central role in the Athenian's account of education (*paideia*, another cognate term) at 643a–644b. As in the present context, the term is closely associated with pleasure (cf. 657c3–6, 667e5–8). *Paidia* is also regularly used in contrast with *spoudê* (verb: *spoudazein*, 'to be serious' as at 636c, 659e, 667e, 673e, 732d; at 643b and 647d it is rendered 'at work'). On this persistent motif in *Laws*, see Jouët-Pastré 2006 and Stalley 1983: 130–1. A striking claim of Book 7 is that singing and dancing at festivals to the gods, which people normally think of as recreation (*paidia*), is in fact a most serious undertaking (803b–804b). The kind of 'recreation' that is about to become the focus of the present context is the drinking party (labelled *paidia* at 666b5, 671e5–6). The Athenian will argue over the course of Books 1 and 2 that the drinking party is an important educational institution (*paideia*) (641a–d, 653a), and thus must be treated as a case of *spoudê* rather than mere *paidia* (673e8; see note ad loc). See also note on 673a7–8.

635c1–2 'hardships, fears, and pains that are unavoidable (*anankaious*)'

Alternatively: '. . . fears and pains that are compelling' (see note on 648d7–e1)

Most likely these are the fears and pains involved in battle. The adjective *anankaious* conveys not only unavoidability but also force and violence—the latter being consistently associated with military contexts. Both senses may be active in the present passage, while the latter predominates in its use at 648d7–e1, where it is translated as 'compulsive'. On an ambiguity in the notion of pain and fear, see notes on 633e1–2, 647c3–4, and 648b7–8.

635c6–8 'they will have no practice at enduring in the face of pleasures (*en tois hêdonais karterein*) and refusing to be compelled (*anankazesthai*) into shameful conduct'
On what counts as 'enduring in the face of pleasures', see note on 634a6–8. Here the range of improper action to which one might be led by the prospect of pleasures is broad—not just failures on the battlefield (as implied at 633d) but any 'shameful' action one might perform because of the prospect of pleasure—hence such endurance is classified under moderation.

635c8–d1 'weakness (*glukuthumias*) in the face of pleasures'
Here *glukuthumia* is used to stand in for the analogue, in the case of pleasures, of being 'defeated by fears' (635d1); thus it invokes what Clinias has identified as the central and worst case of being 'defeated by oneself' (633e3–6). On the connection with *thumos* (spirit, resolve), see note on 633d3.

635d1 'defeated (*hêttômenois*) by fears'
An appeal to the notion of self-mastery and self-defeat originally introduced at 626e and brought up again at 633d. Here 'fears' stands in for 'pains' in the formulation at 633e1–2 (see note ad loc). On the relationship between fear and pain, see note on 633c9–d2.

635d1–4 'their enslavement . . . will be to men who are both able to endure in the face of pleasures and also well versed (*kektêmenois*) in matters of pleasure—utterly bad people'
On enduring in the face of pleasures (*katerein en tais hedonais*, d3), see note on 634a6–8. '[W]ell versed in matters of pleasure' renders the vague expression *kektêmenois ta peri tas hêdonas* (d3–4), which might also be rendered 'masters in the domain of pleasure' (cf. 829c8). The 'utterly bad people' (d4) might be purveyors of illicit pleasures. The Athenian's point may be that lack of self-control in the pursuit of pleasures puts one at the mercy of those who control access to those pleasures (as in the figure of the besotted lover sleeping on a doorstep (*Symp.* 203d, *Phdr.* 252a)), just as failure to

cultivate resistance to the pains and fears of battle may lead to one's capture and enslavement by foes met in battle. In any case, the sort of enslavement and defeat of primary interest to the Athenian here is not at the hands of another person, but by one's own pleasures, pains, desires, and fears—on which see 633e1–2 and note ad loc.

635d5 'slaves in one respect and free (*eleutheran*) in another'
They would be 'slaves' to pleasure (in the sense that they are 'defeated' by their desires for pleasures) but 'free' from compulsion by pains and fears (in that they are not 'defeated' by the pains and fears that urge them to cowardly behaviour). The adjective 'free' (*eleutheros*), introduced here for the first time in the dialogue, has several senses:

(1) The ordinary political sense, in which it means not being a literal slave or subject (*Stsm.* 298c, *Lysis* 208b, *Gorg.* 502d, *Rep.* 351d).
(2) An extended, social sense (whose opposite, *aneleutheros*, is often translated 'illiberal' and applied to the status of the *banausos* (mechanical worker or tradesman—*Laws* 644a5, 741e3; Aristotle, *Pol.* 1338b8–15).
(3) An extended psychological sense (where it means something like self-possession or self-control; see *Rep.* 577d, *Phdr.* 256e, and note on 635d1–4).

635d6 'courageous and free without qualification'
In contrast to the 'lame form of courage' (634a2) praised by Tyrtaeus, courage 'without qualification' would be that involved in the 'complete virtue' described at 631a–c. While freedom is not explicitly mentioned in that context, the Athenian here presents it as a kind of self-mastery (*kreittôn hautou*) that is involved both in courage (resistance to pains) and moderation (resistance to pleasures). 'Qualified' freedom would mean self-mastery on one of these fronts together with self-defeat on the other.

635e1–3 'rushing to judgement . . . like foolish adolescents'
The language recalls the Dorian prohibition against criticism of the laws by young people (634d9–e1).

635e4–636d4

Institutions that cultivate courage undermine moderation

The Athenian ostensibly switches the topic of conversation from courage to moderation (although see note on 635e5–6) and invites Megillus to name Spartan institutions that cultivate the latter virtue. To Megillus' hesitant proposal that the institutions that prepare a city for war also cultivate moderation, the Athenian responds that, on the contrary, they promote two kinds of excess that the legislator needs to guard against: (1) a willingness to resort to force in political contexts (civil strife), and (2) the readiness to indulge in unnatural sexual pleasures. The implication (not drawn explicitly) is that institutions specifically designed for cultivating moderation are necessary to counterbalance the immoderate side effects of the institutions that cultivate courage.

635e5–6 'let us talk about moderation next after courage'
The ensuing treatment of moderation (*sôphrosunê*) indicates that resistance to pleasure, originally introduced under the rubric of courage (633c–d), is the domain of moderation (see 'failure to control one's pleasures', 636c7; cf. 647c7–d8). The strategy of presenting moderation as a form of courage is a device, similar to that employed in the discussion of Tyrtaeus (see note on 628e2–630d1), to introduce a novel idea to the interlocutors in terms of values (e.g. courage) that they already endorse.

635e6–636a1 'superior (*diapheron*) . . . as in the military matters we were just discussing'
Note that it is superiority in war, not in courage, that the Athenian attributes to Cretan and Spartan institutions.

636a2–3 'it seems (*eoiken*) that our communal meals and athletic training (*gumnasia*) . . . achieve both effects (*pros amphoteras*)'
Megillus proposes that the same institutions that cultivate courage will serve to cultivate moderation as well. On the verbal echoes of Megillus' claim in the Athenian's response, see notes on 636a4 and 636a5.

636a4 'What really seems hard (*eoiken dêta . . . chalepon einai*) . . .'
'Hard' (*chalepon*) is the opposite of *rhadion*, and responds to Megillus' use of the latter term at 636a2; 'what really seems' (*eoiken dêta*) responds to his 'it seems' (*eoiken*) in the same line. The upshot of the Athenian's reply (on which see next note) is that the institutions mentioned by Megillus, far from cultivating moderation, in fact breed its opposite.

636a5 'as contradictory in their effects as they are controversial in discussion'
more literally: 'no less disputable in practice than they are in discussion (*anamphisbêtêtôs homoiôs ergôi kai logôi*)'
A difficult phrase, in which the key term, *anamphisbêtêtôs*, is a verbal echo of Megillus' proposal that Spartan institutions achieve 'both effects' (*pros amphoteras*, 636a3). The core notion invoked is *amphisbêtêsis* (literally: 'going (*bainein*) in both (*amphi*) directions'). It is used here in a sense broad enough to include both practical implementation (*ergôi*) and theoretical discussion (*logôi*). In the case of discussion, argument, or theory, 'going in both directions' is disagreement or dispute (as in the standard meaning of *amphisbêtêsis*). In the case of practice or implementation, we may understand it as a tendency to produce opposite effects, as in the example of a training regime that has both good and bad effects on the body (636a6–b1). England, by contrast, construes *anamphisbêtêtôs . . . ergôi* to concern dissatisfaction with the results of implementation. Saunders' use of 'trouble free' for *anamphisbêtêtôs* is preferable in this respect, as it nicely reflects the Athenian's concern with devising institutions that are free from unwelcome side effects, and similarly for Schöpsdau's 'tadellos' (irreproachable), although neither captures the connection with Megillus' *pros amphoteras*.

636a7 'hardly a single regimen (*hen epitêdeuma*)'
The emphasis on the 'single' suggests that the problem is to be solved by multiple practices (*epitêdeumata*) that severally correct for the undesirable effects of each other. To counter the side effect of vigorous military training (which makes citizens eager to fight)

another set of practices is necessary to cultivate good relations among the citizens. The Athenian will propose that the institution of the *sumposion* (drinking party) performs this function (640c–d, 671e–672a).

636b2–4 'a danger in times of faction (*pros . . . tas staseis*), as the youth of Miletus, Boeotia, and Thurii have made clear'
alternatively: 'pose the danger of faction' (Saunders)
Faction is first mentioned at 628b2. The cities of Miletus and Thurii, along with Thebes (in Boeotia), were famous in Plato's day for their civil strife (see Plutarch, *Lysander* VIII; Aristotle, *Pol.* 1307a27–b6; Moore 2005: 175). The Athenian proposes that susceptibility to faction (*stasis*) is exacerbated by the vigorous military training of their youth, which makes them eager for a fight.

636b7–c2 'Your cities in particular are to be criticized for bringing about this effect, yours and any others that put such great emphasis on athletic training'
The link between athletic training (*gumnasia*) and sexual temptation is more evident in Plato's Greek. *Gumnasia* in the literal sense are exercises for which one strips naked (hence the root *gumnos*, naked)—paradigmatically, wrestling with a partner. All the wrestlers would be male, and the communal meals (*sussitia*) were also all-male affairs. For a good example of the sexual innuendo surrounding the gymnasium see *Charm.* 153d–155d and *Symp.* 217c. On sexual activity at gymnasia, see Ephorus of Kyme, *FGrH* 70 F 149. See also O. Murray 1993: 175.

636c2–3 'Whether it is right to be playful or serious about such matters . . . '
Nussbaum 1994: 1630, citing correspondence with Dover, takes this remark to signal that the condemnation of same-sex intercourse that follows (c3–7) is not intended to be taken seriously. However, this is unlikely to be what the Athenian intends, since a recurring theme in his exposition is that the message affirmed in one's playful and

serious activities must be the same; see 643b–d, 659d–e, and note on 635b5. For additional responses to Nussbaum, see Rist 1997 and Moore 2005: 177–80. On Plato's treatment of same-sex sexual relations, see also Gould 1963 and Dover 1978.

636c5–6 'the pleasure of males coupling with males or of females with females is unnatural'
A point reiterated in Book 8, 836c–837a, 838e–839b. For similarly negative evaluations of sexual intercourse between males (but not homoerotic attraction) see *Phdr.* 253d–256e, *Rep.* 402d–403c. On sexual mores in Plato's time, see Dover 1978; Foucault 1978; Halperin et al. 1990; Cohen 1991; and Moore 2005: chapter 1. See also note on 636c2–3.

636c6–7 'one of the greatest outrages arising from failure to control one's pleasures (*akrateian hedonês*)'
'Outrage' (*tolmêma*; alt: brazenness) foreshadows the notion of *tharros* (daring) that will be introduced at 644d1 and used at 649c8–d2 to characterize the impulse to pursue inappropriate gratifications (see Nussbaum 1994: 1627–30). The locution *akrateia hedonês* ('failure to control one's pleasures') is used instead of *hêttô . . . tôn hêdonôn* ('defeated by pleasures') which is used at 633e1–2 to describe defeat in the struggle to be 'master of oneself' (*kreittôn hautou*—626e8). The opposite adjective *enkratês* is used at 645e8, where it is translated as 'in control of himself' (see note on 626e4). As argued in the note on 634a6–8, the pleasures that one struggles against here must be understood not as (A) those arising from homoerotic activity, but rather (B) desires to engage in that activity.

636c8 'Ganymede'
The mythical boy cupbearer to the Olympian gods, abducted by Zeus (*Iliad* 20.231–5), and in later versions of the story (e.g. Plato *Phdr.* 255b–c) sexual partner of Zeus. The Athenian charges the Cretans with introducing the homoerotic element into the story, which is absent from the version in Homer. See Schöpsdau ad loc.

636d2–4 'they saddle him with this tale so that they can be following the god even when reaping this particular pleasure'
A cynical perspective on the stories of the 'divine origin' of the laws introduced at 624a.

636d5–637c3

Happiness requires intelligent selection of pleasures and pains

From his preceding criticism of Dorian societies for indulging in what he castigates as inappropriate sexual pleasures (636b–d), the Athenian here draws a general moral that the law's chief concern is with pleasures and pains: these are 'two springs' from which one must draw intelligently in order to live a happy life (636d–e). This point requires an important qualification to the simple 'resistance model' for virtue that has informed the discussion since 633b. The challenge we face as human beings is more complicated than simply resisting pleasures and pains: we must be intelligent in our selection of which pleasures to resist and which to indulge in, and similarly which pains to endure and which to avoid. When Megillus proposes that drinking parties are an indulgence to be avoided (637a–b), the Athenian comes to the defence of the practice (637b–c) and thereby introduces the issue that will inform the rest of Books 1 and 2.

636d5–7 'virtually the whole subject concerns pleasures and pains, those in cities and those in individual characters (*en . . . idiois êthesin*)'
A prescription about how the interlocutors are to conduct their own inquiry (recalling the description of the proper legislator's attention to citizens' pleasures and pains at 631e–632a), rather than a description of actual legislative practice. The pleasures and pains in 'individual characters' (d7) are presumably those already mentioned at 631e–632a as the legislator's concern; those 'in cities' would include the sorts of pleasant activities that are allowed (or forbidden) to citizens, and the sorts of pain or hardship citizens

would be required or expected to endure (e.g. in military service). Those 'in individuals' correspond to pleasures and pains of type (B), and those 'in cities' to those of type (A), as distinguished in the note on 633c9–d2. On the role of pleasures and pains in motivation see also 644c, 663b, 732e–733d. Aristotle makes a virtually identical claim about the significance of pleasure and pain at *EN* 1104b8–9.

636d7–8 'These two springs flow freely by nature (*metheintai phusei rhein*)'
alternatively: 'these two springs flow naturally without restraint'
The point is that nature disposes us to follow the one and shun the other, so restraint in either pursuit or avoidance must come from some other source—later to be identified as training (*ethos, ethismos*; see note on 655d7–e1). The term *metheintai* foreshadows the related *aneintai* (practised without restraint) and *anesis* (lack of restraint) in 637c1–3.

636d8–e1 'the right one at the right time and to the right extent'
This recalls the doctrine of due measure at *Stsm.* 283c–284e and illustrated at *Laws* 638c5–8—later made famous by Aristotle, *EN* 1106a26–b28. Figuring out the right time, extent, etc. for pleasures and pains will require calculation (*logismos,* 644d2)—hence the inopportune selection is 'unintelligent' (*anepistêmonôs*) at 636e2.

636e1 'lives a happy life (*eudaimonei*)'
On happiness (*eudaimonia*) as the legislator's concern, see 628d and 631b. Here we are told that citizens' happiness (alt: 'well-being'—see note on 628d5) depends on how well they select which pleasures to endure, indulge in, or forgo (and similarly regarding which pains to endure and which to avoid). Compare 631e–632a where the legislator, who provides happiness to the citizens (631b), scrutinizes the pleasures and pains that are involved in their emotional responses. On those pleasures and pains, see note on 636d5–7.

The pleasures of drinking parties

636e4 'That's more or less right'
more literally: 'these things are admirably said, in a way (*kalôs pôs*)'
The expression *kalôs legein* typically means to be correct or right, without invoking the ethical or aesthetic dimensions of the term *kalon* (see note on 646d1).

636e6–7 'the lawgiver for the Spartans quite rightly commanded us to avoid pleasures'
literally: '. . . flee from (*pheugein*) pleasures', as at 635b–d.
The blanket command to avoid pleasures violates the doctrine of due measure just articulated by the Athenian (636d8–e3), which implies that the right pleasures, at the right times, should be allowed by the legislator.

637a5–6 'drinking parties (*sumposia*) with all that they involve'
The *sumposion* (pl. *sumposia*, root of the English 'symposium') was a venerable institution in Athens and other non-Dorian Greek states: an after-dinner ritual in which drinkers reclining on couches sing songs and partake of entertainment ranging from exotic dancers and prostitutes to more refined conversation. See Plato, *Protag.* 347c–d and *Symp.* 176b–e for the range of possible entertainments, as well as Xenophon, *Symposium* 2.1–23. Drinking to the point of drunkenness was an essential feature of the event, as the Athenian emphasizes at 637d5–6. (Many features of the modern Jewish Passover seder derive from the Greek symposium. In the Hellenized world in the centuries after Alexander the Great's conquests, which included the land of the Israelites, the symposium was the epitome of leisured and free entertainment among the ruling class.)

637b2 'even if he has the festival of Dionysus as his excuse'
Dionysus is the god of wine and his festivals in the Greek world typically involved communal drunkenness. See Burkert 1985: 161–7 and Seaford 2006. Even Spartan colonists in the city

of Tarentum engaged in the practice, Megillus notes at 637b3–5—hardly evidence, as England notes, for his earlier contention (636a2–3) that Spartan austerity inculcates resistance to such temptations. In Book 2 the Athenian will shock his interlocutors by claiming that old men like themselves should sing and dance in honour of Dionysus (665b).

637b7 'when practised with discipline (*karterêseis*)'
more literally: 'when practised with endurance'
Endurance (*karteria*), here opposed to 'lack of restraint' (*anesis*), is a recurring motif throughout the *Laws*, especially as a response to pains: 633b, 727c, 840b, 942d. Here, as at 635d, 836d–e, 918c–d, and 955c–d, the endurance is in the face of pleasures, desires, or inducements; cf. the 'battle . . . against yearnings and pleasures' (633d1–2). For a more precise analysis of the restraint involved, see note on 634a6–8. Saunders' translation, 'in men with a certain strength of character', wrongly implies that endurance here is a character trait. The Athenian will soon make it clear, in the case of drinking parties (647c–d), that such strength of character may be cultivated by acts of endurance or restraint by people who do not yet possess the corresponding character trait. At 639d–e the Athenian will concede that the requisite restraint or endurance is lacking in the drinking parties Megillus has observed.

637c2–3 'the lack of restraint in your women at home'
'Lack of restraint' (*anesis*) picks up on *aneintai* in the previous line 'when practised without restraint (*aneintai*)' (c1). The charge of licence against Spartan women is elaborated by the Athenian in Book 7, 806c. Aristotle elaborates on the charge, with language echoing this passage, in *Politics* 1269b12–1270a15. In the cross-cultural tit-for-tat envisaged here by the Athenian, a hypothetical Athenian criticized for the abandon (*anesis*) of his own city's drinking practices responds by pointing out lack of restraint in certain Spartan practices as well. There is no reason to suppose that it is specifically the sexual mores of Spartan women that are invoked here (as in

Saunders' translation 'the easy virtue of your women'). On Spartan women see Pomeroy 2002 and Millender 1999.

637c3–639a1

Principles for evaluating practices

Having identified conflicting practices in Sparta and Athens on the regulation of drinking and women's activities (637a–c), the Athenian here canvasses a variety of different approaches one might take when assessing the merits of practices or institutions. The first, dismissed out of hand, is a version of cultural relativism: there are simply differing cultural practices and none of them is incorrect (637c–d). The second approach appeals to the previously discredited military ethic: the norms of the society that prevails in war are best (637e–638b). The Athenian here rejects it on empirical grounds, and also rejects the criterion of popularity (638d). He proposes to explain a better approach (638c–e).

637c5 'that it is faulty (*kakôs echein*) rather than correct'
more literally: 'that it is bad . . . '
Here *kakôs echein* means the same as *mê kalôs echein* (isn't admirable) at 634d9–e1; see note ad loc and on 637e5.

637c6 'the stranger who is shocked at the unfamiliar ways that he observes'
Since 636a, the Athenian and Megillus have each been playing the part of the stranger (*xenos*) who is affronted by alien customs and unreflectively partial to those of his home state—the Athenian in his repugnance at Dorian homosexual practices (636b–d), and at the licence of Spartan women (637c); the Spartan in his chauvinism for his own city's asceticism (636e–637a) and contempt for rituals involving drunkenness in Athens and other cities (637a–b).

637c7–8 'This is our custom (*nomos*) here and no doubt you do things differently where you come from'
alternatively: 'this is our law here . . . '

This is the all-purpose method for diffusing criticism introduced at 637c4 as the 'single reply' to cross-cultural criticism; it echoes the fifth-century view that law or convention (*nomos*) has no basis in reality (*phusis*); for an especially clear articulation of such a view, see *Gorg.* 482c–484c. The Athenian states unequivocally that the joint project of the dialogue, an inquiry into the merits of different laws, rejects this simple relativism. On the translation of *nomos* as 'custom' see Introduction.

637d2 'excellence or deficiency of their lawgivers'
more literally: 'badness and excellence (*kakias te kai aretês*) in their lawgivers'
The term *aretê*, translated as 'virtue' above (630b–631a, 632e–633a), here indicates accomplishment in the discipline of the legislator; at 627e4 it indicates the excellence of a judge.

637e2–3 'While your people, as you say, abstain completely, the Scythians . . . take their wine unmixed (*akratôi . . . chrômenoi*)'
It is from drunkenness, not wine drinking, that Megillus has said the Spartans abstain (637a–b; see O. Murray 2013: 111–12). Greeks of Plato's day drank their wine diluted with water, even at drinking parties. Some of the most beautiful relics of the material culture of the era are the mixing bowls (*kratêres*) used for this purpose. Drinking 'unmixed' wine was considered uncivilized, and would of course lead more readily to inebriation.

637e5 'an admirable (*kalon*) and happy (*eudaimon*) practice'
'Happy' here, while not idiomatic in contemporary English, indicates either that the practice is conducive to the good life, or is an element or expression of such a good life. On happiness, see note on 628d5. The conjunction here of the adjective 'admirable' (*kalon*) with 'happy' shows the close connection between the notions of the admirable or beautiful (*kalon*) and the good (*agathon*). See notes on 637c5, 641b8–c1, and 667c6–7. On the *kalon*, see note on 630c7.

638a1–2 'we put all these peoples to flight'
Megillus here reverts to Clinias' original proposal that military success is the standard of legislative excellence (626b5–c3), notwithstanding the Athenian's subsequent exposition of the deficiencies of that standard (627c–628d).

638a4 'that tell us nothing (*atekmartoi*)'
Translation following Ast, with Brisson/Pradeau. Alternatively one might render *atekmartoi* as 'inexplicable' or 'mysterious' (Bury, Saunders, des Places, England, Schöpsdau, Lisi); however, the Athenian's point is that such cases provide no evidence or proof (*tekmêrion*) that the victorious people's practices are better.

638b1–3 'The Syracusans subjugated the Locrians, whose laws were thought to be the best in that region, and the Athenians did the same to the Ceians'
The Syracusans under the tyrant Dionysus II conquered the Locrians in 352 BCE—so this reference provides a *terminus post quem* for dating the composition of the present text (five years before Plato's death in 347). In praise of Locrian laws, see Plato, *Tim.* 20a. The Ceians attempted to secede from the Athenian naval confederacy in 364 BCE, but were forcibly brought back into the alliance. For details see Schöpsdau ad loc and Gehrke 1985: 76 ff. Plato himself had visited Syracuse several times by the end of his life and is reported to have made some (spectacularly unsuccessful) efforts to educate Dionysus II in philosophy (DL 3.18–24; see also *Ep. VII*); Vlastos 1981: 215–16 suggests that Plato's experience with Dionysus II led him to abandon the political philosophy of the *Republic* and settle on the 'second-best' politics outlined in *Laws* (739e).

638c5 'cheese'
Reading *turous* (cheese) for the MSS' *purous* (wheat). Thus Saunders 1972, England, Lisi, and Brisson/Pradeau, but not des Places or

Schöpsdau. The Hippocratic corpus contains a similar example involving cheese (*On Ancient Medicine* 20.17–22).

638c7–8 'how and to whom it is served, with what accompaniments and in what condition, as well as the condition of the person who eats it'
These would be specific instances of the variables mentioned in the doctrine of due measure at 636d8–e1 (see note ad loc).

638d4–5 'some thinking the large number on their side settles the matter'
It is not obvious that any party to the present discussion has invoked this consideration (by contrast, it is clearly invoked at *Gorg.* 471e and criticized there and at *La.* 184d–e). Although the Athenian has just pointed out the large number of societies with wine-drinking practices different from the Dorians' (637d–e), he has not concluded from this that their practices are superior, although he will do so in a joking manner at 638e5–6.

639a2–641a3

Goals and leadership of a properly led drinking party

The Athenian proposes that a properly conducted drinking party must have a sober leader. While the order of exposition in this passage is not straightforward, the general line of argument is as follows: a collective undertaking—whether it be a sea voyage, a military campaign, or a drinking party—requires a leader if it is to have any chance of achieving anything good (639a–c, 640a); thus to find fault with a leaderless or ill-led collective enterprise is pointless for those investigating the merits of social practices (639a, 639c, 640d–641a). The drinking parties criticized by Megillus, and indeed all those in the Athenian's experience, fall into the ill-led category (639d–e). So to appreciate the benefits that might come from a drinking party, one must consider what it can achieve under proper leadership. In developing this point, the Athenian indicates without fanfare that the goal of such an enterprise is to increase the bonds of civic friendship among the drinkers (640c–d).

639a9 'Now, is someone a good ship's captain (*chrêstos . . . archôn*) as long as . . . '
Picking up on the importance of having good masters in the example of goat-keeping (639a2–7), the Athenian now turns to the criteria for good leadership, switching the example from animal husbandry to navigation and warfare. The two criteria identified here (639a9–b11) will be applied to the leadership of a drinking party at 640a8–d9: (1) knowledge of how to conduct the enterprise at hand; (2) immunity to the naturally occurring disturbances that are occupational hazards in the enterprise (e.g. seasickness in a naval voyage, fear in a military campaign).

639b5 'leader of armies'
The term *archon*—translated as 'leader' here and at 639c—is rendered by 'master' above in the example of the goats (639a6) and 'captain' in the example of the ships (639a9).

639c1 'gathering (*koinônias*)'
The term *koinônia* (also at 639c6) is used interchangeably with *koinônêma* (639d1), *sunousia* (639d3, 640c1, c9, d2), and *sunodos* (640a4), and is translated as either 'gathering', 'social gathering', or 'assembly' in those contexts. The extension of the term encompasses group undertakings 'of any kind' (640a4–5); thus it applies equally to the collective enterprises that the Athenian has just been discussing, sailors on a ship or soldiers on a military campaign, which are fresh in the minds of his interlocutors (639a9–b11).

639d2–3 'drinking companions, or a drinking party, are one kind of gathering (*sunousian*)'

Here the Athenian makes the crucial move of subsuming drinking parties under the general principle about group activities just articulated at 639c1–6; see note on 640c10–d2. On the translation of *sunousia* see note on 639c1.

639d9–e1 'pretty well none of those I have observed or heard of was conducted properly'
The Athenian here concedes the criticism Megillus levelled at the drinking parties in his experience (637b).

640a5 'the correct thing is for the participants to have a leader'
alternatively: 'there is always a correct leader in each case' (Pangle)
The Athenian's extended point (639a–641a) is both that a drinking party must have a leader (as on the present translation), and that the leader must have the appropriate qualifications (as on the alternative translation), but Pangle goes too far in proposing that the Athenian here implies that the leader of a drinking party, like that of a political community, must be an absolute ruler unlimited by law (Pangle 1980: 397). The Athenian indicates that there will be laws governing drinking parties (671c). The credentials of the leaders of drinking parties will be specified at length in Book 2 as expertise in the 'finer music' of the Dionysian chorus (664b–666d).

640a8–9 'we were just saying that a leader of warriors has to be courageous'
The reference is to 639b. 'Courage' is here understood in the sense of fearlessness in battle. At 646e–649d courage will be presented as a kind of fearlessness, and moderation a kind of fearfulness.

640b7–8 'in peacetime, he will lead friends gathered together in mutual goodwill (*philophrosunês*)'
The link between peace and *philophrosunê* is first invoked at 628c10–11, where they, rather than war and conflict, are identified as the ultimate focus of the legislator. The Athenian here presents the

drinking party as an institution for achieving these social goals of the legislator—a point reiterated more emphatically at 640c9–d2.

640c1–2 'not . . . without disturbances (*athorubos*)'
The adjective *athorubos* echoes the verb *thorubein* (disturb) at 640a12 and b3, where it concerns the fears to which the military commander must be immune. The as yet unspecified disturbances that characterize a drinking party are here portrayed as analogous to the fears that assail the soldier in battle. In the present context, the requirement that the leader be 'sober' (640d4) implies that the disturbance is drunkenness. The disruptive or unruly behaviour at a drinking party is further described at 649a–b and 671a–b.

640c10–d2 'for his job is to safeguard the existing friendly relations among the participants and . . . strengthen them for the future'
more literally: 'for he is the guard (*phulax*) of . . . '
In contrast to the sort of guarding that Clinias identified as central to the goals of the Dorian state (see note on 626a8–b1), the Athenian here talks about 'guarding' peaceful relations of friendship (*philia*) among citizens. He thus implies that a properly led drinking party furthers this civic goal. On friendship as a civic goal, see Book 3, 693b–c; cf. 695d, 698c.

640d4–5 'we must set up as ruler over our drinkers a leader who is sober'
Compare the leadership of the drinkers in Plato's *Symp*. 176c–177d. By the end of that drinking party, Socrates is the only sober participant (223c–d).

640d6 'or by a young and inexpert leader'
'Inexpert' renders *mê sophos*. On the expertise (*epistêmê, phronêsis*) of the leader, see 639b1, 640c9–10. On *sophia* and *phronêsis*, see note on 631c5–6.

641a4 –643a8

Drinking parties claimed to benefit education

Having granted at 640d–e that a collective undertaking is beneficial only when properly led, Clinias now asks, with some impatience, what benefits a city could possibly derive from drinking parties, even if they are conducted by competent leaders (641a–b). The Athenian answers that the benefit concerns education (*paideia*, 641b–d). He warns that a full defence of this claim will require a rather lengthy detour on the topic of education (641e–642a), but his interlocutors reassure him (with uncharacteristic prolixity of their own) that they are willing to hear him out in a speech of any length (642b–643a).

641b1–2 'a properly led (*paidagôgêthentos kata tropon*) drinking party'

Clinias here employs the verb *paidagôgein*, which can be a general term for leadership or guidance, as he uses it here. But it can also mean 'instruct' or 'train' (and is the root for the English term 'pedagogy'), as in the Athenian's reply (b3). The educational connotations of the term, and the use of it here in the passive voice, switches the focus from the activity of the leader (leading, instructing) to the effects on those led, and hence to the notion of *paideia* (education, b6), construed as a cultivated disposition in a person; the latter is the topic to which the Athenian now turns. The related term *agôgê* will be used to invoke the guidance or leadership of calculation (*logismos*) in the figure of the divine puppets at 645a1; see note ad loc.

641b3–4 'a single pupil (*pais*) or chorus properly trained (*paidagôgêthentos*)'

more literally: 'a single child . . . '

The Athenian's reply uses the same verb, *paidagôgein*, that Clinias used in his question (641b1–2; see previous note), and singles out from its compound elements *pais* (child, or in this case, pupil). The institution of the chorus (which performs ensemble song and dance—see note on 654a4–5) is mentioned here for the first time; it will turn out to play an important role in education, as set forth in Book 2 (653c–654b, 664b–d).

641b6–7 'what benefit a city derives from educating people (*paideian tôn paideuthentôn*)'
Here the Athenian switches the verb from *paidagôgein* (lead, train, guide) used by Clinias (see note on 641b1–2) to the related *paideuein* (educate) and the cognate noun *paideia* (education), thus completing the transition to the topic of education, which is next on his agenda (642a).

641b8–c1 'those who are properly educated become good (*agathoi*) men, and as a result do admirably (*prattoien kalôs*) in all things'
That is, education cultivates the virtues enumerated at 631c–d. A more idiomatic translation of *prattoien kalôs* ('do admirably') would be 'do well' or 'succeed' (thus des Places, Lisi, Saunders, Schöpsdau); the sense of the expression here is indistinguishable from that of 'doing one's best' (*arista prattein*) in 628d3, which stands in for 'being happy' (*eudaimonein*); see note on 628d5. As at 637e5 and 657c5–6, doing admirably and being happy (doing well) are very closely connected; see notes ad loc. Brisson/Pradeau's translation ('they conduct themselves as they should') is too narrow to capture the success implied by the term, which includes even victory in war (641c1–2).

641c1–3 'They even defeat their enemies in battle! Education, you see, delivers victory'
Education here includes the military training that cultivates resistance to the pains and fears of battle (see 647b3–7); thus it can be credited with the military success so prized by Clinias and Megillus (626b–c). Of course, the Athenian recognizes that even the courageous are sometimes defeated in battle, as for example when they are

outnumbered (638a–b), but his main point is that education is necessary for such success; 643b4–7 makes a claim of necessity, not sufficiency.

641c3–4 'although victory sometimes undermines education. For many are made insolent by their victories in war'
Insolence (*hubris*) is closely connected to injustice (630b6, 661e2, 662a2). It is a form of shamelessness (*anaideia* 647a10), which will be identified as the fault that training in the virtue of moderation (*sôphrosunê*) seeks to ward off (647a–b, 649a–e). The Athenian will later claim that one can develop hubris as a result of coming into possession of wealth and other goods (649d4–7; see note ad loc), which Clinias has noted are the spoils of military victory (626b2–4).

641c6 'Cadmean victories'
Like a 'Pyrrhic victory', a Cadmean victory sows the seeds of its own undoing. In the founding legend of the city of Thebes, Cadmus slayed a dragon and then planted its teeth in the ground, from which twelve armed warriors sprang up. See Saunders 1972.

641d7–8 'if I am simply to say how things seem to me'
The Athenian's epistemic reticence is repeated at 643a3–4 even as he assumes leadership in the conversation.

641e2–4 'you are trying to figure out what my view (*logon*) is, and I am doing what I can to present it clearly'
Here all pretence that the three interlocutors are on an equal footing in the conversation is abandoned (see note on 625a7). From here on, the Athenian takes charge of the discussion.

641e4–5 'my city' (i.e. Athens)
On the association of Athens with intellectual acuity, see also 626d. The Athenian here appeals to stereotypical intellectual characteristics of the cities of the three interlocutors.

641e7–8 'Sparta is brief of speech (*brachulogon*) and Crete more given to extended thought (*polunoian*) than extended exposition (*polulogian*)'
This slight difference in the stereotypes of Spartans and Cretans flatters Clinias. Perhaps the latter's confident assertions early in the dialogue (625c–626b) display 'extended thought', but they also arguably constitute *polulogia*.

642a4 'correctness in music'
Mousikê encompasses not only music in the narrow sense (instrumental and vocal music), but also dance, poetry, and drama (see Peponi 2012: 4 and note on 666d3). 'Correctness' (*orthotês*) in music will be a major preoccupation of Book 2 (655c–657b, 667b–670e), where it is important to keep in mind that the 'music' in question includes dance as well as song. I thank Greg Scott for stressing the latter point.

The goodwill of the interlocutors

642b4 '*proxenos*' (plural, *proxenoi*)
A *proxenos* represented in his own city the interests of a foreign state, rather like a modern consul, except that a *proxenos* is not a citizen of the city he represents (see Walbank 1978). The character Megillus in *Laws* may have been modelled on the Megillus who led a delegation of Spartan peace envoys to Athens during the Peloponnesian War (circa 408–7 BCE) and was probably a *proxenos* of Athens. Nothing else is known of this Megillus (See Nails 2002: 197–8). Dusanic 1990: 365–6 proposes that the name of the Cretan interlocutor, 'Clinias', evokes the faction of Alcibiades, active at the time of the embassy to Athens by the historical Megillus.

642c2–3 'treated us badly (*ou kalôs . . . errexe*)'
A Spartan locution.

642c3–5 'From listening to this and always defending you against those casting aspersions on your city, I acquired broad feelings of goodwill towards you'
An instance of the kind of training (*ethizesthai*) that shapes feelings of pleasure and pain in the account of education (*paideia*) that opens Book 2 (653a–c).

642c8 'not by compulsion'
Megillus here prefigures the Athenian's emphasis on persuasion (as opposed to compulsion (*anankê*)) as the essential mode of education (see notes on 632b7–8, 648b8–c5). The point (at least as it is developed by the Athenian) is not that the Athenians, unlike for instance the Dorians, are free to become bad (thus England ad loc), but that their education uses gentle and persuasive means rather than forcible and violent ones.

642d2–4 'don't hold back . . . go ahead'
Both injunctions translate *tharrôn*—the verbal form of *tharros* (daring, confidence), which figures prominently in the Dorian ideal of courage that will be one of the main elements of the moral psychology introduced at 644c–d; the Athenian will explore the negative and antisocial side of *tharros* at 647a–649a.

642d5 'divinely good man (*anêr theios*)'
A typically Spartan locution, applied to Tyrtaeus at 629b9.

642d5–7 'Epiminedes . . . visited your city . . . ten years before the Persian war'
Epimenides of Knossos, legendary wonderworker and prophet from the archaic age of Crete (see Morrow 1960: 18), was fabled to have visited Athens during the time of Solon (Plutarch, *Solon* 12.7–12), that is, in the late seventh/early sixth century BCE. Clinias' claim that the visit took place 'ten years before the Persian war' (d6–7) would date it circa 500 BCE, nearly one hundred years later. If Plato's Athenian audience could be expected to notice the discrepancy in

dates, he is portraying Clinias as grossly ignorant of Athenian history. Cf. 677d7–8, where the Athenian jokes to Clinias that Epimenides is 'your friend . . . of practically yesterday'. For discussion of the historical evidence, see Schöpsdau ad loc and Dusanic 1991: 36–43.

642e4 'My ancestors formed ties of hospitality (*exenôthêsan*) with you'
The verb *exenôthêsan* contains the root *xenos* (Stranger), which is ubiquitous as a form of address between the interlocutors; see note on 624a1. Strictly speaking, the ties Clinias mentions were between families, not cities. So he is invoking a connection between the families of Epimenides and the family of the Athenian. One might note that Solon, the celebrated Athenian lawgiver at the time of Epimenides' visit, is Plato's own ancestor (DL 3.1.1).

643a4 'As a first step in our argument (*logon*)'
That is, the argument that drinking parties benefit education (641c8–d9), to which a definition of education has been identified as a necessary preliminary (642a1–b2).

643a7 'the god that is its destination'
The phrase invokes the pilgrimage that the three travellers are making to the cave of Zeus (625a–b) as a metaphor for the general conversation about laws that they are undertaking along the way; the destination of the former here stands in for that of the latter. By contrast, des Places, Saunders, Taylor, England, Schöpsdau, Lisi, and Brisson/Pradeau take the god in question to be the god of wine (Dionysus). However, Dionysus has not been invoked in the immediate context; cf. the similar phrase at 968b9–10, discussed by Nightingale 1993: 283.

643a8 'if it pleases you'
After the Athenian has just placed the route of the discussion in the context of the sacred journey to the god (643a7), Clinias' good-natured response (picked up on by the Athenian at 643d3)

misses the point. It is not because it pleases the Athenian that it is the right thing to do, but because the discussion itself requires it (642a5–6). The notion that pleasure is the criterion of choice will be subject to severe criticism in Book 2 (657c–659c, 667b–668b). On pleasure as a motive for the conversation, see also 625a6 and note ad loc.

IV
EDUCATION, VIRTUE, AND VICTORY OVER ONESELF

643b1–646e2

Having claimed that the value of drinking parties is educational, the Athenian turns now to give a preliminary account of education (643b–644b). It is the process of training the 'pleasures and desires' (643c7–8) of children towards the virtues of citizenship (643e5). Next, he provides a psychological analysis of self-mastery and self-defeat (originally introduced at 626e) in the memorable image of the divine puppets: we are moved by the 'iron cords' of pleasure, pain, and their 'anticipations' as well as by the 'golden cord' of calculation (logismos)*; self-mastery is to be understood as the victory of the golden over the iron cords (644b–645c). As the first step in his explanation of the educational benefits of drinking parties, he claims that drunkenness, while it temporarily lessens self-mastery, ultimately yields an important benefit (645c–646e), later to be identified as the cultivation of moderation (646e–650b).*

Two paradigms for virtue

The account of education presented here (634b–644b) implies a conception of virtue significantly different from the 'victory over oneself' that is praised by Clinias at 626e and that has served as a paradigm for virtue in the discussion of courage and moderation from 632e–636c. On the 'victory' model, pleasures and pains are forces that the virtuous person struggles against and overcomes; thus internal conflict and struggle is an inevitable feature of virtuous experience. The account of education presented at 643b–644b, however, in allowing that pleasures and pains can be trained and therefore properly directed, implies that internal conflict is not inevitable. It thus allows for a conception of virtue on which all of a person's internal motivations are harmonious—that is, directed towards the activities required by justice. That virtue is to be conceived in this way is an easy moral to draw from the Athenian's earlier argument that peace, not victory in war, is the greatest good (627d–628d), although there the Athenian stops short of explicitly drawing that moral (see note on 628c9–11). At the beginning of Book 2, he will explicitly articulate a conception of virtue as 'agreement' (sumphônia) *between pleasures and pains on the one hand, and reasoned judgements on the other (653a–c), and later in Book 1, when explaining how drunkenness can be used to train citizens in moderation, he will quietly deploy this conception of virtue in his construal of the goal of such training (see notes on 647b9–c1, 648c2–3). However, he nowhere explicitly renounces the 'victory' model espoused by Clinias. In fact, the Athenian will continue to invoke it episodically over the rest of Book 1, most notably in the psychology articulated at 644c–645c, where he explicitly invokes self-mastery (victory in such internal conflict) as the paradigm for virtue, illustrated in the figure of the divine puppets (see note on 644b6–7); he will invoke both models in his concluding discussion of drinking parties as a training ground for moderation (see note on 646e3–650b10).*

In continuing to appeal to a paradigm for virtue that he has discredited, but that his opponents accept, the Athenian is pursuing a tactic similar to one he deploys in his earlier discussion of Tyrtaeus, where, even though he has renounced victory in battle as the ultimate good, he argues for the importance of 'virtue as a whole' by appealing to the notion of 'victory' in the 'greatest battle' (see note on 628e2–630d1). In both cases, the Athenian appeals to normative assumptions that his interlocutors endorse in order to lead them to conclusions that they are not initially inclined to accept.

The distinction and complicated transition between these two paradigms for virtue in Laws 1 *and* 2 *tends to be overlooked by commentators. Stalley (1983: 50–3, 58, 62) correctly notes the competing models and observes that Book 1 concentrates on the 'victory' model and Book 2 on the 'agreement' model (but he does not note the full extent to which the 'agreement' model is advanced in Book 1). The two conceptions of moderation identified in Bobonich (2002: 289–90) concern a different distinction (whether the resistance to pleasures is guided by wisdom) and Bobonich himself finds the Athenian endorsing a conception of virtue on which residual conflict with recalcitrant desires is inevitable (Bobonich 2002: 289, 350, 546n122). Similarly, Belfiore (1986: 428–33) takes the* Laws, *in contrast to the* Republic, *to allow that virtue necessarily involves a struggle against conflicting desires; cf. North 1966: 189. By contrast, Laks (2005: 47; 2000: 277), Jouët-Pastré (2006: 42), Frede (2010: 117), Annas (1999: 144), Zuckert (2009: 69), and Wilburn (2012) interpret the self-mastery involved in the puppet analogy as an expression of the 'agreement' model. While there is no doubt that the Athenian's extended commentary on the figure of the divine puppets leaves open the 'agreement' model of virtue, and indeed may be pregnant with it (see note on 645b8–c1), it is equally clear that his initial and explicit motivation for introducing it invokes the 'victory' model. See further the note on 644d7–645c8.*

643b1–644b5

Education (paideia) *defined*

The Athenian gives a preliminary definition of education that exploits the connections between the terms for education (*paideia*) and play (*paidia, paizein*)—all with the same root, '*pais*' (child—see note on 635b5). The goal of education is to channel the pleasures and desires of a child towards the activity that will be his adult occupation; it does so by employing child's play that practises and rehearses the activities of the adult occupation, suitably scaled down for a child (643b–d). The definition is further refined to distinguish education in a more precise and restricted sense, on which a person trained in a trade does not count as 'educated'. Education in this restricted sense is training in virtue (643d–644b). On the conception of virtue thus implied, see note on 643b1–646e2.

643b1–2 'Let me tell you how we should understand education' more literally: 'When I tell you just what we should call education (*ti pote chrê phanai paideian einai*)'

643b5 'right from childhood (*ek paidôn euthus*)'
The reference to childhood picks up on the use of *pais* (child) at 641b3–4, where it is translated as 'pupil' (see note ad loc).

643b6 'both his playtime (*paizonta*) and his serious attention (*spoudazonta*)'
On the contrast between playing and being serious, see note on 635b5. Children's play is serious business, we are about to be told, because it is the earliest stage of the education (*paideia*) that cultivates a person's adult dispositions. On the sort of play that cultivates virtue (the goal of education in the strict sense to be identified in 643d–644b), see note on 647d6–7.

643c7–9 'through playful activities . . . their caregivers try to direct children's pleasures and desires towards what they must do when they are fully grown'
more literally: '. . . towards the place they must reach (*aphikomenous*) when they are fully grown (*telos echein*)'
A further definition of education will be given at the beginning of Book 2 (653a–c), where it is said to shape a person's 'pleasures and pains' from an early age. On 'pleasures and desires' (*hêdonas kai epithumias*) as opposed to 'pleasures and pains', see note on 633c9–d2. While the Athenian does not here specify the 'playful activities' (*paidiôn*) that will train the requisite pleasures and desires (analogous to the would-be carpenter learning to enjoy carpentry by playing with toy hammer and saw), he will indicate in Book 2 that it

is the performance of choral music, in which citizens participate from childhood (664b–d), and whose songs are presented as games (659d–660a); see also note on 647d6–7. On the playful activities in this passage, see Saunders 1972.

643c9 'it is of the utmost importance for education (*kephalaion paideias*) . . . that one receives a correct upbringing (*orthên trophên*)'
Early upbringing of a child in the home (*trophê*) would ordinarily be distinguished from the formal education (*paideia*) comprised of musical and athletic training at the hands of teachers (see note on 642a4, Aristophanes *Clouds* 961–83, and Golden 1990). The Athenian's main point here is that those earlier activities form a necessary foundation ('the essential preliminary skills', 643c4) for the later formal training.

643d1–3 'since this inculcates . . . a passion (*erôta*) for the occupation in which the grown man will need to be completely good'
more literally: ' . . . in which the grown man will need to be complete (*teleion*), in the excellence of the business in question (*tês tou pragmatos aretês*)'
Passion (*erôs*) is one of the feelings that the legislator must supervise in the citizens ('pains, pleasures, desires, and the general intensity of their passions', 631e4–632a1). The qualification *tês tou pragmatos aretês* (d2–3) limits the scope of *teleion* (thus England), and may be understood to anticipate the distinction the Athenian is about to make (643d6–644b4) between a broad and a narrow sense of education. Education in the wider sense cultivates excellence (*aretê*) in the pupil's intended occupation (*aretê* is used in this sense at 627e3–4 and at 637d2). In the narrower sense, captured in the translation 'virtue' at 643e4, and at 630e–631a, the relevant excellence is restricted to accomplishment in the domain of citizenship. In the present context, the 'occupation at which the grown man will need to be completely good', in the cases of interest to the Athenian, is that of the 'perfect citizen (*politên . . . teleon*) . . . who knows how to rule and be ruled with justice' (643e5–6). The Athenian thus

envisages a condition in which well-educated citizens do not feel conflicted about living up to the demands of justice, since their desires and feelings are properly directed. This is to presuppose a conception of virtue very different from the victory model espoused by Clinias (626e, 633d–e); it evokes instead the harmonious internal condition of 'agreement' (*sumphônia*) that the Athenian will identify as virtue in Book 2, 653a–b. See note on 626e2–3 and general note on 643b1–646e2.

643d6 'let's be precise about what we are calling education'
more literally: 'let's not leave imprecise (*aoriston*) what we are saying is education'

643e3 'our discussion (*logos*) . . . is not with those who consider that sort of thing to be education . . . '
The disparagement of 'mechanical' and commercial occupations is a frequent theme in Plato and his contemporaries (Plato, *Rep.* 495d–e, 590c; Aristotle, *Politics* 1337b8–15; Xenophon, *Oeconomicus* 4.2, 6.5). The Athenian will later make the stronger claim that the practice of manual crafts or retail trade are to be forbidden to citizens (846d–e; 919d–e), whose full-time occupation is the cultivation of virtue (806d–807e); see Meyer 2003.

643e3–4 'education . . . right from childhood, directs a person towards virtue'
The virtue (*aretê*) that education in this strict sense cultivates is that of a citizen, called 'complete justice' at 630c and comprising the 'divine goods': wisdom, moderation, justice, and courage (631c–d).

643e4–6 'giving him an appetite and passion to become a perfect (*teleon*) citizen, one who knows (*epistamenon*) how to rule and be ruled with justice (*meta dikês*)'
alternatively: 'a complete (*teleon*) citizen' (cf. 643d8, d2)
On appetite (*epithumia*) and passion (*erôs*), see also 631e4–632a1, 645d7. On the citizen's knowledge (*epistamenon*, 643e6), see note on

644a3–4. Citizens 'ruling and being ruled (*archein te kai archesthai*) with justice' would avoid the civil strife identified as the premier evil in a city at 628a–d. The phrase also recalls the good brothers at 627d–e who are left to 'rule themselves'. For more on self-rule, see note on 644b6–7. (Note that the inclusion of 'being ruled' in the object of the passion distinguishes the perfect citizen from the timocratic person of *Rep.* VIII 549a, who loves ruling, not being ruled.) The qualification 'with justice' (*meta dikês*) will be used again to define shame as being 'justly afraid' (647c7–8). Used here in close proximity to *teleon* (perfect; translated as 'complete' at 643c8 and 643d2), the phrase evokes the 'complete justice' (*dikaiosunên . . . teleian*) at 630c6, used as a variant for 'virtue in its entirety' (630e2–3; see note on 630b2–3), which is the combination of wisdom, moderation, and courage that amounts to justice (631c–d), in contrast to the narrow conception of courage touted by the Dorian apologists (630c).

644a3–4 'any other skill (*sophian*) that does not involve intelligence (*nou*) and justice'
Skill (*sophia*) here applies both to the knowledge of the 'perfect citizen' (643e5) and to the technical expertise of the farmer, carpenter, soldier, merchant, etc. invoked at 643b7–c6 and at 643e1–2. *Nous* here is the wisdom (*phronêsis*) that informs the virtues. Both justice and wisdom are integral to the virtues of the citizens (631c). See notes on 631c5–6 and on 631d5–6.

644a8–b1 'education is never to be disparaged (*atimazein*)'
The first part of the long prologue at the beginning of Book 5 (726a–728a) indicates that disparaging or dishonouring (*atimazein*) something need not involve speaking disrespectfully of it (as, for instance, Callias does of philosophical education at *Gorg.* 484c–485d); the disrespect might consist simply in behaving inappropriately towards it. The Spartan and Cretan constitutions are charged with just such a disregard for education at 666e–667a, given their narrow focus on military training. Note the Athenian's

insistence that the lawgiver must 'mete out honour and dishonour correctly' (631e2–3; 648c1–2).

644b1–2 'first of the very finest things bestowed upon the best of men'
The sense in which education is 'first' is explained in the account that begins Book 2, where education is described as the first step in the cultivation of virtue (653a–c). For a similarly high estimate of the value of education (*paideia*) and upbringing (*trophê*), see Plato, *Phd.* 107d and Aristotle, EN 1104b11–13, 1179b31–4.

644b2–3 'If it ever goes off course and there is the possibility of correcting it'
At the beginning of Book 2, we are told that such deterioration is an inevitable effect of daily life (653c7–9) and that the preservation (*sôtêria*, 653a3) of a correct childhood education is a lifelong project of maintenance and repair (653d–654a). Drinking parties, the Athenian will argue in Book 2, play a crucial role in this project of repair (671b–d).

644b6–c3

Virtue as victory in internal struggle

Having just identified education as the process of making citizens good (644a7–8; cf. 641b8) by appropriately directing their pleasures and pains (643c7–9, 643e5), the Athenian now takes the curious tack of reverting to the very different model of goodness advocated by Clinias at 626e and used as a paradigm for the discussions of courage and moderation at 633d–636c. On this paradigm, goodness consists in struggling against and defeating pleasures and pains; on the competing paradigms for virtue, see notes on 626e2–3, 643b1–646e2.

644b6–7 'we previously agreed that those who are able to rule themselves (*archein hautôn*) are good, while those who are unable to do so are bad'

An interestingly ambiguous statement. 645b2–3 indicates that the Athenian evidently has in mind 626e, where Clinias invoked 'victory over oneself' (626e2) or self-mastery (being *kreittôn hautou*, 626e8) as the greatest achievement. Such 'victory' has functioned as a paradigm for virtue in the treatment of courage and moderation at 633d–636c. However, it is misleading of the Athenian to represent *himself* as having endorsed this conception of virtue. While he agreed with Clinias that victory over oneself is preferable to self-defeat, he objected that a far superior achievement to such victory is internal harmony, where there are no conflicting forces to be defeated (627e–628d). His objection explicitly addressed only the case of a city state and drew no conclusions about an individual person; however, the conception of virtue presupposed in the account of education that the Athenian has just sketched (643b–644b) conforms to the conception of virtue as internal harmony or 'agreement' articulated in Book 2, 653a–c; see notes on 628c9–11, and general note on 643b1–646e2.

It is worth noting, furthermore, that the expression used here, 'rule themselves' (*archein hautôn*), is an odd one to employ to invoke the victory-over-oneself that Clinias considers to be a paradigm of virtue (626e). The expression is not used with such a meaning anywhere else in *Laws*. Rather, Clinias first invokes 'victory over oneself' (*nikân auton hauton*, 626e2), and the Athenian subsequently calls the condition being 'master of oneself' (*kreittôn hautou*, 626e8) and calls its opposite 'being defeated by oneself'—*hêttasthai auton huph' heautou* (626e3–4) or *hêttôn [hautou]*, (626e8). Later, the person who wins the struggle will be called 'in control of himself' (*enkratês*) at 645e8, and the opposite condition is described as 'failure to control one's pleasures' (*akrateia hêdonês*) at 636c7; see note on 626e4. Where the expression 'rule themselves' (*archein hautôn*) does occur in *Laws*, its sense is political or social, rather than psychological. It characterizes the political autonomy of the good brothers in the warring family at 627e1, in contrast with the political subjugation of the wicked brothers, who are ruled (*archesthai*) by their betters (627e3). The expression is used again in this sense at the end of Book 2, where the inebriated participant in a drinking party is described as thinking himself fit to rule (*archein*) his companions as well as himself (671b5–6)—the latter being not victory over oneself (in the sense of *enkrateia* or being *kreittôn hautou*), but autonomy ('no one is going to tell me what to do').

When Plato employs the expression outside of the *Laws*, its primary sense is also social/political; e.g. the young Lysis is not allowed to 'rule himself' but is in the charge of a pedagogue (*Lysis* 208c; cf. *La.* 179a, *Rep.* 590e). On three occasions, Plato does have Socrates use the expression in an extended psychological sense: he accuses Meno of seeking to rule others before he is able even to 'rule himself' (*Meno* 86d); he asks Callicles whether the rulers of cities should be able to 'rule themselves' (*Gorg.* 491d–e); and in the *Republic*, he characterizes the person with a just soul as 'ruling himself' (*arxanta auton hautou*, 443d4; cf. *basileuonta hautou*, 580c2). But in none of these 'psychological' uses is it clear that the expression is intended to capture Clinias' 'victory over oneself' rather than the internal harmony and agreement endorsed by the Athenian; indeed, the relevant expression is clearly used in the latter sense at *Rep.* 443d4 and 580c2. Bobonich (1994:18) wrongly implies that 'rule oneself' is one of Plato's standard terms for enkratic action (on *enkrateia*, see note on 626e4). To be sure, the metaphor of *ruling* is ubiquitous in the tripartite psychology of the *Republic*, where parts of the soul are described as ruling (*archein*) and being ruled (*archesthai*) by each other, or as ruling or being ruled by the person (442c5–d1, 443b1–2, 558d4, 561b4, 590c2–d6, 606d5), and a person is said to rule or be ruled by other persons (579c4–d2, 590e2–591a3). But none of these texts uses the expression 'ruling oneself' (pace Dorion 2007: 135n48). We do find 'rule over oneself' (*heautou archên*) at 561b4 but the context does not attribute self-rule to any of the parties involved. And where we would expect to find the locution, as an elegant contrast with 'rule others' (*allôn . . . archein*) in a passage parallel to *Meno* 86d and *Gorg.* 491d–e, we find instead *heautou . . . akratôr* (*Rep.* 579c7–8), which suggests that *archein heautou* is not the most natural expression to use to invoke the psychological condition of self-control (whether on the 'victory' or the 'agreement' model). Indeed, in *Gorg.* 491d4–e1, Callicles' initial incomprehension of Socrates' question (491d9) marks the psychological sense as one that would not be the first to occur to a native speaker, although he has no objection when Socrates indicates that the expression means the same as the familiar locutions *sôphrona onta kai enkratê auton heautou* (491d11–12; by contrast, Irwin (1979: 190) construes the lines as indicating that 'the many' use *archein heautou* in this psychological sense, a construal that makes it hard to explain Callicles' initial incomprehension).

Thus the Athenian's use here of the expression 'rule themselves' would be likely to strike Plato's intended audience first in its primary, political, sense. Although self-mastery (*to kreittô heautou*) is about to become the topic of conversation, the extended context preceding the present text is the account of *paideia*, from which that topic has been quite absent (see general note on 643b1–646e2). Indeed, the description there of the 'perfect citizen' as knowing how to 'rule and be ruled (*archein te kai archesthai*) with justice' (643e6) deploys the political sense of 'ruling'; thus this sense of the term would be fresh in the reader's mind. Indeed, it is in this political sense of *archein hautôn* (self-rule) that the Athenian can here legitimately represent himself as having agreed that self-rule belongs to the good person, since it is the citizens, possessing the virtues, who engage in the collective project of ruling (*archein*) the polity. Of course it is in its extended, psychological sense that it applies to Clinias' ideal of goodness as self-mastery—and it is such self-mastery that the discussion will now turn to analysing. The ambiguity might well be deliberate on Plato's part, as it allows the Athenian to appeal to the paradigm of virtue that resonates with his interlocutors (the 'victory' model), but without endorsing it himself. On a similar tactical strategy deployed in the discussion of Tyrtaeus, see general notes on 628e2–630d1 and 643b1–646e2.

644b9–c1 'clarify further what we take it [ruling oneself] to be' Clarification is called for because the earlier discussion of self-mastery (626e–627d) did not address the phenomenon as it occurs within an individual person. Mastery of a city or of a family 'by itself' was explained in terms of the better party overmastering the worse (627a7–11, c8–d1), but no attempt was made to identify the 'better' and 'worse' forces at war within a single person. The latter analysis is the task at hand (644c–d); this 'tale of virtue' (as it is described at 645b2) identifies the better and worse parts in a person as, respectively, the golden cord of calculation and the iron cords of pleasure, pain, and anticipation.

644c4–d6

Pleasure, pain, anticipation, and calculation

Having just invoked victory over oneself as a paradigm for goodness (644b; see note on 644b6–7), the Athenian now prepares to illuminate the internal structure of such 'self-mastery'. He does so by distinguishing various items within a single person. There is first of all the distinction between the 'opposing advisors', pain and pleasure (644c4–8). Next there is the distinction between these and their respective 'anticipations' (*elpides*), fear and daring (c9–d1). Finally, there is the distinction between all the preceding items and the 'calculation' (*logismos*) that evaluates them (d1–3). The Athenian does not explicitly attribute these items as aspects to the soul (*psuchê*) but his remarks at 645e5, 646b6, and 649b9 make it clear that he thinks of them as such (cf. 632a4, 635d4, 643d1).

Parts of the soul?

How far does the picture presented here depart from the tripartite theory of the soul of *Republic* 435c–441c? Bobonich (2002: 261–4) correctly notes that the Athenian invokes not parts of a soul, but impulses issuing from a unitary agent (for responses see Gerson 2003; Kahn 2004; Laks 2005: 85–92; Lorenz 2006: 26n18; Sassi 2008: 132; and Kamtekar 2010: 141–3). However, this leaves open the question of whether the Athenian here diverges from the view that there are three fundamentally different types of human motivation or impulse—'appetitive', 'spirited', and 'rational' (for this construal of the tripartite theory of the *Republic*, see Cooper 1984). Most commentators take the Athenian to recognize only a twofold distinction: between rational and non-rational impulses (Müller 1951: 22; Rees 1957: 112–16; Graeser 1969: 102–5; Robinson 1970: 124–5, 145; Fortenbaugh 1975: 24; Schöpsdau 1994: 229–30; Bobonich 2002: 263–4; Sassi 2008: 133–8; Frede 2010: 18). The consensus is that Plato in *Laws* no longer recognizes a distinct category of 'spirited' impulses; the contrary position has been argued by Ritter 1923: 451 and Saunders 1962: 37–8, and a qualified version is defended in Meyer 2012. See also Wilburn 2013a and Renaut 2014.

644c6–7 'we each have inside ourselves two opposite and witless (*aphrone*) advisors, which we call pleasure and pain'
alternatively: 'foolish advisors'; *aphrone* indicates absence of wisdom (*phronêsis*) at 630b7, 733e6, 734c4, 734d1
Pleasure and pain have been identified as the legislator's concern (631e–632a, 636d–e) and as forces to be resisted in moderation and courage respectively (632e–636c). On an ambiguity in how these terms are used, see note on 633c9–d2. The 'pleasures and pains' here identified as internal advisors must be those 'in individual characters' (636d7), which is in keeping with the Athenian's regular invocation of 'pleasures and pains' as a general category (653a–c, 659d, 689a–b) encompassing love and hate (653c), fear and anger and passion (*erôs*, 631e–632a, 645d), yearnings (633d), and desires (*epithumiai*, 643c8). So construed, the category includes both positive and negative feelings about things that have happened (e.g. grief at a loss, joy at a birth) as well as impulses that direct us towards or away from as yet unrealized possibilities (e.g. a desire to retaliate). Here the epithet 'witless advisors' (*aphrone sumboulô*) is not applied to the 'anticipations', fear and daring, that will be introduced next (644c9–10); however, in the parallel passage at *Tim.* 69d1–4 it is applied to them.

On the relation between pleasures and pains, on the one hand, and the anticipations, on the other, see note on 644c9–d1.

644c9 'Besides these two, we have opinions (*doxas*) about the future'
This remark does not indicate whether *doxa* (belief or opinion) is distinctive of the anticipations. Compare 645e1–2, where 'opinions' are listed along with 'perceptions, memories . . . [and] cognitions (*phronêseis*)' as contrasted with 'pleasures and pains and angry feelings and passions' (645d7). See note on 645e1–3. On opinion in fear and daring, see note on 647e3–4.

644c9–d1 'whose common name is "anticipation" (*elpis*) and whose particular names are "fear", the anticipation before pain, and "daring" (*tharros*), the anticipation before the opposite'
For parallel passages about *elpis* (anticipation), see *Philb*. 32b9–c5 and 39d1–5; *Tim*. 69d1–4: cf. *Laws* 864b6–c1. While in many contexts the term *elpis* (plural: *elpides*) means 'hope' (as at *Tim*. 69d3–4 and in the story of Pandora's box in Hesiod's *Works and Days* 60–99), it has a well-attested more general use for anticipation or expectation, where the expected results may be either positive or negative; thus it encompasses both hopes and fears. The Athenian here uses *elpis* in that broader sense, hence the translation 'anticipation'. The positive anticipation invoked here, however, is not hope, but *tharros* (daring), a term that translators often render as 'confidence' (thus Bury, Taylor, Saunders, Brisson/Pradeau and Schöpsdau), but this is too weak to capture the Athenian's point. As he will soon make explicit, he considers *tharros* to be an aggressive impulse for self-assertion in the face of opposition or adversity (647a–d; note the cognate terms *tharraleos* (daring), (*thrasus*) (bold), and *thrasutês* (audacity) at 649c8–10). Hence the translation 'daring' (Pangle: boldness). *Tharros* thus performs some of the functions attributed to the spirited part of the soul (*thumos*) in the *Republic*. The adversarial context for a display of *tharros* gives a double meaning to

'daring before the opposite (*pro tou enantiou*)' (644d1), since *enantios* can also be used for an opponent. See also note on 646e4.

The significance of anticipation?

Why does the Athenian here invoke anticipations in addition to pleasures and pains? Elsewhere, he is content to use 'pleasures and pains' as the general category of non-rational motivation (see note on 644c6–7). One might suppose that the present passage offers a more precise psychological theory, on which pleasures and pains are construed more narrowly as objects of pursuit and avoidance, while daring and fear are the impulses to pursue the one and avoid the other, respectively. Thus Frede (2010: 116–17) proposes that, strictly speaking, what moves a person to act are not the pleasures and pains, but their 'anticipations' (*elpides*). Such a hypothesis, however, would be more plausible if the quartet was pleasure, pain, fear, and desire (as at *Phd.* 83b6–7, *La.* 191d6–7, *Rep.* 430a7–b1, *Symp.* 207e2–3, *Tht.* 156b4–5); but here the Athenian invokes daring (*tharros*) rather than desire. For further discussion see Meyer 2012. Rather than supposing that fear and daring are generic impulses for pursuit and avoidance in a general theory of non-rational motivation, it makes more sense to suppose that the Athenian invokes these specific impulses here because each has a role to play in the account of courage and moderation that occupies the final pages of Book 1 and for which the present passage lays the groundwork. At 646e–649c he will explain that training in courage involves cultivating daring and eliminating certain kinds of fear, while training in moderation involves cultivating a kind of fear (shame), and eliminating inappropriate daring. For further reasons to doubt the theoretical aspirations of the Athenian's comments here, see Frede 2010: 118–20. Bobonich (2002), by contrast, finds a highly developed theory (chapter 3), although not one to which the distinction between pleasures or pains and 'anticipation' is central. Naddaf (2000: 343) finds here a hedonistic theory of motivation.

644d1–2 'against all of these (*epi de pasi toutois*) . . . calculation (*logismos*) as to which of them is better or worse'

'Calculation' (the translation preferred by most scholars today) is an imperfect rendering of *logismos*, which is here contrasted with all pleasures, pains, and anticipations invoked above. The contrast recalls the distinction in the *Republic* between, on the one hand, the rational part of the soul (dubbed the *logistikon*), whose activity is *logizein* (calculation, reasoning, of which *logismos* is the cognate noun—*Rep*. 439d–441c), and on the other hand, the non-rational 'spirited' and appetitive parts, which are characterized as *alogiston* (439d, 441c, 604d). On what *logismos* amounts to in the *Republic*, see Moss 2008, who argues that it involves figuring out how things really are, as opposed to how they immediately appear, and may appeal to a wide range of complex considerations. 'Calculation' may be a misleading rendering insofar as it may seem to imply that only quantitative considerations are involved in *logismos*; 'reasoning' is better in this respect, but its natural referent in English is the process of arriving at a verdict, rather than the verdict itself (and the verdict seems to be at least part—or maybe even all—of what the Athenian has in mind as *logismos* in the present context; it is a *dogma*, 644d3). Similar problems arise for 'reason' as a translation, since idiomatic use restricts this term to the reasons or explanations supporting a verdict. 'Reason' has the further disadvantage that, among scholars of Plato today, it tends to be used for a part or faculty of the psyche (explicitly so on the translation of Brisson/Pradeau), whereas the Athenian is here talking about an activity of the psyche (*logismos* rather than the *logistikon*). The translation 'judgement' (Taylor, des Places) allows *logismos* to be a verdict, but depending on how one construes the relationship of belief to judgement, the term 'judgement' may be too weak to yield a contrast with the 'anticipations' (*elpides*), which were described two sentences earlier as 'opinions about the future' (644c9).

The 'calculations' in question need not be restricted to quantitative comparison, e.g. of short- and long-term pleasures, as Mouracade (2005: 83–4) proposes. Bobonich construes *logismos* as 'practical deliberation' that delivers 'all things considered' judgements about what is 'good or bad for the person in the long run' (Bobonich 2002: 263–7 and passim ch. 3). Wilburn (2012) proposes that *logismos* is a commitment to general principles of rational conduct, distinct from any practical deliberations. However, all the Athenian says here to characterize *logismos* is that it is an assessment of which of the pleasures, pains, and anticipations in us is 'better or worse' (644d2). This suffices for his immediate purpose, which is to elucidate the notion of ruling oneself (644b7), construed as self-mastery (cf. 645b2–3): the person engaged in a struggle to be master of himself (*kreittôn hautou*) is struggling to resist feelings of attraction of which he does not approve. We need not suppose that this is intended as an exhaustive characterization of *logismos*, but we are also given no further indication that a complete theoretical account is intended or presupposed.

644d2–3 'When it [calculation] becomes the common view (*dogma*) of a city, it is called "law"'

more literally: 'which (*hos*), when it becomes the common view . . .' It is implied here that 'calculation' (*logismos*) is a judgement or view (*dogma*); so it is not (simply) a process of reasoning, and certainly not a *faculty* of reasoning (see note on 644d1–2). The claim that law is the common view of the city is repeated at 645a2 (cf. 645a4–5) and is made again in slightly different language at 645b6–8 and 659d1–4. In the latter passages it is not *logismos*, but *logos* that expresses the common view. On the relation between *logismos* and *logos*, see note on 645b4–5. See also Book 4, 713e–714a, where 'law' (*nomos*) is invoked as the name for regulation by reason (*nous*). On *logos* as law, see Moss 2014: 199.

644d4–6 'I am barely able to follow you'

Exactly what part of the preceding exposition poses the difficulty is unclear. The Athenian has invoked (i) pleasures and pains, (ii) anticipations, and (iii) 'calculations', and (iv) he has connected the latter to law. Clinias has already assented to (i) at 644c8; (ii) does not seem particularly arcane; and even (iii) is intelligible as one of the forces at play in internal conflict. So it may only be (iv) that poses the difficulty.

644d7–645c8

The divine puppets

To illuminate the psychological forces just distinguished (644c–d), and fulfil his promise (644b) to explain the nature of 'ruling oneself', the Athenian now invokes the figure of a 'divine puppet' pulled by two different kinds of cords: those of 'calculation' on the one hand (the 'golden cord'), and those involving pleasure and pain and anticipation on the other (the 'iron cords'). Our task in life is to live according to the golden cord, and ruling oneself is to be understood as the victory of that golden cord in its struggle against opposing iron cords. On the difference between such self-mastery and the conception of virtue implied in the account of education at 643b–644b and 653a–c, see notes on 643b1–646e2 and on 645a1.

644d7–8 'Consider each of us, living beings that we are, to be a divine puppet (*thauma . . . theion*)'
Translation following England, with Kurke 2013: 124. Alternatively: 'consider each of us living creatures as . . . ' (Saunders, Pangle). The Athenian's point is not that the puppet model holds for all living creatures, but that it holds for us, even though we are living creatures.

This is the 'image' (*eikôn*) promised by the Athenian at 644c1. 'Puppet' renders *thauma* (literally 'marvel' or 'wonder'). In calling human beings puppets, Frede (2010: 116) points out, the Athenian is not intending to imply that that we are controlled from without, but rather to emphasize the complexity of our inner workings (like the marvel of a wind-up toy to a small child); see also Kurke 2013: 125–6. The image of a human being as a puppet (*thauma*) of the gods is invoked again in Book 7, 804b. On the significance of the image, see Laks 2005: 46–7.

644d8–9 'whether constituted as . . . the gods' plaything (*paignion*) or for a serious purpose (*spoudêi tini*)'
The contrast between the serious (*spoudaion*) and the playful is a motif throughout the *Laws* (636c, 643b, 647d, 659e, 667e, 673e, 732d), treated explicitly in Book 7 (803c–804b, 806d–808c), where humans are again called 'playthings' (*paignion*) of the gods (803c4–5). See note on 635b5 and Jouët-Pastré 2006.

644e1–2 'these various experiences (*pathê*) in us . . . '
The experiences (*pathê*) in question are those just enumerated by the Athenian at 644c6–d3. While the term *pathos* (pl. *pathê*) is often translated as 'emotion' (Saunders; Annas 1999: 142) or 'passion' (Pangle), its scope here is broad enough to include not only the pleasure, pain, and anticipations invoked at 644c6–d1, but also instances of the 'calculation' (*logismos*) introduced at 644d1–2. Megillus has just referred to his own incomprehension as a *pathos* at 644d6 ('that's what I'm feeling too'). Compare the use of *pathêmata* in the parallel text at *Tim.* 69d1–4.

644e2–3 'are like cords or strings that tug at (*spôsin*) us and oppose each other (*enantiai ousai*). They pull against each other (*allêlais anthelkousin*) towards opposing actions (*ep' enantias praxeis*) across the field where virtue is marked off from vice . . . '
In likening the pleasures, pains, anticipations, and calculations of 644c–d to 'cords or strings that tug at us' the Athenian indicates that each of them is, or involves, an impulse that moves the agent to act (thus Bobonich 2002: 261–4). The tug-of-war in which the strings 'pull against each other towards opposing actions' models the kind of internal struggle Clinias has invoked as the universal human condition at 626d–e. The present 'image' (644c1) of the puppet is explicitly intended by the Athenian as an elucidation of the self-mastery that constitutes victory in such a struggle (626e; see note on 644b6–7). Demarcating the field of struggle as 'where virtue is marked off from vice' indicates that the internal struggles of interest to the Athenian are cases in which a person is torn between a virtuous

action and its vicious alternative. On alternative construals of the struggle, see note on 645a1.

644e4–5 'our account (*logos*) singles out one of these pulls (*helxeôn*) and says that each of us must follow it and pull against the other cords (*anthelkein tois allois neurois*), never loosening our grip on it' alternatively: 'reason (*logos*) says . . . ' (Annas 1999: 142); against the translation of *logos* as 'reason', see Moss 2014

The discussion between the three interlocutors has consistently been referred to as a *logos*, as at 633a4; the term is also used for an argument or thesis as at 628e2 and 652a5, and for an evaluative judgement at 653b4–5. The account (*logos*) in the present context extends through ' . . . victorious over the others' at 645b1; it identifies self-mastery as the victory of the golden cord over the iron cords and is presumably the 'tale of virtue' (*muthos aretês*) of 645b2, which elaborates the 'image' (*eikôn*) promised at 644c1. 'Pulls' translates *helxeôn* (genitive plural of *helxis*, cognate with the verb *anthelkei'* (pull against) used at 644e3, e6). The Athenian uses it as a general term for all the 'experiences' (*pathê*) of 644e1–2 (see note ad loc) that 'pull against each other towards opposing actions (*allêlais anthelkousin . . . ep' enantias praxeis*)' (644e2–6). It is here used equivalently with the 'cords or strings' of 644e2.

645a1 'the sacred and golden guidance (*agôgên*) of calculation (*logismou*)'

'Guidance' translates *agôgê*, which is here used by the Athenian to indicate an instance of the 'forces' (*helxeis*) that have just been said to 'pull against' (*anthelkein*) each other (644e3, 6). The term can also refer to education or training, and is used in this way by the Athenian at 659d2 and 819a5; so too *Stsm.* 274b1 and *EN* 1179b31; it is used for physical training at *Laws* 673a9. Later writers typically refer to the Spartan educational system as an *agôgê* (Plutarch, *Agesilaus* 1.1.7–8, *Phocion* 20.4.2–5.1; Athenaeus, *Deipnosophistai* 4.19.41–4, 11.66.13–15). However, Plato also uses the term to refer to psychological impulses or inclination, as he does in *Republic* in the case of the 'conflicting impulse' (*enantias . . . agôgês*) that marks the divided soul (604b3–4), and in *Phaedrus* in the case of the forceful drive of *erôs* (238c1–4). In the present context, the Athenian indicates that the 'golden *agôgê* of calculation' is 'one of these pulls' (e5), since the antecedent of *tautên* (645a1) is *miai . . . tôn helxeôn* (644e4–5).

England's proposal that the 'golden *agôgê* of calculation' in the present passage is the education (*paideia*) invoked at 659d2 is at odds with the Athenian's clear indication here that 'calculation'—no less than pleasure, pain, and anticipation—is one of the 'experiences' likened to 'cords and strings' (644e2) and construed as 'pulls' (*helxeis*, 644e5). Education, by contrast, is a matter of shaping a person's 'pleasures and pains' to agree with a correct *logos* (653a–c, 659d). Insofar as education is a causal process that redirects pleasures and pains, the agent of that process is not calculation, but teachers, trainers, etc. And insofar as education is the trained condition resulting from that process, there is agreement rather than conflict between calculation and the pleasures and pains. On neither alternative can calculation be a party to the sort of tug-of-war depicted in the figure of the puppets.

A number of recent commentators have denied that *logismos* is a party to that tug-of-war. Frede (2010: 217–20) proposes that, strictly speaking, only the iron strings actually pull against each other, while *logismos* plays the very different role of giving them their direction and content. Annas (1999: 142–4) concludes that the 'victory' of the golden string over the iron ones is the condition in which a person's pleasures, pains, desires, etc. are shaped by *logismos*, and similarly Jouët-Pastré 2006: 42. Wilburn (2012: 32–3) proposes that the 'guidance' provided by *logismos* is a general commitment to follow certain rational principles but does not pull an agent towards specific actions.

Such interpretations are at odds with the most natural reading of 644e1–645b1, and appear to be motivated by the assumption that the 'victory' of the golden over the iron cords at 645a–b is the same condition as that of the educated person at 653a–c, whose pleasures and pains agree (*sumphônein*) rather than conflict with *logos*.

However, while the Athenian clearly takes such internal agreement to be a feature of virtue (653a–c)—indeed, he has identified agreement as a different, and better, achievement than the victory over oneself (also called self-mastery) that Clinias has invoked at 626e—he explicitly offers the image of the puppets to elucidate Clinias' and Megillus' very different conception of virtue as self-mastery (644b6–c2; see note on 644b6–7). While the Athenian does not in the end accept his interlocutors' identification of virtue with self-mastery, the point of the present passage is to elucidate what is involved in such self-mastery or victory over oneself. In the divine puppet, the golden *agôgê* of *logismos* is the victorious party in such a conflict. Thus it must pull against, rather than inform, the iron pulls. (On the Athenian's reasons for continuing to elucidate his opponent's victory model of virtue, even after expositing its deficiencies, see general note on 643b1–646e2.)

645a2 'also called (*epikaloumenên*) the city's common law'
A reference back to 644d2–3. Nightingale (1999: 104) takes *epikaloumenên* to be middle rather than passive, and proposes the alternative translation: 'which summons as an ally the common law of the city'. But 644d2–3 supports the present translation, which takes the participle to be passive.

645a2–3 'The other pulls are hard as iron'
more literally: 'the others are hard (*sklêras*) and iron (*sidêras*)'
The subsequent comment that these 'resemble all kinds of different material' (literally: 'resemble all variety of things'—*pantodapois eidesin homoias*, 645a3–4) allows that their shared 'iron' status might not be a matter of having the same material composition. Thus Brisson/Pradeau may go too far in finding here an allusion to the myth of the metals in *Rep*. 414b–415c. The adjective *sidêras* here functions as a synonym to *sklêras* (hard). Thus Saunders translates the phrase 'tough and inflexible'.

645a6 'gentle (*praiou*) rather than violent (*biaiou*)'

This characterization of calculation (*logismos*) continues the thematic opposition between persuasion, on the one hand, and force or violence (*bia*) on the other (see notes on 629a2, 629d2, 632b7–8). Placing *logismos* and law in the gentle and persuasive camp highlights the challenge of achieving self-mastery, which involves having calculation's gentle 'guidance' (*agôgê* (645a7), repeating the term from 645a1) overcome the stronger pull of the iron cords. On the nature of that guidance, see note on 645a1. On law as persuasive, see note on 632b7–8.

645a6–7 'so its guidance requires helpers (*hupêretôn*) if our golden element (*genos*) is to be victorious over the others'
The plural in 'helpers' fits the metaphor of the tug-of-war at 644e2–4, where multiple parties can pull on either side. The nature of the helpers or of the assistance required is not elaborated on here, although the repeated injunction in the preceding lines to 'follow' (*sunepomenon*, 644e5) the pull of *logismos* and 'pitch in with it' (*sullambanein*, 645a5), together with the explanatory *gar* at a5, mark them as calls to the requisite assistance; thus 'each of us' (*hekaston*, 644e6) might be the helpers. Alternatively, the notion of 'helping' or 'assisting' calculation recalls the doctrine of the *Republic*, that the spirited part of the soul (*thumos*) functions as an ally (*summachos*) of the *logistikon* against the appetites (*Rep.* 441e–442b). While the Athenian does not here avail himself of the tripartite psychology of the *Republic* (on which see general note on 644c4–d6), his treatment of the 'anticipations', fear and daring, at 646e–647a invokes many features of *thumos* from the *Republic*—in particular the task of resisting pleasures and pains. Thus the *tharros* that enables a warrior to resist the pains and fears of battle, and the sense of shame (*aidôs*) that enables the just citizen to resist the temptations of illicit pleasures, are candidates for the 'assistants' mentioned here (see Meyer 2012: 358–60 and note on 644c9–d1). These commendable instances of fear and daring play a role in the training process that aims at inculcating moderation and courage respectively, which the Athenian has classified under the general

heading of education (*paideia*) (see 642a). He will later characterize education as a 'pulling' (*holkê*) and 'guidance' (*agôgê*) (659d2); thus Schöpsdau and Brisson/Pradeau (2007: 32–3) propose that it provides the requisite assistance (although see note on 645a1). More speculative hypotheses about the 'helpers' include the idea that it involves the psychological activity of intention or decision (Bobonich 2002: 273–82) and the proposal by Wilburn (2012) that it is deliberation implementing general principles espoused by *logismos*. Nightingale (1999: 104), Klosko (2006: 221), and Renaut (2014: 304) propose that the law is the helper (see note on 645a2).

Conclusions about virtue and self-mastery

645b1–2 'Here is how (*kai houtô dê*) we may vindicate the tale of virtue (*muthos aretês*) that likens us to puppets'
more literally: 'In this way the tale of virtue that says we are puppets would be preserved (*sesôsmenos an eiê*)'
alternatively: 'the tale . . . would achieve its point' (Brisson/Pradeau).
The 'tale of virtue that likens us to puppets' is the 'illustrat[ion] by means of an image' promised at 644c1 and 'our account' (*logos*) at 644e5. A *logos* or *muthos* is 'vindicated' or 'preserved' (*sesôsmenos*) when it can survive objections (as at *Tht*. 164a, 167d; *Rep*. 395b). On the range of the expression, see England ad loc and Brisson 1982: 71–5. The present 'tale' might require vindication because of the incomprehension expressed by the interlocutors at 644d4–6. The vindication offered by the Athenian is given in the lines that follow (645b2–c4), which list the salutary morals to be drawn from the tale. On this reading, the emphatic 'this is how' (*kai houtô dê*, 645b1) is forward looking, and is resumed, by the *houtô kai* in b8. On Saunders' reading ('If we do give our help'), *houtô* in 645b1 refers to the preceding lines.

645b2–5 'It makes clearer, in a way, what is meant by "self-mastery" and "self-defeat", as well as the manner in which a city and an individual person ought to live'

more literally: 'that is (*kai*), it would become clearer in a way what is meant by "self-mastery" . . . as well as that a city and an individual person ought to live'
The translation takes *kai . . . phaneron an gignoito* (b2–3) to be epexegetic of *sesôsmenos an eiê* (b2). The Athenian's point is that we can demonstrate the usefulness of the puppet metaphor by showing how it sheds light on what is involved in self-mastery (a question raised at 644b9–c1; see note on 644b6–7), as well as on the broader question of how we should live.

645b4–5 'a person must grasp within himself the true account (*ton men logon alêthê labonta*) concerning these pulls (*peri tôn helxeôn toutôn*) and live in accordance with (*hepomenon*) it'
alternatively: ' . . . and live following (*hepomenon*) it'
In using the locution 'grasp the account' (*logon lambanein*), the Athenian is employing the vocabulary of the 'agreement' model of virtue that he will articulate at the beginning of Book 2 (see note on 653b3–4). What is the relationship between the *logos* invoked here (and at 653b4–5) and the *logismos* ('calculation') invoked at 644d2 and identified as the golden cord in the puppet? The *logos* is here described as concerned with 'these pulls' (*helxeôn toutôn*, 645b5); that is, about the pleasures, pains, etc. invoked at 644c–d. Thus the logos may be the evaluative judgement ascribed to *logismos* in that earlier context ('which of the [pleasures, pains, and anticipations] is better or worse', 644d2). So construed, the *logos* (account) mentioned here would be an instance of *logismos* (calculation). On the distinction between grasping (*lambanein*) and following (*hepomenon*) the true *logos*, see Moss 2014: 199–200; on *logos* v. *logismos* see also note on 644d2–3.

Note that there are two different ways in which a person might 'live his life in accordance with' a true *logos*/*logismos*: (1) by the victory of one's *logismos* in a struggle against any 'pulls' that it judges to be inappropriate—as at 644e4–645b2; (2) by the absence of any 'pulls' that *logismos* disapproves of—as in the account of virtue articulated at 653a–c. Way (1) would amount to the 'victory over self' that Clinias and Megillus conceive of as virtue. Way (2) would conform to the 'agreement' paradigm for virtue endorsed by the Athenian. On these two models for virtue, see note on 643b1–646e2. As at 644b6–7 (see note ad loc), the Athenian succeeds in articulating his message in a form that both he and his interlocutors can endorse, even in the face of their differing conceptions of virtue.

645b6–8 'a city, having received this account (*logon*) from a god or from the person who understands these matters, must establish it as law'

Assuming that *logos* here is an instance of *logismos* (see note on 645b4–5), the Athenian here applies the point he made at 644d2–3 that the *logismos* ('calculation') internal to a person is an expression of law (*nomos*); on law as an expression of the divine, see 713e–714a and note on 644d2–3.

645b8–c1 'In addition (*houtô kai*), the tale gives us a more lucid articulation (*saphesteron . . . diêrthrômenon*) of virtue and vice'

alternatively: 'it gives us a more evident [alt: clearer] distinction between virtue and vice'

Houtô kai (b8) resumes the *houtô dê* of 645b1, indicating that the Athenian here continues his list of the salutary morals that can be drawn from the puppet metaphor. On what is *saphes* [clear, obvious, evident], see note on 661e3–4; the Athenian's language leaves it ambiguous whether what is rendered more lucid (*saphesteron*) is (i) the distinction between virtue and vice or (ii) the articulation or composition intrinsic to virtue and vice alike. Clinias and Megillus would incline to accept (i), since they think that the distinction between self-mastery and self-defeat is the distinction between virtue and vice (644b). The Athenian, however, rejects such a conception (see notes on 643b1–646e2 and 644b6–7), and (ii) is perfectly adequate to capture his present point: the internal components involved in self-mastery are equally involved in the superior condition that the Athenian identifies as virtue.

645c2–4 'education and . . . the drinking party'
The present discussion is part of the account of education (*paideia*) begun at 643b, which has been proposed as the proper context to demonstrate the value of the institution of drinking parties (642a). Education will be defined more precisely in Book 2 at 653a–c.

645c7–8 'whatever in our present enterprise is worth the effort'
The patience Clinias professed at 642d–e appears to be wearing thin, perhaps because, as the next exchange makes clear (645d1–3), he has no idea what bearing any of the preceding discussion has on the issue of drinking parties.

645d1–646e2

Drunkenness and self-mastery

The Athenian now brings to bear on the topic of drunkenness his preceding discussion of self-mastery and the divine puppets (644c–645c): the iron cords are strengthened by drink, and the golden weakened, with a resulting loss of self-mastery (645d–646a). This result is, however, only a temporary debility that is instrumental to a longer-term benefit, just as vigorous exercise or medical treatment weakens a body in the short term but benefits it in the long run (646b–e). This sets the stage for the Athenian to argue in the next section (646e–650b) that the longer-term benefit of properly supervised drunkenness is the cultivation of moderation.

645d6–8 'Doesn't drinking wine make our pleasures and pains, our angry feelings (*thumous*), and our passions (*erôtas*) more intense?'
If this remark is an application of the puppet analogy (as indicated by 645d1–2), the intensified items must figure among the puppet's 'iron cords' (645a2–3), originally enumerated as 'pleasures and pains' and their anticipations at 644c6–d1. See also general note on 645d1–646e2.

645e1–3 'perceptions, memories, opinions (*doxas*) and cognitions, (*phronêseis*) . . . completely abandon a person who is full of drink' An ascending order of cognitive activities, as at *Tim.* 37a–c; cf. *Tim.* 77b, *Philb.* 34a–c, 38b; for a similar use of *phronêsis* in the plural as a term for episodes of mental activity, see *Tim.* 90b7. On the relation between true opinions and *phronêsis*, see 653a7–9 and note on 632c5.

In the context of the puppet metaphor immediately preceding the present passage (645d1–2), we must understand the present lines to describe a weakening (or incapacitation) of the 'golden cord'. However, it is difficult to construe the listed cognitive states as being characteristic of the golden cord exclusively. For example, the 'anticipations' that figure among the iron cords are explicitly identified as 'opinions about the future' (644c9). And it would be odd if the iron cords did not involve at least sense perception or some kind of representation of content, to the extent that they have intentional objects (cf. the 'pictures in the soul' of *Philb.* 39a–b); see Bobonich 2002: 295–330 and 2010; Lorenz 2006: 95–110; Sassi 2008: 131–3; and Kamtekar 2010: 134–40 for different proposals about how they have content. Thus the Athenian is not entitled to conclude (in the absence of further argument) that a general loss of cognition tips the balance in favour of the iron cords. See Bobonich 2002: 270 for a proposal about how the two effects listed here might interact to yield a loss of self-control. While the Athenian's emphasis here on the drinker's cognitions fits awkwardly with the psychology illustrated by the puppet metaphor (644d–645c), it fits better with the account of education sketched at 643b–644b, on which education gives content and direction to a person's pleasures, desires, etc. A general impairment of cognition would undo this educational effect. (On the different paradigms for virtue implied in these two discussions, see notes on 626e2–3 and 643b1–646e2.)

645e5–6 'his soul returns to the same condition as when he was a young child'

This is the uneducated juvenile condition described at the beginning of Book 2, when a child's pleasures and pains, desires, etc. have not yet been shaped and given their content by musical training (653a–654a) and a young person lacks both *phronêsis* and 'stable correct opinion' (653a), which are two of the items just mentioned as absent in drunkenness. While here the Athenian is about to describe this condition as a lack of 'self-control' (*enkrateia*, 645e8), in Book 2 he describes it as a lack of order (*taxis*). On that juvenile state, see note on 653d7–8. On the locution *enkrateia*, see note on 626e4.

645e8 'least in control (*enkratês*) of himself'
'In control of himself' (*enkratês*) here is used as a synonym for 'master of himself' (*kreittôn hautou* at 626e8) and 'victorious over oneself' at 626e2. See notes on 626e4, 645e5–6, and on 644b6–7.

646a2 'Don't we affirm that this sort of person is the worst (*ponêrotatos*)?'
Inability to control (or master) oneself has been identified as 'most shameful (*aischiston*) and wretched (*kakiston*)' at 626e4 and the person in that condition is classifed as bad (*kakos*) at 644b7. On the different question of whether the corresponding self-control is best (cf. 628c–d), see note on 644b6–7.

646a10 'only a moment ago'—at 641d
The Athenian has now completed the account of *paideia*, which he heralded at 642a (and 643a) as a lengthy but necessary preamble to his explanation of the benefits of drinking parties. He is thus in a position to return to the former question.

646b2 'the two of you have emphatically declared your willingness to listen'—at 642b–e

646b10–c1 'if someone willingly (*hekôn*) brought such things upon himself'

The thesis that no one willingly or voluntarily (*hekôn*) brings bad things upon himself is a central theme in Plato, and core to the so-called 'Socratic Paradox' that 'no one does wrong willingly' (*Protag.* 345e, 358c–d, 358e; *Gorg.* 509e; *Tim.* 86e; *Laws* 731c, 734b, 860d–e); for discussion see Santas 1964; O'Brien 1967; Saunders 1968; and Segvic 2000.

646d1 'Precisely (*kallista*)'
A superlative and elliptical version of *kalôs legeis*, which generally indicates agreement with the preceding statement ('you are right') rather than an aesthetic or ethical assessment of the speaker's words (cf. *Philb.* 31d1, *Tht.* 148a5). Clinias here gives his strong endorsement to the Athenian's preceding statement. Pangle's 'that's a very noble (*kalon*) way of putting it' wrongly implies that the ethical dimensions of the *kalon* are operative here (as they are, for instance, at 630c7, 637e5, 646e11, 654c4–d3). On the range of the *kalon*, see note on 630c7.

V
DRINKING PARTIES CULTIVATE MODERATION

646e3–650b10

We are now told that drunkenness, precisely because it undermines self-mastery, thereby provides an opportunity to battle against 'pleasures and desires' (647d4–5). Indeed, properly supervised drunkenness is a forum in which to cultivate resistance to pleasures and desires, just as the battlefield is a venue for cultivating resistance to fears and pains. These claims develop further the elaborate analogy between courage and moderation originally deployed at 632e–636c, where the paradigm for virtue is victory over self in internal conflict. Here, however, the Athenian characterizes the virtuous condition to be cultivated in terms that fit the alternative paradigm for virtue that is implicit in the account of education at 643b–644b and that will explicitly inform the discussion of virtue in Book 2 (see notes on 626e2–3 and 647b9–c1 and general note on 643b1–646e2). On this new paradigm, virtue is a matter of having appropriately directed pleasures, pains, desires, fears, and so forth (the 'agreement model') rather than being victorious over conflicting internal impulses. On an ambiguity that masks the transition to the 'agreement' model of virtue, see note on 647c3–4.

The Athenian begins by identifying a variety of fear (shame) and of daring (shamelessness) that apply to social contexts (646e–647c). He then argues (on analogy with the case of courage) that shame is to be cultivated by exposure to shamelessness and training against it (647c–d). Drunkenness, he proposes, simulates the conditions in which we are prone to shamelessness (647e–649d), which makes it a valuable method for both testing and training moderation (649d–650b).

646e3–647c2

Varieties of fear and daring

The Athenian begins by invoking the two 'anticipations', fear and 'daring' (*tharros*), identified earlier in the puppet psychology of 644c–645c. He points out that there are appropriate and inappropriate versions of each. While the pair are ordinarily construed as applying to military contexts, where the coward is afraid and the courageous soldier is daring, they have an important application in social contexts, where the just and moderate person has an appropriate fear (a sense of shame) and the shameless person is inappropriately daring. Thus, while a limited kind of daring should be cultivated for military purposes, a far more important trait for the legislator to cultivate in citizens is a sense of shame.

646e4 'two roughly opposing (*enantia*) kinds of fear'
These are the fear involved in cowardice and the sense of shame (*aidôs*) involved in just and moderate behaviour. What the Athenian

means by calling them 'opposing' (*enantia*) is unclear. Perhaps it is that the former kind motivates a person to flee the enemy and the pains of battle, while the latter makes one stand one's ground. Compare the sense of *enantios* at 647a4–5 (see note on 647a4–6 and on 649a4–6).

646e11 'something that is ignoble'
more literally: 'something that is not admirable (*ti tôn mê kalôn*)'
On the translation of *kalon*, see note on 630c7.

647a4–6 'The latter opposes (*enantios*) not only pains and other fears but also the most prevalent and strongest pleasures'
Shame, so conceived, resists opposing impulses in the domains of both courage and moderation (cf. 633c–636c). On an ambiguity in the notion of resistance, see note on 647c3–4.

647a10–b1 'the daring (*tharros*) that is opposed (*enantion*) to it . . . being . . . the greatest evil in private or public life'
This is the daring or brazenness involved in transgressing social norms, as at 647c7–d8; cf. 641c2–7, 649d4–650a5.

647b3–5 'nothing is more effective [sc. than shame] . . . at securing victory and safety in war itself'
Even in the military context, the fear touted by the Athenian outperforms the daring (*tharros*) venerated in the military ethic of the Dorians.

647b9–c1 'So each of us needs to become both fearless and afraid'
As at 648b8 and 649c4, the courageous person is presented as 'fearless' (*aphobos*) instead of *tharraleos* or *thrasus* (bold, daring, 649c8–10). The natural contrast between fear and daring might make the substitution seem a mere stylistic variation. However, in characterizing the courageous person as lacking fear, rather than as victorious in the struggle against the fears in question, the Athenian

conforms to the 'agreement' model for virtue implied in the account of education at 643b–644b, rather than the 'victory' model that informs his interlocutors' conception of virtue. For the analogous point about resistance to pleasures, see note on 647c8–10. On the two models for virtue see note on 643b1–646e2.

647c1 'for the reasons we have explained in the two cases'
more literally: 'for the sake of what (*hôn d' hekateron heneka*) we have explained in each case'
The expression 'for the sake of' (*heneka* + gen.) is familiar teleological language, used to characterize the legislator's activity: just as military matters are to be regulated 'for the sake of' peace, not vice versa (628d8–e1), fearlessness is not an end in itself, to be cultivated in the citizens as an ultimate goal; rather, it has a point or goal (peace) that both limits and gives the point to its pursuit. And even fear has a point, or goal, the Athenian insists, when it fulfils an important social function.

647c3–d8

Cultivating shame by exposure to shamelessness

The Athenian now applies the preceding remarks about shame and shamelessness (646e–647c) to his earlier contention that cultivating moderation requires exposure to pleasures (634a–635d): just as cultivating courage requires exposure to cowardly feelings and practice in fighting against them, cultivating moderation requires exposure to 'shamelessness' and practice at battling against it (647c–d).

647c3–4 'make someone unafraid of various things . . . by exposing him to fear (*eis phobon*)'
Note that the disposition to be cultivated is a kind of fearlessness (*aphobia*; see note on 647b9–c1), not simply the strength to resist the pull of the fears that one feels. We may thus understand as follows

how exposing a person to fear serves to cultivate such a disposition. The trainee is:

(i) led into fearful (fear-provoking) situations, and as a result
(ii) experiences feelings of fear, and
(iii) struggles to resist acting on those feelings.

Repeated success at (i)–(iii) eventually cultivates in the trainee:

(iv) a disposition to not experience feelings of fear in those fearful situations.

The trainee who engages in (iii) will be fighting against 'fears and pains' in the way that Clinias and Megillus take to be central to courage at 633b–e (see note on 633e1–2); thus he will experience the internal conflict modelled by the divine puppets at 644d–645c. By contrast, the courageous person who has achieved (iv) will not experience such internal struggle when placed in situations like (i). The virtue achieved in (iv) fits the Athenian's paradigm of 'agreement' rather than Clinias' paradigm of 'victory over oneself'. The latter occurs at stage (iii) and is thus only an intermediary stage on the way to the agreement in the soul that the Athenian takes to be essential to virtue. On those two paradigms for virtue, see note on 643b1–646e2. Later it will become clear that the 'fears' into which the trainee is led are ambiguous between the fear-provoking situations in (i) and the fearful feelings they provoke in (ii). Thus it will be intelligible to say that a person displays courage by being exposed to 'fears' of type (i) and not experiencing fears of type (ii) when he is so exposed. See notes on 648b7–8, 649c4, and 649c8–10.

647c4 'in a controlled manner (*meta nomou*)'
literally: 'with law'
As England notes, *meta nomou* here is parallel to the characterization of the requisite fear as *meta dikês* in the next line (647c7–8, translated as 'in a just manner') as well as with 'by dint of argument' (*meta logou*) in 647d6.

647c7–8 'justly afraid'
more literally: 'afraid with justice (*meta dikês*)'
The expression *meta dikês* (parallel to *meta nomou* in 647c4) is used again to characterize fear at 671d2 (translated as 'fear with justice'), and it recalls the goal of education at 643b–644b, which is to cultivate citizens who 'know how to rule and be ruled with justice' (643e6). The fear to be cultivated is shame. See note on 647c4.

647c8–10 'To make him victorious in the fight against his pleasures . . . we . . . throw him into the ring with shamelessness and make him wrestle against it'
The shamelessness (*anaischuntia*) that the trainee is made to battle against is manifest in the 'many pleasures and desires that urge him to commit shameless and unjust actions' (d4–5). On analogy with training to resist fears (which cultivates fearlessness—see note on 647c3–4), the present training has the goal of cultivating a disposition in which one is free of shamelessness; that is, one does not experience such pleasures and desires in the situations that naturally provoke them. At 649d–e we are given a sketch of the situations that tend to provoke such feelings in the untrained; the Athenian's point will be that drunkenness simulates those situations.

647c10–d1 'face off against the cowardice within him and defeat it'
'Cowardice' (*deilia*) is often a term for a character trait, but here it is used for a cowardly impulse or feeling (i.e. fear).

647d3 'even halfway towards virtue'
An indication that there can be different stages of achievement on the way to the perfection in moderation (*sôphrôn . . . teleôs*, d4) or courage (*teleon . . . pros andreian*, d1), which is the goal of this training regime. The people who have developed the sort of 'victory over self' praised by Clinias at 626e might be 'halfway' towards virtue, while the complete or perfect virtue of interest to the Athenian would belong to those whose feelings have been trained to 'agree'

(*sumphônein*) with their rational judgements. On the difference between victory and agreement as paradigms for virtue, see note on 626e2–3 and general note on 643b1–646e2.

647d6–7 'both in play and in earnest (*en te paidiais kai en spoudais*)'
A reflection of the claim, implicit in the account of education at 643b–644b, that there is a kind of 'play' or 'recreation' (*paidia*) that cultivates virtue. We are about to be told that drinking parties (explicitly called *paidia* at 635b5, 666b5, and 671e6) provide a forum for battling against shamefulness (i.e. for cultivating moderation). In Book 2 we will be told that regular performance of choral song and dance (also a kind of *paidia*—673d4) is the means by which virtue is to be cultivated. On the distinction between play and seriousness (*spoudê*, here translated as 'in earnest'), see note on 635b5.

647e1–650b10

Wine as a drug to induce shamelessness

Having insisted that cultivating courage and moderation requires exposure to the sorts of fears and desires that a person must learn to resist, the Athenian now raises the possibility of using a drug to stimulate such feelings. A drug that stimulated fear would provide a safe and convenient way to train for courage, with many advantages over conventional methods (647e–648e). While there is no such drug, we do have wine to stimulate the sorts of shamelessness that one must struggle against in order to cultivate moderation (649a–d). Thus wine provides a safe and convenient alternative to conventional training methods—since those conventional methods involve situations in which the 'trainee' is in a position to do serious harm to his fellow citizens (649d–650b).

647e1–2 'has any god given humans a potion (*pharmakon*) for fear?'

This hypothetical potion induces the fears that one must struggle against when training for courage, just as wine (traditionally described as a gift from the god Dionysus—672a5) induces the feelings of fearlessness (shamelessness) to be battled against in training for moderation.

647e3–4 'the more one comes to suppose (*nomizein*) . . . that he has fallen into misfortune'
The Athenian here construes fear much more broadly than as a response to bodily danger, expanding it to include all the feelings responding to apparent misfortune (*dustuchia*) that are identified as the legislator's concern at 632a4–7. This broad characterization of the fear to be combated suggests that the coordinate 'daring' to be combated arises in response to good fortune or prosperity (*eutuchia*; cf. 632a5). See note on 649d4–7. Note that fear, which is classified as an opinion (*doxa*) at 644c9–d1, is here said to involve thinking (*nomizein*) that one is unfortunate. On the connection between feelings of pleasure and judgements that one is doing well, see 657c5–6.

648a4–5 'where in the world might one find such a drink . . . ?'
more literally: 'which beverage found among humans should we say is of this sort?'

648a6–7 'for inculcating courage (*pros andreian*)'
more literally: 'towards courage'
The phrase also occurs in 647d1 (*teleon . . . pros andreian*), where it is translated as 'perfect in courage'.

648b1–2 'a test (*basanon*) for courage and cowardice'
A slight change of focus here, from training (the subject of discussion above) to testing. The testing function will be emphasized below, 649d–650b, but the training function will reclaim the Athenian's attention at the start of Book 2. The shift of focus is understandable, since the circumstances in which one trains to develop a trait

(whether courage, moderation, or any other skill) also reveal the trainee's level of proficiency in that endeavour. Indeed, the diagnostic function will be bound up with the training function as a feedback mechanism and as a motivation for improvement, as indicated by 648b7–c5 and 648d5–e1. See note on 650b7–8.

648b7–8 'lead your citizens into fears (*eis tous phobous*) and test (*elenchôn*) their reactions (*en tois pathêmasin*)'
The Athenian indicates, in the very next clause, that the goal of such exposure is to cultivate fearlessness ('so that . . . you would compel them to become fearless', b8–c1; see note on 647b8–c5). At 649c4, that goal is literally described as 'fearlessness in the presence of fears (*aphobian en tois phobois*)'. Thus the 'fears' into which the trainees are led in the present context must be (i) fear-provoking situations, rather than (ii) actual feelings of fear (see note on 647c3–4 and on 649c8–10). Accordingly, Schöpsdau translates: 'Situations der Furcht'. 'Reactions' (*pathêmata*) recalls the characterization of the puppet's strings as *pathê* at 644e1 (cf. the parallel passage in *Tim.* 69d1). England would translate it 'disturbances'; however, while the feeling of fear is indeed a disturbance (*tarachê*, 632a4), the present passage leaves it open that not every person will experience that disturbance in such a situation.

648b8–c5 'so that by exhorting, chastising, and bestowing honour upon them, you would compel (*anankazein*) them to become fearless (*aphobon*)'
On fearlessness, see previous note. The testing function of the drug is here shown to play a role in its training function (see note on 648b1–2). The trainer is here invited to use exactly the same tools of praise, blame, reward, and punishment that the Athenian attributed to the legislator at 632a–b; here it is made explicit that these are tools for shaping character, not just for evaluating it. We are presented with a model in which a leader (like the coach, a drill sergeant, or a ship's captain 639b–640d) uses praise and blame and reward and punishment to cultivate citizens' character. This would be a case of

being 'compelled and persuaded by honours' (634a9; see note ad loc). On the legislator's use of praise and censure, see notes on 631e2–3 and 634a9.

648c2–3 'heap disgrace (*atimazôn*) upon the disobedient for failing to be exactly as you command'
alternatively: 'anyone who is not persuaded by you (*hostis soi mê peithoito*) to be just as you instruct (*einai toioutos hoion su tattois*) in every respect (*en pasin*)'
The recipient of disgrace would be an example of the citizen 'resistant to persuasion' (*duspeithês*) at 632b8. On the pairing of persuasion here with compulsion just above (648b8), see note on 648b8–c5. Note that the trainer is not simply concerned with how the trainee behaves in the circumstances, but with the latter's frame of mind and with the 'sort he is'; this reflects the fact that feelings and affective responses quite generally are being trained (as on the 'agreement' (*sumphônia*) model of virtue—on which see note on 643b1–646e2).

648c7 'method of training (*gumnasia*)'
Gumnasia (physical training or exercise, including military training) is the cornerstone of Dorian education (see 625c). The related term *gumnastike* is translated as 'athletics' at 672c6 and 673a10; see note on 673a8–10.

648d7–e1 'to escape and overcome the compulsive shaking (*anankaiai diaphorai*) induced by the potion'
alternatively: 'the inevitable shaking . . . '
'Shaking' renders *diaphora*, here used in the medical sense (thus des Places, Schöpsdau), and 'compulsive' renders *anankaia* (in contrast to the more usual translation 'necessary' or 'inevitable' (England, Saunders, Schöpsdau, Brisson/Pradeau, Lisi), which is the sense of the term at 635c1–2. In the present context, however, the Athenian claims that the effect (feeling fear) is avoidable by proper training (see notes on 647c3–4, 648b7–8). Construing the effect as inevitable

fits the 'victory' model for virtue endorsed by Clinias, but not the 'agreement' (*sumphônia*) model espoused by the Athenian; on the two models, see note on 643b1–646e2.

648e1–3 'His virtue would keep him from being seriously tripped up or led astray by impropriety (*hup' aschêmosunês*)'
That is, his virtue keeps him from responding inappropriately (either in feeling or in action) to the frightening circumstances.

648e4–5 'since he would fear the drink's power to defeat any human being'
The fear named here would be an instance of the shame that characterizes the good person (646e–647b), rather than the sorts of fears induced by the hypothetical potion. The potion's 'power to defeat any human being' would be analogous to wine's ability to incapacitate any human drinker if taken in sufficient quantities—i.e. if one continues drinking to the 'final round' (*tên eschatên pôsin*), 648e3.

649a4–6 'what about fearlessness, the excessive and untimely daring to do what we should not? Is there any drink for this . . . ?'
The Athenian now explicitly turns to make the parallel point that wine induces the inappropriate 'daring' (*tharros*) that is 'opposed' to shame at 647a10. The daring is 'untimely' (*akairôs*) because it violates the doctrine of due measure at 636d–e (cf. 'at the wrong time'—*ektos tôn kairôn*—636e2).

649a9–b1 'The immediate effect of drinking wine is to make a person more affable than he was before'
Cf. 671b3–4.

649b2–3 'filled with optimistic expectations and belief in his abilities'
more literally: 'filled with expectation of good things (*elpidôn agathôn*) and ability, in his opinion (*dunameôs eis doxan*)'

This reflects the initial description of 'daring' (*tharros*) as a kind of *elpis* (expectation, anticipation), and *elpis* as a kind of opinion or belief (*doxa*) at 644c9–d1. See notes on 644c9 and 647e3–4.

649b9–c1 'supremely daring (*malista tharrêsomen*)' . . . 'supremely afraid (*malista phobêsometha*)'
The former is the *tharros* required for courage in battle (647b6–7), the latter the sense of shame that characterizes the moderation required in social/peaceful contexts (646e10–647a7). At 647b9–c1 these two desiderata are presented as fearlessness and fearfulness respectively.

649c4 'it is in the presence of fears that we must practise being courageous and fearless'
As is made explicit in the analogous point about moderation (see note on 649c8–10), the 'fears' in whose presence the 'practice' takes place must be (i) fear-provoking situations rather than (ii) actual feelings of fear (see notes on 647c3–4 and on 648b7–8).

649c8–10 'it is in the presence of things that naturally make us especially daring (*tharraleoi*) and bold (*thraseis*) that . . . we must practise at *not* being shameless . . . '
more literally: ' . . . in the presence of those things that, when we experience them (*ha pathontes*), we are naturally (*pephukamen*) especially daring, we must practise being least shameless . . . '
The Athenian here acknowledges a distinction between (i) the circumstances that naturally provoke inappropriate feelings of daring and (ii) the inappropriate feelings that are provoked in those circumstances. As in the parallel case of training against fears just described (649c3–4), it is (i) rather than (ii) that are the necessary context for the exercise of the virtues (see notes on 647c3–4 and on 648b7–8). The goal of practising is to eliminate as far as possible (*hôs hêkista*) the inappropriate feelings of daring, not simply to defeat them when we experience them.

649d4–7 'all these things have such an effect on us: [a] anger (*thumos*), passion (*erôs*), insolence (*hubris*), ignorance (*amathia*), greed, and cowardice—along with [b] wealth, beauty, strength, and everything that by making us drunk with pleasure drives us out of our minds'

An enumeration of the 'things' whose 'presence . . . naturally makes us especially daring and bold' (649c8; see note on 649c8–10). The listed items are heterogeneous: [a] are psychological states or conditions, which we might understand as either instances or causes of boldness. Cowardice (*deilia*, used as at 647c10 for cowardly feelings) might seem an odd item to find on the list, with its suggestion of timidity, but consider for example a case where cowardice leads to traitorous action. By contrast, those in [b] are among the 'human goods' listed at 631c. As a rough approximation, [a] are the pleasures and pains of the citizens that the legislator is supposed to evaluate and shape (631d–632a) while [b] are items whose acquisition or loss are the circumstances in which we 'naturally' (*pephukamen*, 649c8) experience [a]. This passage, taken together with 631d2–632b1, suggests the view that the pleasures and pains we feel at apparent misfortune and good fortune are the causes of, or constitute, the antisocial *tharros* that the legislator trains the citizens to avoid (in particular, when we mistakenly believe that possessing the human goods is the marker of good fortune, without recognizing that the virtues are a precondition of deriving any benefit from them). Thus we are given a reason here why the legislator is supposed to supervise the pleasures that citizens feel in the face of apparent good fortune (*eutuchia*) (632a5). See also note on 647e3–4. The Athenian may also have in mind here a point he develops in later books: that our desire for the human goods has no natural limit, and satisfying it makes it stronger (831d–832b, 918d–919c; see Meyer 2003). Thus a person who acquires great wealth may feel emboldened to seek out more. Such a hypothesis would also explain the previous claim that victory in war (where 'the goods of the vanquished go to the victors'—Clinias: 626b) leads to 'insolence' (*hubris*, 641c5) and hence undermines education. The examples in the present context (649e2–650a7) indicate that the greed or insolence in question concern the pursuit of financial gain or sexual gratification, so we may suppose the latter also figures on the list in [b]. On 'driving us out of our minds', see Bobonich 2002: 270.

Drunkenness as a test for character

649d7–9 'Now for an inexpensive and relatively harmless way, first of all, to test ourselves, and second, get practice in these matters'
Note that both the testing function and the training function of the drug are invoked. See note on 648b1–2.

649e1–2 'provided it is conducted with some care'
That is, under knowledgeable leadership; see 640a–e. The proper leadership of drinking parties will be addressed further in Book 2, 671c–e.

649e3–650a5 'entering into a business deal with the man and exposing oneself to the attendant risks . . . entrusting to [his] care our own daughters, sons, and wives . . . endangering what is most precious to us . . . '
This explains why a 'safe' method of testing (and training) for moderation is desirable. The situations in which it is a challenge to act moderately are ones in which fellow citizens risk being harmed.

650b7–8 'the discipline (*technêi*) that cares for (*therapeuein*) these matters'
more literally: 'the discipline whose business it is to care for these things'
That is, the discipline that cares for (*therapeuein*) the soul by cultivating the virtues (see 649b8–c1, where the verb is translated as 'cultivate'). Here the testing function of the drinking party emphasized in 649e–650b is subsumed under the more general training function; on education (*paideia*) as the process of such cultivation, see 643b–644b; 653a–c; cf. *Rep*. 410c.

650b8–9 'We agree . . . that this is the task of politics (*politikês*)?' The legislator is referred to as a *politikos* (statesman) at 628d6, 657a4, 688a1, 693a6. The conception of politics (*politikê technê*) as care for the citizens' souls is developed at length in the *Gorg.* 464b–c; cf. 513e, 515a–e, and is taken up by Aristotle, *EN* 1102a5–12, who remarks that the Cretan and Spartan legislators have a reputation for making the citizens good and law-abiding.

Book 2

I
EDUCATION, VIRTUE, AND CHORAL PERFORMANCE

(652a1–654d4)

After announcing that drinking parties are a 'safeguard' to education (652a–653a), the Athenian defines education (paideia) *as the condition of having correctly trained 'pleasures and pains'. He distinguishes this condition from 'virtue in its entirety' (653b6). Choral song and dance at festivals to the gods are the means by which such 'education' is inculcated and repaired (653c–654b). Those who have been trained to sing and dance well will take pleasure in what is beautiful or admirable* (kalon) *and be pained at what is shameful or ugly* (aischron), *even if they cannot articulate or understand it (654c–d).*

652a1–653a4

Drinking parties are a safeguard for education

The Athenian has just claimed at the end of Book 1 that drunkenness reveals a person's true character (649d–650b)—a subordinate point in the larger argument, begun at 636e, that drinking parties have beneficial effects on education (*paideia*, 641b–d). His present remarks serve to redirect the discussion back to that larger benefit, which concerns the shaping of character. The role that drinking parties play as a 'safeguard' to that larger benefit will later be explained in the context of the so-called Chorus of Dionysus

(665d–666c, 671a–672a; see notes on 664d1–2 and general note on 671a2–674c7).

652a3 'our natures'
More literally: 'the condition of our natures (*pôs echomen tas phuseis*)' A reference back to the 'natures and dispositions of people's souls' (650b7).

652a3–4 'some great benefit, which we must take very seriously (*axion pollês spoudês*)'
The Athenian will conclude at 673e that drinking parties are a 'serious matter' (*spoudê*) rather than recreation (*paidia*). On the contrast between what is serious (*spoudê*) v. play or recreation (*paidia*), see note on 635b5.

652a4 'properly conducted (*en têi kat' orthon chreiai*) communal drinking'
That is, under correct leadership; cf. 638c–641a, 671d–e.

652a5–6 'The present argument evidently aims to establish that there is'
This goal of the argument was announced at 641c8–d3.

652b1 'if we are not to get tripped up by it (*mê . . . parapodisthômen hup' autou*)'
It is not obvious what potential confusion the Athenian has in mind. Perhaps the caveat refers to the convoluted and oft-interrupted train of argument in which the specific topic of drinking parties is not addressed explicitly, beyond a brief mention at 666b–c, until the end of Book 2. See general note on 671a2–674c7.

652b3–653a1 'recall what we said correct education is in our case (*hêmin*)'
The qualification 'in our case' recalls 643d–644b in Book 1, where education (*paideia*) in the strict sense is identified as training in the

virtues of citizenship, as distinct from training in manual or technical skills. See also 672e5.

653a3 'its safeguard (*sôtêria*)'
alternatively: 'its preservation'
Sôtêria is used in this sense at *Rep*. 425e3. On the range of the term, see England on the present passage. At 654d8 *phulakê* (guarding) is used instead of *sôtêria*. That education (*paideia*) may require 'preservation' or 'safeguarding' was adumbrated in the account of *paideia* in Book 1, which speaks of *paideia* 'going off course' (*exerchetai*) and requiring 'correction' (*epanorthousthai*) (644b2–3). Just ahead, at 653c8, the problem is described as a 'slackening'.

653a5–c6

Education (paideia) *is properly trained pleasures and pains*

The Athenian now specifies the sort of education that is preserved by drinking parties. While the term *paideia* (like 'cultivation' and its cognates in English) can be used to describe both an educational process and the cultivated disposition that results from such a process, the latter sense is operative here, where we are given a further refinement of the conception of education presented in Book 1 (643d–644b). There, *paideia* in a strict sense was distinguished by its goal of inculcating the virtues of a citizen. Here, virtue and *paideia* are defined more precisely and distinguished from each other. *Paideia* consists in the proper cultivation of one's 'pleasures and pains', while virtue 'in its entirety' consists in agreement between those properly trained 'pleasures and pains' and one's *logos* (account).

653a6 'pleasure and pain'
These are the 'witless advisors' identified as 'iron cords' that move a person, according to the metaphor of the puppets in Book 1 (644c–645c). Here they are evidently intended to include love

(*philia*) and hate (*misos*) (653b2–3, b7–c1). On the range of what is included under pleasure and pain, see note on 633c9–d2.

653a7–9 'we are lucky if we have also developed wisdom (*phronêsin*) and stable true opinions (*alêtheis doxas*)'
On the distinction between *phronêsis* and correct belief or opinion (*doxa*), see 632c–d and note on 632c5; cf. note on 632d5–6. Later, at 672c, *phronêsis* is linked to the order (*taxis*) associated with rhythm and harmony which, in the present context, are about to be attributed a large role in *paideia* (653e–654a). In the present context both *phronêsis* and 'stable true opinions' are distinguished from the pleasures and pains that agree (*sumphônein*) with them. Presumably the former are expressed in the 'golden string' in the puppet metaphor of 644c–645c. Note the Athenian's pessimism here about the prospects of either condition being widespread among the citizens.

653a9–b1 'these goods and all that they involve (*ta en toutois*) complete a person (*teleos . . . est' anthrôpos*)'
'All that they involve' might be a reference to the virtues, which at 631b–d are said to be 'divine goods' that 'depend' (*êrtêtai*, 631b7) on *phronêsis*. These are the elements of 'virtue in its entirety' (*sumpasa aretê*, 630b3; cf. 653b6); at 630c5–6 they are said to comprise 'complete justice' (*dikaiosunê telea*; cf. 631c7–8, and note on 630c5–6); thus here they are said to make a person 'complete' (*teleos*). At 631b–c possession of the 'human goods' (health, wealth, etc.) is said to follow from possessing the virtues (see notes on 631b6–8, 631b8–c1, and 631c1–5), but it is unlikely that the human goods are included in 'all that these involve' here, since the notion of a 'complete' (*teleos*) person is strongly connected with the aims of education (see 643d2 and 643e5, where *teleos* and its variant *teleion* are translated as 'completely' and 'perfect'; cf. 643c8–9).

653b3–4 'when we are not yet able to grasp the account (*logon lambanein*), and when we do grasp the account (*labontôn de ton logon*)'

alternatively: '*logon lambanein*' might be rendered 'engage in argument' (thus England)
Logos here (as at 645b4, 659d2, and 696c10) is best construed as an evaluative judgement or verdict rather than as the faculty of reason; thus the popular translation 'reason' is misleading; see the masterful treatment by Moss (2014: 196–202), who notes the parallel between the present passage and *Rep*. 401d–402a. The phrase *logon lambanein* in the text of des Places as well as Burnet's alternative *logôi lambanein* are sometimes used by Plato to indicate a kind of epistemic grasp (as at *Laws* 645b4, *Parm*. 135e3, *Tht*. 208d6–7, *Rep*. 402a2, 534b3)—hence the present translation. But he also uses them with the weaker meaning of 'discuss', or 'examine by argument' (*Laws* 638c2, *Soph*. 246c5–7, *Protag*. 348a2, *Meno* 75d2, *Rep*. 337e3)—hence the alternative translation. On either alternative, the distinction is presumably between those who have not yet reached the age of reason and those who have. These two developmental stages will later be assigned, respectively, to the chorus of the Muses and the chorus of Apollo (664c–d).

653b4–5 'agree with it'
literally: 'agree with the account (*sumphêsôsi tôi logoi*)'
This agreement or concord (*sumphônia,* b6) is later described at 659d–e as holding between a child's pleasures and pains, on the one hand, and the 'correct account (*orthos logos*) articulated by the law' on the other; cf. 696c. Here the agreement is an internal psychological concord between one's 'pleasures and pains' and one's evaluative judgement (*logos*)—when the latter reflects the views expressed in the law (cf. 644d2–3, 645a2) and thus expresses the *phronêsis* or 'stable true opinions' of 653a8. The parties to the agreement are presumably the iron and gold cords in the puppet metaphor of 644c–645c, with *logos* as a virtuous instance of the *logismos* of 644d that is identified as the 'golden cord' at 645a (see note on 645b4–5). An instance of the *sumphônia* invoked here is given at 654c: one takes pleasure in the things one judges to be beautiful (*kalon*) and hates those that one considers shameful (*aischron*). In Book 3 we are told

that, without such *sumphônia,* no one has wisdom (*phronêsis*, 689d4–6). Elsewhere, the verb *sumphônein* indicates agreement between persons (as at 661d4, 662b2, 686b3, and at 634e2 where it is translated 'sing out their agreement') or logical consistency (662e9; cf. *Rep*. 380c3). The verb and its cognates are regularly used in *Rep*. to indicate the relationship between the parts of the virtuous city (432a8, 463e3) and soul (441e9, 442c10).

653b5–6 'because they have been correctly trained (*eithisthai*) by appropriate habits (*ethôn*)'

The translation follows the emendation (*tôi logôi tôi*) favoured by Schöpsdau following Stallbaum; thus Kurke 2013: 164n28. The MSS text lacks the second *tôi* and would be translated: 'agree with the account that they have been correctly trained'.

On MSS text, the Athenian would be claiming that our pleasures and pains express reflexive normative assessments, and that such assessments are the content of the *sumphônia* with *logos* that is characteristic of virtue. Elsewhere, however, the requisite agreement between one's pleasures and plains, loves and hates, on the one hand, and one's *logos* on the other is not so restricted (as at 659d–e, 689d, and 696c; cf. *Rep*. III 401e–402a). 'Habit' (*ethos*) is a term the Athenian will use to describe the process of cultivating or training pleasures and pains (see note on 655d7–e1).

653b6 'this agreement (*sumphônia*) is virtue in its entirety (*sumpasa . . . aretê*)'

The agreement is between one's 'pleasures and pains' on the one hand, and one's *logos* (evaluative judgement) on the other (see note on 653b4–5). In identifying this concord with virtue, the Athenian endorses the 'agreement' model of virtue, rather than the 'conflict' model espoused by his interlocutors in Book 1 (on those two models, see general note on 643b1–646e2). The phrase 'virtue in its entirety' (*sumpasa aretê*) has a different sense here than it does in Book 1 at 630b3, where it refers to the combination of wisdom, moderation, courage, and justice—also called 'complete (*telea*) justice' at 630c6. Here, however, the 'entirety' is that of a whole, as distinct from one of its constituents—*paideia* being a distinguishable feature (the correctly trained pleasures and pains) that is 'part' of the condition of agreement (those pleasures and pains agreeing with *logos*) that constitutes virtue 'in its entirety'.

653c1 'from beginning to end (*mechri telous*)'
This use of *telos* (end, goal) recalls the notion of a 'complete' (*teleos*) person at 553a9, and suggests that the aspect of virtue here singled out as *paideia* persists even in the complete form of virtue ('virtue in its entirety', 653b6), not just in its early stages of development.

653c5–6 'Your earlier remarks about education': at 643b–644b.

653c7–654a8

Choral performance is the medium of education

The Athenian here notes that correctly nurtured pleasures and pains, i.e. education (*paideia*) in the sense just identified (653a–c), require regular maintenance to withstand the stress of human life (653c7–9) and that this maintenance is achieved through choral performance at religious festivals (653c9–654a8). He explains the natural origins of the choral arts: (1) all young animals are naturally exuberant, and prone to voicing sounds and leaping about; and (2) humans naturally enjoy harmony and rhythm (653d5–654a3). Thus choral performance (*choreia*), a combination of song (*ôidê*) and dance (*orchêsis*), is something we are eager to engage in (654a3–5), at least when we are young. Drinking parties, the Athenian will later argue (666b–c, 671a–c), will replicate this youthful condition in the elderly. He does not explain how song and dance shape a person's pleasures, pains, loves, and hates, although some of his presuppositions will emerge over the course of 655d–656b, 659e–660a.

Choral performance at religious festivals maintains education

653c8–9 'education . . . tends to slacken and be undone over the course of human life'
more literally: ' . . . is loosened (*chalatai*) and destroyed (*diaphtheiretai*) in many respects (*kata polla*) . . . '
The MSS text is difficult to construe, as it provides no explicit subject for the verbs 'slacken and be undone'. The present translation follows England in taking *paideia* (in the sense of the cultivated condition) to be the implied subject and *kata polla* to be adverbial. As England points out, Ast's emendation of *kata polla* to *ta polla* would make the Athenian's claim much stronger: that most of *paideia* is weakened and undone by human life. The burdens of life are invoked again at 666a6. See also note on 653d4–5.

653d2–3 'ordained (*etaxanto*) intervals (*amoibas*) of respite from their toils in the form of festivals to the gods'
alternatively: ' . . . respites from their toils in exchange for festivals (*tas tôn heortôn amoibas*)'; parallel language at *Symp.* 202e5 invokes rituals that the gods command (*epitattein*) mortals to perform, and benefits that they promise in exchange (*amoibas*)
The immediate point in the present passage is that holding the festivals commanded by the gods brings humans, in return, the benefit of respite from their toils, in the sense of a holiday from work. The larger point, about to be elaborated, is that these festivals are occasions for the maintenance and repair of *paideia*, which the grind of daily life has 'slackened and undone'.

653d3–4 'the Muses, their leader Apollo, and Dionysus as fellow celebrants'
The Muses are patrons of culture: poetry, song, and dance; the god Apollo is also associated with music and Dionysus is the god of wine, whose festivals involve drunkenness. On the Muses, see P. Murray

2004; on Apollo, see Burkert 1985 and Graf 2009; and on Dionysus, see Burkert 1985, Seaford 2006, and Wildberg 2011. Later in Book 2, these three will be the titular leaders of the three choruses introduced at 664b–665d. They are 'fellow celebrants' (*sunhêortastai*) at the festivals to the gods insofar as these festivals involve the performance of song and dance in which these gods are 'partners in the dance' (*sunchoreutas*, 654a1). The Athenian's point is that by involving the Muses, Apollo, and Dionysus in these festivals (that is, by involving song, dance, and wine), the gods are giving humans a way of restoring the *paideia* that has 'slackened and been undone' (653c8–9) over the course of daily life.

653d4–5 'To set them back on the correct course (*epanorthôntai*)' literally: 'in order that they be set back on the right course'; alternatively: 'in order that they set them up correctly' (England)
This construal takes the verb *epanorthôntai* as passive rather than middle (following Burnet), as it is in the parallel text at 644b2–3. The subject of the verb, (the antecedent of 'them' in the translation) is either humans (thus Brisson/Pradeau; Kurke 2013: 163n15) or their education (*paideia* in the plural at 653c8). Either may be construed as 'set back on the right course' in the sense that the celebrants' pleasures and pains (*paideia*) are cultivated anew during these festivals. England, by contrast, takes the verb to be middle, with the gods as its subject and the festivals as its object. Schöpsdau agrees that this is the natural reading of the text, but prefers an emendation that would make the 'nurture during these festivals' (d5) the object of the verb. On neither of the latter readings, however, does the verb have the restorative force that it has at 644b3 and that is clearly relevant in the present context; nurture (*trophê*), unlike education (*paideia*), does not extend to the cultivated condition. Kurke (2013: 131) proposes that the verb may be understood quite literally as 'set upright again', which, in conjunction with the 'slackening' at 653c8, is intended to evoke the puppets on strings at 644d–645a.

The natural basis of choral dance

653d5–6 'a hymn we hear (*ha . . . hêmin . . . humneitai*)'
more literally: 'a thesis (*logos*) that is intoned (*humneitai*) to us these days';
alternatively: 'a thesis that is intoned by us (*hêmin*)' (Schöpsdau)
The verb *humneitai* continues the festival motif from above; it can also be used of a frequently repeated statement, as at *Laws* 778d7, *Rep*. 549e1, and *Critias* 118b3, as well as of ritual song (*Rep*. 617c3), and of song invoking the Muses (*Critias* 108c4). At *Laws* 799a9 its compound *ephumneisthai* is used of hymns sung at festivals to the gods. On the message of the 'hymn', see note on 653d7–8. While the Athenian stops short of endorsing it in the present context, he invokes it at 672b8–c7 as something he knows.

653d7–8 'It says that every young creature is practically unable to sit still or keep quiet'
Continuing until 654a5, this theory is the content of the 'hymn' invoked at 653d6. It is repeated at 664e3–665a3, 672c1–d4, and 673c9–d5. The two main components of the theory introduced here are:

(i) Young animals are naturally inclined to motion (both of voice and body)—and hence to a prototype of choral dance (cf. 673c–d).
(ii) Humans naturally take pleasure in the order of harmony and rhythm—and hence in choral dance, which is about to be named as the medium for cultivating *paideia* (654a).

Other statements of the theory make explicit what must be assumed to be implicit here:

(iii) The natural juvenile motions are disorderly and indeed display a kind of madness (664e, 666a, 672c).
(iv) The juvenile soul is pliable, receptive to being trained to acquire various kinds of order (664b, 671b–c).

The educational function of drunkenness, eventually to be identified at 666b–c and 671a–672d, is to replicate that pliable juvenile condition (with all its disorderliness) in an adult soul whose education has been 'slackend and undone' (653c8–9), thus preparing it to be retrained in appropriate 'harmonies' and rhythms. Fire is a frequent metaphor for the kinetic juvenile soul, invoking both the latter's frantic disorderliness (666a; cf. 664e) and its malleability: like iron in the fire, capable of being shaped (or reshaped) by a knowledgeable sculptor (671b–c). While the thesis of disorderly juvenile motions recalls the degraded condition of the incarnated soul in *Tim.* 43a–47e, as Schöpsdau notes (cf. Kamtekar 2010: 130–3), the Athenian here casts those motions in a very positive light, taking them to mark the educability of youth, in contrast with the stiffness (and corresponding resistance to education) in the elderly (cf. 665d–e, 666b). Juvenile motions are not so much disordered (as in *Tim.*) as unordered—awaiting the shaping influence of education.

653e1–3 'Some leap and bound as though they were dancing (*hoion orchoumena*) in playful glee (*meth' hêdonês kai prospaizonta*)'
more literally: 'as though . . . dancing with pleasure and playing'
This youthful exuberance and its connection to dance is invoked again at 673a7 with similar language (cf. 657c5–9). On play or recreation (*paidia*), see note on 635b5.

653e3–5 'the other animals do not sense order and disorder in movement (what we call rhythm and "harmony" (*rhuthmos . . . kai harmonia*))'
alternatively: ' . . . do not perceive (*echein aisthêsin*) order and disorder . . . '
It is perception or sensation (*aisthêsis*) of such order (not just pleasure in that perception) that is distinctive of humans, as 664e6–8 makes clear. On the significance of this natural affinity to order, see Mouze 2005: 150; Laks 2000: 277. The *harmonia* invoked by the Athenian is not harmony in the modern musical sense (simultaneous notes of differing pitch), but something more like a musical scale. The Athenian will later specify more precisely that

harmonia is an order (*taxis*) of vocal pitches, while rhythm is order of movement (664e8–665a3)—both vocal movement and bodily movement (672e8–673a1). *Harmonia* is sometimes translated as 'mode' (e.g. the Dorian, Phrygian, and Lydian modes mentioned in the *Republic*—397b–400a; see A. Barker 1990: 14–17 and Rocconi 2003); however, 'mode' won't do as a translation here, so 'harmony' is used as a placeholder for want of a better English counterpart (see England's note on 653e5). Scott (1999: 20–33, and in an unpublished work) argues that *harmonia* should be translated as 'song' or 'music' and *rhuthmos* translated as 'dance' when they occur in the phrase *rhuthmos kai harmonia*; however, the Athenian uses *rhuthmos* and *harmonia* to refer to the structure or order that belongs to song and dance, not to song and dance themselves. Later the Athenian will insist that the *harmonia* and *rhuthmos* in a choral work must be appropriate to its words and gestures (669b–670e).

653e5–654a1 'the gods whom we said were given to us as partners in the dance (*sunchoreutas dedosthai*)'
The gods described at 653d4 as 'fellow celebrants' (*sunheortastas*) are now identified more precisely as fellow performers of *choreia* (choral dance); this indicates that the specific medium of their educational influence is choral dancing. The connection between *paideia* and choral training has already been hinted at in Book 1, 641b3. On the central role of dance in choral performance, see note on 654a4–5.

654a2–3 'gave *us* pleasure in rhythm and "harmony"'
more literally: 'gave us rhythmic and harmonious sensation with pleasure (*tên enrhuthmon te kai enharmonion aisthêsin meth' hêdonês*)'
The educational significance of this pleasure is further elucidated at 660a5–8: a composer can train us to take pleasure in words or gestures simply by setting them into rhythm and 'harmony'. On appropriate rhythms and 'harmonies', see 670a–e.

654a3 'and that is how they set us in motion'
Reading *hêi dê* instead of the MSS *êdê* (with England, Burnet, Saunders 1972, Brisson/Pradeau).

The MSS reading would yield the alternative translation 'and then they set us in motion'; thus Schöpsdau, who nonetheless takes the Athenian to mean that this is a further step made possible by the gift of 'pleasure in rhythm and "harmony" '.

654a4–5 'When they link us together in song and dance we call it a chorus (*chorous*)—from the name for delight (*charas*)'
A *choros* in Plato's time involved both singing and dancing (654b3–4)—unlike a chorus in the sense of the English term today—although the connection to dance is retained in the contemporary notion of a 'chorus line'. The cognate verb (*choreuein*) and abstract noun (*choreia*) are generally rendered 'choral dance' or 'choral performance' in this translation; the concrete noun (*choros*), which refers to the ensemble of performers or to the institution (as in the three choruses of 664b–d), is rendered 'chorus'. On choral song and dance in Plato's day, see Morrow 1960: 302–18; Lonsdale 1993; Athanassaki and Bowie 2011; Peponi 2012: 4–5; Calame 2013; and Billings et al. 2013. See also Prauscello 2014.

654a6–7 'our initial education is through the Muses and Apollo'
Dionysus is here omitted (although mentioned along with the Muses and Apollo at 653d3–4) because the present comment concerns initial (*prôtê*) education—i.e. that of children, who have a natural propensity to engage in the choral activities that will educate them. Dionysus will be invoked later to address the educational challenge of encouraging the elderly to participate in the music that will renew their education (653d4), even though they have lost that enthusiasm for song and dance (665d–666c, 671a–672d).

654a9–d4

Choral training shapes pleasures and pains

Having identified choral performance (a combination of song and dance, 654b3–4) as the medium of education, the Athenian completes his sketch of the properly educated person. Such a person, who 'sings and dances well (*kalôs*)' (654b6–7), will both (a) perform beautiful (*kala*) choral works (654b11–c1), and (b) experience pleasure in beautiful things and distress at ugly things (654c4–d4). While (a) introduces a topic to be treated at length in the next section (654e–660a), which investigates what makes choral works beautiful (further developed at 667b–670e), the emphasis here is on (b), which reflects the definition of education at 653a–c as the correct disposition of a person's feelings of pleasure, pain, likes, and dislikes. On 'beautiful' and 'admirable' as alternative translations of *kalon*, see note on 630c7 and notes below. In the present passage, the Athenian will be moving seamlessly between the aesthetic and ethical senses of *kalon* in a manner that is difficult to lay bare in the translation. The reader is invited to keep in mind that the 'beauty' in question encompasses both ethical and aesthetic quality.

654b6–7 'the well (*kalôs)* educated person would be able to sing and dance well (*kalôs*)'
alternatively: 'the beautifully [admirably] educated person would be able to sing and dance beautifully [admirably]'
The alternative translations take the relevant sense of *kalon* to be aesthetic or ethical. The printed translation construes the adverb *kalôs* in the generic sense in which it is interchangeable with *eu* (well); on the semantic range of *kalon*, see note on 630c7. While 'beautifully' might a defensible translation in the present context, which concerns choral music and the fine arts more generally, and while 'admirably' has the advantage of continuity with the typical translation of *kalon* as 'admirable' in Book 1, both adverbs in English tend to function as superlatives of 'well', and so would give the misleading impression here that the Athenian is overstating the implications of his preceding remark that a properly educated person has received a 'proper (*hikanôs*) choral training' (654b1).

654b11–c1 '"He sings well (*kalôs*)"... provided the things he sings and... dances are beautiful (*kala*)'

alternatively: '. . . provided the things he sings and . . . dances are admirable'
The surface plausibility of the Athenian's suggestion is evident in the Greek: 'he sings *kalôs* (adverb) provided the things he sings are *kala* (adjective)'. On the translation of the adjective, 'beautiful' would be appropriate here if 'the things he sings' are (a) songs and dances (i.e. works of choral art); however, they might also be (b) the gestures and utterances of the choral dancer who performs the song and dance, or (c) the behaviour represented or imitated in such song and dance. In the case of (c) and possibly also (b), the ethical sense of the adjective, captured by 'admirable', would be operative. Since either the aesthetic or the ethical dimension of the *kalon* may be operative here (and quite possibly both, as at 654c4–d4), the translation 'beautiful' is used with the intention that it stand for both. The reader should keep in mind that 'beautiful' is used in a wider sense than is natural in English (see note on 630c7).

Later, at 654e–660a and 667b–670e, the Athenian will investigate the criteria for the beautiful choral art. Here, however, his emphasis is on the behaviour and psychology of the person who has received a proper choral training. This is in keeping with his present focus on education (*paideia*) as a cultivated condition of a person.

654c4–d4

The well-educated person takes pleasure in beautiful things

In this difficult passage—where both the ethical and the aesthetic aspects of the *kalon* are operative, and the translation 'beautiful' is used to capture both (see note on 630c7)—the Athenian sketches three different psychological profiles and asks which is the best educated. While the details of the passage are difficult and disputed, his main point is clearly that the most important educational result of choral training is to have properly cultivated feelings of pleasures and pain (i.e. education as defined at 653a–c).

The three people are contrasted along the following dimensions:

(a) whether they have correct thoughts about what is beautiful and ugly (or admirable and shameful);
(b) whether they have correct pleasures and pains concerning what is beautiful and ugly (or admirable and shameful);
(c) whether they are able to 'adequately render in voice and gesture' what is thought to be beautiful and ugly (or admirable and shameful).

It is clear that the first person is correct on (a), that the second is correct on (c) but not (b), and that the third person is correct only on (b). Difficulties arise because the Athenian begins by asking whether the second is better educated than the first and implies that he is not, but he concludes by proposing that the third is better educated than the second, without indicating the relationship between the first and the third.

England proposes that the second and third persons are instances of the first (reading the first 'than' (*ê*, 654c6) as 'whether'; rejected by Schöpsdau). It makes more sense to suppose that the Athenian makes two successively stronger assertions with the two comparisons:

(i) the second person is less well educated than the first, because he lacks correct pleasures and pains;
(ii) indeed, he is less well educated than *anyone* who has correct pleasures and pains (even if such a person lacks the first person's correct thoughts).

For a different interpretation, on which the third person is the same as the first, see note on 654c9–d3.

654c4–5 'suppose that what he considers (*hêgoumenos*) beautiful (*kala*) really is beautiful and what he considers ugly (*aischra*) really is ugly, and he treats them as such (*houtôs autois chrêtai*)'
alternatively: '. . . what he considers admirable . . . and what he considers shameful . . .'

The first person is here characterized in terms of his beliefs about what is beautiful and ugly (where these notions encompass the admirable and shameful); it is left ambiguous whether the *kala* and *aischra* things are the songs and dances—just invoked at c1—or the actions they imitate. The Athenian thus indicates that choral training cultivates not only one's singing and dancing abilities, but also one's evaluative outlook (views about what is *kalon* and *aischron*). The meaning of 'treats them as such' (*houtôs autois chrêtai*) is not obvious. If the verb *chrêtai* is parallel to the *chreian orthên* at 657c4 (see note ad loc), it might mean that this **first person** has the correct pleasures and pains attributed to the **third person** at 654d1–3. Or it could extend to all ways of conducting oneself properly regarding admirable/beautiful and shameful/ugly things, in which case it would extend to correct behaviour, not just correct feelings.

654c5–9 'Do we hold him to be better educated in choral dance and music (*choreian te kai musikên*) than a person who is able to comply in particular cases with what is thought to be beautiful (*to dianoêthen einai kalon*), using his body and his voice, but who fails to enjoy beautiful things and fails to hate their opposites?'
The second person's speech and actions conform to received standards of the *kalon*, although the passive *to dianoêthen* ('what is thought to be beautiful') leaves it open that this person does not himself believe these standards, which would mark a contrast with the first person. In any case, the salient defect of the second person (as the contrast with the third will make clear) is his failure to feel pleasures and pains in line with these standards. Here, as in the description of the third person (c9–d3), 'using his body and his voice' is ambiguous between performing choral dance, and the speaking the words and doing the actions represented in choral dance (cf. 654e–655a).

654c9–d3 'Or is the better educated person the one who gets it right in his pleasures and pains, embracing what is beautiful [alt: admirable] and offended by what is not, even if he is not quite able to get it right in voice and body or to grasp it in his thought?' **The third person**, in failing to 'get it right' (*katorthoun*) in voice and body, contrasts with the second person's success in this domain, but in 'getting it right' in pleasures and pains, he contrasts with the second's failure. His inability 'to grasp it in his thought' (*dianoeisthai*) contrasts with the first person's correct conception (*hêgoumenos*, c4) of what is *kalon* and *aischron*. On the emendation favoured by England (rejected by Schöpsdau but reflected in the translation of Brisson/Pradeau), the translation would not be 'or to grasp it in his thought' but 'in the way he thinks of it' (*hêi dianoeisthai*); in that case the third person, like the first, would have correct thoughts about what is *kalon*. A different reason for supposing the third is a version of the first, suggested by an anonymous reviewer for the press, is that 'grasping it in his thought' (*dianoeisthai*) may be stronger than 'considering' (*hêgeisthai*), in which case the Athenian's point would be that, regardless of the first's failure to achieve *dianoia* of beautiful things (a higher epistemic standard than mere true belief, perhaps equivalent to 'grasping the account' (*logon lambanein*) at 652b4), his pleasure in the beautiful makes him better educated than the second person. He would be an instance of those in whom 'pleasure and . . . pain . . . develop correctly in [their] souls when [they] are not yet able to grasp the account' (652b2–4). It is not obvious, however, that the Athenian accords such a higher epistemic status to *dianoeisthai*.

II
VIRTUE, NOT PLEASURE, IS THE STANDARD OF CHORAL ART

654d5–660a8

Having stated that beautiful song and dance are the medium by which education is to be cultivated and maintained (654c), the Athenian now asks what such beauty consists in (and indicates that beauty is a matter of correctness). He rejects the popular view that music is beautiful simply insofar as it is pleasant, and proposes instead a standard of virtue: choral song and dance is beautiful insofar as it depicts the speech and actions of virtue (654e3–655b8). Taking pleasure in the behaviour of wicked characters shapes one's own character accordingly (655b9–656b8). Thus it is important for the legislator to establish and enforce standards for appropriate music (656c1–657c2). The view that pleasure is the criterion of correct music derives its apparent plausibility from the intimate relationship between our feelings of pleasure and our evaluative judgements (657c3–658a3). The Athenian urges, on the contrary, that: different kinds of people find different kinds of music most pleasant (658a4–d10); the most authoritative verdict is that of the best educated (658e1–5); and in musical education, the pleasures endorsed by the best educated should be used to shape those of the inferior (658e6–659c5). Thus, he concludes, the proper task for the composers of choral song and dance is to make pleasant the speech and actions of virtue by casting them into the pleasant vehicles of beautiful language, harmony, and rhythm (659c5–660a8).

654d7–e1 'Without this knowledge . . . we could never know whether there is any safeguard (*phulakê*) for education, or where it is to be found'
A reference to the Athenian's stated intention at 653a3 to establish that drinking parties are a safeguard (*sôtêria*) for education. While drinking parties are not presently the focus of discussion, the present question about beautiful song and dance will turn out to occupy (at least some) participants in drinking parties (those members of the chorus of Dionysus whose task is to identify which choral compositions are appropriate for performance—670d–e).

654e3–655b8

Beautiful choral music depicts the speech and actions of virtue

Having concluded that beautiful choral dancing is the medium for education (654a9–c2), the Athenian now turns to consider what kind of choral works are beautiful.

654e3–4 'like hounds in the hunt'
The same image is used at *Parm. 128c*, where the hounds are Spartan. On hunting as a signature Spartan activity, see 633b. Thanks to Henry Newell for the euphony and the cross reference.

654e4–5 'beautiful (*kalon)* gesture (*schêma*), tune (*melos*), song (*ôidên*), and dance (*orchêsin*)'
alternatively: 'admirable gesture, tune . . . '
Gesture (*schêma*) and tune (*melos*) are the material of dance and song respectively, as is clear below at 655a5. See also 672e–673a.

655a1–2 'Will their gestures (*schêmata*) and utterances (*phthegmata*) be alike . . . ?'
Here the Athenian is talking about the behaviour of a real person, not the depiction of such behaviour in song and dance, hence his use of 'gestures' and 'utterances' instead of the more usual pair 'gestures and tunes' (as at 654e4, e9, 655a5, a7; cf. 669c5–8). Strictly speaking, *melos* (tune) is a combination of words (*logos*), 'harmony', and rhythm (*Rep*. 398c11–d9; see also note on 669c3–8). Thus tunes (*melê*) are conceived of as the utterances of a person, and the *schêmata* as the movements of the person's body. When these utterances and movements are set into rhythms and 'harmony', the result is song and dance (655a4–7).

655a3 'How could they, since not even their colouring is?'
The colours invoked by Clinias are presumably those of people's faces or complexions, e.g. the pallor of the coward (thus England). But the Athenian will take the occasion (655a4–8) to introduce an objection to the use of 'good colour' (*euchrôn*)—in a special musical sense—to answer the question he has raised about beautiful choral music at 654d–e.

655a4–8 'it is not correct to speak of gestures or tunes as having "good colour" (*euchrôn*) . . . [but]as having good rhythm (*euruthmon*) or good "harmony" (*euarmoston*)'

The translation reorders the clauses of Plato's sentence. The Athenian objects here to using the expression 'good colour' (*euchrôn*) to describe music, but he will later use the term 'colour' (*chrôma*) to refer to a feature of music (669c4) in a context which, like the present one, invokes the notions of having 'good rhythm' (*eurhuthmon*) and 'good "harmony"' (*euarmoston*, 670b9); he explains that the latter features are a matter of a choral work's rhythm and 'harmony' being appropriate to its gestures and tunes (669b–670d). The Athenian's focus in the present passage, by contrast, is on beautiful gestures and tunes considered independently of their specifically musical features (e.g. 'harmony' and rhythm): his concern is whether they represent the actions and utterances of virtuous people (see 655b3–6 and note ad loc). His objection is not so much to the use of colour to describe music, but to the notion that 'having good colour' is a criterion of 'what is beautiful (*kalon*) in song and dance' (654d5).

655a8–b1 'As for the gesture or tune of the cowardly or courageous person, the correct thing to say is that those of the courageous are beautiful (*kala*) and those of the cowardly are ugly (*aischra*)'
more literally: 'It is possible to speak correctly about the gesture or tune of the cowardly and the courageous, and the correct thing to say is that those of the courageous are beautiful . . . '
alternatively: 'those of the courageous are admirable and those of the cowardly are shameful'
The appropriate term to invoke when characterizing the gestures and tunes of the cowardly or brave men is not 'good colour' but *kalon* and its opposite, *aischron*. The latter terms are used in the sense that invokes both ethical norms ('admirable'/'shameful') and aesthetic norms ('beautiful'/'ugly'). Thus the Athenian's proposal that the actions of the virtuous are *kala* is completely uncontroversial to his interlocutor, who endorses it without hesitation (655b7). On the ethical and aesthetic dimensions of the *kalon*, see note on 630c7.

Bury, by contrast, construes the Athenian as conceding that it is appropriate to invoke colour to describe the gestures and tunes of the cowardly or couragous person—which poses the difficulty that the

Athenian has just denied the appropriateness of such language for gestures or tunes (655a6–7); against Bury's construal, see Saunders (1972 ad loc), followed by Schöpsdau. Moss (2012: 207) goes one step further than Bury and translates 655b1–2: 'the colours of a brave man are *kalon* and those of the cowardly man are *aischron*'; but the antecedents of *ta men . . . ta de* in 655b1–2 are the 'gesture or tune' (*schêma ê melos*) of the brave and the cowardly in 655a9.

655b2–3 'going on at great length about every case'
That is, about all the virtues, not just courage.

655b3–6 'all the gestures and tunes connected with virtue of soul or of body are beautiful—whether this is the virtue itself or its representation—while all those connected with vice are the opposite'
The Athenian will later claim that choral music is a representational (*eikastikê*) or imitative (*mimêtikê*) art (667c10, e10, 668a6–7; cf. *Rep*. 392d–397b). In particular, he is about to say, it imitates the characters (*tropoi*) of different people (655d5; repeated in Book 7, 798d8–9). Thus we may take the representations of virtue mentioned in the present passage to be the gestures and tunes involved in the song and dance of a choral performance. Beautiful tunes and gestures are therefore those that represent the speech and actions of virtuous people. See also Hatzistavrou 2011: 367–8.

655b9–656b8

Taking pleasure in wicked characters shapes one's own character accordingly

We now turn to the pleasures that choral dance elicits in its performers and audience (a topic originally introduced into the discussion at 654d2–3). The Athenian begins by noting that people vary considerably in how pleasant they find different choral works (655b9–c2). He then asks what accounts for this divergence

(655bc3). What follows is an extremely puzzling stretch of text, which may be divided into three parts:

(1) 655c4–d4: questions and opinions about the pleasant and the *kalon*;
(2) 655d5–656a6: an explanation of how a single person could come to have pleasures opposed to what he thinks is *kalon*;
(3) 656a7–b8: an explanation of the dangers of taking pleasure in music that portrays bad characters.

While the relevance of (1), (2), and (3) to the question that elicits them is not immediately obvious, a thread that unites the entire discussion is the assumption, made explicit at 655e1–5, that what we experience as pleasant seems *kalon* (beautiful or admirable) to us. The upshot for the discussion of education through choral music is that choral music must train us to take pleasure in behaviour that is genuinely *kalon*.

655c3 'what . . . is the cause of this divergence (*to peplanêkos hêmas*)?'
alternatively: 'What . . . causes us to stray?' (Brisson/Pradeau)
The verb *planan* (participle: *peplanêkos*) is ambiguous between 'vary' and 'go astray' (i.e. err). When the verb is repeated at the end of this paragraph (655d3), 'go astray' best captures its sense—with *mallon* ('even more') implying that *planan* is on a continuum with the unspeakable error mentioned in d2–3 (although the explanation that follows (655d5–656a5), at least at the beginning, might explain interpersonal, as opposed to intrapersonal variation; see Mouze 2005: 158–9). Here, however, the Athenian may be trading on the ambiguity, saying at least that we stray *from each other* in what pleases us, and perhaps also implying (what he will make clear later is his view) that we thereby stray from the truth. Schöpsdau's translation, 'abweichen', nicely straddles both senses of *planan*, but there is no English term that does the same, although Saunders' 'confusion' comes close.

655c4–d4

(1) Opinions about the pleasant and the kalon

In this difficult and compressed stretch of dialectic, the Athenian considers how to explain the interpersonal variation in musical pleasures that he has just called to our attention. He asks whether the observation that:

(A) what pleases us in choral performance varies from person to person

is to be explained by the hypothesis that

(B1) what is *kalon* [in choral performance] varies from person to person.

Or whether we should reject (B1) in favour of:

(B2) it is only what we think *kalon*, not what is *kalon*, that varies from person to person.

His main opponents are those who endorse pleasure as the criterion of *kalon* music:

(C) music is *kalon* insofar as it is pleasant—

a version of which he articulates at 655c8–d2 (see note ad loc).

Those who espouse (C) are licensed to infer (B1) from (A), so it is not unreasonable for the Athenian to frame the issue, which is ultimately about (C), as a question about (B1). However, he presents his audience with the choice between (B1) and (B2) before he has introduced (C), so it makes sense for him to offer his audience an explanation of why (B1) and (B2) are reasonable options to consider as explanations of (A). This he does at 655c5–8, where he notes two things that 'no one would say'. Together, these amount to a view that the Athenian also clearly endorses:

(D) if something pleases us, we judge it to be *kalon* (see note on 655c5–8).

The combination of (A) and (D) entails that:

(E) what we judge *kalon* [in choral performance] varies from person to person—

which is neutral between (B1) and (B2).

This makes it reasonable to frame the issue as a choice between them.

655c4–5 'Is it that the same works (*t' auta*) are not beautiful (*kala*) for everyone (*hêmin pasin*)? Or that they are, but they just don't seem (*dokei*) to be so?'
alternatively: 'Is it that the same things (*t' auta*) are not beautiful for everyone . . . ?'
The Athenian's language is imprecise and colloquial. He asks his interlocutors to choose between (B1) and (B2) (see general note on 655c4–d4). The antecedent of *t' auta* could be very general (as in the alternative translation: 'the same things'); but in the present context it most likely invokes the choral works just mentioned in b9–c1 (hence the present translation 'same works'). On the rarity of the locution *kalon* + dative in Plato, see Barney 2010: 367.

655c5–8 'Presumably no one would say that the choral dances (*choreumata*) of vice are more beautiful (*kalliona*) than those of virtue, or avow that *he* takes pleasure in the gestures of wickedness while others find enjoyment in a contrary Muse'
As at 655b3–6, the 'choral dances of vice' and the 'gestures' of wickedness are to be understood as depicting the actions of vicious people. The Athenian here makes two claims about what people will affirm:

(1) No one would say that vice is more beautiful (admirable) than virtue.
(2) No one would say that *he* takes pleasure in the gestures and sounds of vice while those with the opposing pleasures take pleasure in virtue.

He offers these as a pair to explain (*gar*, 655c5) why the dilemma he has just posed between B1 and B2 is relevant to the question at hand. (2) concerns precisely the situation in which the explanandum (A) obtains: different people enjoy different choral performances; (2) implies that those who notice the variance between their own pleasures and those of others will affirm that the behaviour they themselves enjoy is virtuous rather than vicious. (1) allows this claim about virtue and vice in (2) to be translated into a claim about what is beautiful/admirable (*kalon*) and ugly/shameful (*aischron*). Hence the two claims together amount to the view that everyone thinks that what they take pleasure in is *kalon* (a version of (D)). They leave indeterminate what one would say about 'those with the opposing pleasures'—so Schöpsdau is wrong to take (1) and (2) as support for (B2) over (B1). In support of (1) see *Gorg.* 482d–e.

655c8–d2 'most people do say (*legousin ge*) that the power to bring about pleasure in the soul is what makes music correct'
Here the original question about beautiful (*kalon*) music is replaced by a question about correct music. This third observation about what people say concerns a doctrine which the Athenian is about to classify as 'impious to pronounce' d2–3. As articulated here, the doctrine is:

(3) Music is correct to the extent that it provides pleasure.

If the correctness (*orthotês*) is to be understood as being beautiful/admirable (*kalon*) (as indicated by 667c6–7) then (3) amounts to: (C) music is *kalon* insofar as it is pleasant, against which the Athenian will later marshal a sustained attack (658e–659c). Thesis (C) is what motivates the wrong choice between the options (B1) and (B2) articulated above. See general note on 655c4–d4.

655d2–3 'but another doctrine is even more likely to lead us astray (*planan hêmas*)'
What 'leads us astray' (*planan hêmas*) will also 'cause . . . the divergence' (*to peplanêkos hêmas*) at 655c3. The Athenian does not explicitly identify the doctrine. What he goes on to describe as pernicious (655d5–656b7) is the condition of being pleased by things that one judges to be wicked. Although one might construe someone with these attitudes as a case that illustrates the Athenian's claim that what is pleasant may diverge from what is *kalon*, he rejects this

way of construing the claim. On the translation of *planan*, see note on 655c3.

655d5–656a6

(2) Enjoying what one calls shameful

We are given first a brief account of the psychological factors giving rise to (i) our verdicts about what is *kalon* and *aischron*, and (ii) our reactions of pleasure and pain. Then that account is employed to explain how (iii) one could come to call something 'pleasant but wicked'.

655d5–6 'choral dances imitate different types of character (*tropôn*) found in all kinds of actions and fortune'
A person's *tropos* is his or her character, as at *Rep*. 329d3. The language here recalls *Rep*. 399a5–c4, which describes the range of vicissitudes in which imitative music will present a dramatic character's response, a theme developed at length in *Laws* 7, 814e6–815d5. Music in general (including poetry and dance) is treated as an imitative (*mimêtikê*) or representational (*eikastikê*) art at 667d–668c; cf. 669e. Imitation is also discussed in later Books: 4, 719c; 6, 764d–e; 7, 796b, 798d, 812b–c, 817b. On this passage, see also general note on 669b5–670a3.

655d6–7 'the performers drawing both on their . . . characters and on imitation (*kai êthesi kai mimêsesi*)'
That is, to perform song and dance characteristic of a courageous person, one either draws on one's own courageous character (*êthos*—used here as an alternative for *tropos* in the previous line) if one has it, or if one lacks such a character, one imitates the actions of a person who has it. In the former case, the performance will be pleasant, according to the account that follows (655d7–e5), but the latter will not (at least for the reasons about to be given). Presumably the

composer makes the behaviour pleasant in the latter case by attaching to it the pleasant media of 'harmony' and rhythm (cf. 654a).

655d7–e1 'When the words . . . comport with a performer's character (*pros tropou*)—either with his nature (*kata phusin*) or with his training (*kata ethos*) or with both—'

On *tropos* as character, see note on 655d6–7. In allowing that some aspects of a person's character are according to nature, the Athenian does not mean that they cannot be altered by training (*ethos*; alternatively, *sunêtheia* as at 655e4 and 655e6–7); he means only that they do not arise from training.

The terms *ethos* and *sunêtheia* are systematically ambiguous between (i) a trained or educated disposition (658e3 and 666d9; cf. 632d6) and (ii) the process of training that yields such a disposition (653b5–6, 663c1, and 656d8). Even the verb *ethizesthai*, which usually invokes the process (659d5 and 660a3), can capture the disposition (as at 673d1, where it is translated as 'propensity'). Both senses (i) and (ii) are operative in the use of *ethos* and *ethizesthai* in Book 3, 681b1–3. These terms are often translated as 'habit' and 'habituate'; however, the English terms have a strongly behavioural connotation, and the Athenian often applies the Greek terms to dispositions to feel, not just to act.

The translation 'training' is nicely ambiguous between senses (i) and (ii), and is used in the present volume for all occurrences of *ethos*, *sunêtheia*, and their cognates, except at 625a5 (see note ad loc). This volume also uses 'training' to translate *gumnazein* (athletic or physical training) at 635c2–3, 626b5, 647c9, 648c3, and 648d3, d7. On the distinction between *êthos* and *ethos*, see note on 625a5.

655e2–5 'will necessarily enjoy them and praise them and call them beautiful (*kala*). But if the choral components run contrary to his nature, type, or training the inevitable result will be that he cannot enjoy or praise them but will instead call them ugly (*aischra*)'

alternatively: 'will . . . enjoy them . . . and call them admirable (*kala*) . . .'

On nature, type, and training, see note on 655d7–e1. We are told here that those choral works just described as 'in accord' with a person's character (*pros tropou*, d7) are pleasant to us, while those that are contrary to our character (*para tropon*) are unpleasant. Presumably this means that for a courageous person it is pleasant to perform songs and dances that depict the words and actions characteristic of courage, and unpleasant to perform songs depicting cowardly actions or words (cf. 669c and Book 7, 802c–e where different rhythms and 'harmonies' are appropriate to different kinds of people). We are also told that such pleasure and pain goes along with the behaviour of praising and calling *kalon* ('beautiful' or 'admirable') the thing that pleases one. This behaviour is the external manifestation of the 'appearance' that the behaviour is *kalon*. Thus here too, as in the dilemma posed above (see note on 655c4–d4), the Athenian assumes that what pleases us seems *kalon* to us. At 657c5–6 the Athenian will state the connection between pleasure and evaluative judgements more explicitly (see note ad loc).

655e5–656a2 'where a person's nature is correct, but his training is the opposite, or his training is correct but his nature the opposite, his praises will conflict with his pleasures, and he will call such choral dances "pleasant but wicked (*ponêra*)" '

more literally: '. . . he will call each of these works "pleasant but wicked" '

The works in question are those in which 'his praises conflict with his pleasures'—with 'praises' used broadly enough to include both positive and negative evaluative judgements (such as the verdict 'wicked' in the next line). Having explained how one comes to take pleasure in choral music and to think it *kalon* (655d5–e5), the Athenian now explains how one can come to have pleasures opposed to what one calls *kalon*. He thus accounts for how people arrive at the view that he claimed at 655d3 is 'even more likely to lead us astray'. The harmful consequences of the straying will be explained next at 656a7–b8. Here we are given the cause of the 'straying': either one's 'nature' or one's training (*sunêtheia*) is incorrect. The Athenian does not simply say that the nature and training are inconsistent, but that one of the two is incorrect; thus he must reject the first horn of the dilemma at 655c4–5.

Note that these remarks concern the experience of choral music; they do not purport to be a general discussion of psychological conflict. The inconsistent response here described (being pleased in what one calls *aischron*) should be distinguished from the phenomena of psychological conflict described in the puppets metaphor in Book 1 (644d–645c), which Mouze (2005: 160) links to the present passage. In the puppets passage, conflicting impulses issuing from the golden and iron strings pull a person in opposing directions: one struggles to do what one's calculation (*logismos*) directs, against the opposing pull of pleasures and pains. But the 'nature' and 'training' invoked here are both aspects of the iron strings; each is treated as capable of giving rise either to the affective response (pleasure/displeasure) or to the evaluative assessment (praising, calling it *kalon* or *aischron*). These evaluative responses are intimately bound up with the pleasures and pains that, according to 653a–c, must be trained (*ethizesthai*) to follow one's *logos*.

656a4–5 'ashamed to sing out their hearty approval'
more literally: 'ashamed to sing out a hearty declaration that these things are beautiful/admirable (*kala*)'

656a5 'although they do enjoy doing so when they are on their own (*par' hautois*)'
alternatively: '. . . enjoy doing so inside themselves'
Taking *para* + dative like French *chez* (as at 656d6; more literally: 'at their own homes'). The alternative, '. . . inside themselves' (Saunders, Brisson/Pradeau, Schöpsdau) is not a standard meaning of *para* + dative, and the Athenian's point is not that such imperfectly educated agents hide the pleasure they feel while performing shameful songs in the presence of their betters, but that their sense of shame either restrains them from engaging in those activities in the presence of better people (or makes them feel shame if discovered in the act),

but that when on their own (or among bad characters—cf. 656b3–4) they enjoy performing them. NB: shame is a version of fear (646e10–647a2), which is one of the iron strings in the puppet image (644c9–d1).

656a7–b8

(3) benefits and harms from choral pleasures

Whereas above (655d–e) the Athenian explained the causes of our being pleased with some choral works and displeased with others, here he considers the effect of such pleasures and pains, with particular focus on the question of whether the choral works to be performed on a regular basis, as part of the educational curriculum, may include (contrary to 655b) songs and dances depicting vicious people. He identifies two harmful consequences of enjoying such performances (656b2–6): one's censure of such people becomes insincere, and one becomes like them oneself.

656b1–3 'It's just like what happens to someone who associates with bad men of wicked character (*ponêrois êthesin*) and comes to enjoy and welcome their company instead of disliking them'
'Character' here translates *êthos*, used in place of *tropos* ('type of character') in 655d5, e3.

We are here given an account of how a person whose nature (*phusis*) is decent comes to have a *sunêtheia* (trained disposition) that is incorrect (as at 655e5–6). Regularly performing (or experiencing) choral art that depicts vicious behaviour is like spending time with vicious people and thereby coming to enjoy their company; the point is repeated at 669b8–c1. See Mouze 2005: 161–4; Hatzistavrou 2011: 362–6.

656b3–4 'When he condemns their wickedness it is as if he is playing a game (*hôs en paidias moirai*) or dreaming'
more literally: 'When he condemns them it is as if he is playing a game and only dreaming of its badness'

Reading *autou tên mochthêrian* in b4, with England; Schöpsdau favours the alternative reading *hautou* (reflexive), which would yield the translation: 'only a dreaming grasp of his own badness'.

In keeping with the general claim above that one's praises and censures go along with one's feelings of pleasure and pain, respectively (655d7–e5), the Athenian here betrays the assumption that those feelings of pleasure and pain affect the security or depth of those evaluations: the person who condemns a bad activity but also enjoys it has an impaired grasp of its badness (on the alternative reading: of his own badness in enjoying it). Thus the person who fully grasps what is *kalon* and *aischron* must love and take pleasure in the one and hate and be pained at the other. For a forceful articulation of the epistemic significance of feeling the right pleasures and pains, see Moss 2012. While proper pleasures and pains will not suffice for wisdom (653a), the Athenian here indicates that they are necessary for it. On 'playing a game' (*en paidias*, 656b3) v. being serious (*meta spoudês*, 656a5), see note on 635b5.

656b7 'this absolutely necessary consequence'
An arrestingly strong claim, which underscores the importance that the Athenian places on early education (644a–b), and choral training in particular, which trains us to 'enjoy' good characters rather than bad ones (654c–655b). See note on 644b1–2.

656c1–657c2

Choral composition must be strictly regulated

Having just established that choral song and dance depicting vicious characters will make its performers vicious (and similarly for virtuous characters), the Athenian now concludes that the legislator (whose concern with making the citizens virtuous was made clear in Book 1, 630c, 631a–c) must exercise strict controls over the choral compositions to be used in education (656c1–8). He hails Egypt as an example of such successful control (656d1–657a2). Only 'beautiful'

(656d7) or 'correct' (657a8) works are to be performed by the youth of the city, and once the standards of such correctness are determined (a task addressed later at 667b–670e) no composer is to be allowed to transgress them (656d5–657a2).

656c1 'where there are good laws'
more literally: 'where laws have been admirably established (*kalôs . . . keimenoi*)'
See note on 634d9–e1.

656c2–3 'education (*paideian*) and recreation (*paidian*)'
A play on the similar words for education and for play, amusement, or recreation. The phrase is restated at 657c3–4 as 'music and recreation'. On the range of the term *paidia*, see note on 635b5. In the present context, as at 635b5, 649d9, 650a6, 657c4, d3, and 685a7, its connection to pleasure is especially salient.

656c4–5 'whatever rhythm, tune, or phrases they please'
Rhythm (*rhuthmos*), tune or melody (*melos*), and words or phrases (*rhêmata*) are the three elements of choral composition invoked at 669b2–3. On *rhuthmos*, see also note on 653e3–5. On the relation between *melos* and *harmonia*, see note on 669c3–8.

656c5–6 'teach it to the youths and children . . . in their choruses'
These are choruses composed of youths and children (see 664b–d). On choral performance, see note on 654a4–5.

656c6–7 'regardless of the effect it may have on their development towards virtue or wickedness'
more literally: 'bringing about whatever may chance regarding (*pros*) virtue or wickedness' (taking *hoti* as the subject of *tuchêi* in c6: thus Schöpsdau, against England)
On England's preferred reading, the effect on the children is to give them whatever character (virtuous or vicious) the poet happens to have. The educational role of choruses is first introduced in 641b.

656d7–8 'the youth of the city must be trained to practise (*metacheirizesthai tais sunêtheiais*) beautiful (*kala*) gestures and songs'
That properly educated youths must perform beautiful (*kalon*) song and dance was asserted at 654b–655d, where both the ethical and aesthetic dimensions of *kalon* are operative (see notes on 654b6–7 and 654b11–c1). On *sunêtheia* as training (as at 666d9–10), see note on 655d7–e1. On choral performance as a way to shape character, see note on 656b1–3.

656d8–9 'Having established which ones are beautiful, and what they are like'
Identifying these standards for *kalon* choral music will be the Athenian's focus from 667b–670e; he will reject the standard of pleasure at 657c–659c; cf. 667b–668b. On what these standards consist in, see note on 656d9–e3.

656d9–e3 'they put these on display in their temples, permitting no painter or anyone else who depicts gestures to introduce new forms (*kainotomein*) or to invent anything that departs from the ancestral tradition'
Here control of the visual arts is used to illustrate the way in which choral compositions are to be regulated. As D'Angour (2006) notes of *Rep.* 424b3–c6, the prohibition is not against composing new works (*aismata nea*, 424c1) but against introducing new musical forms (*tropon ôidês neon*, 424c2); the latter is called *kainotomein* in the present passage (656e2; cf. 657b4–7 and note ad loc). That new songs and dances will be allowed, even encouraged, is indicated at 665c5–7 (see note ad loc). The point of the restrictions invoked here by the Athenian is to make sure that any new compositions are as beautiful (*kalon*) as the old ones (657a1–2). What the requisite musical orthodoxy consists in is not further specified here. Note that he has already given at least a preliminary answer to the question, raised at 654b–e, of what makes songs and dances beautiful: they depict the words and actions of virtuous people (655a–b), but this answer does not identify the specifically musical forms (on analogy

with the styles of painting in the Egyptian example) in which such behaviour is to be depicted.

His later discussion will require that the rhythms and 'harmonies' of the work be appropriate to the gestures and songs (669b–670e). This requirement, in conjunction with the restriction to the depiction of virtuous activities (655a–b), would (on the musical theory of Damon) effectively require that choral works be in the Dorian and Phrygian 'harmonies' (see note on 669c3–8). (These 'harmonies' and rhythms may be the 'kinds' (*tropoi*) and 'forms' (*eidê*) of music invoked at *Rep*. 424b3–c6.) While the Athenian here suggests that it will suffice to display exemplars of the allowed forms, his later discussion will require 'wise judges' to discern whether the appropriate 'harmonies' and rhythms are employed (see general note on 669b5–670a3). On what 'putting on display' consists in, see Rutherford 2013: 72–4.

657a1–2 'exactly the same art (*technên*)'
alternatively: 'exactly the same technique'
An exaggerated claim, according to Griffith 2013: 21–2 and Rutherford 2013: 74–9.

657a4 'An extreme (*huperballontôs*) feat of legislation and statecraft indeed (*men oun*)'
The Athenian here endorses Clinias' remark of 657a3—'that's amazing' (*thaumaston legeis*)—which is not an expression of disbelief (as des Places, England, Schöpsdau, and Saunders construe it), but a confirmation of the Athenian's own '[y]ou will be amazed to hear' (*thauma kai akousai*, 656d5); thus Brisson/Pradeau. Denniston's citation of the passage does not select between affirmative and adversative senses of *men oun* (Denniston 1950: 475).

657a6–8 'it is possible to provide enduring stability to songs (*melê*) that have a natural correctness (*tên orthotêta phusei parechomena*), provided the legislator is bold enough (*tharrounta*)'

The transmitted text poses intractable difficulties (discussed by England, Saunders 1972, and Schöpsdau), some of which are alleviated by construing *tharrounta* as invoking boldness rather than confidence (see note on 644c9–d1). Schöpsdau rightly draws our attention to the threefold occurrence of the verb in this paragraph. On natural 'correctness' (*orthotês*), see note on 657b2–3. For another example of legislative daring on musical matters, see 663d6–e2.

657b2–3 'the standards of correctness in these matters (*autôn . . . tên orthotêta*)'
more literally: 'the correctness in these matters'
The same term, *orthotês*, is used at 657a8. It is clear from the use of 'beautiful' (*kalon*) at 656d7 and 657a1 that the Athenian understands correct music as beautiful (*kalon*) music. He will return to the topic of correctness in music at 667b–670e, where he will assign to the Chorus of Dionysus the task of grasping, or at least applying, the standards of correctness.

657b4–7 'the pursuit (*zêtêsis*) of pleasure and pain in the constant striving after novelty in music (*kainêi . . . mousikêi chrêsthai*) has little power to undermine (*diaphtheirai*) *sanctified* choral dancing (*kathierôtheisan choreian*)'
alternatively: 'the constant striving of pleasure and pain to experience novelty in music . . . '
The phrase 'pursuit of pleasure and pain' must be shorthand for 'pursuit of pleasure and avoidance of pain' since pain is a natural object of avoidance rather than pursuit (634a8, 792d1, 875b8–9), hence its status as an 'opposing advisor' to pleasure at 644c6. The 'novelty in music' (*kainê mousikê*, alt: 'new music') must be what is referred to as 'introducing new forms' (*kainotomein*) at 656e2 (see note on 656d9–e3). *[K]athierôtheisan* (sanctified) recalls the connection of music to religious festivals at 653c–d and the verb is used again for the officially sanctioned music in Book 7 (799a4, 809b6, 813a2). The Athenian's point is that giving the correct musical forms a solid (cf. *bebaiôs*, 657a7) institutional basis in religious rites is a

sufficient and powerful antidote to the natural craving for novelty. On the power of religious norms to combat the attraction of pleasures, see also Book 8, 838a–c. On the new music of Plato's time, see note on 669d2–3.

657c3–660a8

Why pleasure is not the standard for judging choral works

Having established that the goal of musical education is to shape citizens' pleasures and pains, and that therefore legislators must take steps to ensure that only beautiful song and dance are to be performed in the choral performance that is the medium for such cultivation (656d–657b), the Athenian now turns to consider the popular thesis that beauty in music consists simply in its ability to give pleasure. After acknowledging the considerations that give the thesis its apparent plausibility (657c3–658a3), he details at length its specific consequences (658a4–d10), which conflict with the assumption, shared among the three interlocutors, that the verdict of the best educated (specifically the elders) is authoritative on the relative merits of musical compositions (658e1–5). He concludes that the proper procedure for identifying beautiful music is to have the virtuous select the music that will improve the pleasures of the spectators and performers (658e6–659c5).

657c3–658a3

The apparent plausibility of the pleasure criterion

The intimate relationship between feelings of pleasure, evaluative judgements, and choral music gives initial plausibility to the thesis that the best choral music is that which gives the most pleasure.

657c3–4 'correct use (*chreian orthên*) of music and recreation' 'Recreation' translates *paidia,* intended here in the sense of pleasure or amusement, as is clear at 657e4. See 656c2–3 and general note on *paidia* at 635b5; cf. 673a7–8 and note. The notion of 'use' (*chrêia*) here is difficult to construe, as the explanation given in the immediately following lines (657c5–6; see note) cites the intimate relationship between our feelings of pleasure and our judgements of value, rather than a way of 'using' or 'employing' music. 'Use' here might have the same sense as the cognate verb *chrêtai* at 654c5, where someone who has correct views about what is *kalon* and *aischron* 'treats (*chrêtai*) them as such'—where the latter involves feeling pleasure in the things one thinks *kalon*, and distress at those one thinks *aischron* (see note ad loc). Alternatively, it might be the use of music and pleasure as educational media, in which case the account of correct use extends from 657c5 to 660a8.

657c5–6 'When we think we are doing well (*eu prattein*) we are pleased (*chairômen*) and . . . when we are pleased we think we are doing well'
A more explicit statement of the relationship between feelings of pleasure and evaluative judgements than the implications at 655e2–5 (see note ad loc). Not only does one praise and call (*prosagoreuein*) 'beautiful' what one enjoys (655e1–5), but one thinks it good. *eu prattein* is a synonym for *eudaimonia* (happiness); see note on 628d5. On the connection between the beautiful/admirable (*kalon*) and the good (*agathon*—adverb: *eu*), see notes on 637e5, 641b8–c1, 667c6–7.

657c8–d2 'unable to keep quiet . . . eager to dance in a chorus'
'Keeping quiet' (*hêsuchian . . . agein*) encompasses both keeping silent and keeping still, while choral performance (*choreuein*) involves both singing and dancing. The inability to refrain from sound and movement recalls the juvenile propensity to engage in both that is invoked as the origin of choral dance at 653e1–3 and 673a7–8; see notes ad loc.

657d5 'we [elders] set up competitions'

Competitions between choruses were a regular feature of religious festivals in Plato's time (see Morrow 1960: 377–9) and will be an institution in the city of Magnesia as well (764c–765c, 828b–c). Participants in such contests were the 'festival performers' of 657e1. On the training for such competitions, see 665e6–8. On the elders as the proper judges of choral works see 658e–659a and 670a–b.

657d9–e3 'So we don't find entirely off the mark . . . the opinion . . . that the most accomplished and deserving of victory is the one who gives us the greatest pleasure and delight'
It is because we take pleasure in the performances we think are beautiful, and think beautiful those performances that please us (657c5–6; see note ad loc), that we might think that pleasure is the criterion of beautiful performance. Thus Clinias endorses pleasure as the criterion at 658a3. The Athenian endorses a qualified version of the principle at 658e6–659a1, but he rejects the criterion outright at 667e9–668a4; see notes on 668a9–10 and 658e6–9.

658a4–e5

The divergence of verdicts on the pleasure criterion

Those of different age, sex, and education would judge different compositions most pleasant. However, the most authoritative judgement would be from those with the best education, the elders. The Athenian here sets out to raise problems for the pleasure criterion, pointing out that it conflicts with his and his opponents' view that elders should be the judges of musical competitions in which younger performers compete.

658a4 'In these matters . . . "perhaps" is not good enough'
more literally: 'let us not judge quickly (*tachu*) in such a matter'
Here *tachu* refers back to Clinias' answer *tach' an* (a3), translated as 'perhaps' (alternatively: 'probably').

658a5 'divide (*diairountes*) the matter into its parts (*kata merê*)'
On the method of division (*diairesis*), see note on 631a8–b1. The relevant parts invoked over 658a–e are the pleasures of different kinds of people.

658c3 'which one is rightly (*dikaiôs*) the winner?'
Note the assumption that there is a rightful winner. It is to this assumption that the Athenian will appeal in order to discredit the pleasure criterion. Clinias, in taking this question to be 'strange' (c4), as well as in his explanation of that strangeness (see note on 658c4–6), shows that he has no idea that the pleasure criterion puts his own judgements on a footing with those of every other person, a point the Athenian is only about to make.

658c4–6 'How could anyone answer . . . without having listened to each of the contestants himself?'
Clinias responds as if he is being asked which of the performers he himself would find most pleasing, rather than which of them would please the most spectators. In effect, he is adopting the criterion that the Athenian will articulate below at 658e1–4.

658c7–8 'Shall I tell you the strange (*atopon*) reply?'
Clinias has evidently not considered the consequences of the pleasure criterion, about to be drawn, which conflict with his assumptions that the elders are the authoritative judges.

658c10–d8 'if the very small children are delivering the verdict, won't they select the puppeteer? . . . But we old men . . . would declare [the rhapsode] to be the overwhelming winner'
The Athenian predicts that the audience members' verdicts will differ according to age, sex, and education. When he claims, subsequently, that the verdict of his own age and sex class (old men) is the most authoritative, since their training is the 'best by far in any city anywhere today' (658e3–4), the comparison is presumably with that of other age and sex groups. On the different verdicts, see Folch 2013: 342–5.

658e1–3 'you and I at any rate (*ge*) must declare the proper winners to be those selected by our own age group'
One might suppose, given the restrictive *ge*, that this expresses the psychological necessity noted above (655d–656a; cf. 657c) of taking to be most beautiful whatever pleases one the most. But this would not show that the elders' verdict is more authoritative, which the Athenian's next sentence affirms (see note on 658e3–4); see also note on 658c4–6. On the elders as proper judges of music, see Bartels 2012.

658e3–4 'For our training (*ethos*) seems to be the best by far in any city anywhere today'
'Training' here translates *ethos* (see notes on 655d7–e1 and on 656b1–3). It refers to the cultivated disposition, alternatively referred to as *sunêtheia* at 655e4, where it is distinguished from one's *phusis*, as a distinct aspect of one's character (*tropos*) (655d–656a). It arises from musical training (656d7–8). The main force of the present claim is that in any city today, the cultivated disposition of the elders is superior to that of other age groups. The restriction of the comparison to the present (*nun*) might, as England suggests, leave room for the further expertise that members of the Chorus of Dionysus will need (670a–e). At any rate, the Athenian is not seeking to *prove* that the education of the elders is best; he simply appeals to his interlocutors' own assumption that they themselves are the authoritative judges of musical compositions (cf. 657d5–7) to show that this stance conflicts with the pleasure criterion. At 666d8–e1 he will allege that his interlocutors' training was in fact deficient.

658e6–659c8

Music should improve the pleasures of the audience

The judges of choral competitions should not be swayed by the approval of the audience, since the function of music at those festivals (as was said at 654a) is to shape the pleasures and pains of the mass audience, not to reinforce those they already have. Hence the poets should take their standards from the qualified judges, not from the audience.

658e6–9 'I agree with the majority this far at any rate: that music is to be judged (*krinesthai*) by pleasure—not, however, the pleasure it affords any random person. My view is, roughly, that the finest (*kallistên*) Muse delights the best people'
The majority view is stated at 657d9–e3 and will be rejected at 668a9–10 (see note ad loc). Note that the Athenian's positive statement of his view ('the finest Muse . . . ') does not endorse pleasure as the *criterion* by which the best people evaluate music; rather he notes the extensional equivalence between the finest music and that which pleases the best educated. When he says below that such judges require wisdom and courage (659a3–4), he implies that their verdict is an expression of wisdom. Thus there is no substantive conflict between what he says here and his categorical rejection of the pleasure criterion at 668a9–b2. See notes ad loc and Moss 2012: 213. The criteria by which the best educated will judge (*krinein*) music will be detailed at length at 669b–670e. (Hatzistavrou (2011: 367) proposes to avoid the conflict by supposing that pleasure is a criterion for the Athenian only in the sense that good music must be pleasant to the young people it is intended to educate; however, the present passage clearly tells against that proposal.)

659a3–4 'they must possess not only wisdom (*phronêseôs*) but courage as well'
The requirement of wisdom (*phronêsis*) is explained at 659a4–6, and that of courage at 659a6–b1. On the wisdom involved in complete virtue, see note on 653a7–9. Presumably here it is understood to include the expertise outlined at 668b–670e for evaluating musical compositions.

659b4–5 'This used to be possible under the ancient law of the Greeks'

See Book 3, 700a–701e, where the view that music is to be judged by the criterion of pleasure is also roundly rejected.

659b5–6 'the Sicilian and Italian law (*nomos*)'
Here, as in the previous line, *nomos* probably indicates a practice or norm rather than a statute. See Introduction.

659c3–4 'better characters than their own'
'Character' here translates *êthos*—as at 656b1–3 (see note ad loc); it is the 'type' (*tropos*) invoked at 655d5–e5.

659c9–660a8

Composers should present serious content in pleasant media

The Athenian concludes his rejection of the pleasure criterion and draws together the strands of his previous accounts of education and music. The job of the poets is to put into pleasant vehicles (beautiful phrases, 'harmony', and rhythm) the speech and actions of virtue. Songs are 'charms' to make serious matters pleasant.

659c9 'the third or fourth time'
The account of education about to be recapitulated was first sketched in Book 1 at 643b–644b and then set out more fully at the beginning of Book 2, 653a–c. On the relationship between the three accounts, see Mouze 2005: 113–19.

659d1–4 'education is the drawing (*holkê*) and guidance (*agogê*) of children towards the correct account (*logon*) that is articulated by the law and accepted as correct by the worthiest and eldest citizens on the basis of their experience (*di' empeirian*)'
Building on his previous statements that education trains a person's pleasures and pains to agree (*sumphônein*) with one's account (*logos*, 653b–c), and that the elders are the authoritative judges of music

(658e), the Athenian here elaborates that the account (*logos*) in question is:

(1) articulated in the law (cf. 644d2–3, 645a5, b4–8, and note on 644d2–3); and
(2) expressed in the judgements of those elders.

Thus the *sumphônia* (agreement) to be cultivated (659e3) is interpersonal agreement across generations, obedience to the law, and to the elders of the community, in contrast with the intrapersonal *sumphônia* in the 'complete virtue' mentioned at 653b6. On experience (*empeiria*), see also 632d5 and 673c7. The language here recalls the puppet metaphor in Book 1 where the gold and iron cords are pulls (*helxis, agôgê*) that draw against each other (*anthelkein*). On England's proposal that education, as conceived in the present passage, supplies the requisite 'assistants' to the golden cord, see note on 645a1. On the translation of *logos* as 'account', see Moss 2014 and note on 653b3–4. It is also worth noting that *nomos* (law) can also mean 'song' or 'melody' (700b5), and the message 'articulated by the law' (*hupo tou nomou*) in the present passage (659d2–3) is equally the message of the songs about to be invoked in 659e–660a.

659d5 'trained to feel pleasure or pain'
alternatively: 'habituated (*ethizêtai*)'
The same verb is used at 660a3. The habituation or training is what cultivates the *ethos* or *sunêtheia* which is part of a person's character type (*tropos*) (see 655d7–e1 and note ad loc). The cultivated disposition that results is called 'education' (*paideia*) at 653a–c, and it is inculcated by participation in choral song and dance (654a).

659d6 'those who accept the law'
more literally: 'those who are persuaded (*pepeismenois*) by the law'
On the significance of persuasion, see note on 632b7–8.

659e1–3 'Bringing about this "agreement" . . . is the very serious purpose (*espoudasmenai*) of the things that we call "songs" (*ôidas*) (which are really charms (*epôidai*) for our souls)'
A playful etymology meant to make the point that the pleasure afforded by song and dance attracts us to the words and gestures set into these agreeable forms, even if we would not antecedently find those words and gestures agreeable without this pleasant packaging. On songs as charms, see also 664b, 665c, 666c, and Morrow 1960: 309–12; Helmig 2003; and Mouze 2005:165–8. On 'agreement' (*sumphônia*), see note on 653b4–5. On the serious v. the playful, see note on 659e3–5.

659e3–5 'Children's souls . . . can't abide seriousness (*spoudên*), so we perform these charms in the playful guise of songs'
more literally: 'they are performed as play and songs (*paidiai te kai ôidai kaleisthai te kai prattesthai*)'
On the contrast between *paidia* (play or recreation) with seriousness (*spoudê*, e4), see note on 635b5.

659e5–660a1 'We are like those who care for the ill and infirm, who deliberately use pleasant-tasting dishes and drinks to deliver wholesome foods'
more literally: ' . . . who try to serve (*peirôntai . . . prospherein*) wholesome food in pleasant dishes and beverages'
The songs or charms just mentioned are the medium by which the young are to be trained to delight in what their elders recognize to be good, on analogy with the way a child may be trained to take pleasure in wholesome foods by getting used to eating them in pleasant-tasting dishes. By contrast, Moss (2012: 218) implies that 'those who care for the ill and infirm' deliver foods that are naturally pleasant with no need of culinary art to make them appealing. But the Athenian's point here is that the ill and infirm do not find nutritious food appealing, any more than children find appealing the serious business involved in the actions and utterances of the

virtuous. Moss' main concern is to insist that the pleasure afforded by *kalon* music is not contingently connected to the features that make it *kalon*; however, the Athenian's concern in the present passage is not with the pleasantness of *kalon* music but with its message or content, which he claims will not appeal to children or to improperly educated adults. On what makes music *kalon* besides its message or content, see 668e–670e and general note on 668b9–669b4.

660a5–6 'The . . . legislator will persuade the composers to do the same thing with their lovely and laudable phrases (*kalois rhêmasi kai epainetois*), and if he fails to persuade them he will compel them'
alternatively: 'the legislator will use beautiful (alt: admirable) and laudable phrases to persuade . . . ' (Brisson/Pradeau)
The option of persuasion is omitted when the point is restated at 660e2. While it is important that the citizens be persuaded by the legislator rather than simply forced (see note on 632b7–8; cf. 663e1–2), the Athenian does not hold the same scruples about the poets. The 'lovely and laudable phrases' (660a5) are, with the 'harmony' and rhythms about to be mentioned (660a7), the pleasant vehicles for the legislator's message, analogous to the pleasant-tasting dishes in the nutrition analogy (659e5–660a3). On Brisson/Pradeau's alternative construal of the syntax, it is the legislator, rather than the poet, who functions analogously to the nutritionist.

III
THE TEACHINGS OF BEAUTIFUL CHORAL MUSIC

660b1–664b2

In response to Clinias' claim that only Spartan and Cretan cities conform to the standards of beautiful music articulated above (660b1–d10), the Athenian articulates the doctrines that he expects beautiful music will teach. The central teaching is that the just life is happy and pleasant, while the unjust is unhappy and unpleasant, no matter how many advantages the former lacks and the latter contains (660d11–662a8). This thesis is, to the Athenian, as 'obvious' as that 'Crete is an island' (662b4), but to Clinias and Megillus, who have been taught differently in their Cretan and Spartan education, it is quite implausible. After offering a battery of arguments for the thesis and for the importance of persuading citizens to accept it (662c6–663e2), the Athenian concludes with the optimistic assessment that, no matter how implausible a thesis is, poets are capable of persuading children of its truth (663e3–664b2).

660b1–2 'is this how you think poets compose in other cities today?'
more literally: '. . . how they compose (*poiein*) . . .'
'Composing' (*poiein*) here is broad enough to encompass the creative activity of poets as well as of musical composers and choreographers—that is, the producers of works in all the genres of art encompassed by *mousikê* (see note on 642a4). Hence *poiêtês* is translated as either 'poet' as at 659b8, 660e2, 662b5, or as 'composer' 668c2, 669d2, 670b5 (and as both at 669c2); the related *poiêtikos* is rendered 'composer' at 656c3 and 660a4.

660b2–5 'except in my own home and in Sparta, I don't see that things are done in the way you describe. Rather, there is always something new (*kaina*) going on in dance and in the other branches of music'
Clinias has in mind the Athenian's claim that innovation in musical forms (*kainotomein*) is not to be tolerated (656d–657b; see note on 656d9–e3), not his most recent point that the legislator must use this pleasant medium to promulgate wholesome doctrines (659e–660a). It is on the latter front that the Athenian will find Dorian music deficient.

660b6–7 'with the changes guided not by law (*hupo nomôn*) but by unregulated (*ataktôn*) pleasures'
On institutions that cater to the audience's pleasures, see 659a–c.

660c6–d1 'it is never pleasant to inveigh against errors . . . although sometimes it is necessary to do so'
An anticipation of his own impending criticism of Spartan and Knossan music (660d–663e).

660d6–7 'their practice would be more admirable (*kallionôs houtôs*) than at present'
An instance of the ethical/political dimension of the *kalon*, prevalent in the discussion of institutions in Book 1. See note on 630c7.

660d11–661d5

Music must teach that the just are happy and the unjust unhappy

The Athenian here claims that poets must be compelled to affirm a very strong pair of doctrines about the relationship between justice and happiness (660e2–6). He illustrates this by revising a poem of Tyrtaeus (criticized in Book 1, 629a–e) in line with the mandated doctrines (660e7–661a4), and then articulates a further set of doctrines about 'so-called goods' (661a4–d5). On the relationship between the two sets of doctrines, see general note on 661a4–d5.

660e1 'musical education'
more literally: 'education (*paideia*) and music (*mousikê*)'
The two types of *paideia* (education) are 'music' (encompassing poetry, drama, song, and dance) and athletics (*gumnastikê*); see note on 642a4 and on 673a8–10.

660e2–6 'the good man, since he is moderate and just, is happy and blessed—whether he is tall and strong or short and weak . . . [or] wealthy— but . . . the unjust man, no matter whether he is "richer than Cinyras and Midas", is wretched and lives miserably'
'Happy' (*eudaimôn*) here means living well, not simply feeling satisfied or content (see note on 628d5). '[R]icher than Cinyras

and Midas' is a quotation from the poet Tyrtaeus (fr. 12.6 West), which the Athenian is about to revise (660e7–661a4) to fit the doctrines articulated here. Height, strength, and riches are invoked as examples of the 'so-called goods' that the Athenian will enumerate more fully below (661a5–b4). The doctrine that the poets are supposed to promulgate is a combination of (1) a *sufficiency* thesis: that the just person is happy no matter how many of these so-called goods he lacks, and (2) a *necessity* thesis: that the unjust person is unhappy, no matter how many of them he possesses (i.e. justice is necessary for happiness). While Bobonich (2002: 213–14) correctly notes that the Athenian's literal statements here do not on their own entail the *sufficiency* thesis (for they leave open that some minimal level of so-called goods is required for happiness), they do entail it if 'whether he is tall and strong . . . ' is illustrative (meant to invoke all the so-called goods) rather than exhaustive (thus Annas (1999: 45) on the list of goods at 631b–d). For further discussion of the *sufficiency* thesis, see general note on 661a4–d5.

Tyrtaeus rewritten

660e7–9 'Your poet says, if he speaks correctly, "I would not memorialize . . . a man" who fails to accomplish with justice all his so-called admirable (*kala*) achievements'

The poet is Tyrtaeus, whose central role in Dorian education has been discussed in Book 1 (629a–630d). The ensuing pastiche of quotation and paraphrase, which extends to 661a4, is manifestly not what Tyrtaeus said. Thus the Athenian's point is that the Dorian poet does not 'speak correctly'. (Only verbatim quotations from Tyrtaeus are enclosed in quotation marks in the translation.)

Tyrtaeus himself wrote that he will not praise a person who (i) 'outruns the North Wind of Thrace' or is (ii) 'richer than Cinyras or Midas' unless he (iii) 'lays waste the enemy, assailing him at close quarters and emboldened at the sight of bloody slaughter' (fr. 12 West)—a stance that the Athenian criticizes in Book 1 for invoking only a partial and impoverished conception of virtue (629a–630c).

The Athenian here rewrites these verses to have the poet proclaim that he will not praise anyone who accomplishes (i) or (iii) unless they possess justice; he has just quoted from Tyrtaeus at 660e5 to make the same claim about the person in (ii).

The unstated presupposition connecting these putative poetic teachings (which concern who is worthy of praise) to the mandated doctrines of 660e2–6 (which concern who is happy) is that a poet who 'memorializes' or praises a person thereby declares him to be happy.

660e9–661a2 'even one who (*kai dê kai*) in such a condition (*toioutos ôn*) "lays waste the enemy and assails him at close quarters", but is unjust (*adikos de ôn*)'

A multiply ambiguous set of phrases. On the most natural reading of the sentence (followed by Brisson/Pradeau), 'in such condition' (*toioutos de ôn*) means 'without justice'—i.e. *toioutos* (661a1) refers back to *mê . . . meta dikaiosunês* (660e8–9). So construed, these lines are a straightforward application of the doctrine mandated at 660e2–6. However, it is also natural to read the participial phrase, 'but is unjust' (*adikos de ôn,* 661a2), as parallel to and contrastive with *toioutos ôn*—in which case 'in such a condition' would mean 'with justice' and *toioutos* would refer back to *meta dikaiosunês* (660e9). However, the sentence as a whole makes more sense if we construe '*toioutos*' in the first way, in which case the contrast marked by *de* in *adikos de ôn* would not be with *toioutos ôn* (since this too means he is unjust) but with the immediately preceding phrase directly quoted from Tyrtaeus ('assails (*oregoito*) him at close quarters . . . ', 661a1). So construed, the participial phrase modifies the subject of *oregoito* in a1.

661a2–4 'or who is "emboldened (*mête tolmôi*) by the sight of bloody slaughter", or "outruns (*mête nikôi*) the North Wind of Thrace", or achieves (*mête autôi . . . gignoito*) any other of the so-called goods' more literally: 'or one who does not [sc. with justice] feel emboldened . . . or outrun . . . or achieve . . . '

This unwieldy continuation of the relative clause begun at 660e8 (*hos mê . . . meta dikaiosunês prattoi*—'who fails to accomplish with justice . . . ') risks saying the opposite of the message (660e4–6) that the sentence is intended to illustrate. The present translation takes the *mê* in *mête tolmôi . . . mête nikôi . . . mête gignoito* to apply not to the verb but to an implicit predicate phrase *meta dikaoisunês*, which is explicit in the original *hos mê* clause. Without some such implicit supplement, the rewritten Tyrtaeus will be refusing to praise anyone who fails to be emboldened, win races, or acquire other so-called goods. But such a declaration would fail to express the doctrine that the Athenian has just announced the poet will affirm (660e4–6). Matters are even worse if one takes *adikos de ôn* in a2 to modify the subject of the optatives in 661a2–4 (as do Schöpsdau, Brisson/Pradeau, Saunders, Taylor, des Places, Pangle, and apparently England), for then we are faced with the embarrassment that the revised Tyrtaeus is refusing to praise any unjust person who fails to be emboldened . . . etc. Following England, these translators solve the problem by treating the optatives as expressing the poet's wish (that the unjust person not be emboldened, outrun, etc.). This is a desperate measure, since those optatives are syntactically parallel to the optatives in the original *hos mê* clause in 660e8, and thus should be construed as within the scope of that relative clause. Schöpsdau glosses the wish as based on the view (to be articulated below at 661b–d) that such things are not good for an unjust person to have. However, we have not been told that poets will be compelled to wish their subjects well, and the intrusion of such a suggestion here is an unhelpful distraction from the Athenian's clear message. While Plato could have avoided this confusion by writing οὔτε ὃς τολμῷ . . . etc., instead of μήτε τολμῷ . . . , he is probably attracted to the latter because it replicates Tyrtaeus' own εἰ μὴ τετλαίη (fr 12.11 West), and yields the superficially parallel structure: ὃς μὴ . . . πράττοι . . . , μήτε τολμῷ . . . , μήτε νικῷ . . .). As England laments of another passage (632b6): 'It is impossible not to wish that Plato had lived to rewrite this whole passage.'

661a4–d5

So-called goods and bads

Having insisted (660e5–661a4) that the unjust person must be proclaimed unhappy, no matter how many 'so-called goods' (661a4) he has, the Athenian now turns his attention to these so-called goods. While most people call 'good' such things as wealth, strength, keen senses, military prowess, and the like, such things are in fact only good for the good person, and are positively bad for the unjust person. Indeed, their opposites ('so-called bad things') are good for such a person; they are bad only for the just person.

Justice, happiness, and so-called goods

It is worthwhile to consider the relationship between the theses introduced here about about *so-called goods* and *bads*, and the theses of *necessity* and *sufficiency* that are identified, at 660e2–6, as the message to be promulgated by correct poetry:

Sufficiency:

(1) Anyone who is just is happy

Necessity:

(2) Anyone who is not just is unhappy

The doctrines expounded here (661a4–d5) are:

So-called goods: such things as health, good looks, wealth, etc. are:

(3) good to the just person;
(4) bad to the unjust person.

So-called bads: losing or lacking such things as health, good looks, wealth, etc. are in fact:

(5) good for the unjust person;
(6) bad for the just person.

Bobonich takes the so-called goods to be the 'human goods' that are distinguished from divine goods in Book 1 (631b–d), and he proposes that (3), (4), (5), and (6) are intended to elucidate the thesis, articulated in that earlier context, that the human goods depend on the divine (Bobonich 2002: 89, 123–7):

Dependent Goods thesis (631b–d):

Human goods (health, strength, wealth, etc.) depend on the divine goods (wisdom, moderation, justice, and courage), which themselves all stem from wisdom.

A problem for this hypothesis, as Bobonich notes, is that theses (4) and (5) are considerably stronger than the Dependent Goods thesis (thus he takes them to be hyperbolic overstatements by the Athenian; Bobonich 2002: 126–7, 183–4). Moreover, we might add, the Athenian gives no indication that the Dependent Goods thesis is under discussion in the present context (see note on 661a5–b3). If anything, (3), (4), (5), and (6) are invoked here in elucidation of the Sufficiency and Necessity theses—i.e. (1) and (2). But while (4) provides some support for (2), by addressing the main consideration that might appear to count against it, it is hard to see what relevance (3), (5), and (6) have to either (1) or (2). Indeed, (6) might well be invoked to mount a challenge against (1)—e.g. how could a just person who is suffering the afflictions of Job be considered happy?

Perhaps, however, it is a mistake to construe (3), (4), (5), and (6) as providing philosophical grounding for (1) and (2). After all, these are supposed to be attitudes inculcated by poets in musical compositions, the performance of which shapes citizens' feelings of pleasure and pain, starting right from childhood (654a, 659d–660a). In shaping citizens' feelings of pleasure, we are told, music cultivates their judgements about what is beautiful or admirable (*kalon*) and good (see notes on 655e2–5 and on 657c5–6). We may accordingly suppose that poetic compositions inculcate (1) and (2) in the citizens by training them to be pleased with virtuous people and displeased with vicious people, no matter what vicissitudes of life befall those characters. Similarly, the attitudes expressed in (3) and (4) will be inculcated by musical training that cultivates a disposition to be pleased by the so-called goods only if the virtuous person receives them, and to be repelled by the thought of the vicious person receiving them. And correspondingly for (5) and (6), which concern attitudes towards the so-called bads: proper musical education will train the citizens to be pleased when the bad person incurs them, and sorrowful when they happen to the good person. So construed, (1) through (6) express a psychologically coherent set of evaluative attitudes (towards virtue, vice, and the so-called goods and bads) whose polarities and symmetries make it well suited to a medium that paints in broad strokes and has a limited normative vocabulary.

Such a scheme of values is philosophically unrefined. For example, it lacks the resources to answer definitively such questions as whether the good person can be happy on the rack (a question debated by later philosophers), whether happiness admits of degree, whether the so-called goods are components of happiness, or whether a person can be virtuous without possessing a certain level of so-called goods. The latter are questions raised by philosophical readers of Plato today, in a debate over whether Plato actually endorses the Sufficiency thesis (for example, Bobonich 2002: 209–15; Annas 1999: 31–51; Irwin 1995: 343–7). However, if we keep in mind the medium that is supposed to be delivering this scheme of values, and its intended audience, we should be wary of taking the present passage to furnish the materials for identifying Plato's own nuanced answer to these philosophical questions. See also note on 662a7.

661a5–b3 'They say that being healthy is the best, having good looks is second, and wealth is third'

This list of 'so-called goods' (*legomen' agatha*) is not presented as exhaustive. One might suppose, with Bobonich (2002: 123–7), that they coincide with the 'human goods' that are said to depend on the 'divine goods' (the virtues) at 631c. However, it is possible to construe the 'dependence' of the human on the divine goods as involving the possession of the virtues (e.g. wealth is characterized as a 'human good' in terms that suggest it involves wisdom—see note on 631c1–5). On such a construal, the human goods would be the 'so-called' goods conjoined with the virtues. The ranking of the so-called goods in the present passage is not precisely the same as that of the human goods at 631c (which inserts physical prowess before wealth), but it does coincide precisely with the ranking in the popular drinking song (*skolion*) that is quoted at *Gorg*. 451e (see note on 631c1–5). Thus even the present remarks, no less than the preceding attack on Tyrtaeus, are a criticism of popular poetry.

661b3–4 'achieving immortality upon acquiring all these goods'
Note that immortality is not a so-called good in the same way as the other items on the list; its goodness, as presented here, seems to consist in prolonging the goodness of the other so-called goods, if one has them. This is why it is an evil to someone whose life is unhappy (661c4–5); cf. Bobonich 2002: 181. On the striving for immortality, see *Symp*. 207a.

661b5 'you and I on the other hand presumably say'
The 'presumably' is ironic, as the Athenian evidently expects his interlocutors to balk at affirming these doctrines (cf. 661d7–e4). Note that the Athenian switches seamlessly here from the question of what the poets should affirm in their musical compositions to the views of people who have been educated by those compositions. It is because the doctrines that the Athenian has just articulated are not promulgated in the musical education in Knossos and Sparta that Clinias and Megillus do not take them to be 'obvious' in the way that the Athenian will affirm that he finds them obvious (662b3–4).

661c4 'virtue as a whole (*aretês hapasês*)'
The combination of wisdom, moderation, and courage that amounts to justice at 631c–d; see note on 630b2–3.

661c7–8 'cast into corresponding (*hepomenous*) rhythms and harmonies'
An anticipation of the requirement at 669b–670e that the rhythms and 'harmonies' in a musical composition must fit its words and gestures. See note on 670b2–4.

661d1 'my obvious (*saphôs*) point'
The Athenian will use the same language at 662b4 to describe the 'obviousness' of the point that Crete is an island. See Mouze 2005: 188–90, and note on 662b3–4.

This is not what Clinias and Megillus have been taught

661d8–e1 'superlative strength and courage'
'Courage', here and at e7, refers to the trait that in Book 1 is specified not to involve wisdom (630c, 631d; see notes on 630a7–b2 and on 630c6–d1); thus it counts as one of the 'so-called goods' at 661b–d that are not good unless possessed along with virtue.

661e3–4 'I fail to persuade you (*humas*) that a person living like this is obviously (*saphôs*) wretched rather than happy?'
Persuasion (*peithein*) is a recurrent motif in what follows (661e6–664b2). 'You' is here plural, as it is throughout the rest of this section. Even though Clinias first voiced his dissent in his own individual voice (*emoige*, 661d6), both he and the Athenian understand his dissent to be characteristic of the outlook of both Clinias and Megillus. The 'obviously' (*saphôs*) recalls the Athenian's use of the same term at 661d1, to be repeated at 662b3–4 (see notes ad loc). What is obvious to the Athenian is not so to Clinias and Megillus, or in general to those raised under Dorian constitutions.

662a1–3 'If he is unjust and insolent, don't you think it necessary (*ex anankês*) that he lives shamefully (*aischrôs*)?'
alternatively: '. . . don't you necessarily think he lives shamefully?'
The 'necessary' (*ex anankês*) here is ambiguous. While it is natural to read it as part of the content of thought (as on the present translation), it is also possible to read it as governing 'you think' (*humin dokein . . . ex anankês*): 'doesn't it necessarily seem that . . . ?'. The former is suggested by the use of 'necessity' at 662b3–4, on which see note ad loc.

662a7 'Would you at least agree that his life is unpleasant and of no benefit to him?'
Clinias, who has agreed that the unjust live shameful lives (662a2–4), but refused to agree that they also live badly (a5–6), refuses to assent to these further affirmations, both of which concern the alleged unhappiness (badness) of the unjust life: (1) the unjust life is not good for the person who leads it; (2) it is miserable, in the sense that it is painful. 'Of no benefit' (*mê sumpherontôs*; alt. 'of no advantage') here is used as a synonym for 'bad' (*kakos*). The Athenian's later argument (addressed to the mythical legislators at 662e8–663a7, especially the second horn to the dilemma) will allege a difficulty in separating the questions of whether a life is good or bad from whether it is pleasant or painful. His present strategy, by contrast, is strongly evocative of the argument that Plato has Socrates present to Polus in the *Gorgias* for the conclusion that committing injustice is worse than being treated unjustly (474c–475e). There the crucial move is from the premise that injustice is shameful to the conclusion that it is bad, via a premise that appeals to considerations of pleasure and pain. Here Clinias, like Polus, agrees that injustice is shameful, but denies that it is bad, and the Athenian responds by invoking considerations of pleasure and pain. However, in contrast to Socrates in the *Gorgias*, the Athenian does not offer Clinias an argument from the premise about shamefulness to the conclusion about badness. Rather, he simply tries to elicit the conclusion that injustice is

unpleasant and bad. The absence of argument here would be striking to any reader familiar with the *Gorgias*, and this would reinforce the point the Athenian is making: that it is not by argument, but by the affective training of a person's basic evaluative attitudes, that the citizens are to be persuaded of such conclusions; see the end of the note on 661a4–d5.

662b1–664b2

Pleasure, injustice, and persuasion

Clinias' disagreement with the Athenian about whether the just person is always happy, and the unjust person unhappy (661d7–e5) is explained by the fact that Dorian musical education has inculcated in Clinias (and Megillus) the view that injustice is shameful, but not that it is unpleasant and bad (661e6–662a8), whereas the Athenian's education has made it 'obvious' to him that injustice is both unpleasant and bad (662b2–4). In support of his contention that the latter view is what the citizens must be taught (662b4–c5), he offers a battery of arguments (662c6–664b2), on which see general note ad loc.

662b1–2 'We are so badly out of tune with one another that it would take a god to bring us into agreement (*sumphônian*)!'
This responds to Clinias' rhetorical question, 'How could we possibly concede' that injustice is unpleasant and unprofitable?' (662a8). The Athenian's answer is that the views in question are fundamental to a person's ethical outlook, and must be inculcated by musical education. On *sumphônia* (agreement) as a result of musical education, see 659e and notes on 653b4–5, 659d1–4, and 659e1–3. Here, as at 634e, the 'agreement' is interpersonal.

662b3–4 'these things appear so necessary . . . that not even "Crete is an island" is as obvious (*saphôs*)'
The use of 'necessary' here recalls that at 662a1–2, and is connected here to the notion of what seems obvious (*saphôs*). One's musical

education has the effect of making certain normative views seem obvious. The example here, 'Crete is an island', would be one that Clinias' own experience growing up on the island would make obvious to him. See also note on 661e3–4. By contrast, Mouze (2005: 180) interprets this bedrock principle of the Athenian's as distinctively philosophical.

662b4 'If I were a lawmaker'
At the end of Book 3, the Athenian will assume the role of lawmaker for a new city, in conjunction with his two interlocutors. In Book 7 he will outline legislation of the sort he describes here.

662b6 'I would mete out . . . the highest penalty'
This legal penalty is the coercion or compulsion (*anankazein*, 662b5) that accompanies the 'persuasion' (662c5) that the laws also address to the citizens (on which, see notes on 632b7–8 and 662c3–5).

662b7–c1 'to anyone in the land who spread word that there are wicked (*ponêroi*) people who live pleasantly'
That is, anyone who promulgates the pernicious view described at 655d3, 656a1–2 (thinking some things are 'pleasant but wicked'); Clinias in effect expresses such an attitude at 662a.

662c1–2 'or that while some things are beneficial (*lusitelounta*) and profitable (*kerdalea*), others are more just'
The Athenian here expands the list of considerations to which one might appeal in deciding whether to act justly. To the notion of the beneficial (*sumpheron*) already mentioned at 662a7 (see note ad loc), he adds the advantageous (*lusitelounta*) and the profitable (*kerdalea*).

662c3–5 'I would persuade (*peithoim' an*) the citizens to proclaim the opposite'
That the legislator uses the laws to persuade the citizens is a theme hinted at in Book 1, 634a9 (cf. 632b7–8), and developed in detail in

Book 4, where preludes to the laws are aimed at persuading citizens to comply with the mandated behaviour (see note on 632b7–8). The persuasion need not be verbal argument, but can proceed by habituation (*ethê*), praises (*epainoi*), or speeches (*logoi*), as 663c1–2 makes explicit (see note ad loc, as well as note on 663b2–3). This is in keeping with Greek usage, which makes it possible to say that gifts or gold persuade (Euripides, *Medea* 964–5). The persuasion invoked in the present context proceeds via the educational medium of music.

662c6–664b2

Four arguments addressed to the legislator

The Athenian now offers a battery of arguments to establish that the legislator must persuade the citizens that the just life is the most pleasant.

The First Argument (662c–663a): A legislator who fails to teach this doctrine is giving an inconsistent message to citizens.
The Second Argument (663b–c): A legislator who fails to teach this doctrine cannot persuade citizens to be just.
The Third Argument (663c–d): The doctrine is true.
The Fourth Argument (663d–e): Even if the doctrine were not true, it would be the most beneficial for the citizens to believe.

He concludes by noting that music is perfectly capable of convincing the citizens of this, or any other, doctrine (664a–b).

662c6–663a8

The First Argument

The argument is structured as a *reductio ad absurdum* of the thesis, introduced at 662d1–3, that an unjust life can be more pleasant than a just life. It is structured as a dilemma about the relationship between justice and happiness (662d4–6): either (a) the most just life is not the happiest—in which case the legislator, who urges justice upon the citizens, is not fulfilling his mandate of making them as happy as possible (662d7–e9); or (b) the most just life is the happiest—in which case there must be some good that makes it happier than any unjust alternative, without at the same time making it more pleasant, an implication that the Athenian purports to disprove by enumeration of cases (662e9–663a7).

(By contrast, the construal of the argument in Stalley (1983: 62–4) conflates the two horns of the dilemma, while that of Mouze (2005: 181–5) construes the two horns as independent arguments for the conclusion that the just life is most pleasant. Schöpsdau (298–300) correctly identifies the argument's structure.)

662c6–7 'In the name of Zeus and Apollo, my excellent friends' Zeus and Apollo are the legendary divine lawgivers of Crete and Sparta, respectively (624a). The polite address, 'my excellent friends' (literally: you best (*aristoi*) of men') must at this point be ironic, since the Athenian has now disproved his initial assumption (625a) that his interlocutors were raised under the institutions that are adequate for cultivating virtue (excellence).

662d1–3 'Is the most just life the most pleasant, or are there two lives, one of them the most pleasant, the other the most just?' The second disjunct is the thesis to be reduced to absurdity. The superlatives are a change to the formulation of the disputed thesis (and may be anticipating the superlative in the exhortation described at 662e6). However, the thesis the Athenian has set out to establish is not simply that the most just life is the most pleasant life, but that the unjust life is *un*pleasant (662a7). While the present formulation leaves open the possibility that there may be unjust lives that are more pleasant than lives that are less than maximally just, the Athenian has given no indication earlier (nor will he later) that he thinks justice admits of degree. On the significance of this issue, see Bobonich 2002: 213.

662d3–e9

(a) The first horn of the dilemma

A legislator who supposes that the just life and the pleasant life diverge (the thesis to be disproved) here accepts, in addition, the first horn of the dilemma: that the most just life is not the happiest. But then, on the unstated assumption that the legislator exhorts the citizens to live justly (the message of *paideia*—643e), he is open to the charge of legislative misconduct: he has exhorted the citizens to lead lives that are less happy than they would otherwise be. On the assumption that the legislator is supposed to aim at the happiness of the citizens, reflected in the reference to him as 'father' at 662e4 and e7, see 631b3–6. The implication, left unstated, is that a proper legislator is not entitled to this horn of the dilemma.

662d3–4 'the right question to ask next would be'
more literally: 'presumably (*isôs*) we would ask next, if we were questioning correctly (*orthôs*)'
The following question, about the happiest life, is the correct question to ask because it reintroduces the notion of happiness (*eudaimonia*) into the issue, which at present is articulated simply in terms of pleasure. The Athenian's seamless transition here between the issue about whether the just life is happy (660e–661d) and the issue of whether it is pleasant is in keeping with the close connection he has noted between the judgements about goodness and feelings of pleasure (657c).

662d7–e1 'their position (*logos*) would be very strange (*atopos*); however, I would prefer not to attribute such a position to the gods, but rather to our ancestral legislators'
It would be impious to charge the gods with the kind of neglect and malfeasance that such an admission would invite (as argued at length in Book 10). Thus it is not the legendary divine lawgivers, Zeus and Apollo, but the human legislator, Minos or Lycurgus (624a, 630d, 632d), to whom this question should be addressed.

662e4–5 'Didn't you wish for me to live the happiest life?'
Legislation aims at the happiness of the citizens (631b).

662e6–9 'A legislator or father who took such a position would be very strange (*atopos*) and quite at a loss (*aporos*) to stay in agreement (*sumphônountôs*) with himself'
The verb 'agree' (*sumphônein*) recalls both (a) the internal agreement (*sumphônia*) between feelings and evaluative judgements that belongs to fully developed virtue (653a–c) as well as (b) the interpersonal agreement between citizens (634e, 662b). Here, however, lack of agreement is the internal inconsistency typically elicited in a Socratic-style cross-examination, portrayed in dialogues such as *Euthyphro, Charmides, Laches, Gorgias, and Republic I* (e.g. *Gorg.* 482b–c); in such contexts, the resulting condition of the inquirers is typically described as *aporia*, which is recalled here by the adjective *aporos*.

662e9–663a7

(b) The second horn of the dilemma

Here the legislator who proposes to divorce the just from the pleasant takes the second horn of the dilemma introduced at 662d1–3: the most just life is happiest. This presents him with the challenge of identifying the feature(s) of the just life that recommend it over all others (since it is, *ex hypothesei*, happiest—i.e. best) without contradicting his original contention that an unjust life may be more pleasant. The Athenian invokes two examples of the sorts of features that the law will recommend in such a life, and points out the absurdity of denying that they also make the just life pleasant. Presumably he intends to generalize the point to all such features. While the Athenian does not draw the moral explicitly, his point is probably that we are left without a reason to deny that the just life is the most pleasant.

662e11–663a1 'what good (*agathon*) and admirable (*kalon*) thing the law commends (*epainei*) in such a life that outstrips pleasure' more literally: '. . . that is superior (*kreitton*) to pleasure'
A difficult phrase in a compressed argument. '[O]utstrips [alt: superior to] pleasure' (*tês hêdonês kreitton*) is immediately glossed as 'separated (*chorizomenon*) from pleasure' (663a2). Perhaps the idea is that if (as the opponent alleges) the just life is best but not the most pleasant, then there must be things that make it good but that are not pleasant. That the laws commend or praise (*epainei*) was stated in Book 1 at 632a, and the close connection between praises, judgements of goodness, and feelings of pleasure is affirmed at 655c–656b and 657c (see general note on 655c4–d4).

663a3–4 'are renown and praise good (*agathon*) and admirable (*kalon*) but unpleasant, while ill repute is the opposite?'
In *Republic* II, renown and praise are identified as two of the 'prizes' for justice, and ill repute as one of the wages of injustice, according to popular opinion and poetry (362e–363e). There, Socrates is charged with arguing that justice is preferable to injustice even without these rewards; here, however, the Athenian voices no objection to having the legally sanctioned poetry invoke these as attractive features of justice (on this see Mouze 2005: 184). His point is that such features are not unpleasant.

663a5–7 'what about neither wronging (*adikein*) anyone nor being wronged (*adikeisthai*) by anyone? It is surely not the case that this is unpleasant but good and admirable (*kalon*), while the contrary is pleasant but shameful (*aischron*) and bad (*kaka*)?'
Neither doing wrong nor being wronged is invoked again in Book 7 (829a), and is another of the benefits of justice invoked in *Republic* II (358e–359b). The Athenian here claims that this situation is not 'separated from pleasure' (663a2). His point is most effective if the contrast is between (a) the conjunction of wronging no one and being wronged by no one and (b) the conjunction of wronging others and being wronged by others; (a) is the benefit one gets from living

under institutions of justice, which saves us from the miseries of (b). One might worry that these considerations do not address the objections of a would-be free rider or the possessor of a ring of Gyges, but once again, as with the first feature (reputation), the question is what general set of attitudes the laws (via legally sanctioned musical training) must inculcate in the populace. The mandated songs and dances will not articulate philosophical arguments (like those Socrates offers in *Republic*) to the effect that justice is preferable to injustice. Rather, they will make the populace favourably disposed to justice, and antagonistic to injustice. Note that the argument in the present passage is addressed to the legislator, not to the citizens.

663b1–6

The Second Argument

The Athenian now gives a second set of reasons why legislators must teach the citizens that the just life is most pleasant. He points to the good consequences of promulgating the doctrine. He invokes the legislator's goal of making the citizens willing (*hekontes*) adherents to the life of justice, together with the psychological thesis that we do willingly only what is, on balance, pleasant.

663b1–2 'the doctrine (*logos*) that does not divorce the pleasant and the just or the good (*agathon*) and the admirable (*kalon*)'
Clinias endorses the contrary doctrine when he allows that injustice is shameful (*aischron*—opposite of *kalon*), but he balks at saying it is bad (*kakos*—opposite of *agathon*) (662a1–8). On the connection between the good and the admirable, see note on 637e5.

663b2–3 'even if it accomplishes nothing else, can persuade a person to be willing to live a just and pious life'
more literally: '. . . is persuasive (*pithanos*) towards being willing (*ethelein*) to live a just and pious life'

Note that persuasiveness here includes success at forming motivation (willingness), not just at instilling belief. On the connection between persuasion and willingness, and the translation of *ethelein* by 'willing', see note on 663b4–6.

663b3–4 'any doctrine that denies this'
Examples of such denials would include Clinias' refusal to assent to the thesis at 661e6–662a8, as well as, by the principles of 655d–656b and 657c, any music that portrayed injustice in a favourable light (thereby making it pleasant).

663b4–6 'since nobody would willingly be persuaded to do (*hekôn etheloi peithesthai prattein*) anything that failed to yield more pleasure than pain'
The Athenian's claim is not that we can never be persuaded to take a course of action that we believe will be unpleasant on balance (contra Stalley 1983: 64), but rather that we will not agree to do such an action willingly or wholeheartedly (*hekôn*). While sometimes the distinction between acting *hekôn* and acting *akôn* corresponds to the difference between intentional and unintentional behaviour (as at 700e1, 734b2–4, 860d–e, 862a4, 865a–b, d, 866b7, 866c7, 879a9–b1, 943e1), at other times it marks a distinction within intentional behaviour between those actions performed willingly or gladly and those performed under constraint or without consent (as in the examples of the 'unwilling (*akontôn*) subjects' at 832c4; the property owner who does not consent to the destruction of his belongings at 846a5; the family members who refrain from incest 'perfectly willingly' (*ouk akontes*) at 838a6; and those who are prevented *akôn* by unforeseen circumstances from fulfilling their contracts at 920d4; see also 846a5). In contrast to 627e2–3, where *hekontas* marks the former distinction (see note ad loc), the present context uses *hekôn* to mark the latter distinction. 'Willingly' translates the phrase *hekôn etheloi*, whose component terms have roughly the same sense—the latter verb tending to function as the verbal version of the former adverb. In the context of persuasion (*peithesthai*), *hekôn* or

ethelein indicates that the agent's action is not simply what he does under constraint or for want of a better alternative (as at 663e2), but is what he has been persuaded to do wholeheartedly (as at 671c7). Thus Plato will pair *ethelein* with *prothumoteron* (eager, enthusiastic, as opposed to reluctant) at 666c4, where it indicates a person's willingness to sing in public (cf. 697d8); *hekontes* is used to the same effect at 670c9. Book 4 develops the theme that the citizens must be willing (*ethelein*) to be obedient to the rulers of the city (701b5)—alternatively stated with the adverb *hekôn* (700a5)—or 'easily persuaded (*eupeitheis*) by the laws': 715c; cf. 718c. The present passage should be compared with 732e–734e in Book 5—which also connects what one would choose willingly (*hekousion*—733d8) to what is more pleasant; cf. Laks 2005: 45–7; Stalley 1983: 66–70; and notes on 632b7–8 and on 663c2. On the distinction between *hekôn and akôn*, see Meyer 1993: 9–14.

'Pleasure' and 'pain' here are ambiguous between (a) the affective states cultivated by *paideia* (pleasures and pains such as love and hate, etc.) and (b) the bodily sensations and experiences one could get from engaging in certain actions. It is in virtue of the latter that Clinias and others might think the life of justice can be less pleasant than a life of successful injustice. But it is pleasures and pains of the former sort that the Athenian has connected with judgements of goodness at 654c–d. On the conflation of these two types of pleasure, see note on 633c9–d2.

The distortions of distance and perspective

663b6–c1 'Now objects viewed from a distance appear hazy to most people, especially to children, but the legislator will dispel the haze and clarify our judgement'
more literally: 'objects viewed from a distance make most people dizzy (*skotodinian . . . parechei*) . . . but the legislator will bring our opinion (*doxan*) into the opposite condition, dispelling the darkness (*to skotos aphelôn*)' (reading *d' hêmin* at b7–8, following des Places and Schöpsdau, in place of the MSS *d' ei mê*)

The object in the distance is a metaphor for the expected pleasures just mentioned at 663b5–7. Unlike the observation in *Protag.* that future pleasures may appear smaller than they really are (356a–c), the Athenian here indicates simply that they are indistinct. The task of the legislator, therefore, will be to provide us with the clear and unambiguous expectation that living justly will be pleasant and living unjustly unpleasant. On the means by which he does so, see note on 663c1–2. Mouze (2005: 188) proposes that the 'perspective from afar' is that of the unjust soul mentioned below at 663c2–4 (so too Moss 2012: 215–16); however, the mention of children here makes it more likely that the perspective is that of the uneducated soul. Keuls (1978: 85–6), by contrast, proposes that the view from afar is the correct view.

663c1–2 'He will persuade (*peisei*) us, however he can, by means of [1] training (*ethesin*), [2] praises (*epainois*), and [3] doctrines (*logois*)'

A specification of the means by which the citizens are to be 'persuaded' to act justly; *peisei* here explains *peithesthai* at 663b4. (1) The 'training' (*ethesin*; alt: 'habits'; see note on 655d7–e1) is the musical training invoked at 655d–656b and 656d; for discussion, see Mouze 2005: 181–8. (2) On the legislator's use of 'praises', see 632a. Praises are also expressed in poetry, such as that of Tyrtaeus (660e–661a). (3) The doctrines would include those that the poets are required to promulgate at 660e–661c. On the wide range of what can count as 'persuasion' (*peithein*) in Greek, see note on 662c3–5. On the significance of persuasion in the *Laws*, see note on 632b7–8.

663c2 'because (*hôs*) matters of justice and injustice are subject to perspective (*eskiagraphêmena*)'

alternatively: 'that (*hôs*) matters . . . are subject to perspective'

On the alternative construal, taken by England, Taylor, Saunders, Brisson/Pradeau, Pangle, and Schöpsdau, the clause *hôs eskiagraphêmena . . .* states what the legislator will persuade (*peithein*) the citizens to believe (which lines c1–5 explain in greater detail).

However, nowhere else in *Laws* does Plato use *hôs* + participle to indicate the content one is persuaded to believe. Rather, the verb takes an accusative + infinitive construction (661e4, 710c2, 906b8–c1) or *hôs* + indicative (646a8, 885d2, 903b4, 905c4–6, 913c1–2, 933a3–7). It makes more sense to suppose that the present construction (*hôs* + participle) gives the legislator's reason for persuading the citizens, which is a psychological observation that belongs to legislative inquiry; it is not the content or message to be imparted by legislation or education (the latter is what is affirmed unanimously by 'the whole community, all their lives long, in their songs . . . stories, and . . . judgements'—664a3–6). The upshot for the legislator is that the way to instil in the citizens a clear and unambiguous impression that the just course of action is more pleasant is to cultivate justice in the citizens.

Shadow-painting (*skiagraphia*) is a painter's technique that gives the illusion of depth to a two-dimensional picture observed from a distance (see Keuls 1978 and Pemberton 1976). Thus the metaphor may invoke either deception or perspective; the latter is emphasized in the following lines (663c2–5). See Schöpsdau ad loc.

663c2–d5

The Third Argument

The argument takes as its first premise the psychological observation made at 663c2–5. It may be summarized as follows:

(1) Unjust things appear pleasant to the unjust person but unpleasant to the just person. (663c2–5)
(2) A better soul is more authoritative in its judgements than an inferior soul. (663c7–d1)
(3) The just person has a better soul and the unjust person a worse soul. [unstated]
(4) Therefore, the unjust life is really the way it appears to the just person. [unstated; from 2, 3]
(5) Therefore, the unjust life really is unpleasant. (663d3–4; from 1, 4)

One might worry that the argument equivocates on the understanding of pleasure and pain. To the extent that (1) has been established so far (e.g. at 655d–656b), it concerns the pleasures and pains that are within the scope of *paideia*: affective states with intentional objects, such as those that good people experience when observing virtuous behaviour depicted in choral song and dance (or when engaging in such behaviour themselves). But the pleasures and pains that Clinias had in mind when he balked at affirming (5) at 662a7–8 presumably include (predominantly) those of human experience, e.g. bodily pleasures from eating, drinking, and sex, as well as pains of various bodily afflictions. Is the Athenian here conflating the pleasures and pains of these two sorts? A similar ambiguity occurs in Book 1; see note on 633c9–d2.

663c2–5 'When considered from the perspective opposite to the just person's—that is, from the standpoint of one's own injustice and wickedness'

more literally: 'when appearing (*phainomena*) to someone who is in the opposite condition to the just person (*tôi tou dikaiou enantiôs* [*sc.* *echomenôi*]), that is, considered (*theôroumena*) from the standpoint of one's own injustice and wickedness (*ek men adikou kai kakou heautou*)'

alternatively: 'appearing in the opposite manner to what is just' (Schöpsdau and Brisson/Pradeau, following England's construal of the MSS text) or 'manifestly opposed to the opinion of the just person' (Lisi, Allameda), or 'to the enemy of justice' (Saunders, with a textual emendation)

The MSS text poses several difficulties (see Saunders 1972), but on any of these construals, the Athenian's main point in these lines is that from the perspective of the just person, just things are pleasant, while from that of the unjust person, they are unpleasant. This is premise (1) in the argument that continues through 663d5. See note on 663c2–d5.

663c7–9 'Now which judgement shall we say is more authoritatively true (*tên d' alêtheian . . . kuriôteran*)—that of the worse soul or that of the better?'
Clinias' answer (663d1) opts for the latter. It functions as premise (2) in the argument of 663c2–d5; see note ad loc.

663d2–4 'So it is necessary that the unjust life is not only more shameful . . . but also in truth more unpleasant than the just . . . life'
Strictly speaking, only the second conjunct is the conclusion (5) of the present argument (663c2–d5). But Clinias conceded the first conjunct at 662a2–8, where he also rejected the second.

663d5 'So it would seem . . . at least as far as the present argument goes'
Clinias is not convinced by the argument, which is insufficient to convince a person who has not received a proper musical education that justice is more pleasant than injustice (see note on 662b3–4 and general note on 662b1–664b2); his own Dorian upbringing has failed to expose him to the 'training, praises, and doctrines' (663c1–2) that will make him find justice more pleasant than injustice.

663d6–e2

The Fourth Argument

Having just given an argument for the truth of the doctrine that the just life is the most pleasant, the Athenian now claims that, regardless of its truth, there is no doctrine that is more beneficial for the citizens to believe.

663d6–e1 'even if matters were not as the present argument maintains, could any halfway decent legislator . . . tell a lie more beneficial than this?'

One might compare the legislator's hypothetical appeal to falsehood here with a similar use of falsehood 'for the sake of the good' at *Rep.* 382c–d and 414b–e. On how pernicious the 'lie' would be, see note on 664a2–3.

663e1–2 'not because they are forced, but willingly (*hekontas*)'
On 'willingly', see note on 663b4–6.

The persuasive power of music

663e4 'persuasion, it seems, is not an easy matter'
This remark by Clinias might indicate his own failure to be persuaded by the Athenian's third argument (663c2–d5). The Athenian will respond (663e5–664a8) by pointing to the ease with which music (broadly construed to include poetry and fables) can cultivate belief in even the most implausible doctrines.

663e5 'the Sidonian's tale (*to men tou Sidôniou muthologêma*)'
alternatively: 'the tale about the Sidonian'
The tale concerns Cadmus, legendary founder of Thebes (invoked in Book 1 at 641c), of whom the story is told below (663e8–9) that he sowed dragon's teeth in the ground, from which armed warriors sprouted. The story is a foundation myth for the city of Thebes, and thus the sort a legislator might incorporate into the official musical education of a city. Sidon is a coastal city in modern-day Lebanon, just to the north of Tyre, the legendary birthplace of Cadmus. 'The Sidonian' might refer to Cadmus himself or to the source of the far-fetched tale; England proposes that 'Sidonian' may be standing in for 'Phoenician' (both Sidon and Tyre were Phoenician cities), and notes the use of the latter adjective at *Rep.* 414c4 to mark a fanciful or false tale.

663e10–664a1 'he can persuade the souls of the young of whatever he wants'

Recall that it is the condition of youth that is the primary focus of education, for it is the souls of the young that are open to being shaped by music (see note on 671b8–c2). These are trained to have the requisite attitudes before they are capable of employing arguments (*logoi*; see 653b). The task of the legislator is to design institutions that will maintain these attitudes over the course of a life. On these institutions, see note on 664a3–6.

664a2–3 'All he needs to figure out (*skopounta aneuriskein*) is what doctrine will deliver the greatest good to the city should he convince them of it'
The same combination of verbs is used at 626a5–6 and 656e4 to characterize the inquiry into the goals and methods of proper legislation begun in Book 1; *skopein* alone or its cognates is used of that endeavour throughout Book 1 and into 2: 635d7, 636d5, 638b9, 645d3, 649e2, 658a5. Thus we may suppose that the discovery to which the Athenian here refers is that of the order of divine and human goods from Book 1, 631b–d, where all goods depend on the possession of justice (there conceived as a combination of wisdom, moderation, and courage). There is no suggestion that the city will be benefited at the expense of the citizens—for all the benefits to the city enumerated at 631b–d are possessed by individuals. Note that the claim whose truth is said to be irrelevant to the question at hand is not whether justice is good for the citizens, but rather whether it is pleasant and injustice unpleasant.

664a3–6 'use every means . . . to ensure that the whole community (*sunoikia*), all their lives long, are of one voice on this topic—in their songs (*ôidais*), in their stories (*muthois*), and in their judgements (*logois*; alt: doctrines, arguments)'
The 'means' of achieving this unanimity 'all their lives long' will be the institution of the three choruses, to which the Athenian will turn next (664b–d). He here makes more precise the claim in Book 1 that the whole community must 'sing out their agreement' (*sumphônein*,

634e1–2; cf. 659d–e). The community consensus will be expressed in the songs sung, the stories told, and in the *logoi* (here translated as 'judgements') affirmed by its members. So construed, the latter are instances of the *logos* translated 'account' at 645b and 653b (cf. 696c); see Moss 2014. Alternatively, the *logoi* could be the doctrines mentioned along with 'training [and] praises' as the legislator's means of persuasion at 663c1–2 (thus Saunders, Brisson/Pradeau, and Schöpsdau). They are also the contents of the laws (see note on 659d1–4). On songs: 654a–b, 656d, 659e; on stories: 636c–d, 645b, 663e, 664d, 682a.

664b1–2 'I don't see either of us as capable of disputing these points'
A reflection of the Dorian's lack of facility in argument, mentioned also at 641e.

IV
THE INSTITUTIONS OF CORRECT EDUCATION: THE THREE CHORUSES

(664b3–666d2)

Having established that a proper legislator will ensure that the musical works used in education (paideia) *depict the just life as happy and pleasant (660e–664a), the Athenian now specifies the institutions that will structure the lifelong programme of musical education by which 'the whole community, all their lives long' will be 'of one voice on this topic' (664a4–6). In keeping with his pronouncement that it is by regular performance of choral music that the citizens will receive their initial education and that education will require subsequent maintainance and repair to undo the corrosive effects of everyday life (653c–654a), he now specifies three different types of chorus in which citizens will participate, at different times of their life, each dedicated to one of the three deities identified as the patrons of musical education at 653d. When citizens are children (under 18 years old) they will sing in the chorus of the Muses; as young adults (from 18 to 30 years old) they will sing in the chorus of Apollo; and those beyond 30 will perform in the chorus of Dionysus. The latter chorus, which will occupy most of the Athenian's attention for the rest of Book 2, turns out not to be a chorus in the strict sense that involves performing ensemble song and dance in public at religious festivals; rather, it is a drinking party (665d9–666d2). Thus it is with his account of the chorus of Dionysus that the Athenian makes good on his promise to specify an important educational role for drinking parties (652b–653a).*

The three choruses introduced

664b4–5 'all choruses (and there are three of them) should direct their charms (*epaidein*) at the souls of children, which are still young and pliable'
The three choruses are specified further at 664c4–d4. See Prauscello 2014: 152–9. This is the first mention that there will be three of them, but the number does not seem to surprise Clinias, perhaps because there were known to be three choruses at Spartan festivals. (Plutarch, *Lycurgus* 21.2 says a chorus of old men would lead, followed by a chorus of young men in their prime, then a chorus of children.) Clinias' question at 664d5–7 concerns the nature of the third chorus, not their number or composition. On songs as charms for the souls of children, see 659e (repeated at 665c, 666c). On the plasticity of young souls (which will figure in the final account of the benefit of drinking parties), see 666b–c, 671b–c, and note on 653d7–8.

664b6 'all the beautiful (*kala*) doctrines we've gone through'
alternatively: 'all the admirable [or splendid] doctrines . . . '
Presumably these are the doctrines articulated at 660e–663e (about justice, happiness, and pleasure), as well as those at 631b–632d (about divine and human goods). On the translation of *kala* see note on 630c7.

664b7–8 'that the gods call the same life both most pleasant and most excellent'
A restatement of the thesis insisted on at 662b–663e as central to the message of musical education—with the substitution here of 'most excellent' (*aristos*) for 'most just' (*dikaiotatos*) in the former context (662d2–3), a minor variation given the gloss on justice as 'virtue as a whole' (*aretês hapasês*, 661c4; see note ad loc). An additional change in the present context is the specification that the gods affirm the thesis in question (as at 634e2), perhaps indicating, as England notes, that such an attribution is supposed to have especial force with children (although compare a similar invocation of divine authority at 838b–c).

664c1–2 'speaking truth to the highest degree and . . . more likely to persuade . . . than if we were to proclaim any other doctrine'
Recalls 663b2–3. See note ad loc.

664c3 'What you say must be conceded (*sunchôrêteon*)'
A surprising concession, given Clinias' earlier refusal to make such an admission at 662a and his grudging response to the argument that concludes at 663d5. Perhaps the Athenian's substitution at (664b7–8) of the 'most excellent' (*aristos*) life for 'most just' at 662d2–3 allows Clinias to interpret the claim in light of his own, Dorian, conception of excellence (cf. Tyrtaeus fr. 12.13). Or perhaps the argument at 663c–d has been more convincing than his response at 663d5 would appear to indicate. Clinias' inability to mount a defence of the contrary position (664b1–2) might also be relevant.

The chorus of the Muses

664c4 'the chorus dedicated to the Muses and consisting of children'
The age range is specified more precisely at 666a4 as those up to 18 years old. On the Muses as patrons of culture, see note on 653d3–4.

664c5–6 'take the stage, singing out such doctrines (*ta toiauta*) . . . before the entire city'
The choruses are conceived of as performing in a theatre before the general public assembled for a festival performance (665e; cf. 653d–654a), as was typical of choral performances in Plato's day. See Morrow 1960: 302–18. 'Such doctrines' (literally: 'such things'—*ta toiauta*) are presumably the doctrines just mentioned at 664b3–8.

The chorus of Apollo

664c6–d1 'the chorus of those up to 30 years old, calling upon Paean Apollo as witness for the truth of what they affirm (*tôn legomenôn*), and praying that he grace the youth with persuasion'
These young adults are at a later developmental stage than the children in the chorus of the Muses. On the developmental psychology of 653a–c, they would be at the stage of 'grasping the account' or 'engaging in argument' (*logon lambanein*, 654b4; see note on 653b3–4). How far these adult singers go towards understanding the doctrines they affirm in their songs is not addressed here; calling on Apollo as a witness is an appeal to authority, not to reasons. In any case, as choral performers, they will be singing and dancing to a set text, not engaging in the give and take of rational argument. The 'youths' (*neoi*) to be persuaded might be the children in the first chorus (as *neoi* is used at 653d7, 664e4), but the adjective can also be used to distinguish younger adults from the elderly, as at 631e1 and 666b2 (see note ad loc).

The chorus of Dionysus

664d1–2 'a third chorus . . . will consist of those over 30 and up to 60 years of age'
This will be called the chorus of Dionysus at 665a8–b2. It will be assigned two main functions: (A) it performs a 'finer music', which evaluates musical compositions and selects those that are beautiful and appropriate for use in education (668b, 670a–e). (B) It is a

drinking party in which inebriation replicates, in adults, the juvenile condition of educability by music invoked at 653d–654a, thus allowing the music performed on these occasions to restore their 'education' (666b–c and 671a–671e). (A) and (B) are developed in largely independent treatments and the Athenian makes no explicit attempt to connect them (although see notes on 667b1–3 and on 671e1; cf. Schöpsdau on 671a1–672a4). See also Prauscello 2014: 160–72.

Note the very wide range of ages for this chorus, which encompasses what the Hippocratic writer of *De Hebdomadibus 5* identifies as three distinct 'seasons' of life: that of 'man' (*anêr*) (28–49 years), 'elder' (*presbutês*) (50–56 years), and 'old man' (*gerôn*) (over 56 years). In developing functions (A) and (B), the Athenian will be almost exclusively interested in the 'elders' and 'old men' in this chorus, as much of what he says about their stiffness and other signs of old age (e.g. 666b–c) are unlikely to be general characteristics of those only recently over the 30-year mark—not to mention their position of authority (665d, 670d–e)—although even those at the younger end of the age range will have lost the juvenile volatility that, as he will explain in 671a–672d, is replicated in drunkenness. Note that the three interlocutors refer to themselves both as 'elders' (*presbutai*) (685a, 712b–c, 769a) and as 'old men' (*gerontes*) (634e–635a, 658d, 715d–e). On the age range of the chorus, see also notes on 665d1–4, 670a7–b2, and 671e1, and O. Murray 2013: 115.

664d2–4 'those who are beyond all that (*tous meta tauta*) and no longer up to the challenge of singing will be allotted the role of storytellers (*muthologous*) . . . about these same characters (*êthôn*)'
'Beyond all that' (*meta tauta*) might mean beyond the age of 30 to 60 (thus England, Brisson/Pradeau, Saunders, Schöpsdau), in which case this is a fourth age group, distinct from the membership of the chorus of Dionysus. But, as England notes, this would be an unusual use of the expression, and there is no reason to suppose that the ability to sing is coextensive with the age range of the three choruses; after all, the Athenian implies at 670a–b that some 50-year-olds will not be 'fit to sing'—hence 'beyond the ability to sing' is a more likely

meaning (thus Morrow 1960: 314). At 671e1 the Athenian assigns to those 'over 60 years old' the role of supervising the conduct of drinking parties; however, the inability to sing cited in the present passage is hardly a credential for the office of exercising that wise leadership; see note on 671e1. Alternatively, Pangle translates *tous meta tauta* as 'those who come on after these' (i.e. those who perform after the third chorus). In any case, the Athenian's concern in the present context is to have all citizens participate in the collective affirmation of the 'beautiful doctrines' of 664b5–6, regardless of their ability to sing; 'about these same characters' (664d4) indicates that the content of the stories told by this group will be the same as that of the songs performed by the choruses.

664d5–6 'the third choruses'
The plural reflects the assumption that there will be multiple choruses for each age group.

664e3–5 'At the beginning of our discussion . . . we said that all young creatures have a fiery nature'
A recapitulation of the theory introduced at 653d5–654a5, with the addition that the young have a 'fiery' (*diapuros*) nature, a detail repeated at 666a–c and 671b–c; the latter points to the malleability of the young (cf. 664b5) and their unique susceptibility to the influence of education. For fuller discussion of the theory, see note on 653d7–8. Belfiore (1986: 425–6), by contrast, construes the fieriness as the lack of self-control attributed to the young at 645e.

665a2 'the combination of the two (*to sunamphoteron*) is called a chorus'
The combination of ordered bodily movement (dance) and ordered vocal movement (song) is what constitutes a chorus; see 654a–b and 672e–673a.

665a4 'to join and lead our choral dance'
more literally: 'to be fellow choral dancers (*sunchoreutas*), and lead the chorus (*chorêgous*)'

This repeats claims made at 654a1–5. On the role of dance in choral performance, see note on 654a4–5.

665b3–4 'A Dionysian chorus of elders sounds exceedingly strange, on first hearing'
The Athenian has just given his first indication, in the previous line, that the third chorus is dedicated to Dionysus, the god of wine and drunken revelry (see 637b and note on 637b2). On the oddness of the suggestion that a chorus of elders should dance in honour of Dionysus, see O. Murray 2013: 114–15.

665b7–8 'an account (*logou*), I think, of the way in which it would be reasonable (*eulogon*) for this to take place'
The 'way', it turns out, will involve a drinking party rather than a public choral performance (666b–c).

665c2–5 'That every man (*andra*) and child (*paida*), free person and slave, female and male . . . should perpetually sing to itself those charms that we discussed'
'[M]an and child' marks the contrast between adult and juvenile, with emphasis on stage of life, rather than gender (since both 'female and male' are included). The Athenian here indicates that community members of any age, social status, or gender will be involved in affirming the 'beautiful doctrines' of 664b. That the whole city must give voice to the same opinions: 634e, 662b–c; that the songs inculcating this unanimity are charms: 659e, 664b, 666c.

665c5–7 'with some alteration (*aei metaballomena*) or other and at any rate with sufficient variety to please the singers'
The Athenian here acknowledges the powerful attraction of the pleasure provided by variety. Earlier, he inveighed against alterations to the basic forms of musical compositions (656d–657b). The variation he endorses here must therefore involve variation *within* the sanctioned forms so that the citizens will not have to sing over and over *ad nauseam* a limited menu of songs; thus new songs can be

introduced into the canon over time (cf. *Rep.* 424b–c). It is not to variety as such that the Athenian objects, but to the pursuit of variety that leads to abandonment of those features essential to making the music beautiful and appropriate for education. Thus Rutherford 2013: 72 and Kowalzig 2004: 47. See also Rep. 424b–c and note on 656d9–e3.

665d1–4 'whose collective age and wisdom (*phronêsesin*) makes it the most persuasive (*pithanôtaton*) group of citizens . . . those with the greatest command (*kuriôtaton*) of the finest and most beneficial songs'
This description, like 'divine men' at 666d6, would seem to fit the oldest members of the Dionysian chorus—those for whom the label 'elder' would be appropriate, rather than those at the younger end of the spectrum (see note on 664d1–2). On wisdom (*phronêsis*) coming with age (if it comes at all), see 653a7–9 and note ad loc. '[M]ost persuasive' (*pithanôtaton*) recalls the concerns of 663b–664c. On the laws embodying the wisdom of the elders, and citizens being persuaded by the laws, see 659d–e. The characterization of the music performed by this chorus as 'the finest songs' will be repeated at 667b1–3 and reflects the invocation of the 'finest music' (*mousa kallistê*) at 658e8. On the relation between this characterization of the elders' music and the Athenian's later claim that it is 'finer than that of choruses' (667a10), see notes on 666d11–e1, 667b1–3, and 670e3–4.

Drinking parties are the forum for the chorus of Dionysus

665d9–e1 'As a person advances in age (*gignomenos presbuteros*), doesn't he become increasingly reluctant to sing?'
This reticence of the elders contrasts with the characteristic eagerness of youth to sing and dance (653d–654a, 657d, 664e–665a, 672c, 673c–d). The function of drunkenness, to be invoked at 666b–c, will be to restore that eagerness.

665e2–3 'feels especially embarrassed (*aischunoit' an*)—the more so the older (*presbuteros*) and more moderate (*sôphronesteros*) he has become'
more literally: 'feels especially ashamed . . . '
In Book 1, shame (*aischunê* or *aidôs*) is the kind of fear that the legislator must cultivate in the citizens (647a–c; cf. 671d). Here, as in that earlier context, it is associated with the virtue of moderation (*sôphrosunê*). Earlier in Book 2 shame is what one feels when performing actions that one thinks pleasant but wicked (*ponêros*) (656a–b). Here we see the feeling is associated with a natural self-consciousness—thus the translation 'embarrassed'. The term *presbuteros*, unlike the English 'elderly', connotes not just advanced years but seniority and greater respectability. While these senior performers are not performing songs or dances representing shameful behaviour, and thus have no reason to feel ashamed on those grounds (cf. 656a), they are no doubt aware of the technical imperfections of their performance resulting from age-related loss of agility and vocal range. While there is nothing unseemly about the behaviour their song and dance would imitate, it might well be unseemly (*aschêmôn*—cf. 666c9) for stiff-limbed or rough-voiced elders to imitate it via the very public medium of choral dance.

666a5–8 'We would explain (*didaskontes*) that one should not pour additional fire into the bodies or souls of our youth, but rather be mindful of their excitable condition (*emmanên . . . hexin*)'
more literally: 'their maddened [alt: frantic] condition'
Such explanation (or more literally, instruction) would presumably be in a legislative preamble addressed to the parents of children (or to those charged with carrying out the law). One would not need to convince the children themselves of the reason for the restriction. On the madness of youth, as expressed in the impulse to disordered movement and sound, and the connection between fire, madness, and drunkenness, see 672b–d. On legislative preambles, see note on 632b7–8.

666a6–7 'the burdensome toils (*ponous*) of life'
See 653c–d and note on 653d2–3.

666b1–2 'the young must abstain completely from drunkenness'
'Young' (*neos*) here is contrasted with 'children' (*paides* at 666a4)—even though the latter can also be referred to as *neoi*, as at 666a8 (see note on 664c6–d1). The young who may partake of wine but not in drunkenness are the young adults between 18 and 30 years old, as contrasted with the older adults in the chorus of Dionysus.

666b2 'a person approaching (*epibainonta*) 40'; that is, in one's third decade
alternatively: 'upon reaching 40' (Belfiore: 425; LSJ)
The present translation, like that of Saunders, Brisson/Pradeau, and Taylor, follows England, whose case is strengthened by Schöpsdau. The alternative rendering would leave those between 30 and 40 years old unaccounted for in the drinking regulations. On the lack of precision with which the Athenian notes the age range of the chorus of Dionysus, see notes on 664d1–2, 671e1, as well as Morrow 1960: 318, Schöpsdau on 664d5–665d6, and O. Murray 2013.

666b3 'at the end of a communal dinner'
literally: 'in the communal meals (*en tois sussitiois*)'
On the communal meals (*sussitia*) in Dorian society, see Book 1, 625c–626b. The Athenian will include the *sussitia* among the institutions he legislates for the new colony of Magnesia (see note on 625e2–7). Such establishments for communal eating will also be venues for communal drinking, and the drunkenness that is integral to the Dionysian function of the third chorus. On the question of whether women will participate in such rituals, see Schöpsdau 2003.

666b4–5 'that rite (*teletên*) and recreation (*paidian*) for the elders (*presbutôn*)'
There is some variation in the MSS as to whether it is the elders (*presbutôn*) or the 'more elderly' (*presbuterôn*). Those 'approaching

40' (666b2) would not be classified as *presbutai* (elders) according to the age classifications of *De Hebdomadibus* (see note on 664d1–2). On age classes more generally, see Davidson 2006. On *paidia* (recreation, play) see note on 635b5.

666c1–2 'like iron that becomes pliable when placed in the fire'
The image is repeated at 671b–c; see note on 653d7–8.

666c3–6 'Wouldn't he be more willing to sing with enthusiasm (*an etheloi prothumoteron . . . aidein*) . . . ?'
On being willing (*ethelein*; alt: *hekôn*) and being enthusiastic (*prothumôs*), see note on 663b4–6.

666c6 'those songs that we have repeatedly said are charms'
At 659e, 664b, 665c.

V
THE FINER MUSIC OF THE DIONYSIAN CHORUS

666d3–671a1

Having established that the chorus of Dionysus will not sing publicly in choral competitions at religious festivals, but privately in drinking parties (665d–666c), the Athenian now proposes that the music it is to 'sing' will be 'finer' than that performed in choruses (666d–667b; cf. 665d–e); indeed, he will argue (670b–e) that it requires an education more advanced than mere choral training. He proposes first that the faults of Dorian musical education can be attributed to the absence of such music (666d–667a), and then proceeds to give a detailed account of that 'finer music' (667a–670e). The latter is revealed to be the expertise for judging choral works, which the Athenian elaborates in considerable detail (667b–670a) and distinguishes both from the expertise of composers and from that of choral performers (670a–e). While these expert evaluations by the elders are not 'song' or music in the narrow sense (words set to 'harmony' and rhythm), the Athenian is prepared to say that the elders 'sing' this music (670d).

666d3 'what kind of sound (*phônên*), or music (*mousan*)'
'Sound' here is broad enough in scope to include not just song or speech but utterance more generally, leaving it open that it will not be song, strictly conceived, that the elders engage in. This fits the requirement, articulated at 670d, that the members of the third chorus are in the business of judging which songs are beautiful. The term *mousa* (repeated in a similar context at 667a10–b1; see note ad loc) can mean 'song' (as at 829d6), but admits of the broad scope of the cognate *mousikê*, which includes music, dance, and literature, and can encompass learning broadly conceived (see note on 642a4)—so that philosophy can be called a kind of 'music' at *Phd.* 60e–61a; cf. *Tim.* 88c (see Morrow 1960: 313–14). Saunders (1972: 10) proposes that this 'music' will be the philosophical inquiries of the Nocturnal Council introduced in Book 12 (961a–b; 964e–969c).

666d8–10 'the only type of song (*ôidên*) we are capable of is what we learned to sing in our own choral training (*sunêtheis . . . genomenoi*)'
'Training' (*sunêtheis*) might also be translated as 'accustoming' or 'habituation'; the related noun *sunêtheia* is used at 655e4 and 6 and is translated 'training'. On training, habituation, and music, see notes on 653b5–6 and 655d7–e1. The Athenian's point here is that his interlocutors are able to sing the songs they were trained to sing in their youth, but, lacking the 'music finer than that of the choruses and the public theatres' (667a10–b1) whose nature is detailed at 670a–b, they lack the resources to reflect critically on the adequacy of those songs. Note his earlier comment that Clinias' understanding of Cretan institutions is 'well trained' (*gegumnasthai*) (626b5, see note ad loc). Such a training allows Clinias to identify the goal of Cretan institutions, but it does not enable him to see the deficiency in the choral compositions that communicate this message.

666d11–667b4

Dorian musical education fails to employ the finest kind of song

The Athenian charges that the Dorian societies in Crete and Sparta lack the 'finest kind of music' (666e1) that belongs to the chorus of Dionysus (cf. 665d); and that this has resulted in educational practices that cultivate the impoverished range of virtue criticized in Book 1 (see 628c–630c). Tyrtaeus is once again singled out as a poet who expresses that impoverished conception. The finest kind of 'song' will later be identified as expertise in discriminating which choral or poetic compositions are beautiful, and which are not (668b, 670b–e). Presumably we are meant to conclude that it would reject the poetry of Tyrtaeus as unsuitable for use in education.

666d11–e1 'you are missing out on the finest kind of song'
Perhaps an allusion to Pindar *Paean* 6.181–3 (see Rutherford 2013: 82n32). The 'finest kind of song' is ambiguous. In the context of the immediately preceding lines, it must be the music that will be identified as 'finer than that of choruses', indeed as 'the finest variety' (667a10–b3). This 'music' (assigned to the chorus of Dionysus at 670d–e) is the expertise that judges musical compositions (see notes on 670a3–6 and 670e3–4). However, the criticism of Dorian educational practices in the present paragraph, and especially the invocation of the poetry of Tyrtaeus (whose educational inadequacy is emphasized at 629a–630c in Book 1 and 660d–661d in Book 2) imply that the musical compositions used in Dorian education themselves fall well short of the 'finest'. Likewise, the 'finest song and music' invoked at 668b4–6 must be musical compositions rather than the expertise that evaluates them. On this ambiguity, see also the notes on 667b1–3 and 670e7–8.

666e1 'your legal systems are fit for an army camp'
As Clinias in effect claimed at 625c–e.

666e2 'the inhabitants of a city'
The notion of a city (*astu*) contrasts both with the army camp just mentioned, and with the rural context about to be invoked. It connotes both peace and refinement.

666e6 'stroke him and tame him (*psêchôn te kai hêmerôn*)'
'Tame him' (*hêmerôn,* e6) recalls the goals of musical education (*mousikê*) as articulated in *Rep*. 441e–442a, 554d; in contrast with military or athletic training (*gumnastikê*), which rouses spirited ferocity, *mousikê* soothes and gentles the spirit to make it suitable for the peaceful, cooperative project of civic life; cf. *Laws* 935a.

667a1–2 'a capable participant in the affairs of a city or town- . . . even more warlike than the warriors of Tyrtaeus'
more literally: 'someone capable of governing (*dioikein*) a city or town . . .'
This is the citizen who 'knows how to rule and be ruled with justice' (643e6). The earlier reference to Tyrtaeus is at 630a–c.

667a3–4 'courage as fourth in virtue, not first'
The ranking is explained in Book 1 at 630c–d and 631c–d.

667a6–7 'again casting aspersions on our lawgivers'
As at 630d, where the Athenian politely deflects the charge; cf. 634c, 635a–b.

667a10–b1 'if there is a kind of 'music' (*mousan*) finer than that of choruses and public theatres'
The nature of the 'music' that is 'finer' (*kalliô*; alt: 'more beautiful') than what one learns by being trained to perform in a chorus is delineated at 667b5–671a1 (summarized at 670e5–8; cf. 669a7–b3 and in notes on 670a3–6, 670e3–4). That finer music is 'music' in the broader sense, which includes learning more generally; see note on 666d3. The music 'of choruses and public theatres' is music in the

narrower sense of song and dance. On an ambiguity between these two domains of comparison, see notes on 667b1–3 and 666d11–e1. On the range of the related term *mousikê*, see note on 642a4. On the translation of *kaliô*, see note on 630c7.

667b1–3 'let us try to assign it to those whom we said were embarrassed by the latter kind but eager to partake of the finest variety'

A reference back to 665e–666c, where the Athenian says that the elderly members of the chorus of Dionysus would be embarrassed to sing in public choral performance, but willing to sing in drinking parties, where wine will loosen their age-induced stiffness. That earlier passage, however, does not indicate that the singers' eagerness or lack thereof has anything to do with the kind or calibre of the music to be performed, although, in the passage immediately before it, the Athenian does indicate that the chorus of elders will sing 'the finest songs' (665d1–4; see note ad loc). In the present context, the 'finest variety' (667b2–3) is the music 'finer than that of choruses' just mentioned at 667a10–b1, whereas in the earlier passage, wine is said to renew the elders' enthusiasm for singing the 'charms' to be sung by the whole population (665c4; cf. 666c6)—which is the Athenian's general characterization of choral song (659e1–5). On the ambiguity in the notion of 'finer music', see note on 666d11–e1. Perhaps Plato here trades on that ambiguity in order to connect the largely self-contained account of

(A) the 'finer music' (666d3–671a1)

with what would otherwise be a continuous discussion of

(B) the use of drunkenness by the Dionysian chorus.

The latter resumes at 671a2 as if it were continuous with the discussion that ends at 666d2. On the connection between (A) and (B), see notes on 664d1–2, 671e1.

667b5–668b8

Pleasure, correctness, and the evaluation of representational art

Having just proposed that the chorus of Dionysus will practise a kind of music that is 'finer than that of the choruses and the public theatres' (667a10–b1), the Athenian now begins to elucidate the nature of that 'finer music'. He here takes the preliminary step of revisiting the issue, originally raised in 657c–659c, of whether pleasure is the criterion of correct music. He sketches a general account of the (very limited) conditions in which anything is to be judged by the criterion of pleasure (667b–668a), and gives specific reasons for supposing that music, as a representational art, is not to be judged by the pleasure it provides (668a–b). Rather, it is to be judged by how accurately it represents its intended object (668b).

Correctness

The Athenian appeals frequently in this discussion to the notion of correctness (*orthotês*) or what is correct (*orthos*), and the notion will be especially important in the sequel, where the musical expertise of the Dionysian chorus is specified (668c–669b, 670b). As he deploys the notion here, correctness applies to any activity or object that has a goal (a good or worthwhile objective—see note on 667d9–e3), and it consists in success at achieving that goal. Thus correctness of food consists in its being healthy, correctness of learning consists in its reaching truth (667b–c), and correctness of a likeness consists in accurately depicting its intended object (667c–d). It is only in the case of things that yield only harmless pleasures and occur for the sake of these that pleasure is the criterion of correctness. Where more significant benefits (and their corresponding harms) are at stake, it is those benefits, rather than pleasure, that provide the standard for correctness.

So conceived, correctness is a matter of goodness, of successfully living up to the standards that apply to the activity or object in question. The correctness of music has been a preoccupation of the Athenian since early in Book 2. While his original question (654e–655c), what kinds of song and dance are beautiful (*kalon*), does not invoke the vocabulary of correctness, he restates the issues as the question of what kind of music is correct (655d1, 657a8, b3). Accordingly, in the present context, the Athenian identifies the 'correctness and benefit' of something as 'what is good and beautiful in it' (667c7), and indicates that the search to identify the music that is 'finest' must seek 'the kind that is correct' (668b5–6). (Matters are more complicated by 669b1–3; on which see note on 669a9–b3.)

667b5–6 'anything that brings us enjoyment (*hosois sumparepetai tis charis*)'
more literally: 'what is accompanied by enjoyment'
The verb *sumparepesthai* (repeated at 667e2 and used interchangeably with forms of *parakolouthein* in 667c5 and *parepesthai* in 667d2) means to accompany or follow closely.

667b6–8 'Either this very feature on its own [sc. enjoyment] is the most important (*spoudaiotaton*) thing about it, or else what is most important is a certain correctness (*orthotêta*) or, third, a benefit (*ôphelian*)?'
What is *spoudaion*—often contrasted with what is 'in play' (*paizonta*, see note on 635b5)—is translated as 'serious' in other contexts. Here the superlative form of the term is used to pick out the proper criterion of evaluation and is translated as 'most important'. While the Athenian distinguishes correctness from benefit as the second and third items on the list, he will treat the two as a unit ('its correctness and benefit', 667c1) in the examples of food and learning (667b8–c8). Presumably these are cases in which correctness consists in providing a benefit. (In other cases, e.g. representation, correctness consists in likeness rather than benefit—cf. 667d9–10.) By contrast, Hatzistavrou (2011: 368–371) proposes that correctness and benefit

coincide even in the case of musical representations. On correctness, see also note on 667d9–e3 and general note on 667b5–668b8.

667b9–c1 'enjoyment (*charin*), which we might call "pleasure" (*hêdonên*)'
'Pleasure' (*hêdonê*) seems to be the generic term here, with 'enjoyment' (*charis*) indicating the type of pleasure that comes from some other worthwhile feature of an activity. See also 667c6, d1–3, e3–4, and note on 667e2–4.

667c6–7 'But its correctness (*orthotêta*) and benefit (*ôphelian*), what is good and beautiful in it (*to eu kai to kalôs*)'
alternatively: '. . . what is good and admirable in it'
The Athenian here indicates that correctness is an instance of being good and *kalon* (*eu kai kalôs* [*sc. echein*]). This is in keeping with his restatement, as an issue about 'correctness of music' (655d1, 657a8, b3), of the issue that he originally articulates (654e–655c) by asking what kinds of song and dance are beautiful (*kalon*). On the relationship between correctness and goodness ('*to eu*'), cf. 668d1–2 and notes on 631b5 and 634d9–e1. On the alternative translation, see note on 630c7.

667c10–d1 'Now consider the representational arts (*technai eikastikai*). Their business is to produce likenesses (*homoiôn ergasiai*)'
more literally: '. . . those arts that are representational in that they produce likenesses'
This representational activity will later be described as 'imitation' (*mimêsis*) at 667e10; music is identified as a representational art at 668a6–7.

667d1–3 'any pleasure that accompanies their product, should any pleasure arise, is appropriately called "enjoyment" (*charin*)'
more literally: 'the concomitant occurrence of pleasure in them (*to . . . gignesthai*), if it should occur (*ean gignêtai*), is most rightly (*dikaiotaton*) called enjoyment'

A difficult phrase. While the Athenian here invokes the representational arts as instances of the things that 'bring us enjoyment' (667b5–6), the qualification 'should any arise' (*ean gignêtai*, d2) indicates that he is not claiming that such arts always produce pleasure when they succeed in producing a likeness. Moss (2012: 218) takes this passage together with 667e4 to express the view that accurate representations of human virtue are naturally pleasant. However, the Athenian simply makes a distinction between (a) pleasures that arise in conjunction with representational success (or other forms of correctness) and (b) pleasures that are not so accompanied. He reserves the label 'enjoyment' (*charis*) for the former; see also note on 667e2–4.

667d5–7 'the correctness in such cases would be produced (*exergazoito*), roughly speaking (*hôs epi to pan eipein*), by accuracy (*isotês*) in quantity and quality'

Accuracy (more literally: 'equality', *isotês*) is invoked as a specific kind of correctness (*orthotês*); an accurate picture of a house need not have the dimensions equal to those of the house, but it will preserve the same relative proportions (cf. 668b7 and the example at 668d7–e5). At 668a3 such accuracy is referred to as truth (*alêtheia*). See also Hatzistavrou 2011: 371–2.

The qualification 'roughly speaking' (*hôs epi to pan eipein*) indicates that the statement is rough or approximate. The locution is rare in Plato (cf. *Laws* 917a4–5, *Euthyd.* 279e6) and occurs only occasionally in Aristotle (e.g. *GA* 732a20, *HA* 573a28) as a variation on his more regular locution '*hôs epi to polu*' (e.g. *GA* 725b17, *Phys.* 196b11, *An. Pr.* 32b10); the latter is also used by Plato (*Stsm.* 294e1, 295a4, *Rep.* 377b7, *Laws* 792b1, 875d4–5); in both authors it typically marks a claim as rough in the sense of admitting of exception (see Jones 2013: 7n16). Here, however, it is unlikely that the Athenian means to allow that, in some exceptional cases, correctness in representative arts is not a matter of accuracy. The qualification might acknowledge that '*isotês*' (literally equality) does not perfectly capture the target phenomenon: it is the terminology rather than the generalization that the Athenian marks as rough.

667d9–e3 'the only thing that would be correctly judged (*hêdonêi krinoit' an . . . orthôs*) by pleasure is what provides neither benefit nor truth nor likeness . . . Rather, it comes to be solely for the sake (*heneka*) of this very thing'
'[B]enefit . . . truth . . . likeness' are the different criteria for correctness (*orthotês*) just canvassed at 667b–d. The teleological language here ('for the sake of') reveals that correctness is a matter of success in achieving a goal, such as truth, likeness, etc. See general note on 667b5–668b8.

667e2–4 'enjoyment (*charitos*), which those other things bring in their wake, but when it occurs without them, is best called "pleasure" (*hêdonên*)'
more literally: 'the very thing that follows in the wake of the others (*sumparepomenou tois allois*), enjoyment, which, when none of them accompanies it (*hotan mêden autêi toutôn epakolouthêi*), is best called . . . '
The 'other things' (*tois allois*) are the benefit, truth, and likeness just mentioned (667d10). The pleasures that accompany such results merit the specific label 'enjoyment' (*charis*); but those that arise independently of them receive only the generic label, *hêdonê*; see note on 667d1–3.

667e6–8 'I also call it "recreation" (*paidian*) when it produces neither harm nor benefit worthy of serious mention (*spoudês ê logou axion*)'
This demarcation of *paidia* is recalled at 668a10–b1. On the range of the notion, see note on 635b5. Here its connection to pleasure, as well as the contrast with the serious matters (*spoudê*), are to the fore. The restrictive definition of the term articulated here underlies the claim at 673e8 that drinking parties must not be treated as mere recreation.

667e10–668a1 'no imitation is to be judged by pleasure and false opinion'
'[B]y false opinion' (*kai doxêi mê alêthei*) explains 'by pleasure' (*hêdonêi*). The explanation makes sense in the light of 655c–656b, where the Athenian has indicated that what we experience as pleasant thereby appears (*dokein*) to us to be beautiful, and vice versa (see note on 655e2–5 and general note on 655c4–d4).

668a1 'In particular, accuracy should never be'
more literally: 'in particular, no equality should be (*kai dê kai pasan isotêta*)'
On the translation of *isotês* by 'accuracy', see note on 667d5–7.

668a1–2 'simply because someone thinks so, or fails to enjoy something'
These would be instances, respectively, of judging imitations by the criteria of 'false opinion' and 'pleasure' just invoked (see note on 667e10–668a1). In keeping with the principles articulated in 665c4–d4 (see note ad loc), failing to enjoy an imitation would amount to thinking (*dokein*) that it is not beautiful (*kalon*). But the Athenian has just argued in the present context (667a8 ff.) that the beauty or correctness of a representation is a matter of its accuracy, which does not depend on what people think or feel about it.

668a3 'an imitation is to be judged in terms of its truth above all else'
Here 'truth' is used instead of 'equality' (*isotês*; alt: 'accuracy') for the correctness characteristic of representational art. Cf. 667c5–8, where truth is said to be the standard of correctness for learning (*mathêsis*).

668a6–7 'music, we say, is representational (*eikastikên*) and imitative (*mimêtikên*)'
The two adjectives are used equivalently here (cf. 668b10–c1). Choral songs and dances were described as 'imitations (*mimêmata*) of characters' at 655d5; also in Book 7, 798d9. The notion of

'representation' (*eikastikê*) is invoked for the first time at 667c10–d1, and its product is called *mimêsis* at 667e10. On music that (scandalously, to the Athenian) is not representational, see 669e5–670a3.

668a9–10 'So we should be least prepared to accept it when someone says that music is to be judged (*krinesthai*) by the pleasure it gives'
The Athenian's remark here is in superficial tension with his limited endorsement of the principle at 658e6–659a1, but in the present context he continues to believe that the elders will enjoy the music that they identify as best (670d7–e1), and in the former context he indicates that their judgement is an expression of knowledge (see note on 658e6–9). The former passage does not credit the elders with a judgement based on unreasoned intuition. They will enjoy the music that in their wisdom they recognize to be beautiful, and it is their grasp of its beauty that is the basis of their discrimination.

668a10–b1 'unworthy of our serious attention'
That is, it would count as mere recreation or play (*paidia*), as defined at 667e6–8.

668b2 'the kind [of music] that achieves likeness (*echousan tên homoiotêta*) in imitating what is beautiful (*tôi tou kalou mimêmati*).' alternatively: '. . . achieves likeness to an imitation of what is beautiful'
Following Schöpsdau, the present translation takes the dative (*tôi . . . mimêmati*) not as object of '*homoiotêta*' (likeness), but as instrumental, indicating the means by which the likeness is achieved. The alternative construal of the dative yields the alternative translation (thus Brisson/Pradeau, des Places, Saunders, Taylor, Pangle; rejected by England). Against the latter construal, there is no indication in the surrounding context that the likenesses produced by representational arts (cf. 667c10–d1) are likenesses of imitations, rather than of originals. The Athenian has earlier implied that the gestures and tunes of beautiful choral music are representations of

beautiful (alt: 'admirable') actions and utterances (655b2–6); on representation and imitation of the beautiful, see also note on 669a9–b3. On 'beautiful' as a translation of *kalon*, see note on 630c7.

668b4–6 'those who seek out the finest song and music must . . . search for the kind . . . that is correct'
The 'finest music' here must be music in the narrower sense of song and dance; however, the 'finest music' under discussion over this whole passage (667a–670e) is music in a different sense: the expertise by which the elders will identify correct song and dance. On ambiguities in the notion of the 'finest' or 'finer' music, see notes on 666d11–e1, 667a10–b1, and 667b1–3.

668b9–669b4

Evaluating representational works of art

Having just argued at some length (667b–668b) that music is a representational art which is to be evaluated (*krineisthai*) in terms of its representational accuracy, the Athenian here turns to consider what a wise judge must know in order in order to apply those standards to a particular work of art. He begins (668c4–e5) by distinguishing two questions:

(1) What is the object being represented?
(2) How accurately does the work of art represent it?

In keeping with the immediately preceding discussion (667b–668b), he refers to (2) as a matter of the 'correctness' of the artwork (668c7, d1, d9). Thus we may understand him to be introducing (1) as a prior question that must be addressed in order to answer (2).

He concludes (668e7–669b3) by refining the criteria of evaluation captured in questions (1) and (2), and stating that they are insufficient to determine whether a work of art is beautiful. At least in the case of choral music, a wise judge must also know a third thing:

(3) how well the representation employs 'phrases, tunes, and rhythms' (669b2–3).

This third criterion will be elaborated at some length at 669b–670e, where knowledge of it, characterized generally as knowledge of what is 'harmonious and well rhythmed' (670b9) is identified as the 'finer music' or 'superior education' characteristic of the Dionysian chorus. Most commentators, however, construe (3) as a specifically moral assessment of the work of art—against which, see the notes on 669a9–b3 and 669c3–8.

Assessing representational accuracy

668c4–6 'in order not to misjudge a particular composition'
more literally: 'he who will not to be mistaken about a . . . composition'
The judgement in question is the verdict of the 'true judge' of music at 659a5 and the 'wise judge' of art at 669a9–b3. As noted by Schöpsdau, the Athenian here shifts from arguing that music is to be evaluated by its representational accuracy (667b5–668c3) to asking what one needs to know in order to make such an evaluation.

668c5–7 'one must recognize just what it is (*ho ti pot' estin*) . . . its nature (*tên ousian*)—just what it intends (*ti pote bouletai*), what it actually represents (*hotou pot' estin eikôn ontôs*)'
The repeated '*pote*' gives intensive force to the questions, a colloquial use that is ubiquitous in Plato. At 669a9 'what it is' (*ho te esti*) is listed as the first of three things that the wise judge must know. Here it is explained by the rest of the quoted phrase. The 'nature' (or substance, *ousia*, c6) could either be the nature of the object represented (i.e. a sufficiently determinate conception to allow one to determine the accuracy of the representation) or it could be the nature of the representation (e.g. that it is a representation of a horse); in the latter case, 'nature' is explained by the following clause '*ti pote bouletai . . . ontôs*' (c6–7). '[W]hat it intends' (*ti . . . bouletai*) indicates that representation (*eikastikê*) or imitation (*mimêsis*, 667e10, 668a6) is a goal-directed activity; it has a target object of which it intends to produce a likeness (Halliwell 2002: 69), and its success is to be judged on how similar its product is to that target

object. (On the relationship between goal-directedness and correctness, see note on 667d9–e3.)

668c7–8 'one will hardly discern whether the intention is carried out correctly (*tên orthotêta tês boulêseôs*) or misses the mark'
more literally: '. . . the correctness or error of its intention'
It is ambiguous whether the 'correctness' of the intention is the correctness of having such an intention, or success in carrying it out. One might note, in favour of the latter (endorsed by England and Schöpsdau), that *orthotês* has consistently been used to refer to representational accuracy (667c–668b), and the immediately following comment (668d1) uses '*to orthôs*' ('whether it is correct') in that sense. The simple point here, as illustrated at 668d8–e5, is that in order to tell whether a work of art achieves representational accuracy, one needs to know what it purports to represent: 'what it is'. In effect, 668c4–8 affirms that knowing the second of the three things required of the wise judge at 669a9–b3 ('how correct it is') requires knowing the first ('what it is').

668d1–2 'if one fails to recognize whether it is correct (*to orthôs*), will one ever be able to discern (*diagnônai*) whether it is good or bad (*to ge eu kai to kakôs*)?'
The question 'whether it is correct' (*to orthôs*) concerns the correctness just invoked at 668c7–8, that is, how accurately the artwork represents its intended object. '[W]hether it is good or bad' (*to ge eu kai to kakôs*) is (*pace* England) the same question raised at 667c6–7 with the phrase 'what is good and beautiful/admirable (*to eu kai to kalôs*)'; it is the overall evaluative question addressed by the 'wise judge' of 669a9. Thus the present passage summarizes the message of 667b5–668b8: a work is to be evaluated or judged (*krineisthai*) according to whether it is correct, and the standard of correctness in the case of representational arts is accurate representation. The main difference between the two passages is that the former presents the evaluation of the work as being simply a matter of assessing its representational accuracy (see note on 667c6–7), whereas in the

present passage, by contrast, knowing whether the work is an accurate representation is identified only as necessary for answering the evaluative question. Indeed, at 668e7–669a4, the Athenian will indicate that it is not sufficient (see note on 669a5–6). A wise judge of choral art needs to know, in addition, a third thing: 'how well worked' the composition is (*hôs eu . . . eirgastai*, 669b1–3). England and Schöpsdau, on the basis of construing that third question as a specifically moral evaluation of the work of art, identify it with the question about 'good or bad' (*to ge eu kai to kakôs*) in the present passage. Whatever the merits of their interpretation of the third criterion (criticized in the note on 669a9–b3), Saunders oversteps in translating *to ge eu kai to kakôs* in the present passage as 'its moral goodness or badness'. In any case, if the intended object of representation in choral art is beautiful or virtuous behaviour (see notes on 669a9–b3 and 669c3–8), then the representational accuracy of a work will entail its moral adequacy; thus there would be no reason to suppose the third criterion is the specifically moral requirement.

668d8–e5 'Suppose . . . a person did not know the bodies being imitated'

An example to support the claim at 668c4–8 that one must know what is being represented (e.g. a spider or a horse) in order to assess the accuracy of the representation.

669a2–4 'Is it necessarily the case that someone who recognizes these things (*tauta*) is thereby (*êdê*) in a position to recognize whether the work of art is beautiful (*kalon*), or whether it falls short of beauty (*kallous*) in some way?'

'These things' (*tauta*) are (1) what the intended object of representation is and (2) how accurately the work represents that object; these are about to be identified as the first and second items of knowledge required of the wise judge at 669a9–b3. The Athenian here switches his focus, without warning, from the *necessity* of answering (1) and (2) if one is to evaluate a work of art as good or bad (668c4–e5) to the *insufficiency* of (1) and (2) for grounding such evaluations.

'[W]hether the work of art is beautiful (*kalon*), or . . . falls short of beauty (*tou kallous*) in some way' concerns the same general evaluative question as the phrase *to eu kai to kalôs* at 667c6–7 (see note ad loc), and the phrase *to ge eu kai to kakôs* at 668d1–2; beauty (*to kallos*) is the cognate noun of the adjective *kalon* (beautiful, noble, admirable; on the range of the term, see note on 630c7). On the general evaluative question addressed by the 'wise judge', see note on 669a7–9. (By contrast, Ferrari (1989: 105) takes the Athenian to be implying that (1) and (2) are sufficient grounding for such evaluations in the case of paintings; however, the Athenian will endorse Clinias' negative answer to this question; see note on 669a5–6.)

669a5–6 'But then, virtually all of us would recognize which pictures are beautiful (*ta kala tôn zôiôn*)!'
Clinias answers the Athenian's question of 669a2–4 in the negative, and the Athenian will endorse that answer at 669a7 (*orthotata legeis*). As noted by Schöpsdau, those who construe Clinias' answer as affirmative (e.g. Pelosi 2010: 56 and Hatzistavrou 2011: 377) overlook the significance of the construction '*an*' + imperfect, which marks Clinias' remark as counterfactual. Not everyone, Clinias here implies, is a good judge of the merits of a work of visual art, but we all would be if such judgements simply amounted to an assessment of how accurately the works depict their objects (e.g. if evaluating the merits of a Rembrandt self-portrait was simply a matter of judging how accurately it depicted the painter's face). Such judgements of representational accuracy involve the first and second things a 'wise judge' will be required to know at 669a7–b3; thus the current point provides a premise in the argument for the conclusion there that such a judge must also know a third thing. See note on 669a9–b3.

'Pictures' here translates *zôiôn*, whose primary meaning is 'animals' (and is translated thus by des Places, Taylor, and England, following Ast). However, the term also has an established use (esp. in the plural) for pictures or paintings (LSJ s.v. II; cf. Aristotle *Catg.* 1a2–3) and is translated accordingly by Saunders, Schöpsdau, and Brisson/Pradeau in the present passage. See Saunders 1972: 10.

Three things a wise judge of art must know

669a7–9 'So, for each representation (*eikona*), whether in painting or in music as a whole, doesn't a wise judge (*emphrona kritên*) need to have the following three things?'

Having just endorsed (*orthotata legeis*, 669a7) Clinias' reply (669a5–6) that knowing (1) what object is being represented by a work of art and (2) how accurately it depicts that object does not thereby put one in a position to judge whether that work of art is beautiful (*kalon*), the Athenian here concludes that there is, in addition, a third thing that a 'wise judge' must know. The wise judge must be one who pronounces on the question for which (1) and (2) have just been declared insufficient—that is, whether a work of art is beautiful (669a3–4); this is what the 'true judge' of 659a5 does, who, like the the unqualified judges with whom he is contrasted (the verb '*krinein*' is ubiquitous through 657e–659a), addresses the question that has occupied the Athenian's attention since early in Book 2, 654e: what sort of choral song and dance is beautiful? That question is variously expressed in the present context as a concern with 'the good and beautiful' (*to eu kai to kalôs*, 667c7) in a work of art, or 'whether it is good or bad' (*to ge eu kai to kakôs*, 668d1–2), or whether the work is 'beautiful (*kalon*), or . . . falls short of beauty' (669a3). Making such a judgement will be identified as the task of the chorus of Dionysus, which 'selects' the musical work that is 'most beautiful' (*eklogês . . . tou kallistou*, 670e7–8).

669a9–b3 'One must know [1] first of all what it is (*ho te estin*), next [2] how correctly it is rendered (*hôs orthôs . . . eirgastai*), and [3] third, how well the particular representation is rendered (*hôs eu . . . eirgastai*) in phrases (*rhêmasin*), tunes (*melesi*), and rhythms (*rhuthmois*)'

The first two criteria have been expounded in 668c4–e5. They concern (1) the work's intended object of representation and (2) the accuracy of its representation (regularly described as a kind of 'correctness', 667b5–668a5). The Athenian claimed earlier

(668a6–c3) that representational accuracy, rather than pleasure, is the proper basis for evaluating works of representational art. Here that position is refined. In addition to representational accuracy as expressed in (1) and (2), a beautiful work of art must also satisfy a third criterion: (3) that it be 'well . . . rendered in phrases, tunes, and rhythms'.

There is a tendency among commentators to disregard the significance in (3) of the qualification 'in phrases, tunes, and rhythms', which invokes the same three media of choral composition originally invoked at 656c4–5. (Hatzistavrou (2011: 375), for example, translates the passage as if it qualifies all three criteria, and Janaway (1995: 178) omits the qualifying phrase altogether in his translation.) Question (3) is then conflated with the general evaluative question faced by the wise critic of a work of art. The latter, for example, is articulated at 668d1–2 as *to ge eu kai to kakôs* ('whether [the work] is good or bad'), where it is distinguished from the 'correctness' of the work; and one might suppose (with Schöpsdau and England) that in that passage the Athenian makes the the same distinction between (2) and (3) as in the present passage. Similarly, in 668e7–669a4, immediately preceding the present passage, the Athenian has distinguished between, on the one hand, the representational accuracy of a work (which he has been consistently calling its 'correctness'—667c–668b) and, on the other hand, its beauty (*to kalon*)—the latter term being used to articulate (3) at 670e6. Thus it might seem that in 668e7–669a4 the same distinction is captured as the difference between (2) and (3) in the present passage. On this basis one might conclude that (3) concerns the beauty of a work of art (thus Hatzistavrou 2011: 376 and A. Barker 2013: 397–8). However, this interpretation of (3) makes no sense of the fact that 668e7–669b3 amounts to an argument from the *premise* that knowing (1) and (2) is insufficient to determine whether a work of art is beautiful, to the *conclusion* that some third thing must also be known—sc. in order to answer that question. On pain of irrelevance, the third thing a wise judge needs to have must be the answer to a question distinct from whether the work of art is beautiful, although necessary for answering that question.

England would bracket as an interpolation the phrase 'in phrases, tunes, and rhythms' (669b2–3; rejected by Schöpsdau), since it articulates (3) in terms specific to music in the narrow sense, while the three criteria have been introduced as applying to all representational art ('whether in painting or in music as a whole', 669a7–8). However, an abrupt shift from generic to specific would not be out of character for the Athenian's exposition. In any case, if the interpretation of (3) defended below is correct, (3) is easy to reformulate at the requisite level of generality. Roughly, in any work of representational art, the media of representation must be consistent with each other and with the object that is represented.

669b5–670a3

The third criterion explained

There is considerable disarray among commentators as to how to understand (3), the third criterion invoked at 699b2–3. On the most natural way of reading the text, (3) concerns how well the composer has employed the various musical elements in the composition, how well rendered (*eu . . . eirgastai*) it is 'in phrases, tunes, and rhythms' (669b1–3; cf. 656c4–5). What counts as being well rendered in this respect is explained in the following passage (669b5–670b7), which details the particular 'difficulties' presented by music (669b5–6). The passage, which catalogues errors in musical composition, makes specific and repeated mention of tunes, rhythms, and words; it requires that the 'harmonies' and rhythms in a choral work be compatible with each other and with the melodies (*melê*) and gestures (*schêmata*) that are set in those structures (see note on 669c3–8). Thus we may conclude that (3) in the present text, being 'well . . . rendered in phrases, tunes, and rhythms', is a matter of such internal consistency—a supposition confirmed by the Athenian's identification of expertise at assessing such rhythmic and harmonious appropriateness as the specialized competence of the Dionysian chorus at 670b8–671a1 (see notes below and 812b9–c8). We might call such internal consistency in a work of art its 'integrity'. So interpreted, the third criterion may be construed as a general requirement, of any work of representational art, that the media of representation be consistent with each other and with the object of representation; on the generality of (3) see note on 669a7–9.

Most commentators, by contrast (e.g. England, Saunders, Schöpsdau, and most recently Pelosi 2010: 56–7; Hatzistavrou 2011: 380–1; and A. Barker 2013: 400), construe the ensuing discussion of fitting 'harmonies' and rhythms (669b5–670b7) as pertaining to criterion (2)—the representational accuracy of the composition—and they interpret (3) as a moral or ethical assessment of the artwork, variously understood to concern its suitability for inculcating virtue (Schöpsdau; England; Halliwell 2002: 67–8; Mouze 2005: 198–205) or the moral quality of the behaviour it represents (Morrow 314; Stalley 1983: 126–7, 129; Hatzistavrou 376; Pelosi 56–7; A. Barker 2013: 401; see also Ferrari 1989: 104–5). However, while it is evident that the Athenian takes the question of whether a work of art is beautiful or admirable (*kalon*) to involve a moral or ethical assessment (witness his requirement at 655a–b that beautiful songs and dances be those 'of virtue'—see note on 655b3–6), it is a mistake to suppose that criterion (3) expresses that moral requirement. Call this supposition the 'moral interpretation' of (3).

The obvious embarrassment faced by the moral interpretation of (3) is that the long catalogue of mistakes made in musical compositions (669b5–670b7), which follows immediately upon the introduction of (3), does not concern the moral defects of those compositions, but rather their failure to use appropriate 'harmonies' and rhythms in the songs and dances. We are to suppose that having stated the inadequacy of judging a work of art on (1) and (2) alone—its representational features—the Athenian announces that (3), its moral adequacy, must also be taken into account, but then proceeds to ignore the question of moral adequacy and give a lengthy discussion of additional considerations that go into the assessment of (2). Moreover, the Dionysian chorus' signature expertise in 'harmonies' and rhythms (670b–d) would be irrelevant to the criterion (3) here introduced—even though expertise in the 'third thing' is attributed to them at 670e3–5 (see note ad loc and on 670e5–6). The proposal by Halliwell (2002: 68) that (2) and (3) respectively concern the correctness and benefit invoked in the argument against the pleasure criterion at 667b is open to a similar objection.

This 'moral' interpretation of (3) is nonetheless preferred by commentators as the price of avoiding a variety of problems. For example, it is sometimes supposed that the alternative to the 'moral' interpretation of (3) is a narrowly technical reading—as on the translations of Jowett and Taylor—according to which (3) is a matter of how well the words, songs, and gestures in a choral work succeed in representing their intended object (thus Morrow 1960: 314n55). On such a narrowly technical reading, (3) would collapse into (2)—which is at odds with the Athenian's clear message that (3) is an additional consideration not captured by (2). Schöpsdau, by contrast, supposes that the alternative to the 'moral' interpretation is to suppose that (3) concerns the quality of the composition's workmanship; so construed, (3) would be distinct from (2), the work's strictly representational adequacy. But this alternative, he claims (p. 324), has the unacceptable consequence, given the Athenian's claim at 670e5 that the poets need not know 'the third thing', that the expertise of the poet does not extend to assessing the technical workmanship of poetic compositions. Thus, Schöpsdau concludes, (3) must concern a higher expertise than the poet's technical expertise. However (as will be argued in the note on 670e6–7), it is perfectly intelligible for the Athenian to distinguish between the poet's knowledge of 'harmonies' and rhythms (which is knowledge of how to produce them, that is, to set words and gestures into 'harmonies' and rhythms) from expertise as to whether the 'harmonies' and rhythms so employed are appropriate to the words and gestures. On the 'integrity' interpretation it is the latter expertise that pertains to (3) and is the special province of the Dionysian chorus.

Once we distinguish the question addressed by the third criterion from the question of whether the work of art is beautiful (which will depend on all three criteria), it is intelligible to ask which of the three criteria identified in the present passage (669b1–3) expresses a specifically moral requirement for beautiful works of art. The evidence for supposing that there is such a requirement points clearly towards the first criterion as the locus of the moral restriction, for it asks what object is being represented (or imitated) by the work. Choral music, we are told, imitates or depicts actions and characters (655d5; cf. 798d9), and the Athenian states emphatically, early in Book 2, that the words and gestures portrayed in beautiful choral music must be those of virtuous people (655b; see note on 655b3–6). Accordingly he indicates closer to the present context that serious music, unlike the trifling sort that aims only at harmless pleasure, is engaged in the business of 'imitating what is beautiful' (668a9–b2; see note on 668b2). Thus we may conclude that the reason why a 'wise judge' of music must know 'the first thing' (what the work represents) is not simply in order to know the second thing (how accurate the representation is), but more importantly because the answer to that first question will disqualify those works that imitate behaviour or character that is not *kalon* (admirable, beautiful).

Thus it is criterion (1) that expresses the moral requirement on beautiful music: that the object of representation in beautiful music must be virtuous behaviour. Criterion (2), by contrast, requires that such behaviour be represented accurately. Criterion (3) introduces a consideration in addition to (1) and (2). As an examination of the next paragraph (669b5–670b6) will reveal, the first two criteria ask whether the gestures and words in a choral work accurately represent the behaviour of virtuous people, while the third criterion asks whether the 'harmonies' and rhythms employed in the work are appropriate to the behaviour depicted (see note on 669c3–8). (By contrast, Schipper (1963) denies that (1) and (2) concern representational features of music, and construes (3) as pertaining to intrinsic features of 'harmony' and rhythm, rather than to the fit between these and the words and gestures. Hatzistavrou (2011) also underestimates the significance of the question of fit.) It may be argued that the 'harmonies' and rhythms are themselves representations of character (thus Hatzistavrou 2011: 382–3; A. Barker 2013: 399–400); if that is correct, then (3) as well as (2) will concern representational properties of music. But (3) and (2) would still be verdicts of different kinds of expertise. On the interpretation of (3) defended here, we may say that (2) concerns the representational aspects of the work (words and gestures) whose 'correctness' is more generally accessible to the ordinary person (parallel to the ordinary person's ability to judge whether a painting is an accurate picture of an animal—cf. 668e7–669a4), while (3) concerns aspects of the work ('harmony' and rhythm) whose representational properties are grasped only by specialized musical expertise. On such a construal, the Athenian distinguishes between the second and third items of the competent judge's knowledge *not* because only the former concerns the representational accuracy of the musical composition, *but* rather because assessing the representational adequacy of 'harmonies' and rhythms (as opposed, for instance, to words and figures) is a matter of specialized knowledge. In particular, the analogy with painting emphasizes that (2) concerns how well the choral work has represented the external manifestation of virtue, while (3) concerns how well its 'harmonies' and rhythms replicate the internal psychic structure of virtue. Assessing (2) will be within the competence of a well-educated person, while assessing (3) requires the specialized training of the Dionysian chorus. The special expertise of the composers concerns none of (1), (2), or (3).

Mistakes made by human composers

To elucidate the 'third thing' that a wise judge of art must know (669ab2–3), the Athenian enumerates a variety of mistakes made by human composers:

(A) They employ mutually inconsistent compositional elements (phrases, melodies, gestures, rhythms) in their imitation of human beings (669c3–8).

(B) They attempt to represent multiple distinct objects as if they were a single thing (669c8–d5).
(C) They employ compositional elements without any representational intent (669d5–670a3).

(A), (B), and (C) constitute a series of increasingly severe deviations from the principle of correct composition that is stated more succinctly at the end of the paragraph (670b2–6). This is the view that a tune (*melos*) has 'correctness' (*orthotês*, 670b4) or is 'well rhythmed' (*eurutbmon*) and 'harmonious' (*euarmoston*, 670b9) if it employs the 'harmony'/mode (*harmonia*—see note on 653e3–5) or rhythm that is appropriate to its words or phrases (*rhêmata*) and its gestures (*schêmata*). In effect, the principle requires that the distinctively musical aspects of the work—'harmony' and rhythm—be in keeping with its more narrowly representational features—the words and gestures (see note on 669c3–8). Expertise in assessing whether this is the case is identified as the 'finer music' to be practised by the elderly judges (a point repeated at Book 7, 812b–c), and this, the Athenian claims, requires training beyond that of the ordinary citizen who is drilled in choral performance (670b8–671a1).

669b5–6 'let us not omit to state the difficulties we face in the case of music'

The difficulties or challenges in the present context may be those faced by judges of music who might, for example, find amusing (*gelôta*, 669d4) rather than pernicious the musical practices about to be denounced as mistaken (669c3–670a3). Or they may be difficulties faced by people who indulge in the wrong kind of music. The latter is suggested by 669b8–c1, and the former by the repetition of 'difficult' (*chalepon*) in the superlative at 669c1, where mistakes in music are 'extremely difficult to notice' (*aisthesthai*); see note on 669a9–b3. On either construal, the difficulty would stem from the fact that music is pleasant, and pleasure, as discussed in Book 1, is an extremely 'difficult' or 'hard' opponent (*tôn . . . chalepôtatôn*, 634b5–6; see note ad loc). On the range of the term *chalepon* (hard, difficult) see note on 629d2. On the wide scope of 'music', see note on 642a4.

669b8–c1 'Not only is making a mistake here (*hamartôn*) extremely harmful, since one will come to welcome evil characters (*êthê kaka philophronoumenos*)'
That is, by participating in the wrong sort of song and dance. The harms are detailed at 656b1–4.

669c1 'but it is extremely difficult (*chalepôtaton*) to notice (*aisthesthai*)'
What is difficult to notice is that one is making a mistake, perhaps because even the mistaken varieties of music about to be enumerated (669c3–670a3) are pleasant to the uneducated. See also the note on 669b5–6.

669c3–8 'the blunder (*examartoien*) of composing words (*rhêmata*) suitable for men and then giving them the colour (*chrôma*) or tune (*melos*) of women, or attaching rhythms of the servile and slavish to the tune and gestures of the free'
On rhythms and tunes appropriate to women, men, slaves, etc., see 802d–e. On their relationship to different character types, see *Rep.* 398c–400a and Hatzistavrou 2011: 382–3.

The alleged 'blunders' illuminate, by negative contrast, the third criterion to be used by the wise judge of representational art (669b1–3). A positive exposition of the criterion is given at 670b2–6: the rhythm and the *harmonia* of a tune (*melos*) must be appropriate to it. The present passage, by contrast, substitutes '*melos*' (tune) for '*harmonia*': it is not a composition's '"harmony" and rhythm', but its 'tune (*melos*) and rhythm' that must be appropriate to its words and gestures, as well as to each other. This slight variation reflects the conception of *melos* as a compound of *harmonia*, rhythm, and *logoi* (*Rep.* 398d); any given *melos* involves a specific *harmonia*. The additional mention, in the present passage, of gestures (*schêmata*) ensures that the requirement of fit applies not just to song, but to dance as well. On gestures and tunes (or gestures and words) as the material of dance and song respectively, see notes on 654e4–5 and 655a1–2. On 'colour', see note on 655a4–8. On *harmonia* (mode), see note on 653e3–5; on *melos* (tune), see also note on 670c2–3.

669c8–d2 'they would never mix together animal and human voices, the sounds of instruments, and every kind of noise, yet purport to be imitating a single thing'

This second poetic 'blunder' involves an even greater deviation than the first from the principle that a musical work must provide a consistent representation of a single entity. While the first mistake is that of combining opposing elements (slavish and free) in the representation of a single person, this second error involves the incoherence of imitating different types of animate and inanimate entities as if they were a single entity. Thus Hatzistavrou 2011: 381–2; compare *Rep.* 397a–b. The Athenian makes a different complaint about 'mixing' musical styles at 700a–701e.

669d2–3 'Human composers . . . spin these elements into a great jumble'

more literally: ' . . . weave such things together (*emplekontes*) and pour them together (*sugkukôntes*)'

The Athenian is mixing his metaphors. The 'human composers' are the practitioners of the so-called 'new music' of Plato's time, on which see A. Barker 1984: ch. 7; Csapo 2004; and D'Angour 2006.

669d4–5 'a source of laughter (*gelôta*) for people who are in what Orpheus calls the "prime season of delight" '

alternatively: 'providing objects of derision to men who . . . ' (England)

Orpheus is a legendary musician and poet (see R. Edmonds 2013 and Brisson 1993), mentioned by Plato at *Philb.* 66c, *Ion* 533b, 536b. See Kern 1922: 86 fr. 10 and Brisson/Pradeau v1, 358n90.

669d5–6 'It is not enough that composers confound these things, they also wrench them apart'
more literally: 'The composers both see all these things jumbled together (*horôsi panta kukômena*) and they wrench them apart'
alternatively: 'they see these things . . . and the poets tear them apart'
'Composers' (*poêtai*, d2) is the subject of the previous sentence, and so is naturally construed as the subject of *horôsi* in the present phrase. The alternative is to take the verb's subject to be the 'men . . . in the prime season of delight' (d4–5) in the immediately preceding subordinate clause (thus Brisson/Pradeau and Pangle), or (less plausibly) the subject of '*gignôskein*' (recognize) in e3 (England, following Stallbaum). Pangle is wrong to construe *kai eti diaspôsin* . . . (d6) to be within the scope of *horôsi* ('they see . . . that the poets are guilty of separating . . . ').

669d7–e2 'bare speech (*logous psilous*) . . . bare lyre or reed pipe (*psilêi kitharisei te kai aulêsei*)'
While '*psilos*' when applied to *logoi* (words, speech) often means 'prose', here it indicates words not set to music—i.e. not structured by *harmonia* and rhythm (thus England; cf. Hatzistavrou 2011: 380n18; Martin (2013: 316–18) takes the present passage to forbid the performance of the Homeric poems). When applied to the playing of musical instruments '*psilos*' means 'without words'. The instruments invoked here are the *kithara* (a small lyre) and the *aulos* (a double-reed pipe). The latter's name is commonly translated 'flute', which is unfortunate in that a flute is not a reed instrument; 'reed pipe' is also imperfect, in that it does not distinguish the *aulos* from the *syringx* (Panspipe). Greg Scott has suggested 'double-oboe', for lack of an equivalent modern instrument.

669e2–4 'This makes it extremely difficult to recognize what the wordless rhythm and "harmony" intends (*ho ti te bouletai*)'
While the previous musical errors catalogued since 669b5 consist in making inconsistent representations (see note on 669c8–d2), this

third error is to fail to use music as a representational medium at all. What it 'intends' (*ho ti te bouletai*, e4) is the object imitated or represented by a work of art (see note on 668c5–7).

670a1 'other than to accompany dance and song'
more literally: 'other than as subordinate (*hupo* + accusative) to dance and song'
This indictment of non-choral music reflects the requirement that music be used as a representational medium. See 668a–c and note on 669c8–d2.

670a1–3 'The bare employment of either instrument (*psilôi de hekaterôi . . . chrêseôs*) is completely unmusical showmanship (*pasa tis amousia kai thaumatourgia*)'
It is 'unmusical' in the sense that it displays an absence of learning (*mousikê* in the broad sense; see note on 666d3). In this case it displays ignorance of the representational function of music. See note on 670a1. On 'bare' (*psilos*), see note on 669d7–e2.

670a3–671a1

The elders' expertise in 'harmony' and rhythm

The 'finer music' of the Dionysian chorus (invoked at 667a10; see note on 667b1–3) is expertise in the appropriateness of 'harmonies' and rhythms. This is distinct from the expertise of the composers, and from that of trained choral performers.

670a3–6 'our inquiry is not into what we *shouldn't* do when we have reached our thirties or gone past 50 and are availing ourselves of the Muses, but rather what we should do'
The present inquiry answers the question posed at 666d3–4: what kind of music will be sung by the chorus of Dionysus, whose membership is specified as 'those over 30 and up to 60 years of age' (664d2). The Athenian has answered that their music must be 'finer than that of choruses' (667a10), and he demarcates the scope of

that finer music by detailing the 'three things' a wise judge of music must know (667b5–669b4). The catalogue of musical errors starting at 669b5 begins as an elucidation of the 'third thing'. The present comment notes that the catalogue has gone beyond what is necessary to fulfil this function. Only the initial mistake listed violates the third criterion—see note on 669c3–8—while the second and third are increasingly egregious violations of the first and second. On the age range of the chorus of Dionysus, see also notes on 664d1–2 and 671e1.

670a7–b2 'those who have reached 50 and are fit to sing (*aidein prosêkêi*) must have received an education better than that of the choral Muse'
At 812b9–10, the age given for those who receive this superior education is 60. The question of being 'fit to sing' recalls those 'no longer up to the challenge of singing' (*ou gar eti dunatoi pherein ôidas*, 664d3; see note on 664d2–4).

670b2–4 'They must have keen perception and knowledge of rhythms and "harmonies". How else could one recognize the correctness of tunes (*orthotêta . . . tôn melôn*) . . . ?'
This is what is taught by the 'education better than that of the choral muse' just mentioned (670a7–b1). As discussed in the lines immediately following, it is knowledge that discerns which tunes are 'harmonious and well-rhythmed' (670b9), which is to say that they 'have the appropriate features' (670c2–3)—viz. the appropriate 'harmony' and rhythm. As elaborated in 669c3–8, the 'harmony' and rhythm in a song or dance must be appropriate to the words and gestures and to each other. Thus a wise judge of a choral work must be able (a) to identify its 'harmony' and rhythm ('keenly perceptive'—*euaisthêtôs*, 670b3); and (b) know what character type each of these fits (male, female, free, slavish, etc.). On 'harmonies' and rhythms, see note on 653e3–5. (On the difference between this knowledge of 'harmonies' and rhythms and the expertise attributed to the poets or composers at 670e6–7, see note ad loc.)

The term *orthotês* here, in contrast to the cognate term used in 669b1–3, does not invoke representational accuracy. There, the correctness of a representation consists in its accuracy; here the correctness of a tune consists in its having 'harmony' and rhythm appropriate to its message.

670b4–6 'which of them should be in the Dorian "harmony", and whether the rhythm the composer has attached to a tune is correct or not'
The Dorian is one of the four *harmoniai* ('harmonies' or 'modes') discussed at *Rep.* III 398c–399c (cf. *La.* 188d,193d–e), but which are not named or enumerated elsewhere in *Laws*, even in the discussion of harmony and rhythm in Book 7, 802c–e; see note on 669c3–8. Even if England is right to bracket these phrases as a later gloss not written by Plato, the explanation they provide is surely correct. See also note on 653e3–5.

670b8–9 'able to recognize (*gignôskein*) what is and isn't harmonious (*euarmoston*) and well rhythmed (*euruthmon*)'
This is specialized expertise in the appropriateness of specific 'harmonies' and rhythms (the third criterion of 699b1–3), not the universal human capacity to take pleasure in the perception of 'harmony' and rhythm invoked at 654a2–3. See notes on 669c3–8 and on 670c2–3.

670b9–c1 'simply from having been drilled at singing to the reed pipe and marching in rhythm'
A reference to the sort of education Clinias and Megillus have received (666d8–10; cf. 667a8–b3).

670c2–3 'the tune (*melos*) with the appropriate features is correct'
The features are 'harmony' and rhythm, which must be appropriate to the behaviour represented by its words (see note on 669c3–8). A *melos* here is not a 'tune' in the narrow sense that excludes lyrics, but a combination of words, 'harmony', and rhythm (*Rep.* 398c11–d9).

On 'correct' as applied to tunes, see note on 670b2–4. On the range of the term *melos* see Calame 1998: 107–9.

670c5–6 'Suppose a person does not even recognize what features a tune has. Will he ever be able to do what we said—that is, recognize whether it is correct (*hôs orthôs*) in any given case?'
alternatively: 'correct in any respect (*hotôioun*)' (Saunders)
Such a person does not recognize what 'harmony' and rhythm a tune (*melos*) has, and hence is not in a position to assess 'whether it is correct' (*hôs orthôs*, 670c6) as deployed in a particular composition (v. erroneous in one of the ways catalogued at 669b–d); 'what we said' refers back to the questions about correctness raised at 667b–668e. On what such correctness consists in, see note on 670c2–3.

670c9 'Those singers . . . whom we encourage and in a way even compel (*anankazomen*) to sing willingly (*hekontas*)'
On the willingness of the singers, see notes on 663b4–6, 665d9–e1, and 665e2–3. On the contrast between willingness and compulsion (*anankê*) or force (*bia*), see 663e1–2 and note on 632b7–8. On persuasion v. compulsion see note on 634a9.

670d5–6 'they will be able to select what is appropriate (*ta prosêkonta*). This is what is fitting (*prepon*) for people of their age and character to sing'
more literally: '. . . the appropriate ones, which (*ha*) it is fitting for people of their age . . . to sing' (Schöpsdau)
alternatively: '. . . select the songs that are appropriate for people of their age and character to sing' (Brisson/Pradeau and Saunders)
'[W]hat is appropriate' (*ta prosêkonta*) are songs that have appropriate 'harmonies' and rhythms (cf. the same term at 670c2). Thus the elders are applying the third criterion of the wise judge of 669b1–3 and they do so in fulfilment of their general mandate to select the beautiful songs and dances to be performed by the choruses of citizens. Against the alternative translation, which construes the relative pronoun '*ha*' as restrictive rather than attributive, the task

the Athenian has set for the chorus of Dionysus is not simply to identify songs that are appropriate (*prepon*) for their own age and nature. All the citizens, young and old, must sing songs with appropriate (*prosêkonta*) 'harmonies' and rhythms, and it is the business of the elders to select the songs with these features.

670d6–7 'and when they do, they not only enjoy the harmless pleasures of the moment'
more literally: 'singing thus, they not only enjoy . . . '
On harmless pleasures, see 667d9–e5. 'Singing thus' (*houtôs . . . aidontes*) encompasses both the 'finer music' that selects the songs that are appropriate for choral performance, and the actual singing of those songs—the latter apparently being the method by which the younger singers are taught the selected songs.

670e1–2 'they also guide the younger singers towards the appropriate embrace (*aspasmou prosêkontos*) of worthy characters'
alternatively: ' . . . set an example in the appropriate embrace . . . '
A reminder that music trains a person's affective responses. The term *aspasmos* (embrace; alt: liking, loving), whose verbal form is employed at 654d2, belongs to the 'pleasures and pains' whose proper training constitutes education (*paideia*), in which an educated person 'hate[s] what one should hate (*misein*) and love[s] what one should love (*stergein*)' (653c1–2); cf. 919e5 where *aspasmos* is substituted for *philia* as the opposite of *misein* (hate).

The 'younger singers' here might be members of the choruses of the Muses and of Apollo (664b–d). They might also be the younger members of the chorus of Dionysus, whose age range begins just after 30 (664d1–2; see note ad loc). The Athenian has just assigned the discriminatory expertise in 'harmonies' and rhythms to 'those who have reached the age of 50 and are fit to sing' (670b1–2). Given that the performance context of the Dionysian chorus is a drinking party (666b–c), the leadership here would be that of the 'sober leaders' who lead their juniors in a properly conducted drinking party at 640d.

670e3–4 ‘the skill they practise (*paideian . . . metakecheirismenoi*) is more exact (*akribesteran*) than that of the common run, and even that of the composers themselves’

more literally: ‘the education (*paideia*) they practise . . . ’ (on *paideia* as the result of training, see general note on 653a5–c6)

This ‘more exact’ education is the ‘finer music’ of the Dionysian chorus (667a10–b3), which allows one to discern whether a tune is ‘harmonious and well-rhythmed’ (670b8–9; see note ad loc). On the comparison with the choral training of the ordinary person, cf. 666d8–e2, 670a7–b2, 670e2–3. On the comparison with the training of the composers, see note on 670e5–6. On specialized musical knowledge, see also *Tht.* 178d, *Rep.* 398e, 400b.

670e5–6 ‘there is no need for a composer to recognize the third thing, whether the imitation is beautiful or not’

The ‘third thing’ is probably the third of the ‘three things’ that a ‘wise judge’ must know, enumerated at 669b1–3: ‘how well rendered (*eu . . . eirgastai*) the particular representation (*hêtisoun eikonôn*) is’. In the present restatement, ‘imitation’ (*mimêma*) is substituted for ‘representation’ (*eikôn*) in the original locution (as licensed by 668a6–7) and ‘beautiful’ (*kalon*) is substituted for ‘well rendered’ (*eu . . . eirgastai*); on the close connection between the good and the beautiful (*kalon*) evident, for instance, at 667c7, see note on 637e5. Alternatively, since the third thing is here glossed as ‘whether the imitation is beautiful’, one might take it to be the general evaluative question about the work of art articulated at 669a3–4: whether the work of art is ‘beautiful, or . . . falls short of beauty’; thus Ferrari 1989: 107 and Hatzistavrou 2011: 383–4. However, that question is answered in the ranking of choral compositions as ‘finest’, ‘second’, and so on at 670e7–8, where knowledge of ‘all three’ things is identified as necessary for making the ranking. (On the difference between the three criteria, and the question of whether the work of art is beautiful, see note on 669a9–b3.)

670e6–7 'All [a composer] needs to know, basically (*schedon*), are "harmony" and rhythm'

The composer's knowledge 'about "harmony" and rhythm' (*to de harmonias kai rhuthmou*, e6)—marked as an imprecise phrase by *schedon* ('basically')—must concern different matters than the expertise that allows the wise judges to discern which choral works have appropriate 'harmonies' and rhythms (670b8–c3, 670d1–5). We may understand the difference as follows: the composer's expertise is in setting words and gestures into 'harmonies' and rhythms, but does not extend to discerning which 'harmonies' and rhythms are appropriate to which words and gestures (witness the mixing and matching decried at 669c3–8). Thus the composers are unable to perform the task assigned to the wise judges of music: to select which choral works are 'harmonious (*euarmoston*) and well-rhythmed (*eurhythmon*)' (670b8–9). The higher expertise of the judges will involve not simply discriminating one 'harmony' from another (the Dorian from the Lydian, for example, which a composer is competent to do), but also discerning the sort of character to which each 'harmony' is appropriate (e.g. that the Dorian is appropriate to courage). The latter discrimination involves knowing that the Dorian 'harmony' replicates the psychic structure of courage (see note on 669c3–8), an expertise distinct from the composer's knowledge of how to produce a tune in the Dorian 'harmony'. To deny such discriminatory expertise to composers is thus not to deny them competence in their craft—as Schöpsdau worries, p. 324; see note on 669a9–b3. Hatzistavrou proposes that the composers know the same things about 'harmony' and rhythm as the wise judges know, only less expertly; i.e. they know which 'harmonies' and rhythms go together (Hatzistavrou 2011: 382–3). However, the Athenian has just said that composers make serious blunders on this front (669b–670b). The composers are skilled in composing song and dance (by setting words and gestures into 'harmonies' and rhythms), while the judges are skilled in assessing whether the 'harmonies' and rhythms employed are suitable to their subject matter. A different error is attributed to the composers in Book 7, 801b9–c7.

670e7–8 'These people (*tois de*), by contrast, must know all three, in order to select (*tês eklogês heneka*) what is most beautiful (*kallistou*) as well as what is second (*deuterou*)'
alternatively: '. . . what is finest (*kallistou*) as well as what is second'
'These people' are the elderly singers invoked at the beginning of the paragraph (670c8–9), who are also the wise judges of 669a9, who the Athenian has said must know 'three things' in order to determine whether a work of art is beautiful (669a9–b3). Here that determination is expressed in the ranking of musical works as 'most beautiful' (*kalliston*), 'second', etc.; on the significance of this ranking, see also note on 670e5–6. England and Brisson/Pradeau (359n94), by contrast, suppose that 'what is second' is to be understood as the second of three stages of education that they find sketched at 670d1–5. On this interpretation, 'what is *kalliston*' would be the 'finer music' invoked at 667a and attributed to the Dionysian chorus, which selects the musical compositions that are fit for educational purposes. In support of the former interpretation against the latter: *tois de* (e7) is governed by the expression *anankê . . . gignôskein* (e5)— so 'all three' (e7) are what the wise judges *know*, just like the 'three things' of 669b1–3. Still, there has been a persistent ambiguity in the Athenian's use of the 'finer/finest music': whether it concerns the ranking of choral music against a better variety practised by the Dionysian chorus, or whether it concerns the ranking of choral compositions, as in the competitive context reflected at 657d–659c. See note on 666d11–e1. On the translation of *kalon* by 'beautiful', see note on 630c7.

VI
DRINKING PARTIES

671a2–674c7

The Athenian now fulfils his long-deferred promise to explain his provocative assertion that drinking parties have important educational benefits (641a–d, 652b–653a). His strategy for defending that claim in Book 2 has been to introduce the so-called chorus of Dionysus (664c–665b), about which he has made two main claims:

- *(A) Its members will perform in drinking parties, rather than in public choral competitions (665c–666c).*
- *(B) The music they will perform is 'finer than that of choruses' (667a10–b1) and amounts to the expertise that discriminates which choral compositions are fit to play a role in education (666d–670e).*

While (B) clearly identifies an important educational function, it bears no obvious relation to the specifically Dionysian aspect of the chorus that is specified in (A) (see note on 667b1–3). Thus the Athenian now turns to focus on the benefits that arise from (A). He has already stated that drinking wine on such occasions will loosen up the older members of that chorus, and overcome their embarrassment at singing (666b–c). Here, he connects that point to the general theory of the natural basis of choral music introduced at the beginning of Book 2, 653d–654a: drunkenness returns the adult soul to the kinetic youthful state that makes it amenable to the cultivating effects of music (671a–672d). Thus properly conducted drinking parties have the important function of renewing the education that, from the beginning, the Athenian has said 'tends to slacken and be undone over the course of human life' (653c8–9). Pulling together the strands of his discussion of drunkenness in Book 1, he characterizes the goal of education as the cultivation of shame (671c–d; cf. 646e–647b), and insists that drinking parties will have this educational benefit only if the drinkers are supervised by capable leaders (671d–e; cf. 640c–e). This raises the question of whether those capable leaders are to be identified with the elders who, in narrative (B) above, discriminate what music is fit to sing, in which case the two main claims the Athenian makes about the chorus of Dionysus are linked (on which see note on 671e1).

Finally, after a brief excursus on the necessity of including a discussion of athletic training in a complete account of education (672e–673d), the Athenian concludes his treatment of drinking parties by noting that they are serious business rather than recreation, and that in fact the consumption of wine should play an extremely limited role in the life of a city (673d–674c).

671a3 'we were right (*kalôs*) in our earlier defence (*boêtheian*) of the chorus of Dionysus'
more literally: 'that we did well (*kalôs*) to defend the chorus . . . '
At 665b the Athenian surprised his interlocutors by claiming that the chorus of older citizens will be dedicated to Dionysus. At 666b–c the activities of that chorus are revealed to be those of a drinking party, the institution disparaged by Megillus in Book 1 (637a–b), so the Athenian's 'defence' of the chorus of Dionysus in effect defends drinking parties against the criticisms of Megillus.

671a5–b1 'a gathering (*sullogos*) of this sort inevitably becomes more boisterous as the drinking proceeds—an unavoidable feature, we originally supposed, of these events as they take place nowadays' (reading the MSS' *gignomenôn* instead of des Places' *legomenôn* in b1)
A 'gathering (*sullogos*) of this sort' is a drinking party (*sumposion*), discussed in Book 1 at 637a–641d, with the growing boisterousness described at 649a–b. 'As they take place nowadays' (*peri tôn nun gignomenôn*) reflects the Athenian's concession at 639d–e that such parties, as they are currently conducted, are largely indefensible.

671b5–6 'fit to rule both himself (*archôn . . . heautou*) and the rest of the company'
more literally: 'sufficient (*hikanos*) to rule both himself . . . '
This description (a doublet of 649a9–b3) captures both the lack of self-restraint on the part of individual drinkers, and the incipient conflict and hostility between drinkers (671e7–672a2) that arises in the absence of a sober leader (cf. 640e5) directing the proceedings. On the expression 'ruling oneself', see note on 644b6–7.

671b8–672d10

The benefits of drunkenness

Having recapitulated (671a2–b7) the incipient lawlessness and lack of restraint in drinking parties that led Megillus to deride the practice in Book 1 (637a), the Athenian now casts those same features of drunkenness in a favourable light. The disorderly condition of the drinkers replicates in those no longer young the juvenile volatility that makes the young amenable to the shaping influence of musical training.

The restorative function of drunkenness

The specifically restorative education role identified here for drunkenness has been under-appreciated by commentators, so it is worth stressing that the argument of 671b8–672d10 presents drinking parties as an institution for restoring shame and self-control in adults, not for cultivating that condition in the first place. While the depiction of drinking parties in Book 1 as forums for battling and detecting shamelessness (649a–650b) mentions no age restrictions, the detailed account of *paideia* over the course of Book 2 has made it clear that those under 30 years old will be educated by participating in the chorus of the Muses and of Apollo. It is only those old enough to have lost their natural juvenile eagerness to participate in song and dance who will be 'softened up' and made educable again in drinking parties (see note on 671b8–c2). Thus England on 671e2; Stalley 1983: 55; and Morrow 1960: 442 (discussed by Schöpsdau: 337) are wrong to suppose that the Athenian is proposing drinking parties for the young as well as for the old. A failure to appreciate the restorative function of the drinking parties, and hence the central role of drunkenness in its activities leads Morrow (1960: 316–17) to propose that they are forums for cultivating the 'finer music' attributed to the Dionysian chorus (and similarly Wilamowitz (1920: Vol. 1, 210) supposes that its activities are analogous to that of Plato's Academy)—endorsed in part by Schöpsdau: 337. If there is to be a role for that 'finer music' in the drinking parties here endorsed by the Athenian, it will have to play a role in securing educational benefits from drunkenness. That role will be the same as it plays for the chorus of the Muses and of Apollo: to select the music that is fit to be sung in these choruses (and hence in the drinking parties that are the venue of the chorus of Dionysus). See note on 671e1.

671b8–c2 'Didn't we say that when this happens the souls of the drinkers are like iron in the fire? They become softer and more youthful, receptive to the influence of a skilful educator who can shape (*plattein*) them'
A reference to the theory of youthful volatility and the human susceptibility to the pleasures of 'harmony' and rhythm introduced at 653d5–654a5 and repeated at 664e3–665a3, 672c1–d4, and 673c9–d6 (see note on 653d7–8), as well as to the Athenian's observation at 666b5–7 that wine lessens the crabbedness and inhibitions of old age. While the youthful soul has previously been described as pliable (664b5) and fiery (666a5), those previous passages do not state explicitly the claim of the present passage: that the condition of juvenile volatility is also a condition of plasticity, and hence of educability.

671c7–8 'and make him willing to do (*ethelein poein*) just the opposite'
On *ethelein* as 'being willing' see note on 663b4–6.

671c8–d2 'Against the shameful boldness that is filling him they can send in the finest opponent: fear with justice (*meta dikês*)'
This fear, also called shame (671d2–3), is first mentioned in Book 1 and recommended as a means to combat the boldness (*tharros*) of antisocial behaviour (646e–647b). It is described as 'involving justice' (*meta dikês*) at 647c7–8.

671d5–7 'As guardians and assistants of these laws, there will be undisturbed (*athorubous*) and sober commanders for the inebriated'
A reference back to the sober leaders of drinking parties invoked in Book 1 at 640b–641a as analogues to the military leader who is undisturbed (*mê thoruboumenos*) by fear (640b3; cf. 672a3); the

office of 'guardians of the laws' (*nomophulakes*) will be introduced at 752d–755b; see also note on 632c4.

671d9–e1 'he who cannot willingly obey (*ethelein peithesthai*) his leaders'

On willingness and persuasion, see note on 663b4–6. Here *peithesthai*, which encompasses both persuasion and obedience, has the latter sense, while at 663b5 the same locution *ethelein peithesthai* is translated by 'willingly be persuaded'.

671e1 'those over 60 years old'

This age designation would put the 'sober commanders' of the drinking party beyond the upper age specified for the chorus of Dionysus at 664d1–2: 'those over 30 and up to 60', whose performance context has been identified as a drinking party (666a–c, 671a–d). This would imply that the all-important role of providing wise supervision to drinking parties does not belong to members of the chorus of Dionysus. Thus Schöpsdau identifies these 'over 60-year-old' leaders with 'those beyond that' (*tous de meta tauta*) at 664d2–3 who are assigned the task of telling stories, rather than singing in the chorus of Dionysus. However, the Athenian nowhere explicitly marks 60 as an upper age limit for that chorus. At 664c–d, his concern is to include all citizens in the communal project of affirming the doctrines of beneficial music, and 'those beyond that' at 664d2–4 are specified in terms of their inability, not their age (see note on 664d2–4). Clinias' question at 665b4–6, 'will those over 30 . . . and even up to 60 . . . really perform a chorus in his honour?', expresses surprise at the extension of Dionysian activities to include 60 year olds, and would be equally applicable to those even older. At 670a–b no upper limit is given to the age range, only an indication that the membership goes 'beyond 50', which is consistent with the age designation in the present passage. On the variation with which the Athenian specifies the age range of that chorus, see Morrow 1960: 318; Schöpsdau at 664d5–665d6; O. Murray 2013: 114.

While England (seconded by Schöpsdau at 671d5–e3) rightly notes that the sober leaders of the unsober first mentioned in Book 1 at 640d4–7 are implied to be older than the drinkers they supervise, this poses no obstacle to supposing that both the drinkers and their sober leaders are members of the chorus of Dionysus. The age range of that chorus is unusually broad (see note on 664d1–2) and the Athenian has already made discriminations within it, singling out the older members as the practitioners of the 'finer music' specified in 667b–670e; the wise judges who select the compositions that are suitable for choral performance must have 'reached 50' (*pentêkontoutas*, 670b1), alternatively specified as 'having reached 60' (*hexêkontoutas*, 812b9–10). These passages imply a leadership role within the chorus for its older members (cf. 'leaders of the younger singers', 670e1), and one might reasonably ask whether the leadership function extends to acting as the sober superintendents of the drinking parties in which other members of this chorus perform. The Athenian never says so, and indeed, has done practically nothing to integrate the accounts of the Dionysian chorus as (A) participants in a drinking party and (B) practitioners of that finer music (see notes on 664d1–2 and on 667b1–3). Still, an affirmative answer to this question would connect (A) and (B), and provide a rationale (otherwise missing) for identifying (B) as distinctively Dionysian: the older members who, according to (B) select the music to be performed by younger members would be *eo ipso* providing the requisite guidance to the drinking party in (A). If, on the other hand, the sober leaders of the inebriated are even older than the members of the Dionysian chorus, we must suppose that inebriated wise judges are in need of an even wiser leadership, a point for which the Athenian has not prepared his audience. (Against Schöpsdau's proposal to identify that leadership with those described at 664d2–4 as too old to sing: the latter are hardly specified in terms that imply superior wisdom.) It is entirely possible that the designation 'over 60' in the present context is simply a misremembering by the Athenian (or by Plato) of the designation 'gone past 50' at 670a5 for the age of the practitioners of (B), just as their designation as having 'reached 50' (*pentêkontoutas*) at 670b1 is later misreported at 812b9–10 as having 'reached 60' (*hexêkontoutas*).

In any case, the Athenian's emphasis in the present context is not on the credentials of the leaders of drinking parties, but on the benefits to the inebriated of a properly conducted drinking party. Nor is he here concerned, as he is concerned in 664b–d, to specify the age range of the three choruses.

671e5–6 'this sort of drunkenness and recreation (*paidia*)'
Here, as at 666b5, drunkenness at a drinking party is described as a kind of recreation (*paidia*); however, at 667e6–8 the *paidia* is construed more narrowly for pleasures with no significant benefit or harm at stake (see note ad loc), and at 673e8 wine is forbidden to be used for recreation (*hôs paidiai*). On the range of the term, see note on 635b5.

671e7–672a1 'unlike today, when they part as enemies'
Such hostility arises from the loss of self-restraint in individual drinkers, each of whom thinks himself fit to rule over the others (671b3–6; see note on 671b5–6).

672a5–6 'roundly (*haplôs*) condemn the gift of Dionysus'
Megillus gave such an unqualified condemnation at 637a–b. The blanket nature of the condemnation is criticized by the Athenian on methodological grounds at 638c–640e.

672a7–8 'Indeed, I could go on and recount the greatest good he has given us—only I am hesitant to do so'
more literally: '. . . one could say more on the subject, although . . . I am hesitant to recount the greatest good . . . '

672b4–5 'driven out of his mind'
more literally: 'had the mind (*gnômê*) of his soul (*psuchê*) destroyed'

The condition contrasts with the intelligence (*nous* and *phronêsis*) invoked in 672c and recalls the 'manic' (*emmanê*) condition of youth at 666a7. See note on 671b8–c2.

672b7–8 'I leave it to those who think they have sound judgement about the gods to pronounce on such matters'
In Book 10 the Athenian will reject all stories about the gods that fail to portray them as good and beneficent (885b; cf. *Rep*. 379a–383c).

672c2–5 'before it possesses its proper intelligence (*phronêsin*), it raves and shouts at random (*ataktôs*) and . . . jumps about in disorder (*ataktôs*)'
The Athenian here connects the madness associated with drunkenness and the cult of Dionysus to the juvenile volatility originally invoked at 653d5–654a3. With this new emphasis, he stresses the lack of orderliness (664e6) and apparent madness (666a7) in the natural juvenile motions, which contrast with the order (*taxis*) embodied in 'harmony' and rhythm. Here order is linked to *phronêsis*, on which see note on 653a7–9. On Dionysus see note on 637b2.

672c6–7 'we called these the origins (*archas*) of music (*mousikês*) and athletics (*gumnastikês*)'
The reference is back to 653d5–654a3, which identifies our natural affinity for 'harmony' and rhythm and our natural juvenile volatility as the two roots of choral dance. 'Athletics' (*gumnastikê*) is not in fact mentioned in the earlier passage. Its mention here anticipates the Athenian's upcoming introduction of the topic (672e). He will soon state that dance is a kind of 'athletics' (673a), and will identify the natural juvenile impulse to bodily movement (invoked at 653d) as the origin of athletics (673c9–d6). On the translation of *gumnastikê* as 'athletics', see note on 673a8–10.

672c9–d3 'that in the case of us humans, this origin (*tên archên tautên*) gives rise to (*endedôkenai*) a sense of rhythm and 'harmony',

and that Apollo and the Muses and Dionysus among the gods are responsible for this?'
alternatively: '. . . that a sense of rhythm and harmony yields this origin . . . ' (Schöpsdau)
A difficult sentence, which continues to elaborate the theory of 653d5–654a3 (cf. 673c9–d5 and note on 672c2–5). This 'origin' (*tên archên tautên*) is the condition of disorderly juvenile movement referred to in the previous paragraph (672c6) as the (plural) '*origins*' of music and gymnastics. Schöpsdau's alternative is motivated by the worry that the juvenile condition cannot be the origin of the sense of rhythm etc., since all animals have the former, while only humans have the latter; thus he proposes that 'this origin' (*tên archên tautên*) is the object rather than the subject of 'gives rise to' (*endedôkenai*), with 'the sense of rhythm' (*tên aisthêsin*) as the subject. But then the Athenian would be claiming that the sense of rhythm is the source of the juvenile propensity to disorderly movement. The worry is better addressed by allowing that the expression 'A gives rise to (*endedôkenai*) B' need not mean that A is causally sufficient for B (thus England: the juvenile condition is like the field in which the later sense of rhythm grows). So construed, the sentence fits the Athenian's larger point in the present context, which is to identify the educational benefits of drunkenness by noting that it replicates the juvenile condition of disorderly motion. The educational significance of that juvenile condition is not that it inevitably gives rise to our sense of 'harmony' and rhythm, but that it is a crucial feature of the conditions in which music cultivates the human soul.

672d5–7 'The story other people tell (*ho tôn allôn logos*) . . . the story we are telling now (*ho de nun legomenos*)'
more literally: 'the account (*logos*) other people give . . . the one we are giving'

672d8–9 'given to us as a potion for instilling shame (*aidous*) in the soul and health and strength in the body'
The Athenian has explicitly argued only for the claim about the soul. The mention of effects on the body (cf. its use for 'bodily training' at

674b4) may anticipate the discussion of athletic training that he is about to introduce (672e1–673d9).

672e1–673d9

Athletics distinguished from music

The Athenian here notes that 'athletics' (*gumnastikê*) is a topic that must still be discussed. It is 'one half' of choral performance insofar as the latter involves the motion of the body (dance); however, the preceding discussion of choral music has focused on its vocal aspects, and its role in cultivating the soul. The physical aspects of dance make it a kind of athletic training, like the military training that Book 1 notes is the focus of Dorian education (625c–626b, 666e). These two types of athletics will be treated at length only in Book 7 (dance) and 8 (military training). On the translation of *gumnastikê* as 'athletics', see note on 673a8–10.

672e5 'choral performance (*choreia*) as a whole is pretty much (*pou*) the whole process of education (*paideusis*)'
A theme of Book 2 has been that education (*paideia*) is the condition of having correctly nurtured pleasures and pains (653a–c) and that it is produced by a process that centrally involves choral performance, a combination of song and dance. Here that educational process is called *paideusis* (educating).

672e9 'its distinctive feature (*idion*) is gesture (*schêma*). The other part, vocal movement, has tune (*melos*) as its distinctive feature'
On dance as manifest in gesture (*schêma*) while song is manifest in tune (*melos*), see 654e–655b.

673a3–5 'vocal activities that reach the soul and cultivate virtue' more literally: '. . . that reach the soul, since they are [a kind of] education in virtue (*hôs aretês paideian*)'
Reading *hôs aretês paideian*, with des Places and Schöpsdau, instead of the MSS *pros aretês paideian*. The phrase perhaps reflects the

restricted scope of 'education' (*paideia*) demarcated in Book 1, 643d–644b, which excludes training in trade skills, and includes only the training that is directed 'towards virtue' (*pros aretên*, 643e3–5; see note on 652b3–653a1). On music as what cultivates *paideia*, the 'initial virtue', see 653b2, 654a6–7.

673a7–8 'bodily movements, which we call "dance" when they are performed as recreation (*ha paizontôn orchêsin eipomen*)'
alternatively: 'which we called recreational dance' (Brisson/Pradeau, Saunders, Bury)
The implicit contrast is between bodily movements done in play or recreation (*paidia*), here given the label 'dance' (*orchêsis*), and those done for a more serious (or painful) purpose (see Schöpsdau on 672e1–673d9). The former are the 'playful' juvenile movements described as 'leap[ing] and bound[ing] . . . in playful glee (*prospaizonta*)' at 653e1–3; the 'recreation' involved in dance is also invoked at 657c3–d7, where *paidia* is translated as 'recreation' (see note on 667e6–8). The seriously intended bodily movements will include the athletic training and military exercises that dominate Dorian education; their painfulness is emphasized at 633b–c. The Athenian, who allows that dance is a part of music insofar as it involves rhythm (672e8–9; cf. 655a5–6), here points out the features that it has in common with military training, and thus make it a part of *gumnastikê*. Alternatively, Brisson/Pradeau (361n114) propose that the *paizontôn orchêsin* ('la danse de ceux qui s'amusent') is dance that is not joined with choral song—i.e. playful movement that is not necessarily rhythmic. On such a construal, the Athenian is classifying *gumnastikê* as a kind of dance. On the present construal, by contrast (taken also by Pangle), the general category is bodily movement, with dance and *gumnastikê* as subcategories.

673a8–10 'let us call the skilled guidance (*entechnon agôgên*) towards that bodily condition (*epi to toiouton autou*) "athletics" (*gumnastikê*)'
alternatively: 'let us call the skilled guidance . . . "physical training" '

The term 'athletics'—used here to translate *gumnastikê*—should be understood as encompassing all physical training (as in North American English usage); the English term 'gymnastics' is no longer a suitable translation, since it typically refers to a single sport (tumbling, vaulting, etc.) whereas the Greek term is much broader and includes military training (*Rep.* 404b7; cf. the close synonym *gymnasia* at *Laws* 625c7, 636b1). The present definition of *gumnastikê* as training that cultivates bodily excellence (*sômatos aretês*, a8) serves to distinguish it from *mousikê*, which has just been defined as cultivation of the soul (*aretês paideian*, a4). See notes on 672c6–7, 673a7–8. The Athenian has no use here for the point made in *Rep.* III that *gumnastikê* also cultivates the soul (410b–c).

673b5 'Sir, you are talking to Cretans and Spartans here!'
On the importance placed on athletics in Cretan and Spartan institutions, see Book 1 625c–d, 633a–d.

673c6–7 'considerably more experienced in it than in the previous one'
The antecedent of 'it' is 'this discipline' (*tautêi têi technêi*, c6). The Athenian's comment recalls his criticism in Book 1 that the Dorian states lack adequate institutions for training pleasures (635b–d), which makes them deficient at education, conceived of as the training of pleasures and pains (643b–d). The use here of *technê* (discipline; alt: 'skill') to refer to both music and athletics reflects the reference to the latter as a 'discipline leading' (*entechnon agôgên*) to virtue at 673a9.

673c9–d1 'Now this kind of recreation (*paidias*) has its origin in the natural propensity (*eithisthai*) of all animals to jump about'
'Natural propensity' translates *eithisthai* (alt: habit), elsewhere translated by 'training'; see notes on 632d5–6 and on 655d7–e1. The recreation (*paidia*) in question must be athletics (*gumnastikê*), which has just been announced as the topic of discussion (thus Schöpsdau; see also note on 673d7–8). Against this, one might worry that in

673a7–8 only one kind of athletics—dance—has been identified as a recreation (in the phrase *paizontôn orchêsin*), while the other kind involves hard, often painful, work (see note on 673a7–8). However, the Athenian has earlier shown his willingness to count the frolicking movements of young animals as a kind of play and dance (653e6, a passage that gives the context for 673a7–8). Even though such movements do not count as a dance (*orchêsis*) in the strict sense here identified (as involving rhythm, which only humans have), they are clearly instances of the kind of bodily movement distinct both from non-recreational hard physical training and from rhythmic dance. It is these juvenile movements that the Athenian here invokes as the origin (*archê*) of all athletics.

While the present paragraph (673c9–d5) invokes the two 'parts' of choral performance (*choreia*), *mousikê* and *gymnastikê*, that are already distinguished at some length at 672e1–673b4, it does not (as Schöpsdau claims) merely recapitulate those earlier remarks, for the Athenian goes beyond that earlier discussion by identifying the juvenile animal impulse to movement as the origin of *gymnastikê*. By contrast, 672c–d treats the disorderly manifestation of that impulse as a necessary preliminary to the introduction of order through song and dance.

673d7–8 'Having gone through the one part of the subject . . . we will next try to go through the other'

These 'parts' are the two halves of choral performance (*choreia*) identified at 672e1–673b4 as (1) music, the subject of the previous discussion, and (2) athletics, (*gumnastikê*), still to be discussed. This gives additional support to construing 'this kind of recreation' in 673c9 as athletics (see note on 673c9–d1).

The Athenian will not in fact address the topic of athletics until Books 7 and 8 (dance: 795d–796e, 813b–816d; hunting: 823b–824a; military training and athletic competition: 829b–c, 830a–835b). On the range of activities included in *gumnastikê* (athletics), see note on 673a7–8.

673d10–674c7

The limited role of wine in social life

The Athenian here adds the 'finishing touches' (*ton kolophôna*, 673d10) to the discussion of drunkenness that has been the enduring (if often submerged) focus of his discussion since the topic was introduced in Book 1 (637a). While at 671a–672d he made good on his promise to identify the educational benefits of drinking parties, he here rounds off that discussion by noting the very limited extent to which the practice of drunkenness (or even the consumption of wine) will be a part of the social life of a well-governed polity.

673e3 'as a serious matter (*hôs ousês spoudês*)'
In contrast with 'as a form of recreation' (*hôs paidiai*) at 673e8. On the recurring contrast between play and seriousness, see note on 635b5.

673e5 'to practise and cultivate moderation (*tou sôphronein heneka meletês*)'
In Book 1, drinking parties are presented as a forum for cultivating moderation, analogous to the battlefield as a forum for cultivating courage (647c–649c).

673e6–7 'does not abstain from them but cultivates mastery over them'
In Book 1 the Dorian societies are characterized as 'abstaining' from pleasures (635b–c, 636e–637b).

673e8 'it treats the activity as a form of recreation (*hôs paidiai*)'
(Rather than a serious matter, as at 673e3.) At 666b5, drinking wine in a symposium is referred to as recreation (*paidia*), but the definition of *paidia* at 667e6–8 requires that no great harm or benefit be at stake, and the burden of the argument throughout Book 2 has been that drinking parties provide a 'great benefit, which we must take very seriously' (652a3–4). On *paidia*, see note on 635b5.

673e9–674a1 'anyone who wishes to drink whenever and with whomever he wishes and in conjunction with any activity whatsoever'
In contrast with the drinking parties led by sober leaders who will direct the proceedings, as prescribed at 640c–d; a reflection of the methodological point at 638c–e.

674a3–4 'I would go beyond even the Cretan and Spartan practice'
The practice of forbidding drunkenness (637a), but not banning wine altogether (see note on 637e2–3).

674a4–5 'and vote for the Carthaginian law that prohibits all wine drinking to soldiers on campaign'
Translation following Saunders 1972, Schöpsdau and Brisson/Pradeau, against England's alternative: 'to the Carthaginian law . . . I would add . . . '. Presumably the long list of prohibitions down to 674b6 exceeds what one might reasonably understand the Carthaginian law to encompass (cf. [Aristotle], *Oikonimika*, 1344a33, which corroborates the authenticity of the ban on drinking while on campaign); however, the grammar of the sentence includes all the prohibitions within the scope of that law: 'to a short Carthaginian law the Athenian attaches a long Platonic tail' (Saunders 1972: 12). Morrow (1960: 442n150) proposes that the Athenian intends the prohibitions to apply only in a city that, contrary to 673e3–5, treats wine as a recreation rather than a serious matter. However, the prohibitions are consistent with the restrictions on wine-drinking and drunkenness articulated in the description of the three choruses at 666a–b, and the end of the present paragraph infers from the prohibitions a conclusion that applies to 'any city' (674c2).

674a7–b3 'even in the city itself, no slave . . . nor . . . any . . . officials . . . ship captains . . . jurors . . . on active duty, nor . . . any person who is about to participate in important deliberations'

This list of participants in the civic life of the community contrasts with the military context just discussed (674a5–7). All those listed have a function to perform within the city, which presumably depends on their possessing the alert senses and unimpaired judgement that, as the Athenian has emphasized at 645e1–3, are compromised by drinking wine.

674b7 'no one in their right and lawful mind (*tois noun te kai nomon echousin orthon*)'
more literally: 'no one with a correct (*orthos*) mind (*nous*) and law (*nomos*)'
A play on the common expression 'have sense' or 'be in one's right mind' (*noun echein*), perhaps reflecting the connection between rational judgement (*logismos* or *logos*) and law (*nomos*) invoked at 1, 644c–d, 645a–b. On correctness of law, see 627d3, 657b3, 659d2, d4.

674c2–3 'Once all agricultural and dietary matters have been arranged (*takta*)'
These arrangements are discussed in Book 8 (842b–848c), with no mention of wine.

Bibliography

Texts, translations, and commentaries

AMMENDOLA, G. (1953). *Platone: Nomoi, Scelta e Commento* [selection and commentary]. Naples: Loffredo.

AST, D. F., ed. (1814). *Platonis Leges et Epinomis* [edition and commentary], 2 vols. Leipzig: Weidmann.

BRISSON, L. and Pradeau, J.-F. (2006). *Platon: Les Lois, traduction, introduction, et notes*, 2 vols. Paris: Flammarion.

BURNET, J., ed. (1907). *Platonis Opera.* Oxford Classical Texts. Oxford: Clarendon Press.

BURY, R. G. (1926). *Plato, with an English Translation.* Loeb Classical Library, Vols. IX and X, *Laws*. Cambridge, MA: Harvard University Press.

ENGLAND, E. B. (1921). *The Laws of Plato,* the Text edited with Introduction, Notes, etc., 2 vols. London and Manchester: Longmans, Green & Co. and University of Manchester Press.

JOWETT, B. (1924). *The Dialogues of Plato, translated into English, with analyses and introductions,* Volume 5: *Laws, Index*. New York: Oxford University Press.

LISI, F. L. (1999). *Platón, Diálogos,* vol. VIII et IX. Translation into Spanish. Madrid: Gredos.

PANGLE, T. (1980). *The Laws of Plato, translated with Notes and an Interpretive Essay*. Chicago: University of Chicago Press.

PLACES, E. DES (1951). *Platon: Les Lois Livres I et II.* Greek text and translation; introduction by A. Diès and L. Gernet. Paris: Belles Lettres; repr. 2006 (6th printing).

PLACES, E. des and Diès, A. (1951–6). *Platon: Oeuvres Complètes XI–XII. Les Lois*, texte établit et traduit, 4 vols. Paris: Belles Lettres.

RITTER, C. (1896). *Platons Gesetze: Kommentar sum griechischen Text.* Leipzig: Teubner; repr. 1985.

SAUNDERS, T. (1970). *Plato: The Laws*, translated with an Introduction. London: Penguin Books.

SAUNDERS, T. (1972). *Notes on the Laws of Plato*. London: University of London Institute of Classical Studies. Bulletin Supplement 28.

SCHANZ, M., ed. (1879). *Platonis opera quae feruntur omnia ad codices denuo collato*, Vol XII.1: Leges I–VI. Leipzig: Tauchnitz.

SCHÖPSDAU, K. (1994). *Platon: Nomoi (Gesetze): Buch I–III. Übersetzung und Kommentar*. Göttingen: Vandenhoek und Ruprecht.

SCHÖPSDAU, K. (2003). *Platon: Nomoi (Gesetze): Buch IV–VII. Übersetzung und Kommentar*. Göttingen: Vandenhoek und Ruprecht.

SCHÖPSDAU, K. (2011). *Platon: Nomoi (Gesetze): Buch VIII–XII. Übersetzung und Kommentar*. Göttingen: Vandenhoek und Ruprecht.

STALLBAUM, G. (1859–60). *Platonis Leges et Epinomis*, Vol. X, sec. i–iii. *Platonis opera onmia* [edition with annotations]. Gotha / Erfurt: Hennings.

TAYLOR, A. E. (1934). *Plato: Laws*, translated with an Introduction. London: J. M. Dent and Sons.

Books and articles

ANDERSON, J. K. (1985). *Hunting in the Classical World*. Berkeley: University of California Press.

ANNAS, J. (1993). *The Morality of Happiness*. New York: Oxford University Press.

ANNAS, J. (1999). *Platonic Ethics Old and New*. Ithaca: Cornell University Press.

ANNAS, J. (2010). 'Virtue and Law in Plato' in Bobonich, ed. 2010, 71–91.

ATHANASSAKI, L. and BOWIE, E. (2011). *Archaic and Classical Choral Song: Performance, Politics, and Dissemination*. Berlin: de Gruyter.

BARKER, A. (1984). *Greek Musical Writings*, Vol. 1: *The Musician and his Art*. Cambridge: Cambridge University Press.

BARKER, A. (1990). *Greek Musical Writings*, Vol. 2: *Harmonic and Acoustic Theory*. Cambridge: Cambridge University Press.

BARKER, A. (2013). 'The Laws and Aristoxenus on the Criteria of Musical Judgment' in A.-E. Peponi, ed. 2013b, 392–416.

BARKER, E. (1918). *Greek Political Theory: Plato and his Predecessors*. London: Methuen.

BARNEY, R. (2010). 'Notes on Plato on the *Kalon* and the Good'. *Classical Philology* (Special Issue: *Beauty, Harmony and the Good*) 105: 363–77.

BARNEY, R., BRENNAN, T., and BRITTAIN, C., eds. (2012). *Plato and the Divided Self.* Cambridge: Cambridge University Press.

BARTELS, M. (2012). '*Senex Mensura*: an Objective Aesthetic of Seniors in Plato's *Laws*' in *Aesthetic Value in Classical Antiquity*, Proceedings of the Penn-Leiden Colloquium 2010. Leiden: Brill, 133–58.

BELFIORE, E. (1986). 'Wine and the Catharsis of Emotions in Plato's *Laws*'. *Classical Quarterly* 36 (2): 421–37.

BENARDETE, S. (2000). *Plato's 'Laws': the discovery of being.* Chicago: University of Chicago Press.

BICCHIERI, C. (2006). *The Grammar of Society: the Nature and Dynamics of Social Norms.* Cambridge: Cambridge University Press.

BILLINGS, J., BUDELMANN, F., and MACINTOSH, F., eds. (2013). *Choruses, Ancient and Modern.* Oxford: Oxford University Press.

BOBONICH, C. (1994). 'Akrasia and Agency in Plato's *Laws* and *Republic*'. *Archiv für Geschichte der Philosophie* 76: 3–36.

BOBONICH, C. (1995). 'Plato's Theory of Goods in the Laws and the Philebus'. *Proceedings of the Boston Area Colloquium in Ancient Philosophy* 11: 101–39.

BOBONICH, C. (2002). *Plato's Utopia Recast: His Later Ethics and Politics.* New York: Oxford University Press.

BOBONICH, C., ed. (2010). *Plato's Laws: a Critical Guide.* Cambridge and New York: Cambridge University Press.

BOLOT, R. (2006). *Greek Political Theory.* Oxford: Blackwell.

BRANDWOOD, L. (1990). *The Chronology of Plato's Dialogues.* Cambridge: Cambridge University Press.

BRENNAN, T. (2012). 'The Nature of the Spirited Part of the Soul and its Object' in Barney et al., eds. 2012, 102–27.

BRILL, S. (2010). 'Psychology and legislation in Plato's Laws'. *Proceedings of the Boston Area Colloquium in Ancient Philosophy* 26: 211–51.

BRISSON, L. (1982). *Platon: les mots et les mythes.* Paris: La Decouverte, 2nd ed. 1994.

BRISSON, L. (1993). *Orphée: poèmes magiques et cosmologiques.* Paris: Belles Lettres.

BRISSON, L. (2012). 'Soul and State in Plato's *Laws*' in Barney et al., eds. 2012: 281–308.

BRISSON, L. and PRADEAU, J. F. (2007). *Les Lois de Platon*. Paris: Presses Universitaires de France.

BURKERT, W. (1985). *Greek Religion*. Cambridge MA: Harvard University Press.

CAIRNS, D. (1993). *Aidôs: the Psychology and Ethics of Honour and Shame in Ancient Greek Literature*. Oxford: Clarendon Press.

CALAME, C. (1998). 'La poésie lyrique grecque, un genre inexistant?'. *Littérature* 111: 87–110.

CALAME, C. (2013). 'Choral Practices in Plato's *Laws*: Itineraries of Initiation' in A.-E. Peponi, ed. 2013b, 87–108.

CARONE, G. (2002). 'Pleasure, Virtue, Externals, and Happiness in Plato's *Laws*'. *History of Philosophy Quarterly* 19 (4): 327–44.

CARTLEDGE, P. (1979). *Sparta and Lakonia: A Regional History*. London: Routledge.

CARTLEDGE, P. (2002). *Hellenistic and Roman Sparta: a Tale of Two Cities*, 2nd ed. New York: Routledge.

COHEN, D. (1991). *Law, Sexuality, and Society; the Enforcement of Morals in Classical Athens*. Cambridge: Cambridge University Press.

COOPER, J. M. (1984). 'Plato's Theory of Human Motivation'. *History of Philosophy Quarterly* 1: 3–21.

COOPER, J. M. (1996). 'Reason, Moral Virtue and Moral Value' in M. Frede and G. Striker, eds., *Rationality in Greek Thought*. Oxford: Clarendon Press, 81–114.

COX, C. A. (1998). *Household Interests, Property, Marriage Strategies, and Family Dynamics in Ancient Athens*. Princeton: Princeton University Press.

CSAPO, E. (2004). 'The Politics of the new Music' in P. Murray and P. Wilson, eds. 2004, 207–48.

D'ANGOUR, A. (2006). 'The New Music: So What's New?' in S. Goldhill and R. Osborne, eds., *Rethinking Revolutions through Ancient Greece*. Cambridge: Cambridge University Press, 264–83.

D'ANGOUR, A. (2013). 'Plato and Play: Taking Education Seriously in Ancient Greece'. American Journal of Play 5 (3): 293–307.

DAVID, E. (1978). 'The Spartan *Sussitia* and Plato's *Laws*'. *American Journal of Philology* 99: 486–95.

DAVID, E. (1993). 'Hunting in Spartan Society and Consciousness'. *Échos du monde classique/Classical Views* 37: 393–414.

DAVIDSON, J. (2006). 'Revolutions in Time: Age-class in Athens and the Greekness of Greek Revolutions' in S. Goldhill and R. Osborne, eds., *Rethinking Revolutions through Ancient Greece*. Cambridge: Cambridge University Press, 29–68.

Denniston, J. D. (1950). *The Greek Particles*, 2nd ed. Revised by K. J. Dover. London: Duckworth; repr. 1996 Indianapolis: Hackett Publishing.

Destrée, P. and Hermann, F.-G., eds. (2011). *Plato and the Poets*. Leiden: Brill.

Diehl, E. (1971). *Theognis*, 2nd ed., revised by D. Young. Leipzig: Teubner.

Dorandi, T. (2013). *Diogenes Laertius: Lives, Teachings, and Sayings of Famous Philosophers*. Cambridge classical texts and commentaries 50. Cambridge: Cambridge University Press.

Dorion, L.-A. (2007). 'Plato and *Enkrateia*' in C. Bobonich and P. Destrée, eds., *Akrasia in Greek Philosophy: from Socrates to Plotinus*. Leiden and Boston: Brill, 119–38.

Dover, K. J. (1974). *Greek Popular Morality in the Time of Plato and Aristotle*. Oxford: Basil Blackwell; repr. with corrections 1994 Indianapolis: Hackett.

Dover, K. J. (1978). *Greek Homosexuality*. Cambridge, MA: Harvard University Press.

Dusanic, S. (1990). *History and Politics in Plato's Laws* [monograph in Serbian with English Summary pp. 359–89]. Belgrade: The Serbian Academy of Arts and Sciences.

Dusanic, S. (1991). 'Epimenide le Cnossien et les thèmes historico-politiques des *Lois* de Platon'. *Epigraphica* 53: 25–57.

Edmonds, J. M. (1931). *Elegy and Iambus*, 2 vols. Loeb Classical Library. London: Heinemann.

Edmonds, R. (2013). *Redefining Ancient Orphism*. Cambridge: Cambridge University Press.

Ferrari, G. R. F. (1989). 'Plato on Poetry' in G. A. Kennedy, ed., *The Cambridge History of Literary Criticism*. Cambridge: Cambridge University Press, 92–148.

Folch, M. (2013). 'Unideal Genres and the Ideal City: Comedy, Threnody, and the Making of Citizens in Plato's *Laws*' in A.-E. Peponi, ed. 2013b, 339–67.

Fortenbaugh, W. (1975). *Aristotle on Emotion*. London: Duckworth.

Fossheim, H. (2013). 'The Prooimia: Types of Motivation, and Moral Psychology' in Horn, ed. 2013, 87–104.

Foucault, M. (1978). *The History of Sexuality*, Vol. 1, translated by R. Hurley. New York: Vintage Books.

FREDE, D. (2010). 'Puppets on Strings: Moral Psychology in *Laws* Books 1 and 2' in C. Bobonich, ed. 2010, 108–26.

FREEMAN, K. (1950). *Greek City States*. London: Macdonald.

GEHRKE, H.-J. (1985). *Stasis: Untersuchungen zu den inneren Kriegen in den grieschen Staaten des 5. und 4. Jhr. v. Chr.* München: Beck.

GERSON, L. P. (2003). *Knowing Persons: A Study in Plato*. Oxford: Oxford University Press.

GOLDEN, M. (1990). *Childhood and Children in Classical Athens*. Baltimore: Johns Hopkins University Press.

GÖRGEMANNS, H. (1960). *Beiträge zur Interpretation von Platons Nomoi*. Munich: Beck. (*Zetemata* 25)

GOULD, T. (1963). *Platonic Love*. London: Routledge.

GRAESER, A. (1969). *Probleme der platonischen Seelenteilungslehre*. Munich: Beck. (*Zetemata* 47: 102–5)

GRAF, F. (2009). *Apollo*. New York: Routledge.

GRIFFITH, M. (2013). 'Cretan Harmonies and Universal Morals: Early Music and Migrations of Wisdom in Plato's *Laws*' in Peponi, ed. 2013b, 15–66.

GROTE, G. (1846–56). *History of Greece, from the Earliest Period to the Close of the Generation contemporary with Alexander the Great*. London: J. Muray.

GUTHRIE, W. K. C. (1978). *A History of Greek Philosophy*, vol. V: *The Later Plato and the Academy*. Cambridge: Cambridge University Press.

HALLIWELL, S. (2002). *The Aesthetics of Mimesis: Ancient Texts and Modern Interpretations*. Princeton: Princeton University Press.

HALPERIN, D., WINKLER, J., and ZEITLIN, F., eds. (1990). *Before Sexuality: the Construction of Erotic Experience in the Ancient Greek World*. Princeton: Princeton University Press.

HATZISTAVROU, A. (2011). 'Correctness and Poetic Knowledge: Choric Poetry in the *Laws*' in P. Destrée and F.-G. Herman, eds., *Plato and the Poets*. Leiden: Brill, 361–85.

HELMIG, C. (2003). 'Die Bedeutung and Funcktion von ἐπῳδή in Platons *Nomoi*' in S. Scolnicov and Brisson, eds., 2003, 75–80.

HODKINSON, S., POWELL, A., CARTLEDGE, P., eds. (1999). *Sparta: New Perspectives*. London: Duckworth.

HOOKER, J. T. (1980). *The Ancient Spartans*. London: Dent.

HORN, C., ed. (2013). *Platon: Gesetze/NOMOI*. Klassiker Auslegen 55. Berlin: Akademie Verlag.

IRWIN, T. H. (1979). *Plato: Gorgias, Translated with Notes*. The Clarendon Plato Series. Oxford: The Clarendon Press.

IRWIN, T. H. (1995). *Plato's Ethics*. New York: Oxford University Press.

IRWIN T. H. (2010). 'The Sense and Reference of *kalon* in Aristotle'. *Classical Philology* (Special Issue: *Beauty, Harmony and the Good*) 105: 381–96.

IRWIN, T. H. (2011). *The Development of Ethics*, vol. 1: *From Socrates to the Reformation*. Oxford: Oxford University Press.

JANAWAY, C. (1995). *Images of Excellence: Plato's Critique of the Arts*. Oxford: Clarendon Press.

JONES, R. E. (2013). 'Wisdom and Happiness in *Euthydemus* 278–282'. *Philosophers' Imprint* 13 (4): 1–21.

JOUËT-PASTRÉ, E. (2006). *Le jeu et le sérieux dans les LOIS de Platon*. Sankt Augustin: Academia Verlag.

JOUËT-PASTRÉ, E. (2012). 'Les *Lois*, un paradigme politique possible' in Lisi, ed. 2012, 113–26.

KAHN, C. H. (2002). 'On Platonic Chronology' in J. Annas and C. Rowe, eds., *New Perspectives on Plato, Modern and Ancient*. Washington, DC: Center for Hellenic Studies, 93–127.

KAHN, C. H. (2004). 'From *Republic* to *Laws*' [review essay on Bobonich 2002]. *Oxford Studies in Ancient Philosophy* 26: 337–62.

KAMTEKAR, R. (2010). 'Psychology and the Inculcation of Virtue in Plato's *Laws*' in Bobonich, ed. 2010, 127–48.

KENNELL, N. (1995). *The Gymnasium of Virtue: Education and Culture in Ancient Sparta*. Chapel Hill, NC: UNC Press.

KENNELL, N. (2009). *Spartans: A New History*. Malden, MA and Chichester, UK: Wiley-Blackwell.

KERN, O. (1922). *Orphicorum Fragmenta*. Berlin: Weidmann.

KEULS, E. C. (1978). *Plato and Greek Painting*. Leiden: Brill.

KLOSKO, G. (2006). *The Development of Plato's Political Theory*, 2nd ed. Oxford: Oxford University Press.

KOWALZIG, B. (2004). 'Changing Choral Words: Song-dance and Society in Athens and Beyond' in P. Murray and P. Wilson eds. 2004, 39–65.

KRAUT, R. (1979). 'Two Conceptions of Happiness'. *The Philosophical Review* 88: 167–97.

KRAUT, R. (2013). 'An Aesthetic Reading of Aristotle's Ethics' in Verity Harte and Melissa Lane, eds., *Politeia: Essays in Honour of Malcolm Schofield*. Cambridge: Cambridge University Press, 231–50.

KURKE, L. (2013). 'Imagining Chorality: Wonder, Plato's Puppets, and Moving Statues' in Peponi, ed. 2013b, 123–70.

LAKS, A. (2000). 'The Laws' in C. Rowe and M. Schofield, eds., *The Cambridge History of Greek and Roman Political Thought*. Cambridge: Cambridge University Press, 258–92.

LAKS, A. (2005). *Médiation et coercition: Pour une lecture des Lois de Platon*. Villneuve d'Asq: Presses Universitaires du Septentrion.

LANE, M. (1998). *Method and Politics in Plato's Statesman*. Cambridge: Cambridge University Press.

LAWLER, L. B. (1964). *The Dance in Ancient Greece*. London: A & C Black.

LEAR, G. R. (2006). 'Plato on Learning to Love Beauty' in G. Santas, ed., *The Blackwell Guide to Plato's Republic*. Malden, MA: Blackwell Publishing, 104–22.

LISI, F., ed. (2001). *Plato's Laws and its Historical Significance*. Sankt Augustin: Academia Verlag.

LISI, F., ed. (2012). *Utopia, Ancient and Modern: Contributions to the History of a Political Dream*. Sankt Augustin: Academia Verlag.

LONSDALE, S. (1993). *Dance and Ritual Play in Greek Religion*. Baltimore: Johns Hopkins University Press.

LORENZ, H. (2006). *The Brute Within: Appetitive Desire in Plato and Aristotle*. Oxford: Oxford University Press.

MARTIN, R. (2013). 'The Rhetoric of Rhapsody in Plato's *Laws*' in Peponi, ed. 2013b, 313–38.

MATHIESEN, T. J. (1999). *Apollo's Lyre: Greek Music and Music Theory in Antiquity and the Middle Ages*. Lincoln, NE: University of Nebraska Press.

MEYER, S. S. (1993). *Aristotle on Moral Responsibility*. Oxford: Basil Blackwell; reissued with a new introduction (2011), Oxford University Press.

MEYER, S. S. (2003). 'Plato on the Moral Dangers of Labour and Commerce' in Scolnicov and Brisson, eds. 2003, 207–14.

MEYER, S. S. (2006). 'Plato on the Law' in H. Benson, ed., *A Companion to Plato*. Oxford and Malden MA: Basil Blackwell.

MEYER, S. S. (2008). *Ancient Ethics*. New York: Routledge.

MEYER, S. S. (2011). 'Living for the sake of an Ultimate End' in Jon Miller, ed., *Aristotle's Nicomachean Ethics: a critical guide*. New York: Cambridge University Press, 47–65.

MEYER, S. S. (2012). 'Pleasure, Pain and "Anticipation" in *Laws* I' in Patterson et al., eds. 2012, 311–28.

MILLENDER, E. G. (1999). 'Athenian Ideology and the Empowered Spartan Woman' in S. Hodkinson, A. Powell, and P. Cartledge, eds., *Sparta: New Perspectives*. London: Duckworth, 355–92.

MOORE, K. R. (2005). *Sex and the Second-best City: Sex and Society in the Laws of Plato*. London: Routledge.

MORGAN, K. (2013). 'Praise and Performance in Plato's *Laws*' in Peponi, ed. 2013b, 265–93.

MORROW, G. (1960). *Plato's Cretan City: An Historical Interpretation of the Laws*. Princeton, NJ: Princeton University Press.

MOSS, J. (2008). 'Appearances and Calculations: Plato's Division of the Soul'. *Oxford Studies in Ancient Philosophy* 34: 35–86.

MOSS, J. (2012). 'Art and Ethical Perspective: Notes on the *kalon* in Plato's *Laws*' in A. E. Denham, ed., *Plato on Art and Beauty*. London: MacMillan, 205–20.

MOSS, J. (2014). 'Right Reason in Plato and Aristotle: on the Meaning of *logos*'. *Phronesis* 59: 181–230.

MOURACADE, J. (2005). 'Virtue and Pleasure in Plato's *Laws*'. *Apeiron* 38 (1): 73–85.

MOUZE, L. (2005). *Le législateur et le poète: une interprétation des Lois de Platon*. Villeneuve d'Ascq: Presses Universitaires de Septentrion.

MÜLLER, G. (1951). *Studien zu den platonischen Nomoi*. Munich: Beck. (*Zetemata* 3).

MURRAY, O. (1993). *Early Greece*, 2nd ed. Cambridge, MA: Harvard University Press.

MURRAY, O., ed. (1999). *Sumpotika: a Symposium on the* Sumposion. Oxford: Clarendon Press.

MURRAY, O. (2013). 'The Chorus of Dionysus: Alcohol and old age in the *Laws*' in Peponi, ed. 2013b, 109–22.

MURRAY, P. (2004). 'The Muses and their Arts' in P. Murray and P. Wilson, eds. 2004, 365–98.

MURRAY, P. (2013). '*Paides Malakôn Musôn*: Tragedy in Plato's *Laws*' in Peponi, ed. 2013b, 294–312.

MURRAY, P. and WILSON, P., eds. (2004). *Music and the Muses: The Culture of Mousike in the Classical Athenian City*. Oxford: Oxford University Press.

NADDAF, G. (2000). 'Literacy and Poetic Performance in Plato's *Laws*'. *Ancient Philosophy* 20: 339–50.

NAILS, D. (2002). *The People of Plato: a Prosopography of Plato and other Socratics*. Indianapolis: Hackett Publishing.

NAILS, D. and THESLEFF, H. (2003). 'Early Academic Editing: Plato's *Laws*' in Scolnicov and Brisson, eds. 2003, 14–29.

NIGHTINGALE, A. (1993). 'Writing/reading a Sacred Text: a Literary Interpretation of Plato's *Laws*'. *Classical Philology* 88 (4): 279–300.

NIGHTINGALE, A. (1999). 'Plato's Lawcode in Context: Rule by written law in Athens and Magnesia'. *Classical Quarterly* 49: 100–22.

NORTH, H. (1966). *Sophrosyne: Self-Knowledge and Self-Restraint in Greek Literature*. Ithaca: Cornell University Press.

NUSSBAUM, M. C. (1994). 'Platonic Love and Colorado Law: The relevance of Ancient Greek Norms to Modern Controversies'. *Virginia Law Review* 80 (7): 1515–1651.

O'BRIEN, M. M. (1967). *The Socratic Paradoxes and the Greek Mind*. Chapel Hill, NC: The University of North Carolina Press.

OSTWALD, M. (1962). 'Review of Görgemans (1960)'. *Gnomon* 34: 231–41.

OSTWALD, M. (1986). *From Popular Sovereignty to the Sovereignty of Law*. Berkeley: University of California Press.

PATTERSON, R., KARASMANIS, V., and HERMANN, A., eds. (2012). *Presocratics and Plato*. Las Vegas: Parmenides Publishing.

PELOSI, F. (2010). *Plato on Music, Soul, and Body*. Cambridge: Cambridge University Press.

PEMBERTON, E. (1976). 'A Note on *Skigraphia*'. *American Journal of Aesthetics* 80: 82–4.

PEPONI, A.-E. (2012). *Frontiers of Pleasure: Models of aesthetic response in archaic and classical Greek thought*. Oxford: Oxford University Press.

PEPONI, A.-E. (2013a). 'Choral Ant-Aesthetics' in Peponi, ed. 2013b, 212–39.

PEPONI, A.-E., ed. (2013b). *Performance and Culture in Plato's Laws*. Cambridge: Cambridge University Press.

PODLECKI, A. (1984). *The Early Greek Poets and their Times*. Vancouver, BC: University of British Columbia Press.

POMEROY, S. B. (2002). *Spartan Women*. Oxford: Oxford University Press.

PRAUSCELLO, L. (2014). *Performing Citizenship in Plato's Laws*. Cambridge: Cambridge University Press.

REES, D. A. (1957). 'Bipartition of the Soul in the Early Academy'. *Journal of Hellenic Studies* 77 (1): 112–18.

RENAUT, O. (2014). *Platon: la médiation des émotions: l'éducation de* thymos *dans les dialogues*. Paris: Vrin.

RIST, J. M. (1997). 'Plato and Professor Nussbaum on Acts "contrary to nature"' in M. Joyal, ed., *Studies in Plato and the Platonic Tradition*. Aldershot: Ashgate, 65–82.

RITTER, C. (1923). *Platon: sein Leben, seine Schriften, seine Lehre*, vol 2. Munich: Beck.

ROBERTS, J. (1987). 'Plato on the Causes of Wrongdoing in the *Laws*'. *Ancient Philosophy* 7: 23–37.

ROBINSON, T. M. (1970). *Plato's Psychology*. Toronto: University of Toronto Press; 2nd ed. 1995.

ROCCONI, E. (2003). *La parole delle Muse: la formazione del lessico tecnico musicale nella Grecia antica*. Rome: Quasar.

ROWE, C. (2012). 'Socrates in the *Laws*' in Patterson et al., eds. 2012, 329–48.

ROWE, C. and SCHOFIELD, M. (2008). *The Cambridge History of Greek and Roman Political Thought*. Cambridge: Cambridge University Press.

RUTHERFORD, I. (2001). *Pindar's Paeans*. Oxford: Oxford University Press.

RUTHERFORD, I. (2013). 'Strictly Ballroom: Egyptian *Mousikê* and Plato's Comparative Poetics' in Peponi, ed. 2013b, 67–83.

SAMARAS, T. (2010). 'Family and the Question of Women in the *Laws*' in Bobonich, ed. 2010, 172–96.

SANDAY, E., ed. (2013). *Plato's Laws: Force and Truth in Politics*. Studies in Continental Thought. Bloomington: Indiana University Press.

SANTAS, G. (1964). 'The Socratic Paradoxes'. *The Philosophical Review* 73 (2): 147–64.

SASSI, M. (2008). 'The Self, the Soul, and the Individual in the City of the *Laws*'. *Oxford Studies in Ancient Philosophy* 35: 125–48.

SAUNDERS, T. (1962). 'The Structure of Soul and State in Plato's *Laws*'. *Eranos* 60: 37–55.

SAUNDERS, T. (1968). 'The Socratic Paradoxes in Plato's *Laws*'. *Hermes* 96: 421–34.

SAUNDERS, T. and BRISSON, L. (2000). *Bibliography on Plato's Laws* by T. Saunders. Revised and completed with an additional bibliography on the *Epinomis* by L. Brisson. International Plato Studies 12. Sankt Augustin: Academia Verlag.

SCHIPPER, E. W. (1963). 'Mimesis in the Arts in Plato's *Laws*'. *The Journal of Aesthetics and Art Criticism* 22: 199–202.

SCHOFIELD, M. (1999). 'The Disappearance of the Philosopher-King'. *Proceedings of the Boston Area Colloquium in Ancient Philosophy* 13: 213–41.

SCHOFIELD, M. (2006). *Plato: Political philosophy*. Oxford: Oxford University Press.

SCHÖPSDAU, K. (2003). 'Sussitien für Frauen: eine platonische Utopie' in Scolnicov and Brisson, eds. 2003, 243–56.

SCOLNICOV, S. and BRISSON, L. (2003). *Plato's Laws: from Theory into Practice.* Proceedings of the VI Symposium Platonicum. Sankt Augustin: Academia Verlag.

SCOTT, G. L. (1999). 'The *Poetics* of Performance' in S. Kemal and I. Gaskell, eds., *Performance and Authenticity in the Arts.* Cambridge Series on Philosophy and the Arts. Cambridge: Cambridge University Press, 15–48.

SCOTT, G. L. (unpublished). 'Plato's Well-educated Men, the Dancers: *harmonia kai rhuthmos* as "Music and Dance" ', Chapter 2 of *Aristotle on Dramatic Musical Theatre: The Real Role of Literature, Catharsis, Music, and Dance in the* Poetics.

SEAFORD, R. (2006). *Dionysos.* London and New York: Routledge.

SEGVIG, H. (2000). 'No one Errs Willingly: the meaning of Socratic Intellectualism'. *Oxford Studies in Ancient Philosophy* 19: 1–45.

SHOREY, P. (1922). 'Review of England'. *Classical Philology* 17: 153–5.

STALLEY, R. F. (1983). *An Introduction to Plato's Laws.* Oxford: Basil Blackwell.

STALLEY, R. F. (1994). 'Persuasion in Plato's *Laws*'. *History of Political Thought* 15: 157–77.

STRAUSS, L. (1975). *The Argument and the Action of Plato's Laws.* Chicago: University of Chicago Press.

TIGERSTEDT, E. N. (1965–74). *The Legend of Sparta in Classical Antiquity*, 2 vols. Stockholm and Uppsala: Almqvist & Wiksell.

VANHOUTTE, M. (1954). *La philosophie politique de Platon dans les 'Lois'.* Louvain: Publications Universitaires.

VIDAL-NAQUET, P. (1981). *Le chasseur noir.* Paris: La Découverte.

VLASTOS, G. (1981). 'Socratic Knowledge and Platonic Pessimism' in *Platonic Studies*, 2nd ed. Princeton: Princeton University Press, 204–17; originally printed in *The Philosophical Review* 66 (1957): 226–38.

WALBANK, M. (1978). *Athenian Proxenies of the 5th Century BC.* Toronto: Stevens.

WEST, M. L. (1993). *Greek Lyric Poetry.* Oxford: Oxford University Press.

WILAMOWITZ-MOELLENDORFF, U. VON (1920). *Platon*, 2 vols. Berlin: Weidmann.

WILBURN, J. (2012). 'Akrasia and Self-Rule in Plato's Laws'. *Oxford Studies in Ancient Philosophy* 43: 25–53.

WILBURN, J. (2013a). 'Moral Education and the Spirited Part of the Soul in Plato's *Laws*'. *Oxford Studies in Ancient Philosophy* 45: 63–102.

WILBURN, J. (2013b). 'Tripartition and the Causes of Criminal Behavior in *Laws* IX'. *Ancient Philosophy* 33: 11–134.

WILDBERG, C. (2011). 'Dionysos in the Mirror of Philosophy: Heraclitus, Plato, Plotinus' in R. Schlesier, ed., *A Different God? Dionysos and Ancient Polytheism.* Berlin: De Gruyter, 205–32.

ZUCKERT, C. (2009). *Plato's Philosophers: the Coherence of the Dialogues.* Chicago: University of Chicago Press.

ZUOLO, F. (2012). 'Plato's Political Idealism and Utopia in the *Republic*, the *Laws*, and the *Timaeus-Critias*' in Lisi, ed. 2012, 39–60.

Index

Entries in **bold** indicate page numbers in the translation.